SO-AZB-063

GOURMET'S
GUIDE
CHEESE

GOURMET'S
GUIDE
CHEESE

Brigitte Engelmann

Peter Holler

h.f.ullmann

Wine recommendations by Markus Del Monego
(indicated by "Sommelier's recommendation").

© 2008 Tandem Verlag GmbH
h.f.ullmann is an imprint of Tandem Verlag GmbH

Original title: *Das Feinschmecker-Handbuch Käse*
ISBN (original German edition) 978-3-8331-5023-4

Original idea and basic concept: André Dominé
Main author: Brigitte Engelmann
Text contributions: Peter Holler, Elke Hoffmann, and Bettina Offermann,
edited by Brigitte Engelmann
Project management: Ulrike Reihn-Hamburger
Specialist editors: Peter Holler and Bettina Offermann
Proofreading: Tobias Büscher and Christina Kuhn
Picture editors: Brigitte Engelmann, Anne Williams, and Felicitas Pohl
Arrangement: e.fritz, berlin 06
Layout: e.fritz, berlin 06, and Agilmedien GbR
Cover design: Martin Wellner
Cover illustration: Robert Hardt, Rincon2 Medien GmbH, Cologne

© 2009 for the English edition: Tandem Verlag GmbH
h.f.ullmann is an imprint of Tandem Verlag GmbH

Translated by Susan Ghanouni, Mo Croasdale and Katherine Taylor in association with
First Edition Translations Ltd, Cambridge, UK
Edited by Jenny Knight in association with First Edition Translations Ltd, Cambridge, UK
Typeset by The WriteIdea in association with First Edition Translations Ltd, Cambridge, UK

Printed in China

ISBN 978-3-8331-5082-1

10 9 8 7 6 5 4 3 2 1
X IX VIII VII VI V IV III II I

If you would like to stay informed about forthcoming h.f.ullmann titles, you can request
our newsletter by visiting our website **(www.ullmann-publishing.com)** or by
emailing us at: newsletter@ullmann-publishing.com.
h.f.ullmann, Im Mühlenbruch 1, 53639 Königswinter, Germany
Fax: +49(0)2223-2780-708

FOREWORD

Cheese is one of the oldest foodstuffs known to mankind. No sooner had we learnt, all those millennia ago, that female animals could be milked than the first cheese made from curdled milk appeared. It just needed to be pressed and left for a few days. This remains the basic principle of cheese production today.

Over the centuries, cheese production spread to wherever milk-producing animals were kept. Cheese is therefore the most diverse natural product after wine. Despite today's worldwide cheese industry, however, traditional cheese dairies are fortunately still able to hold their own. Raw milk cheese is the ultimate among cheeses: Unpasteurized, non-sterile cheeses remain alive and undergo a natural evolution and maturation process that fascinates every gourmet.

While cheese production demands tremendous expertise, absolute discipline, and healthy hygiene, its maturation (French *affinage*) requires an almost scientific understanding of cheese chemistry as well as the corresponding equipment. The affineur's senses of smell and taste are also faced with considerable challenges, requiring resourcefulness in order to enable every single cheese to reach its gustatory peak. No other foodstuff offers such diverse and sophisticated enjoyment: From delicate, floral aromas to restrained fruitiness and nutty hints through to the very intense, uniquely complex fragrance and flavor nuances of fully ripened cheeses. Cheese is not only enjoyment, it is a lesson in life.

CHEESE SECRETS
A cultural history of cheese

Precisely when cheese was first produced from the milk of domestic animals will remain an uncertainty forever. There are enough very reliable references to the fact that livestock were being milked in Thessaly and Macedonia about 6500–5000 BC, however. Milk is venerated in the earliest creation myths as mankind's first foodstuff. An Indian myth explains the origins of the cosmos with the image of curdling milk. In a Nordic saga, the cosmic cow Audumla gives birth to the first humans and suckles the giant Ymir. The goat, its milk, and its cheese are accorded special significance in Greek mythology, with the goat Amaltheia secretly raising the baby Zeus and protecting him from his father Cronos. In Roman mythology, a she-wolf nurtures Romulus and Remus, the founders of the Eternal City, with her milk.

Cheese production, too, has been known for several millennia. Magical powers were attributed to herdsmen, and cheese was served as a sacrifice to appease the gods, with consecrated cheese allegedly being able to heal illness. The first cheeses eaten by people were probably sour-milk cheeses born of chance: It was discovered that milk curdles after a while at specific temperatures, the whey separating from the curds, which dry out further when placed in woven baskets to drain. The discovery of rennet was probably also due to chance: The drink containers for travellers were often made from the stomachs of lambs or kids.

Exposed to temperature and shaking on the back of the horse or camel, the milk in the animal-skin pouch automatically turned

Left: Inseparable—the herdsman and his herd.

into rennet cheese. It was from such "coincidences" that a culture of cheese production developed about 5000 BC in Mesopotamia, biblical Palestine, the Black Sea region, Asia Minor, Egypt, and North Africa. The first graphic records of the extraction and processing of milk are to be found in Mesopotamia, with livestock breeding and milk products even having played a role among the ancient Sumerians: A relief in the Temple of Ur (2500 BC) portrays cowsheds, milking, and the churning of butter, the last being a method still practiced today in the region between the Euphrates and the Tigris. The knowledge of cheese production had been nurtured in the Middle East in early times, long before the Romans discovered their love of cheese. It is also known that the people of the Bronze Age (2000–1000 BC) used perforated pots for cheese production.

North of the Black Sea, traces of cheese were also found in fur pouches in the frozen graves of the Scythian tribe (first century BC)

Above and right: In many countries livestock breeding and dairy farming are still carried out as they were in the past. Above in Mongolia, right in the Sahel.

Left: Even in the pre-Christian age sheep and goats served mankind as important suppliers of milk for making cheese.

who, like other equestrian peoples—such as the Kirghiz, Kalmyks, and Tatars—produced a form of cheese.

Literary references to cheese appeared with the ancient Greeks and later the Romans. Cheese was an important means of bartering, an indispensable daily foodstuff, a delicacy for feasts, a sacrifice, and an aphrodisiac all in one. Hence Homer's talk of precious cheese about 800 BC in his *Odyssey* and the fact that, in the *Iliad*, the heroes of the battle for Troy sustained themselves with wine containing grated cheese. The Greek physician Hippocrates (about 460–375 BC) was familiar with popular goat's milk cheese, and the philosopher Aristotle (384–322 BC) mentioned a cheese made from goat's or sheep's milk that was blended with mare's or donkey's milk. Cheesecake, cheese tartlets, and cheese recipes with honey were known in Athens in the fifth century BC, and a kind of warm cheese-cake was eaten on Samos—again in pre-Christian times. Even the Bible contains references to cheese as a foodstuff. In the First Book of Samuel, Jesse sends his son David to his brothers, who are fighting the Philistines: "Take for your brothers ... these ten loaves of bread and run to your brothers in the army, and take these ten cheeses and bring them to the commander."

Aristotle, not only a philosopher but also a naturalist, paid a great deal of attention to cheese production and milk quality. In his time deer rennet was considered the preferred coagulant, but rennet from a calf's or kid's stomach was also commonly used, or else rennet from the flowers and juice of a variety of plants.

The ancient Greeks produced their Tyrós cheese with all kinds of flavoring ingredients such as pepper, caraway, and pine kernels. They were even familiar with a variety of refining methods, placing the cheese in salt, vinegar, or grape must baths, or else smoking it. It is certain that the ancient Greeks developed the art of cheese making further and brought it to Sicily, southern Italy, and—via Massilia, present-day Marseilles—to France.

The ancient Romans also became familiar with cheese, by trading in Greek slaves. The poet Virgil sang the praises of cheese in the following words: "What is milked in the early morning and during the day is pressed into curd cheese late in the evening, what is milked at twilight with the setting sun is on its way in the early morning, in the cheese basket the shepherd takes it to the towns. Or it is salted a little and kept aside for the winter."

The Romans loved to dine on fresh cheese with figs, but there were also baked dishes or salads made with cheese. The cheese was smoked over a straw fire, placed in a salt bath, and treated to an apple must bath, or the milk was flavored with herbs or pine cones. Cheese, olives, and raisins made up the meagre rations of the Roman soldiers, and cheese was as popular with the simple people as it was among the nobles. In his book about agriculture written about AD 60, the farmer Columella describes, among other things, the production of a hard cheese via a process very similar to that for the making of Emmental.

It would appear that France and the alpine countries have the Celts to thank for the further development of the art of cheese making in the pre-Christian era. The Celts' settlement area extended from Gaul, present-day France, over the Alps as far as the Italian Po plain, where they encountered the Etruscans on a more or less peaceful basis. The Celts were considered to be skilled craftsmen and a people with a sophisticated culture, as well as being highly familiar with livestock breeding. As in Rome, there was also an independent cheese culture in the Celtic Gallic region, and a brisk cheese trade probably took place between the Roman and the Celtic tribes.

The Germanic tribes were less imaginative in the development of cheese. Although they also became familiar with their cheese types during the ongoing skirmishes with the Romans and the Celts, it was only sour-milk and fatty curd cheese that continued to feature on the daily menus of the German peoples. Nevertheless cheese

Right: The daily milking was a strenuous task. Today it is usually carried out by milking machines.

Below: The first stop, before breakfast even, is the barn to milk and feed the animals.

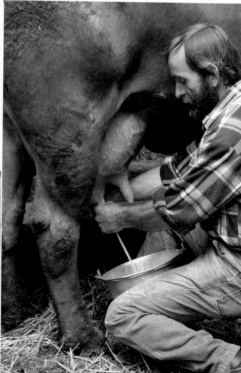

production using rennet and shaped cheeses was not unknown to them.

Initially, sour-milk cheese also predominated among the Nordic peoples. In Iceland, occupied by Norway in the early Middle Ages, a tale from the tenth-century Njal saga—which incidentally also tells of ancient Germanic customs—refers to large cheese wheels made in early times.

Despite all the political and economic upheavals between the Roman imperial and the Carolingian eras, cheese production continued to be fostered, albeit without significant further development. Cheese was traded within the Ostrogoth and Visigoth dominions as well as in those of the Langobards and their provinces. Cheese production and trading on a larger scale only really began about the year 1000, with the development of larger settlements and towns.

MIDDLE AGES AND MODERN AGE

Cheese production was given a major boost during the Middle Ages, not least due to Charlemagne, an enthusiastic cheese fan who actively supported the spread of the expertise available at the time. It was this era that saw the start of the cheese diversity that continues to exist today. In Italy cheese varieties such as Parmigiano, Gorgonzola, Taleggio, and Pecorino, as well as the *pasta filata*

Parmegiano Reggiano has been known in Italy since the days of the Romans...

...as have blue-veined cheeses such as Gorgonzola.

types, have been in existence since the days of the Romans. In Switzerland, Schabzieger and Sbrinz existed by the year 1000.

Gruyère and Emmental from the alpine regions may be traced back to the twelfth century. Appenzeller cheese has been documented since 1282. In France not only is written mention made of the famous Roquefort in 1070, but many of the soft cheeses from northern France go back to the twelfth century. On the North Sea coast, in what is today the Netherlands and Belgium, cheese production was an important economic sector during this time, with Dutch Gouda and Edam conquering the world—these cheeses were to be found at the Paris markets as early as 1148. The weekly cheese market in Alkmaar in Holland is reminiscent of this tradition.

Between the eleventh and fourteenth centuries, it was the monasteries that formed the focus of the art of cheese making. It was also the monks who used expensive copper kettles to make cheese instead of the stone or clay containers that had been common until then. Cheese gradually developed into important merchandise and a means of payment of the tithes due to the monasteries. In mountainous areas the farmers, for example, bought themselves free of the monasteries in order to be able to farm their pastures collectively, producing large cheeses such as Appenzeller (Switzerland), Beaufort (France), and Fontina (Italy), as we still known them today. When international trade began to

The soft cheese Taleggio goes back to the days of the Romans.

Hard cheese production in the Alps dates back to the twelfth century.

Above: Despite industrial production methods, the cheese dairy retains its handcraft character.

Left: The cheese industry today is characterized by the most modern of technology.

prosper in the fourteenth century, the hard cheeses in particular became important trading goods. Soft cheeses, on the other hand, remained a local specialty due to their shorter shelf life and therefore unsuitability for being transported over long distances. From the fourteenth to the end of the seventeenth century, the economies of large areas of Europe were considerably weakened by warfare (religious wars, the Hundred Years' War, the Peasants' War, and the Thirty Years' War) and its aftermath. This also meant a severe setback for the cheese industry. The pastures were laid to waste, livestock numbers decimated, and farmers made destitute.

Cheese production and trade in Europe then underwent a revival from the eighteenth century. Scientific research during the Age of Enlightenment brought with it new insights into the components of milk and cheese and into the process of making cheese. During the nineteenth century, scientists such as Cohn, Pasteur, Liebig, Metchnikov, and Tyndall set about researching the mysterious procedures of the cheese dairy. More and more came to be known about the effects of microorganisms and bacteria, and about the ripening as well as the flavor and aroma creation in cheese. Industrial cheese production then began to take hold with the use of laboratory-produced starter cultures and rennet for the souring and coagulation of the milk. The emergence of the railways enabled the transportation of sensitive soft cheese varieties over large distances, thus making them available to connoisseurs all over Europe.

Many cheeses today are still produced according to traditional methods and recipes, even if the processing has become easier with the help of machines. The cheese maker continues to play an important role. Many specific cheese specialties have or had disappeared from the market, but the commitment of traditional and local producers, as well as the revival of consumer awareness and the demand for natural, unadulterated foodstuffs, has meant that cheese specialties from the farmyard, the pasture, and the monastery have been able to experience a renaissance.

IT ALL BEGINS WITH MILK

Like all mammals, human beings are nourished by milk alone during the first weeks of life. A mother's milk contains all the vital ingredients: Minerals, nutrients, sugar, and fat. Milk is therefore more than just a drink; it is also a substantial foodstuff. It is an important source of calcium for our bodies and is therefore essential for bone development. Milk plays a much more important nutritional role in central and northern Europe than in other continents. Entire peoples in Africa, Asia, and South America, for example, lack the enzyme lactase that breaks down milk sugar, without which human beings are not able to digest milk. This derives from the fact that this enzyme is no longer produced by the body after weaning if milk products are not consumed thereafter.

MILK COMPONENTS

The animal takes in the individual components of the milk ingredients as nourishment. The raw materials ingested from plants and herbs are converted to milk in the mammary glands of the cow, goat, or sheep. Sheep and goats have two mammary glands, while cows have four, and other animals even more. In ruminants, bacteria convey the matter ingested with the food into the first stomach to start with. The cellulose is digested, and less valuable substances are converted into higher quality substances such as inferior amino acids that are transformed into high grade amino acids. In the stomach of the cow, sheep, and goat vegetable protein is converted into high value animal protein with the help of bacteria. The individual

Left: The animal ingests all of the milk ingredients as nourishment.

substances reach the cells via the bloodstream and there they are assembled into milk protein, milk fat, and milk sugar. Salts and minerals are conveyed directly to the tiny cavities of the glandular cells. In addition to protein, fat, and carbohydrates, milk also provides vital minerals, particularly phosphorus, calcium, potassium, and magnesium, diverse trace elements, and especially the vitamins A, D, E, and K, as well as vitamin B complexes, enzymes, and water. The proportions of the individual ingredients differ between the various animal species.

The milk's fat content depends on the animal's breed and on feeding and farming methods, as well as on the lactation phase (the period during which the female animals produce milk) and the milking. The fat content of the milk is at its highest at the end of the lactation phase. The milk fat is present in the form of small globules surrounded by a protein covering.

These globules average 0.005 mm in size. Due to the low specific weight of the milk fat, the globules rise to the top and form a layer

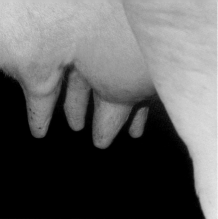

Above: The milk is at its richest and the fat content at its highest at the end of the lactation phase.

Right: No other foodstuff is monitored as strictly as milk.

Left: Milk products provide vital minerals and vitamins.

of cream if the milk is left to stand. In order to accelerate the cream formation during industrial processing, the milk is heated to 104–122 °F (40–50 °C) before it is skimmed in a centrifuge, where it is spun so fast that the fat globules separate as cream. What remains is skimmed milk. Some of the cream is then sometimes added back to the skimmed milk in order to achieve the precise fat content required in the milk. A distinction is normally made between full cream milk (3.5% fat), low fat milk (1.5–1.8% fat), and skimmed milk (0.3% fat). The less fat the milk contains, the lower its concentration of the fat-soluble vitamins A, D, E, and K. Low fat milk has lost about 60% of these vitamins. Ultimately the precise fat content of a finished cheese can only be determined by industrial production. This is generally not possible in farmyard manufacture, which lacks the technical means for the precise adjustment of the fat content.

Farmyard producers prefer to work with the natural fat content. Consequently, the fat in dry matter indication in farmyard cheeses is often only an approximate value.

The formation of the milk proteins is aided by amino acids. The protein content is also strongly dependent on the breed, farming methods, feeding, and lactation phase. Milk protein comprises casein, the actual basis of cheese, and whey protein (albumin and globulin). While the protein in casein can be obtained only by souring, whey protein can be precipitated only by heating to at least 158 °F (70 °C). The extraction of liquid (whey) during cheese production concentrates the protein in accordance with the quantity of liquid extracted. The whey can be extracted in a variety of ways: By cutting up the coagulated milk or by means of temperature control, through the passing of time, and by various means of souring. A softer or a harder cheese is obtained depending on the combination of these factors.

Milk sugar or lactose acts as a nutrient for the lactobacilli. These bacteria play a role in cheese production and have a positive influence on shelf life and quality. Lactobacilli convert the milk sugar into lactic acids, which in turn ensure the precipitation of the milk protein. This is especially important for the production of sour-milk products, but the process also influences taste and consistency in cheese production, so a sufficiently high quantity of milk sugar needs to be available.

The calcium content of the milk is of special significance for cheese production. If milk did not contain calcium, it would not be possible for it to coagulate with rennet. The concentration of mineral salts is also dependent on the animals' food. The lecithin contained in the milk acts as a natural emulsifier, which is necessary because fat and water do not combine by themselves. The lecithin encases the fat globules in the milk and keeps them suspended in the water.

HOMOGENIZATION, PASTEURIZATION, STERILIZATION

It was pasteurization, sterilization, and modern refrigeration technology that enabled the expansion of cheese production. Industrial production necessitates the transportation and storage of large quantities of milk from a variety of regions, which makes pasteurization indispensable. The disadvantage is that today hardly anyone knows the flavor of raw, fresh milk any more. The heating of the milk reduces the germs to a minimum and kills off any pathogens that may be present. Heated milk ensures that, with hygienic processing, only the required added lactobacilli develop. Industrial cheese production requires the addition of calcium chloride, however, because the calcium naturally present in the milk, which is required for it to coagulate after the addition of rennet, is bonded during heating. The characteristic milk flavor is diminished by heat treatment. This is expressed dramatically in the words of the cheese compendium of the Grands Seigneurs du Fromage: "Pasteurized

Right: Stainless steel plant ensures hygienic processing.

Below: The farmers bring the fresh milk to the dairy immediately.

milk is dead milk and you cannot make living cheese out of dead milk." In addition to the undesired germs, the heating unfortunately also destroys almost all of the milk's microbial flora, which determine the characteristic flavor of the milk and therefore that of the cheese as well. Nevertheless, despite pasteurization there are still outstanding cheeses produced today, otherwise we would simply have to dismiss industrially produced Edam and Gouda.

Pasteurization is in fact superfluous for milk which is to be turned into cheese within 24 hours. The raw milk used for cheese needs to be of an especially high quality.

As with wine, the French as the greatest advocates of raw milk cheese speak of *terroir* when it comes to cheese, namely the ideal interaction between animal breed, pasture, and climate. It is no wonder that the best cheeses come from areas where the milk-producing animals feed on hearty, healthy food in lush pastures. The plant species in the pastures have a determining influence on the robust, flavorsome aroma of the later cheese specific to the type and region.

It is not just the EU bureaucrats in Brussels who make it very difficult, if not impossible, for the small, traditional producers to make delicious cheeses full of character from their raw, untreated milk, however. The regulations governing the production of raw milk cheese in the cheese dairy are among the strictest imaginable. Especially strict attention has to be paid to both hygiene and to the health and living conditions of the animals.

HOMOGENIZATION

The layer of cream settles on the top if the milk is left to stand for a few hours at the farmyard. The milk is homogenized in order to delay this process. This involves compressing it through fine nozzles at 122–158 °F (50–70 °C). The large fat globules are thus broken up very finely and acquire a uniform (homogeneous) size. The lecithin is then better able to fulfill its task as the emulsifier of fat and water.

A further advantage of homogenization is that the uniform size of the fat globules gives the milk a more full-bodied taste.

PASTEURIZATION AND STERILIZATION

Germs in the milk cannot always be avoided, even under hygienic conditions. They can cause disease and infections if they do get into the milk and proliferate. Pasteurization and sterilization (i.e. the heating of the milk) provide effective protection against pathogenic bacteria. Any germs that may be present are killed off, meaning that the milk may be kept for longer as well. With the exception of ultra-heat treated milk, pasteurized fresh milk can be kept refrigerated for about three to four days. The loss of water-soluble vitamins may be up to 10%.

DISTINCTION BETWEEN FOUR PASTEURIZATION PROCESSES:

- Extended heating:
The milk is heated to 144–149 °F (62–65 °C) over a period of half an hour.

- Short time heating:
The milk is heated to 162–167 °F (72–75 °C) over a period of 15–30 seconds.

- High temperature heating:
The milk is heated to at least 185 °F (85 °C) over a period of four seconds.

- Ultra-high temperature heating:
The milk is heated to 275–300 °F (135–150 °C) over a period of two to six seconds. This produces so-called UHT milk, which has a shelf life of about six weeks, with vitamin losses of 5–20%.

For sterilization, the milk is heated to 248 °F (120 °C) for about 20 minutes. This milk has a shelf life of several months but, in the worst cases, has lost up to 99% of its vitamins.

CHEESE PRODUCTION
How milk is made into cheese

Cheese is the delicious result of a method of solidifying flavorsome and healthy milk and making it suitable for storage. The solid (protein, fat, milk sugar, vitamins, and minerals) and the liquid components of the milk have to be separated from one another in order to turn milk into cheese. This is done through souring and thickening the milk, during which process the protein contained in milk—casein—coagulates. The process may be triggered naturally by the lactobacilli present in the milk or else by the addition of a vegetable or animal enzyme known as rennet.

The means of souring itself determines the type of cheese that will be derived from the coagulated milk. In the case of rennet cheese, the casein is of course coagulated through the addition of rennet. The actual cheese making begins as soon as the milk has coagulated. What is now a gelatinous mass is broken down into so-called curd grains by cutting or stirring in order to precipitate the liquid part of the milk: The serum or the whey. For hard and semi-hard cheeses, the broken-down grains are then also heated (cooked), causing the curd grains to shrink and even more whey to drain off. The majority of cheeses are rennet cheeses—such as Emmental, blue-mold cheese, and Camembert—or semi-hard cheeses such as Gouda and Edam, to name some examples.

Sour-milk cheeses are derived from souring the milk with lactobacilli. What remains once the whey has drained off is sour-milk curd cheese, the starting product for fresh cheese (today these cheeses are sometimes also coagulated with rennet).

Left: The curd and whey separate when the coagulated milk is cut.

The junket is cut (1), and whey is produced as a by-product (2). The curd is heated again for hard cheese (3). The curd is shaped and left to drain (4, 5, and 6). The salt bath prior to ripening (7) encourages the formation of the cheese rind.

This cheese mass may be eaten fresh or slightly ripened. The most well-known examples of this type of cheese are fresh cheeses, Harz cheese, Mainz cheese, German hand cheese, and cooked cheese (Kochkäse).

Cheese is also made from the whey that has drained off. It still contains enough protein for it to be able to solidify and to make whey cheese specialties such as Zieger (Switzerland), Ricotta (Italy), Manouri (Greece), and Brocciou (France/Corsica).

The curd is placed in perforated molds from which the whey is able to drain off. In the case of hard and semi-hard cheeses, the draining of the whey is further facilitated by compression. The molded cheeses are sprinkled with salt or dipped in a salt bath. The salt extracts further liquid from the curd, ensuring that the cheese has a stronger flavor and a firm rind. After salting, the cheeses are left to dry and ripen with different temperatures, humidities, and surroundings.

During the ripening it is ultimately the microorganisms (bacteria, molds, and/or yeasts) that ensure the protein and fat break down and form flavoring substances. Typical examples include the red bacteria responsible for the strong flavor of Münster cheese, the white-mold cultures in Camembert and Brie, and the blue mold in Roquefort.

The type of milk used—whether raw milk or heated milk, skimmed or full-cream milk; the type of souring selected; the temperature of the milk during the coagulation process; whether the curd grains were heated again; the shape and size of the cheese; the pressure used during compression; the salting; the type, location, and duration of the ripening; if and which bacteria or mold cultures were added—all of these factors contribute to the development of the cheese's characteristic properties. The variety and combination of these features enable the production of an astounding number of different cheeses.

The size and consistency of the curd grains play an important role in the consistency of the subsequent cheese. The smaller the curd grains, the more whey is able to escape and the firmer the cheese will be. The larger the curd grains, the softer the cheese will be. With some especially smooth cheeses, the coagulated milk is placed in perforated molds without the curd having been cut. Curd grains for hard cheeses are about the size of a rice grain; for semi-hard cheeses the curd grains need to be about the size of a hazelnut, and for soft cheeses at least the size of a walnut. The curd mass is heated in order to solidify the curd grains and to extract the liquid even more for hard cheeses with an extremely long shelf life. The higher the temperature, the harder the cheese. Hard cheeses that are produced without further heating of the curd mass need to ripen for months, even years—irrespective of their size—in order for the curd grains to lose the liquid contained.

The degree of compression also has a determining influence on the cheese later. For the production of soft cheese, the pressure of the cheese mass's own weight is sufficient for solidifying the curds. The harder the cheese is to be, the more it needs to be compressed in order to extract the whey from the cheese.

The basic ingredients—milk, lactobacilli, rennet

The milk has to coagulate first in order for it to be turned into cheese. The coagulation takes place either by itself, due to the lactobacilli contained in the milk, or through the addition of cultures or enzymes.

LACTOBACILLI AND CULTURES
In the cheese dairy, cultures are a combination of selected microorganisms that perform a specific task during cheese production. A culture's most important microorganisms include the lactobacilli that are naturally present in the milk and the ambient air.

The warmer the ambient temperature, the quicker these germs multiply. Microorganisms enable the conversion of milk sugar into lactic acid. At a specific concentration the lactic acid then allows the milk protein to precipitate, causing the milk to coagulate and protecting the cheese against decaying bacteria at the same time. Lactobacilli play a key role in the formation of flavor and of the holes in the ripening cheese. All of these bacteria have a variety of different strains with differing properties. The breeding programme of high performance milk producers has led to enough milk being available, but the natural lactobacilli necessary for cheese production are often lacking. The milk therefore needs to be artificially inoculated with bacteria cultures prior to cheese production. The work of the lactobacilli is often supported by enzymes as well. Cultures may also contain special microorganisms in addition to the lactobacilli that are used only for specific cheese types. Examples include the propionic acid bacteria—a bacteria strain that ensures

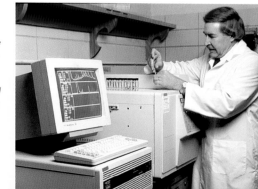

Right: Analysis, control, and monitoring in the laboratory before and after cheese production.

Below right: The fat content is determined according to the proportion in the dry matter.

Below: Microorganisms and bacteria cultures are indispensable for the modern cheese dairy.

the formation of large, distinct holes in the cheese due to its ability to form carbon dioxide gases. The cheese is still elastic at this stage, so that the gas is unable to escape and forms bubbles inside in a process similar to that of yeast activity in dough.

RENNET

Rennet ferment is an enzyme traditionally obtained from the calf's stomach, but it is also present in the stomachs of other young animals. The history of rennet cheese goes back a long way, even though the scientific explanation of how it works only followed very much later. Shepherds used to carry their daily milk ration in pouches made from the dried stomachs of animals. The milk they carried in them converted to cheese sooner or later, however, because these pouches still contained residues of the digestive enzyme rennet. The calf's stomach lining produces the substance prochymosin, which is broken down into the enzyme rennet in the acidic environment of the stomach contents, helping the young animal to digest its mother's milk better. This rennet is able to convert milk to a gelatinous substance within a short space of time. The milk protein is precipitated, and the milk coagulates and thickens. The more rennet is added and the higher the temperature of the milk, the firmer the cheese will be.

Milk-coagulating enzymes of vegetable origin are also used in cheese production in addition to the various types of animal rennet, especially in the Mediterranean region: Plant extracts such as the juice of the fig tree or thistle petals, for example, have been used since antiquity as a milk coagulant.

MILK PRE-RIPENING

Pre-ripening the milk prolongs its freshness, which is required for some cheeses. The addition of a certain amount of lactobacilli culture (curdled milk, buttermilk, or yogurt) to the chilled milk is sufficient for pre-ripening. The lactobacilli are thus able to acclimatize and to multiply to a limited extent.

The herb yellow bedstraw (*Galium verum*) also causes milk to coagulate. Vegetable rennet tends to play a secondary role in cheese production, however.

Microbial rennet has been used in the cheese dairy for almost 40 years now. This rennet substitute comprises enzymes obtained by microbial means from molds, which can be produced in whatever quantity is required. Cheese produced with microbial rennet is suitable for vegetarians. The use of microbial rennet has come to play an important role in industrially produced cheese because supplies of natural animal rennet are no longer able to keep up with increasing cheese production.

Genetically engineered rennet substitutes have been available since 1990. Often used for cheese production in the USA, these substitutes remain the subject of dispute in Europe.

In principle, all varieties of rennet cause milk to coagulate, but they do have different renneting properties and are not suitable for all types of cheese.

VITAMINS AND MINERALS

Every piece of cheese contains the milk ingredients in a concentrated form. Many nutrients are therefore present in greater quantities in cheese than they are in milk. Cheese provides the body with high quality protein, vital vitamins (A, D, E, and K), and easily digestible milk fat, as well as valuable minerals and proteins. Cheese is unbeatable as a source of calcium and protein.

Hard cheese in particular occupies a top position as a source of calcium. The reason is simple: a great deal more milk is needed to produce hard cheese than to make the same weight of yoghurt or fresh cheese—the calcium concentration is therefore much higher. The production of 4 oz of hard cheese requires nearly 2¾ pints of milk on average (100 g requires 1.2 l), while the same quantity of extra-hard cheese needs just over 3 pints (1.3 l). The reduced water content means that the minerals and proteins are more concentrated in hard cheese. The harder the cheese—that is, the less water it contains—and the less fat it contains, the higher the concentration of nutrients. A further health factor with hard cheese is the low milk sugar content. The long ripening over many months, sometimes even years, means that the lactose (milk sugar) is broken down completely. This is especially important for people with lactose intolerance.

FAT CONTENT

The somewhat obscure abbreviation FDM means "fat in dry matter" and indicates the fat content of the cheese. The fat content in the dry mass has little in common with the absolute fat content of the cheese. However, it is this absolute fat content that is of great interest to the consumer and is indicative of how much fat the cheese really contains. The reason why it is not simply the percentage fat content of the cheese that is given, as is the case with other foodstuffs, is easily explained. Cheese is subject to constant change; it loses moisture and therefore weight during ripening. The proportion of fat therefore increases in relation to the water content during the ripening process—it is not a fixed measurement. The dry mass, however, comprising fat and protein, barely changes at all during ripening. In addition to the consistency, the fat content of the cheese also plays an important role when it comes to the nutritional value, flavor, and aroma, the majority of aromas being able to develop only in the presence of fat.

There are eight fat content stages altogether. The fat content or the fat content stage must be indicated for all cheese types—with the exception of sour-milk cheese, which always belongs to the low fat stage.

Double-cream stage	min. 60% FDM, max. 85%
Cream stage	min. 50% FDM
Full-fat stage	min. 45% FDM
Fat stage	min. 40% FDM
Three-quarter fat stage	min. 35% FDM
Half-fat stage	min. 20% FDM
Quarter-fat stage	min. 10% FDM
Low fat stage	less than 10% FDM

FAT CHEESE IS NOT THAT FAT AT ALL

An initial glance at a lovely, creamy soft cheese with 70% FDM might have you thinking that it is out of the question for figure-conscious consumers, but such concerns are unfounded because the actual fat content of such cheeses is in fact much lower.

How is the absolute fat percentage calculated, then? It is very simple if you are familiar with the average dry mass percentages of the different cheese groups. There is a practical equation for determining the approximate fat content. The percentage of fat in dry matter has to be multiplied by the following values: By 0.3 for fresh cheese, by 0.4 for Mozzarella, by 0.5 for soft cheese, by 0.6 for semi-hard cheese, and by 0.7 for hard cheese. If you want a precise value, you may use the following rule of thumb: (FDM x dry matter) ÷ 100 = absolute fat content as a percentage.

Here is an example: The soft cheese mentioned above with 70% FDM has an average dry matter content of 50%. The absolute fat content of this soft cheese therefore amounts to just 35% (70 x 50) ÷ 100 = 35.

Hard cheese	ca. 70 %
Semi-hard cheese	ca. 60 %
Semi-soft cheese	ca. 55 %
Soft cheese	ca. 50 %
Processed cheese	ca. 50 %
Fresh cheese	ca. 30 %

Ripening and the art of affinage

It is through ripening that a cheese develops its varietal character. Cheeses ripen very individually, depending on their shape, size, age, and type. During this time the microorganisms convert cheese from a foodstuff into a delicious luxury article. Bacteria, enzymes, yeast, and molds are busy at work during the ripening process, jointly ensuring the conversion of the different ingredients, serving as a nutrient medium for the ripening bacteria, breaking down fatty acids, and converting the milk protein into valuable amino acids. The cheese becomes easier to digest, developing texture as well as its varietal flavor and aroma. A cheese tastes best when it has reached the ideal degree of ripeness. This can take just a few hours or days, depending on the type of cheese, but can also take many months, sometimes even years.

The more handcrafted the cheese production method, the greater the extent to which the milk is untreated and the more natural the ripening room, then the greater the influence of the ripening process on the end product. Natural caves, such as the famous Roquefort caves, for example, have a very specific microclimate.

An expert uses a cheese borer to remove a sample in order to check the degree of ripening.

Temperature and air humidity are determining factors for the ripening process.

Industrial production attempts to replicate such microclimates in modern ripening rooms. Sometimes, however, special natural yeasts, bacteria, or fungal spores are added to the milk intended for the cheese, to the curd mass, or to the young cheese in order to replicate the original product, which develops under conditions as close as possible to the natural conditions.

Higher or lower temperatures in the ripening room or differences in humidity cultivate specific bacteria. A soft cheese with a bloomy rind, such as Camembert, needs 95% air humidity, while 80% is sufficient for a hard cheese, and a goat's milk cheese needs just 75% air humidity. The propionic acid bacteria, which are responsible for the holes in the cheese due to their releasing carbonic acid gases (see box above), only start working at a specific temperature. More carbonic acid gases are released at relatively warm temperatures, producing larger holes in the cheese.

The cheese dairy's master cheese ripener is responsible for the correct coordination of the ripening process from the start through to the end product. Affineurs, however, who are usually passionate cheesemongers, also understand the art of ripening. To some extent an affineur sees himself as an artist who buys the young cheese from the best producers and then dedicatedly attends to its ripening according to his secret recipes in his own ripening cellar. Each cheese needs careful handling. Some require washing

Regular maintenance and cleaning of the rind is an absolute must.

The rind is brushed with salt water in order to prevent mold forming.

in brine, beer, or schnapps, while others are dusted with wood ash or are ripened in leaves, hay, or herbs. Many cheeses are simply rubbed, brushed, washed, and turned over. A glance or a touch is enough for the cheese master to tell what is still lacking and when the cheese has reached its optimum ripeness. A Camembert needs to be nurtured and groomed for about three weeks only, while a semi-hard Cantal needs up to six months. Only conscientious handling produces a balanced flavor, intense aroma, optimum texture, and attractive appearance. This is what distinguishes an affineur's masterpiece from a straightforward dairy product.

When it comes to the ripening of cheese, a distinction is made between those cheese types that ripen from the outside toward the inside and those that ripen from the inside outward. Sour-milk cheeses or rennet cheeses with exterior mold, such as Camembert or Brie, ripen from the outside toward the inside, as do those forming a creamy layer such as Münster cheese or Limburger. In the case

Right page: Cheese with interior mold growth ripens from the inside outward.

Left: A ripeness test to assess the aroma, perforation, and texture.

Below: Natural caves have a very specific microclimate.

of ripening from the outside toward the inside, the microorganisms on the surface proliferate very quickly and form enzymes that break down the proteins entering the cheese. The breakdown of the proteins makes the cheese soft in the middle.

Cheeses with interior mold growth ripen from the inside outward. The best-known example is Roquefort, its mold cultures also being used with many other blue-veined cheeses. These cheeses do not become softer with increasing ripeness but instead remain semi-hard.

CHEESE FAMILIES

If you were to ask a variety of cheese experts how many types of cheese there are, you would get a different answer in every case. The reason: Some cheeses are eaten both fresh and after ripening for a number of months, meaning that they are available as fresh cheese but also as soft, semi-hard, or hard cheeses, depending on the water content. Italian Ricotta is an extreme example: It can be eaten fresh when it is just a few hours old but, if it is salted during the production process, Ricotta can also be grated as hard cheese following several months of ripening. This has provided a basis for establishing basic categories, however.

Classification according to the means of coagulation is the oldest means and distinguishes between sour-milk cheeses and rennet cheeses. These boundaries have become blurred today because both coagulation methods are often combined with one another. A further distinction is made according to the "milk source" (cow, sheep, or goat). The water content in the fat-free cheese mass and the texture forms the basis of a largely uniform, international classification, in which the abbreviation WFF stands for "water fat free." This international criterion distinguishes between six groups.

CHEESE GROUP	WFF
Hard cheese	up to 56 %
Semi-hard cheese	54-63 %
Semi-soft cheese	61-69 %
Soft cheese	60-73 %
Processed cheese	> 67 %
Fresh cheese	> 73 %

Left: The astounding diversity of cheese types leaves nothing to be desired.

The classification according to the water content in the fat-free cheese mass does not apply to whey cheese and whey-protein cheese, cheese which is sold either in or without liquid (cheese in brine, whey, or oil), or *pasta filata*.

Germany classifies its cheese groups according to the water content in the fat-free cheese mass (WFF) as hard, semi-hard, semi-soft, soft, fresh, processed, and sour-milk cheeses. In France, on the other hand, the cheese groups are based on criteria such as appearance, milk type, and production method, giving rise to the following cheese groups: Fresh cheese, soft cheese with white mold, soft cheese with washed rind, semi-hard cheese, semi-hard cheese, hard cheese, blue-veined cheese, processed cheese, goat's cheese, and sour-milk cheese.

FRESH CHEESE

In the past its limited shelf life meant that fresh cheese was produced for the maker's own consumption only, but modern refrigeration options now enable individual fresh cheeses to be distributed outside their specific regions at a national and even an international level.

Fresh cheeses do not require ripening and are ready for consumption directly after production. However, they can be eaten slightly matured or once they have been preserved by salting, smoking, or drying. Fresh cheese usually comprises cow's or goat's milk and is normally produced in the following way: The milk is soured by means of lactobacilli and curdled. Rennet is added if full-cream milk is used, while skimmed milk requires a starter in order to stimulate the lactobacilli. The milk curdles very slowly at low temperatures (about 68 °F / 20 °C). The curdling takes between 10 and 24 hours, depending on the temperature. The resulting gelatinous mass is then cut very roughly and left to stand for a while, and the cheese mass is placed in molds in which it drains for a further six to eight hours. The drained mass is pressed slightly in order to obtain a somewhat firmer curd cheese. The water content of fresh cheese is very high and its shelf life is correspondingly short (one to three weeks at about 39 °F/34 °C). The fat content can vary significantly, depending on whether skimmed milk or milk enriched with cream is used.

There are a number of exceptions that deviate from the production process described here. Mascarpone, for example, is made from heated cream curdled with citric acid, Ricotta and Zieger are obtained by heating the whey. Fresh cheeses include cottage cheese, full-cream, and double-cream cheese, as well as curd cheese in a variety of fat categories.

Cottage cheese is not really curd cheese, and comprises layers of fresh cheese with differing fat contents that are ladled by hand. Cottage cheese is a special type of fresh cheese and has a characteristic grainy consistency achieved by separating out the protein without the addition of rennet, simply by souring the skimmed milk. The characteristic flavor is obtained by adding cream to the resultant cheese grains.

The curd grains absorb the cream to a certain extent and then become "covered" in cream on the outside. Cottage cheese is made

Curd cheese production: The whey drains off after being curdled with rennet, and the fresh cheese is stirred and then placed in containers for sale.

from skimmed milk and the fat content is increased afterward through the addition of cream.

On the farm, cottage cheese production normally takes about three days and involves four steps: Souring, curd preparation and subsequent heating, the washing of the curd, and the addition of fat in the form of cream.

Fresh cheese should have a mildly sour and aromatic flavor and a delicate, creamy consistency. It does not have a strong taste of its own and it is therefore ideal for combining with fresh and raw ingredients. It is then known as fresh cheese spread. New fresh cheese creations featuring herbs, spices, vegetables (such as garlic and tomatoes), nuts, or fruit are continually appearing on the market.

SOFT CHEESE

Soft cheeses owe their creamy consistency to their high water content. They reach their optimum maturity and flavor very quickly and have a short shelf life in comparison to that of hard cheese.

Soft cheeses are small and usually flat, enabling them to ripen quickly through to the core. Their flavor extends from creamy and mild through to robustly aromatic, their consistency from elastic through to runny. Soft cheeses have a characteristic rind formation, a distinction being made between soft cheeses with white mold and those forming a coating or with washed rinds.

With soft cheeses the ripening takes place from the rind toward the centre. The rind flora includes enzymes—bacteria or molds—that break down the protein and infiltrate the cheese mass, causing it to become soft with increasing ripening. If the ripening process is triggered by mold, then the cheese is known as soft cheese with mold. Soft cheeses that ripen as a result of bacteria are known as red smear or red culture cheeses because the bacteria, which thrive in the salty environment, form a smooth coating. There are also soft cheeses that ripen simultaneously as a result of bacteria and mold, however.

The production of soft cheese is based on the principle of rennet cheese production. It is made from cow's, goat's, or sheep's milk that is curdled by adding rennet. Semi-skimmed, full-cream, or milk enriched with cream can be used, with about 3 pints of milk required to produce 1 lb of cheese (8 l for 1 kg). The rennet is added at a temperature of 82–86 °F (28–30 °C) and curdles at this temperature in about two hours. The curd separated from the whey is not cut at all, or else only very roughly, and then carefully ladled into perforated molds in several stages so that the whey is able to drain off properly. After a number of hours the cheese in the mold is turned over and left to drain further. The cheese is then firm enough to be taken out of the mold and to be salted if required. It is left to rest on racks in the drying room for several days, during which time it is turned regularly and sprayed with mold culture.

About a week later, once a fine layer of mold has formed on the surface of the cheese, it is placed in the cool, ripening cellar with a temperature of 46–50 °F (8–10 °C). The young cheese needs to be turned regularly in order to ensure that the surface mold is able to develop evenly. Depending on the size and shape of the cheese, the optimum ripeness is achieved in two to five weeks, at which point the cheese is elastic and the white mold flora has developed reddish patches.

With the exception of a few deviations, the production of soft cheeses with washed rinds is largely similar to the method that is described above. After having coagulated, the curd is cut into walnut-size pieces, after which it is placed in the mold. The molds are sometimes placed on top of one another in order to compress them slightly.

The well-drained cheese can be removed from the mold after four days of regular turning and then salted, before being left to drain for several days. In the ripening cellar with a temperature of 50–57 °F (10–14 °C) and an air humidity of about 95%, the cheese is

washed regularly with brine or else brushed and turned. The washing with brine prevents the formation of mold and encourages the formation of the linens bacteria which, depending on the type, form a reddish or a yellowish, dry to humid coating. The bacteria strain can also be added to the milk prior to adding the rennet. Beer, wine, schnapps, or herbs are added to the brine for some cheeses. Depending on the size and shape, a cheese with a washed rind ripens over a period of between four weeks and four months. Such cheeses are stronger in flavor and do not have the characteristic mildly acidic flavor of a soft cheese with mold. The reason for this is the fact that the bacteria feed on the lactic acid in the cheese. The somewhat stronger aroma comes from the oxidization of the fatty acids.

SEMI-HARD CHEESE

Semi-hard cheeses have an elastic, firm texture and are easy to cut.

In some countries semi-hard cheese is also referred to as semi-soft cheese. Semi-hard cheeses, too, are primarily rennet cheeses. With semi-hard cheeses the distinction is based not only on consistency (water content) but also on whether a rind has formed. Semi-hard cheeses come with or without a rind, with a red coating, with mold on the outside, with yeasts on the rind, or with a wax, paraffin, or plastic coating. It is primarily the water content in the fat-free dry mass that is the determining factor in whether a semi-hard cheese is semi-hard or, indeed, semi-soft. The higher the water content, the more moist and soft the cheese will be. Semi-hard cheeses ripen for a shorter period than hard cheeses but longer than soft cheeses. The distinction between one and another cheese group is therefore blurred. Depending on the ripening period, the size, and therefore the water content of the final cheese product, some semi-hard cheeses are closer to soft cheeses, while others may be classified as hard cheeses. Nevertheless, you will always find references defining semi-hard cheeses as both soft cheeses and hard cheeses. It should also be remembered that the water content for specific cheeses can vary in different countries, so that a cheese is defined as a hard cheese in one country and as a semi-hard cheese in another country. What semi-hard cheeses have in common is the slight heating of the curd during the production process, the curd sometimes being washed beforehand.

The consistency of semi-soft cheeses (*fromage à pâte demi-molle*) places them between semi-hard and soft cheeses. The group of semi-soft cheeses includes the French Reblochon and St. Nectaire, for example, and the German Butterkäse. In Italy the semi-soft cheeses such as Taleggio and Bel Paese are known as *formaggi stagionati mature* (ripe soft cheese). The group of semi-soft cheeses also includes cheeses with mold on the inside such as Roquefort, Gorgonzola, Stilton, and a variety of blues.

Semi-hard cheeses (*fromage à pâte demi-dure*) make up the second group. The distinctions between young hard cheeses are again blurred. Classic semi-hard cheeses include the Dutch Gouda and Edam, for example, and the German Tilsit. With semi-hard cheeses the draining of the whey is supported by additional pressing. Semi-hard cheeses are subjected to less pressing than hard cheeses but more than semi-soft cheeses.

HARD CHEESE

Hard cheeses also belong to the group of rennet cheeses. They have the lowest water content, and that reduces with the increasing ripeness of the cheese, giving hard cheeses a long shelf life and making them capable of being stored for long periods. Hard cheeses have a firm to very firm—sometimes hard—texture. What the majority of hard cheeses have in common is the significant subsequent heating of the curd, known as "cooking." Hard cheeses that result from a particular processing of the curds—such as Cheddar, Cantal, and Colby, for example—are not heated. Semi-hard cheeses, which ripen for a very long time, can also become hard cheeses, as can infused and kneaded cheeses (Mozzarella, Kashkaval) and even fresh cheese (Ricotta), which becomes hard due to the addition of salt and long ripening (see relevant chapters).

A further determining factor is that hard cheeses ripen evenly throughout. The ripening process takes place in both directions, from the outside to the inside and also from the inside outward. A hard cheese achieves its full flavor and characteristic aroma only after a long period of storage and ripening, which can last from a number of months to several years, depending on the type of cheese. With this cheese category it is the classics such as Emmental, alpine cheese, Cheddar, and Parmiggiano Reggiano (Parmesan) that come to mind immediately, but cheeses such as the Italian Pecorino and Provolone, and Kashkaval which is common in eastern Europe, also belong to this group. The hard cheeses may also be divided into a further two types: Cheeses with holes (Appenzeller, alpine cheese, Emmental, Greyerzer) and those with no holes or barely visible holes (Parmiggiano Reggiano, Grana Padano, Sbrinz, Pecorino). Cheeses that undergo heating with hot water and the kneading of the curd followed by pulling (see infused and kneaded cheeses) also belong to the hard cheese group after the appropriate period of ripening.

Hard cheeses include a multitude of cheeses that differ in terms of shape, consistency, rind formation, and flavor.

The size of the curd grains and the strength of the compression influence the later consistency: The lower the compression strength, the softer the cheese will be later; the greater the compression strength, the harder it will be. The cheese is salted dry or in a salt bath. It is then salted once again after drying off to enable a firm rind to form.

The fresh cheeses ripen in a humid cellar at differing temperatures and are turned regularly. The cheeses then undergo further handling, depending on their subcategory. The washing with unsalted water prevents the formation of mold and red cultures. This method is used with cheeses such as Tamié, Asiago, and some Trappist cheeses. Another option is the dry cleaning of the rind by brushing, as is done with Cantal and Cheddar. Washing with slightly salted water enables the formation of a small amount of red coating, which then becomes covered with mold.

Some cheeses are left to dry out slowly while the rinds are regularly rubbed or brushed dry. Some kinds are allowed to develop a small layer of mold on the surface, which is then pressed on by hand—as is the case with Tomme de Savoie, for example. This makes the rind thicker.

ALPINE CHEESE

A considerable number of hard cheeses, with the exception of Parmiggiano Reggiano, originate from the alpine regions. These cheeses used to be made from milk gathered from different farms during the pasture season from June to September and brought in to a collection point. This collective milk supply was then processed into wagon-wheel-size cheeses and, once ripe, divided amongst the farms at the end of the season. For a hard cheese such as Emmental, for example, full-cream or skimmed milk is heated to 90 °F (32 °C) and propionic acid bacteria (see below) are sometimes added to promote the formation of the holes. The milk is left to curdle for about 30 minutes after the rennet is added. The curd is then cut up very finely and heated again, to about 127 °F (53 °C). The heating extracts further liquid from the fine curd grains so that it becomes more elastic. The curd is then lifted out of the kettle with a linen cloth, in which it is pressed for about 24 hours while being turned several times. The pressure exerted at this stage is very significant and can easily reach 2 tonnes for a cheese weighing 265 lb (120 kg). The degree of compression means that a very large quantity of milk is required: 25 gallons of milk produce no more than about 13–18 lb of hard cheese (100 l of milk produces about 6–8 kg).

The cheese is placed in a salt bath for about a week after pressing. The cheese is again salted several times following the salt bath in order to increase the flavor and to ensure better rind formation. Following a drying period of 10 to 14 days, cheeses that are intended to develop holes (Emmental, Greyerzer, Appenzeller, and alpine cheeses) are placed in a warm fermenting cellar, where the propionic acid bacteria are able to flourish at 71–75 °F (22–24 °C) and form the characteristic holes.

All other cheeses are placed directly in the ripening cellar. The actual ripening takes place under high air humidity of 90% and significantly cooler temperatures, namely at 54–57 °F (12–14 °C). The cheese is rubbed or brushed with water regularly during the ripening process. Some types, such as Gruyère, are deliberately washed with brine in order to encourage the formation of red cultures.

Hard cheese is especially hard close to the rind, and the flavor here is also more intense owing to the treatment during ripening. It is softer and milder on the inside. The optimum ripening period is reached after six to twelve months, namely once a little brine has collected in the cracks or holes in the cheese or the salt has crystallized to form small white dots or holes in the cheese.

INFUSED, KNEADED, AND FILATA CHEESES

The key feature in the production of infused, kneaded, and filata cheeses is the infusion of the soured, finely cut curd with hot water, followed by the kneading of the then malleable cheese substance.

The infusing and kneading of the cheese produces a typically fibrous to foliated texture. This texture is still easily recogniz-able in young cheeses, while older cheeses lose the foliated texture and appear layered or granular. The blanching with hot water reduces the microflora contained in the cheese and gives the infused and kneaded cheeses their own characteristic flavor. The infusing and kneading also make the cheeses malleable and pliable. The group of infused and kneaded cheeses includes the Italian *pasta filata* cheeses, which are cheeses made from "pulled" curd. These cheeses are made by pulling the infused and kneaded cheese substance into strips and strands (*filare*) that are cut to the required length before being woven, pressed into molds, or cut into smaller pieces (*mozzare*). The best known examples of the Italian *pasta filata* cheeses (*formaggi a pasta filata*) are of course Mozzarella, along with Scamorza, Provolone, Caciocavallo, and Ragusano.

Infused and kneaded cheeses are not only produced in Italy, but are also widespread in southeastern Europe, where the pulling stage is usually omitted, however. The curd is kneaded and reshaped before the malleable cheese is pressed into round molds. Examples include Kashkaval (Romania, Bulgaria, the former Yugoslavia), Kasseri (Greece), Oštiepok (Slovakia), Păpufli de cafl (Romania), and Kaflar peyniri (Turkey). The cheeses are salted and usually then left to ripen over several months. The curd, which is obtained from the soured, cut-up and recompressed curd grains, is sometimes also eaten fresh. In southeastern Europe such curd is known as Cafl or Kafl.

Although the Italian *pasta filata* cheeses are the most widespread, the pulling of malleable cheese substances is also known in eastern Europe with Parenica (Slovakia), for example, and Parenyica (Hungary). The production of *pasta filata* cheeses is also widespread in the USA, where they are known as stretched curd-type cheeses. Also popular are the so-called string cheeses, sold in strips as a snack, either smoked or unsmoked. In Canada, Mozzarella cheese with a low fat content is simply known as pizza cheese.

CHEESE WITH INTERIOR MOLD

Cheeses with interior mold are usually made from cow's or sheep's milk, more rarely from goat's milk. These are cheeses streaked or interspersed with blue or green mold. In France they are known as Bleu or Fromage bleu and Persillé or Fromage persillé, while in Anglo-Saxon countries they are referred to as blue or blue cheese, and blue-veined cheese or blue-green veined cheese. In Spanish-speaking regions such cheeses are known as Azul or Queso azul. The molds that spread through the interior of the cheese and contribute to their distinctive appearance and flavor are various strains of *Penicillium roqueforti*.

Full-cream milk is traditionally used for cheeses with interior mold and the cheeses are correspondingly fatty, most of them having about 50% FDM. From 1⅓ gallons of milk the yield is about 1 lb of cheese (10 l make about 1 kg). The rennet is added to the milk at a temperature of 82–90 °F (28–32 °C) and the coagulation period is about one hour. The curd is then carefully broken up and stirred slightly. Cheeses with interior mold belong to the group of semi-hard cheeses, but the curd is not compressed in this case. The curd grains need to remain elastic so that the mold is later able to spread evenly through the cheese. The curd is then ladled into cylindrical molds in which the cheese then drains for three to four days, being turned frequently during this time. After being removed from the molds, the cheese is salted dry and left to dry for four to six days. It is then injection time: The cheese is pierced with a long needle and injected with the required blue or green mold cultures. Outside air is able to penetrate the cheese via the pierced air passages, where it circulates and thus encourages the mold growth from the inside. With some cheeses the mold cultures are added earlier, at the stage when the rennet is added to the milk or when the curd is cut. With these cheeses the later injection of the mold cultures is not necessary, but the piercing of the air passages is still required.

Following the injection, the cheese ripens for several weeks to several months, depending on the type, at a temperature of 46–50° F (8–10 °C) and high air humidity (90–95%). This often takes place in natural caves or grottos which are home to specific microorganisms. During this time, the ripening takes place from the inside to the outside. The cheese is packed in aluminum foil once the mold has worked its way through to the edge, preventing further mold growth. The cheese continues to ripen in the foil with the cheese protein being broken down further, and the cheese becomes creamier and more liquid with a butter-like consistency. Some 100 different flavoring agents develop during the ripening process. With strongly salted cheeses (such as Roquefort), the rind needs to be scraped occasionally so that the red bacteria, which flourish in a salty environment, are not able to spread. With Gorgonzola, on the other hand, the formation of this red coating is encouraged by washing the cheese with brine.

SOUR-MILK CHEESE AND BRINE CHEESE

Sour-milk products are the longest known types of cheese. The starting product for sour-milk cheese is sour-milk curd that is processed either fresh or ripened, depending on the type. Sour-milk curd is produced without the addition of rennet, contains no fat, and has a higher dry mass than that of curd cheese. Well-known sour-milk

cheeses include Kochkäse and Olmützer Quargel, Harz cheese, and Handkäse, for example.

The basic mass is obtained by heating skimmed milk to 72–79 °F (22–26 °C) and adding sour milk, buttermilk, or frozen cultures. The mass is then left to stand for 14–18 hours. The curd is cut into pieces about ⅓ in (1 cm) in size and left to rest for half an hour. Once the whey has separated, it is slowly heated in a water bath and churned for about 15–30 minutes so that the curd becomes firm. The sour-milk curd is drained in a cloth, during which time it is also compressed slightly. Table salt and bicarbonate of soda are added before the curd is then finely ground in a mincer. It is then placed in molds in layers. The yeasts in the loosely layered curd then begin to break down the acids. Depending on the cheese variety, the cheese has to "sweat" for two to four days at a temperature of 68–77 °F (20–25 °C) and high air humidity, meaning that it releases liquid due to the added salt. For this reason it is also turned over regularly and placed on a new underlay. Sometimes the cheese is placed directly in the ripening cellar, and in these circumstances the ripening and deacidification process lasts slightly longer. The cheeses become glassy on the surface after five to six days. When they reach this stage they are washed with a salt solution and red culture before being placed in the ripening room at a temperature of 59 °F (15 °C). There they continue to be rubbed with the salt solution and turned on a regular basis. The cheese is ripe when the core is no longer white.

Brine cheeses are white cheeses that were originally usually made from sheep's milk. They are typical of warmer countries in the Balkans and eastern Mediterranean area. Brine cheeses ripen in a brine with a salt content of 4–10%. The salted fresh cheese is placed in wooden, metal, or plastic molds in layers, and these are then closed so that they are airtight. Sometimes they are left to ripen for several months. Prominent brine-cheese-producing countries are Bulgaria, Greece (Feta), and Romania—as well as Turkey, where the mild, slightly salty sheep's milk cheese Beyas peynir, for example, is widespread. A similar situation also applies in the countries of the former Soviet Union. Today white cheeses are produced all over the world, most of them from cow's milk.

KOCHKÄSE

Also known in Austria as Glundner Käse and in France as Cancaillotte, Kochkäse is made from ripened sour-milk curd which is melted by cooking it. Kochkäse is therefore also classified as a processed cheese.

The curd is deacidified with yeasts in order for it to be able to ripen. The crumbled curd is then layered to a height of about 2 in (5 cm) in a ripening box. A little bicarbonate of soda may be added in order to speed up the deacidification. The curd is covered with a damp cloth and left to stand for three to four days at a warm temperature, during which time it is also stirred occasionally. The curd is ripe once the curd particles have become glassy. This is followed by the cooking, with butter, salt, and spices being added as flavor enhancers. The curd is heated to 167–194 °F (75–90 °C), while being stirred continuously until it has become homogeneous with a honey-like consistency. The hot curd is then placed in small containers and the thin Kochkäse obtained in this manner can be spread once chilled.

Processed cheeses are made by heating cheese with or without the addition of emulsifying salts. Processed cheese is available in all fat categories—in slices, wedges, cubes, and in cake shapes. Depending on the variety, they may have a smooth, spreading, or slicing consistency. The flavoring ingredients used include mushrooms, peppers, ham, herbs, walnuts, and many others. Intermediate layers and coating with other ingredients often provide a distinct contrast to the mild emulsified, piquant flavor.

Processed cheeses were developed specifically to enable the problem-free preservation and transportation of cheese products.

Before the advent of processed cheeses at the beginning of the twentieth century, Dutch cheeses had been subjected to heat treatment and preserved in tins. It was at about the same time that the German chemist Hermann Lassig had his process for producing processed cheese without the addition of emulsifying salts patented at the patent office in Kiel. He melted skimmed-milk cheese with butter and full-cream milk over low heat, placed the mixture in molds, and left it to set. A number of years later Walter Gerber and Fritz Stettler from Thun in Switzerland came up with the idea of preserving Emmental by heating it. In 1911, they brought onto the market a packaged Emmental that they had produced using emulsifying salts (at that time citric acid salts). A few years later, an American of German descent, J. L. Kraft, produced a processed Cheddar using monophosphates as emulsifying salts. It was from this point in time that processed cheeses began to take hold all over the world.

Younger, ripened cheeses were finely ground to produce the cheese mass. Today the mass is heated at high pressure with sodium phosphates or other emulsifying salts (polyphosphates) at a temperature of 248 °F (120 °C) and liquefied. The melted mass is placed in molds and sets as it cools. The heat treatment and the addition of emulsifying salts stabilize the processed cheese physically, chemically, and bacteriologically. The cheeses used as the raw material usually come from overproduction or are cheeses that are not put on the market due to minor blemishes. Processed cheese is a high quality convenience product that is temperature resistant—it is even able to withstand tropical temperatures.

WHEY AND WHEY-PROTEIN CHEESE

Whey cheese is made by extracting the water from the whey and adding cream, butter, or else fresh milk. Whey-protein cheese comprises a curd-like mass that is obtained by souring and heating whey or skimmed milk, or a mixture of the two. Whey and whey-protein cheeses contain all of the milk's valuable, nutritionally relevant whey proteins. Sweden boasts a long tradition of whey cheeses made from goat's milk (Gjetost), as does Norway. Other well-known whey cheeses come from Italy (Ricotta), Corsica (Brocciou), and Greece (Manouri), while the Schabzieger cheese has been known in Switzerland since the thirteenth century.

SHEEP'S MILK CHEESE

Some of the most famous and most popular cheeses are made from sheep's milk—namely the French Roquefort, the Italian Pecorino, and the Greek Feta. Creamy sheep's milk, which contains almost double the fat content of cow's milk, is especially well suited to cheese making. Cheeses made from sheep's milk largely come from hot, dry regions.

The production of sheep's milk cheese is comparable to that of cow's milk cheese in principle but, unlike cow's milk, sheep's milk is always processed as full-cream milk. Sheep's milk is often combined with cow's or goat's milk. The addition of cow's milk largely serves to extend the sheep's milk yield, which is limited and available only at specific times, while the addition of goat's milk refines the taste. With their higher lactose content, sheep's milk cheeses always have a slightly more acidic flavor in comparison to cow's milk cheeses. Sheep's milk cheese can also be enjoyed as cream or soft cheese during the sheep's lactation period. Part of the milk is made into longer-lasting hard cheese, however, in order to ensure that sheep's milk cheese is available for the rest of the time.

GOAT'S MILK CHEESE

Like sheep's milk, goat's milk is not skimmed prior to being made into cheese, and it is sometimes combined with sheep's or cow's milk for reasons of flavor. In France, home to some of the most well-known goat's cheese specialties, goat's milk cheeses produced from combined sheep's and cow's milk are known as *mi-chèvre*, these being made of 50% goat's milk. Cheeses made solely from goat's milk are known as *chèvre*. The characteristic goat's cheese aroma derives from specific fatty acids which are formed a while after milking. Very freshly processed goat's milk has a neutral taste and the cheese flavor is correspondingly subtle. Modern processing methods mean that the typically 'goaty' flavor of goat's milk cheese is now a thing of the past.

The production of goat's milk cheese differs little from that of its cow's milk relatives. The fact that the curdled goat's milk is soft means that the cheese making has to be handled particularly carefully. The delicate curd is also the reason for goat's milk cheeses usually being produced as small cheeses, which also have a very creamy texture.

Goat's milk is curdled by means of lactobacilli and/or rennet, the whey is separated off, and the curd is cut. After draining, this is a fresh cheese with a mild, slightly acidic character. If the cheese is to ripen further, it is then rubbed with salt solution and stored. Special mold cultures are added to some cheese varieties. The ripening period, which can take one to two weeks or else several months, depends on the size of the later cheese and the desired aroma. The longer the cheese ripens, the more piquant the aroma.

One of the particular refinement methods used with goat's milk cheese is the sprinkling of the cheese with ash. The ash often comes from the burnt wood of grape vines. It is then combined with a little salt and sprinkled over the cheese, offsetting the humidity and encouraging the formation of the rind. The ash on the rind of a goat's milk cheese is entirely harmless. Goat's milk cheese is sometimes also wrapped in leaves or placed in flavored olive oil.

RAW-MILK CHEESE

Cheese fans swear by raw-milk cheese as being the only cheese that exhibits the full character of the milk. It is produced from unprocessed milk that has not been pasteurized, skimmed, or homogenized and that is made into cheese just as it was milked. In order to retain the natural bacterial flora, the milk used for raw-milk cheese may not be heated above 104 °F (40 °C). This bacterial flora in the milk changes according to the time of the year, the microclimate and the animal feed, and is responsible for the characteristic flavor of the respective cheeses. The milk from animals that feed on fresh grass in the spring and summer pastures has a different flavor from that of animals kept in barns and fed on hay and silage. Many raw-milk specialties are made from the milk of very specific breeds of milk-producing animals. For alpine cheeses, these include especially robust breeds of cow that are well adapted to the alpine climate. The bacteriological and physiochemical quality of the milk is therefore higher but the milk yield is much lower.

The regulations governing the production of raw-milk cheese are among the strictest imaginable in a cheese dairy. Special attention has to be made to hygiene as well as to the health and well-being of the animals. The milk for raw-milk cheese is collected from the farmers on a daily basis and in some areas the farmers even bring the milk to the cheese dairy in the morning and in the evening. The cheese making and affinage for the production of raw-milk cheese usually involve long-established, handcraft methods.

ORGANIC CHEESE

Organic cheese producers dispense with many of the additives commonly used in conventional cheese production, with the rind not being treated with preservatives, for example. In addition to organic milk, other ingredients such as herbs and spices also come from organic sources. The cultures, enzymes, and ingredients used may not be demonstrably genetically modified.

HANDLING CHEESE
Cheese is good for you

Not only does cheese taste good, it is also good for our health. It is a true multitasker among foodstuffs, containing high quality protein and easily digestible fat. The milk sugar (lactose) is broken down while the cheese ripens, meaning that the majority of cheese varieties contain practically no carbohydrates. People suffering from lactose intolerance are therefore able to enjoy the majority of cheese varieties without any problem. With each piece of cheese containing a concentration of the milk ingredients, cheese is a source of many vital vitamins and minerals. This is especially true of hard cheeses which, with their low water content, have a higher concentration of nutrients than is the case with fresh cheese with its higher water content.

HIGH QUALITY PROTEIN
Milk and cheese protein has a high biological value and contains many essential amino acids (protein-building blocks). Milk protein also increases the biological value of other foodstuff proteins—such as those in bread or potatoes, for example. A cheese sandwich or a cheese and potato bake therefore provides the optimum complement of essential amino acids.

FAT AS A FLAVOR CARRIER
The milk fat contained in milk and milk products is especially easy to digest, is quickly absorbed by the intestines, and also contains the fat-soluble vitamins A, D, and E. Many of the flavoring agents that characterize the different cheese varieties are fat soluble.

Flavoring agents derive from the fatty acids during the ripening of the cheese and the fat in cheese is therefore an important flavor carrier.

VITAL MINERALS AND VITAMINS

Calcium, indispensable for the development and preservation of bones and teeth, is the most important of all the minerals contained in cheese. Calcium is also required for many metabolic processes and plays a very significant role in the prevention of osteoporosis. There is no other foodstuff with such an abundance of calcium in such an easily utilizable form as milk and milk products, including cheese of course. Adults are able to meet their daily calcium requirement by eating about 4 oz (100 g) of semi-hard or hard cheese daily.

Milk and cheese are among the foodstuffs that are rich in magnesium. Magnesium performs vital tasks with regard to muscle work and the interaction between nerves and muscles.

Vitamin A is especially important for the eyes, but also for the functioning of the mucous membranes and for normal growth. Cheese provides both vitamin A and its precursor beta-carotene, which the body converts to vitamin A. The B vitamins that are contained in cheese are known as cell vitamins. They assist the body in obtaining energy from protein, fat, and carbohydrates, as well as playing a role in hematosis and the breakdown of the body's own substances.

Children like it mild

An adequate supply of calcium is especially important for growing children. The cheese varieties popular with children—including Allgäu, Emmental, Gouda, Edam, and Butterkäse—contain large quantities of this vital nutrient and 4 oz or so (100 g) of cheese is enough to meet the daily requirements of a school-age child. Scientists at the University of Dijon have established that the determination of the foods we enjoy the most takes place at nursery-school age. It is therefore recommended that parents begin "practicing" with their offspring at an early age in order for them to acquire the taste for cheese as a primary health food. It is important that the child is not overburdened with strongly flavored varieties. The mild cheeses ranging from Butterkäse to Gouda are ideal for getting started, while fresh and processed cheeses are popular spreads on bread. Children have a natural preference for soft foodstuffs that can be chewed easily. Cheese is also found in dishes familiar to children all over the world: Pizza, cheeseburgers, and spaghetti with grated cheese. Anything that children are able to eat with their hands tastes especially good of course, and cheese sticks, Mozzarella sticks, and crumbed or fried Emmental slices are therefore ideal for tempting children in the direction of cheese.

Buying cheese is a question of trust

The quality has to be right in order to be able really to enjoy cheese, while the multitude of cheese varieties and brands makes the choosing more and more difficult. Buying cheese is a question of trust and it is therefore worth relying on an expert. Competent advice is especially important with international and rare cheese specialties. Cheese experts in a specialist shop or delicatessen know their range and know where the cheeses come from. They will sell you your chosen cheese at optimum ripeness and will advise you on your choice. Well-organized cheese counters with expert advice can also be found in discerning specialist departments in some supermarkets. Here you will find mainly the most common varieties and will be able to try one or two of the cheeses before deciding what to purchase. The range in the large supermarket refrigerators is limited. Normal supermarkets do not have the personnel resources to be able to provide their own expert cheese department, and so they generally resort to pre-packaged goods that are usually industrially produced.

Competent advice is especially important with international cheeses.

Well-organized cheese counters can also be found in some supermarkets.

Assessing cheese quality

A "normal" cheese fan is also able to assess the quality of a cheese by using their eyes, nose, ears, sense of touch, and palate. In doing so the focus is on criteria such as aroma, texture, degree of ripeness, and the rind.

SIGHT

The external appearance of the cheese does provide some indication of its inner quality. It should have a uniform shape, and the surface and the sides should be even—not shrunken or bloated. The rind should not exhibit any cracks or folds but should enclose the whole cheese. This is an indication of careful production. In the case of cheeses with surface mold, the mold flora should be distributed evenly over the whole cheese. The color of the surface mold may vary between snow white and cream colored through to ochre-yellow, depending on the variety and ripeness of the cheese. It should definitely not deviate from the characteristic color of the cheese in question, however. When cut, the cheese texture should also exhibit the consistency characteristic of the particular cheese variety.

Cheese experts know their range and are happy to advise you on your selection.

The external appearance of the cheese provides an indication of its inner quality.

HEARING AND FEELING

The quality of a cheese can also be established by hearing, but this does need a certain amount of practice. Once you have heard the characteristic sound audible when tapping the rind of a relatively hard, ideally ripened, and carefully produced cheese with your fist, finger, or a small hammer, then you have a comparative basis for checking the next cheese. A dull sound is indicative of too many cavities in the cheese. If the sound is faint then the cheese substance is probably too compact. With a soft cheese the elasticity of the cheese and the degree of ripeness are easily tested by pressing your finger on the rind. The more the rind gives in to the pressure, the riper the cheese; the greater the resistance, the fresher the cheese.

SMELLING AND TASTING

Your nose and palate can tell you a great deal about the flavor and aroma of a cheese. The cheese must not be too cold when you are carrying out this means of assessment, otherwise the aromas will not yet have developed. The test is best carried out one to two hours after taking the cheese out of the refrigerator. The distinction is made between pleasant, clear, fresh, sweet, and sour aromas, while moldy, grassy, and ammonia-like aromas are characteristic of some cheese varieties. However different the characteristic aromas may be, the aroma of the milk used should always be perceptible because every type of milk—be it cow's, sheep's, or goat's milk—has its own aroma. The taste buds on the tongue enable the perception of the sweet, sour, salty, and bitter tastes. The different flavor and aroma components of the cheeses combine on the palate initially, and then on the tongue by means of the fragrance, aromas, and taste, providing a complex gourmet experience.

EU PROTECTION FOR REGIONAL SPECIALTIES

Quality guarantees are a tremendous help when buying cheese specialties from other countries. Many European cheese specialties form part of the exclusive circle of foodstuffs enjoying EU-wide protection. Depending on their properties, regional products can be entered in the EU register as "protected designation of origin," "protected geographic indication," or "traditional specialty guaranteed," thus protecting them from imitation. A total of around 750 foodstuffs and agricultural products from 21 EU countries enjoy such protection. The spectrum extends from cheese, meat and meat products, fish and crustaceans to fruit, vegetables, olives, vinegar, and oil through to upmarket bakery products and beer. In France there are 44 cheese varieties alone that enjoy EU origin protection, in Italy the number is 33, while in Spain there are 19 varieties, to name just a few traditional cheese-producing countries. Cheeses that enjoy origin protection are clearly labeled with the individual country codes.

The product is either bred and/or produced and/or processed in the region in question, but the raw materials do not have to come from the region.

The products must be produced from traditional raw materials, according to traditional compositions or traditional production and/or processing methods.

The product must originate from the region in question, where it must also be processed and produced. The raw materials used also have to derive from the region.

The EU Commission's objective with this protection is to provide guidelines for the consumer. It is Brussels' intention that, given the multitude of products available on the market, the consumer is given clear, concise information about their origins in order to be able to make the best choice. The geographic details and designation of origin therefore indicate that a product derives from a specific region and that there is a correlation between the quality, reputation, and particularities of the product and its geographic origin. Many of the products enjoying EU-wide protection are produced according to traditional recipes, while the climatic and geographic characteristics of the region can also have a specific influence on the flavor of the products. The characteristic flavor, the special production method, and a long tradition make each foodstuff with protected origin a culinary experience.

The best way
to store cheese

Cheese is a living natural product that continues to ripen from the day it is produced. Cheese prefers cool but not cold temperatures. The fat in cheese is light sensitive, with exposure to light altering the taste of the cheese. Cheese should therefore always be stored in the dark.

REFRIGERATION

Only very few of today's households have a larder or a cellar at the right temperature, so cheese is usually stored in the refrigerator. The cheese does need to be taken out of the refrigerator at least an hour before eating in order for the full cheese aroma to be enjoyed.

Humidity during storage can influence the quality of the cheese, as can temperature changes. Temperature fluctuations cause the surface of the cheese to become damp, while the cheese will continue to ripen too quickly if it is too warm. As bacteria proliferate at warm temperatures, cheese stored in a warm place may also develop a bitter taste, while temperatures that are too cold may also make cheese bitter. Cheese must be protected from drying out during storage and an ambient humidity of 80–90% is ideal. The vegetable drawer is generally the best place in the refrigerator for storing cheese. If you have a cool, well-ventilated natural cellar or larder with a constant temperature of about 50 °F (10 °C), then the cheese should be stored on a slatted frame. A cloth dampened slightly with wine or salt water and spread over the cheese on a rack, without coming into contact with it, is ideal.

ONGOING RIPENING

When stored at temperatures of between 37 and 48 °F (3–9 °C), cheese reaches optimum ripeness by the use-by date indicated on the packaging. Soft cheeses taste best when they are well ripened, but they can then be kept for a few days only from this point in time. The ripening process is interrupted if they are stored at too low a temperature. Fresh cheese does not continue to ripen and should be eaten as fresh as possible. It is therefore best stored where it is very cool, namely directly under the freezer compartment at about 36 °F (2 °C). Slightly ripened fresh cheese is best stored in the middle of the refrigerator at about 39–45 °F (4–7 °C). Processed cheeses also do well when stored at cool temperatures.

GOOD AND BAD MOLD

Cheese mold, be it on the surface or on the inside, is harmless cultured mold bred especially for the production of different cheese varieties. The harmful foodstuff mold which develops in the case of the extended and inappropriate storage of fruit, vegetables, or bread and which is also present—albeit invisibly—in places on the surface of the foodstuff, seldom occurs in milk products. Undesired wild mold on hard or semi-hard cheese should always be removed thoroughly. Moldy fresh, soft, or semi-hard cheese should be thrown away.

Cheese varieties with cheese mold should always be packed separately so that the mold spores do not spread to other cheeses, as they may do if a variety of cheeses are packaged together in foil. For example, if a semi-hard cheese is stored together with a soft cheese with surface mold, then mold can develop on the rindless surface of the semi-hard cheese. This also happens with a cut cheese, where the surface mold can develop on the cut surface of the cheese. This transmission is harmless, however, and does not compromise the flavor.

FREEZING

Cheese may be frozen, but this should only be done in emergencies and for a short period of time. It is better to buy the cheese fresh from the cheese counter. The cold interrupts the ripening process and compromises the flavor and aroma, especially in the case of soft cheeses. Hard cheeses are least affected by freezing because they contain the least water. Fewer ice crystals are formed and the texture of the cheese does not change as much, although it may become crumbly due to the extreme cold. To freeze them, the pieces of cheese should be packed individually in freezer bags, pressing out as much of the air as possible. The cheese will keep for up to six months, depending on the fat and water content (the more fat and water it contains, the shorter the period for which it will keep). The individual pieces of cheese should ideally be left in the refrigerator overnight to thaw.

Airtight plastic containers are suitable for storing cheese.

A fresh piece of tomato or apple underneath the cheese cover ensures sufficient humidity.

Soft cheeses with a coating are best kept in their original packaging.

PACKAGING

Cheese is best bought in one piece. A single piece of cheese with rind does not dry out as quickly and keeps much better than if it is sliced. With cut cheese it is important to protect the cut surface from drying out without robbing the cheese of the air it needs to breathe. Semi-soft and semi-hard cheeses are usually covered with a wax and paraffin layer that protects them from drying out, so that only the cut surfaces need to be protected. Freshly cut surfaces are best covered with aluminum foil (blue, green, and white mould cheeses) or breathable plastic wrap (hard, semi-hard, and sour-milk cheeses). For short term storage each type of cheese should be wrapped individually in aluminum, plastic wrap, or waxed paper. The plastic wrap or aluminum foil should be pierced with a needle a couple of times so that the air is better able to circulate. Soft cheeses with a coating and sour-milk cheeses are better off in their original packaging, but should be wrapped in a further layer of foil or wax paper after opening.

Should a cheese begin to "sweat" as a result of inappropriate storage (globules of fat on the surface) or become too dry, then the globules can be wiped off—a dry cheese can still be used for grating and baking.

SENSITIVE CHEESE

Sensitive soft cheeses need the right packaging as they do not have any protection of their own. The packaging also needs to enable the further ripening of the cheese. Soft cheese is best protected in paper-lined aluminum foil, with further protection in the form of a wooden or cardboard carton. This protects the sensitive cheese from pressure while allowing it to breathe at the same time. Soft cheese that is bought without packaging is best wrapped in waxed paper. Plastic wrap is suitable only for shorter storage periods because it can cause the rind to soften quickly.

One option is to pierce the plastic wrap with a needle to allow the air to circulate and then to wrap it in a damp cloth. Damp cloths protect the cheese from drying out, but if the moisture comes into direct contact with the cheese the rind can become soft and viscous.

"FRAGRANT" CHEESE

Some soft cheeses give off a strong aroma that overpowers all of the other foodstuffs in the refrigerator. The "stinkers" should therefore be stored in an airtight container apart from other foodstuffs. Another option is to place strong-smelling cheese in a plastic bag which is then blown up like a balloon and sealed with an elastic band. This form of packaging does mean that it needs to be used up quickly because harmful mold can develop quickly. Mild varieties should generally be stored apart from strong-smelling varieties. Several semi-hard and hard cheeses can be stored in the same container without any problems, however.

PLASTIC CONTAINERS

Airtight plastic containers are also suitable for storing cheese. Condensation may gather on the lid, so cheese stored in a plastic container should also be wrapped in paper so that moisture does not drip onto the cheese. Special plastic containers with adjustable ventilation slots are more suitable if the cheese is to be stored for several days.

CHEESE COVER

Cheese covers are especially suitable for cheese that is to be eaten soon or that still needs to ripen further at room temperature. A fresh tomato wedge or a piece of apple underneath the cover also ensures sufficient humidity. The individual varieties need to be packaged separately if the cheese is to be kept under the cover for a longer period.

Pieces and portions

Cheeses come in a wide variety of shapes and sizes. They can be small and cylindrical, flat and round like a large cake, sometimes no bigger than a coin; they also come as rolls, blocks, as flat medium-size blocks, as cubes and rectangles, and as wagon wheel size, very heavy blocks. The right cutting technique means not only that unnecessary waste is avoided but also that the cut cheese simply looks more appetizing, providing a feast for the eye as well.

Processed cheese wedges are wrapped separately in foil without the need for cutting them through. Round and rectangular soft cheeses are cut into small pieces like a cake. Blue-veined cheeses are also cut like a cake, while tall cylindrical cheeses are sometimes cut in half through the middle beforehand. Small, flat cheeses are best cut into two halves. Sticks, rolls, and long, thin blocks are cut into thick slices. Spherical-shape cheeses are best cut into quarters. Large, rounded blocks are first cut through the middle and half a hexagonal piece is then cut from their middle, the cheese then being sliced thickly as far as this piece. Large hard cheeses are cut into quarters and then into thick slices. A large cube is best cut into blocks and a rectangular cheese into cubes.

CUTTING EQUIPMENT

The different cheese varieties require individual treatment. While all cheeses can be cut with a knife in principle, one or two items of specialist cutting equipment are worth having, depending on the consistency of your favorite cheese. A selection of such equipment is presented below.

Extra-hard cheeses are best broken up and not cut. This is done using the tip of a small, short, almond-shape hard cheese knife to lever out large pieces diagonally. The cheese is also broken up into smaller pieces for serving in this way.

A flexible cheese wire is used for cutting up larger cheeses. With semi-hard and hard cheeses the rind is first removed from the section of the cheese that is to be cut so that the wire is able to glide though the cheese effortlessly. The cheese wire should be pulled through the cheese quickly to avoid "steps" forming on the cut surface. A wire is also ideal for cutting semi-soft cheeses with interior mold, which are often slightly crumbly. Since these cheeses usually have a slightly sticky texture it is recommended that they be cut directly after taking them out of the refrigerator. The warmer and therefore softer the cheese is, the more difficult it is to separate the slices after cutting. A cheese wire also enables even slices to be cut smoothly from semi-soft blue-veined cheeses, rolled fresh cheeses, and soft cheeses—for which the wire is attached to a handle. With its firm handle a cheese spade is easy to hold, has a wide, sharp blade, and is very stable, but it does have only a limited cutting width. It can be used to cut larger pieces of firm hard cheese and firmer semi-hard cheeses without any problem. Cheese can of course be cut with a knife as well. A stable cheese knife with a wide blade is best used for cutting larger pieces of hard and semi-hard cheeses. The blades are often grooved to prevent the cheese from sticking. A soft cheese knife with its two-pronged tip is best suited to cutting smaller pieces of cheese and for cutting soft cheese. The prongs can be used to place the cheese pieces directly on the serving plate. The majority of such knives have a serrated edge in order to ensure that the cheese pieces come away from the blade easily. Blunt knives are in fact much better suited to cutting cheese than sharp knives. Warming the knife slightly by placing it in hot water, for example, means that the blade glides through the cheese like butter. A cheese plane is especially suited to shaving thin strips from blocks of hard or semi-hard cheese, while the rind is also easily removed using a cheese plane. A girolle is a specialist piece of cutting equipment used to shave cylindrical hard cheeses with a rotating knife. The cheese forms small rosettes which are very decorative on the cheese platter.

A cheese grater is well suited to low fat hard cheese and extra-hard cheese. The finely grated cheese is ideal for sprinkling on soups, sauces, and pasta dishes. Cheese graters with small, straight perforations are best suited to firm semi-hard cheeses and the grating produces thin strips of cheese. A grater with larger holes which produces larger strips is better for semi-soft cheeses. Both thin and large strips of cheese are ideal for baked dishes and as a salad ingredient. A variety of cheese mills are also available for grating pieces of cheese, and they come with a range of fittings and also often with an electric motor.

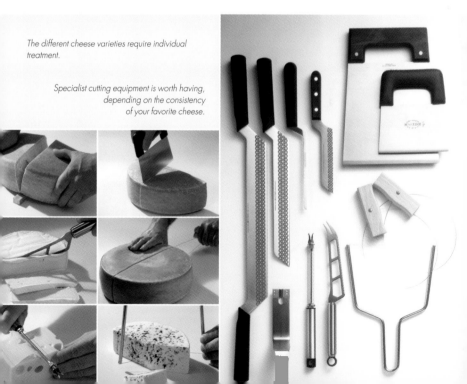

The different cheese varieties require individual treatment.

Specialist cutting equipment is worth having, depending on the consistency of your favorite cheese.

Serving and enjoying cheese

Cheese tastes good anywhere, anytime. From a simple cheese sandwich to a grand buffet appearance—cheese adapts to our requirements like hardly any other foodstuff.

WITH OR WITHOUT RIND?

The pure, varietal cheese flavor can only be enjoyed if the rind is removed. The rind is washed with brine, wine, beer, or other ingredients, as well as being brushed and handled. Some rinds can contain fermentation and bitter components that develop during ripening. Cheese rind therefore often has a very bitter, intense, and not always pleasant taste. The rind should be cut off, with the exception of young white mold cheeses, fresh cheeses, or young goat's cheeses. The rind protects the cheese from drying out and is therefore a kind of natural packaging. With non-biologically produced cheeses, the rind of hard and semi-hard cheeses often contains traces of natamycin, a preservative applied to the surface of the cheese to prevent the development of mold.

Some cheeses are spooned ...   *... while others are enjoyed on bread ...*

THE CHEESE PLATTER

It is the highlight of any buffet and the conclusion to a celebratory menu—the cheese platter. Be it a rustic cheese platter with whole pieces of cheese or one with sophisticated decoration, the right selection is what is important. The cheese varieties should always be served on a material that does not influence the flavor of the cheese, such as wood, marble, glass, porcelain, or plastic. The cheeses should be laid on the platter without their wrappings and cut into pieces. For the cheese to be enjoyed to the full it needs to have the right degree of ripeness and the right temperature, between 60–64 °F (16–18 °C) so that its aroma is able to develop fully.

A cheese platter should provide a selection, and it is therefore good to combine a variety of flavors and textures. A selection of between four and five cheese types is sufficient for a small platter. A classic composition takes the different taste preferences into account. Hard and semi-hard cheeses, soft cheeses with exterior mold, blue-veined, fresh, and red culture cheeses should definitely form part of the selection. A composition of various types and shapes of cheeses from a single family of cheeses can be appealing. Fewer varieties at different stages of ripeness provide a special treat for real cheese connoisseurs. Calculate 5–7 oz (150–200 g) of cheese per

… and still others add a touch of sophistication to special meals.

Hardly any other foodstuff provides such a wide diversity of indulgent options.

person, while 3–4 oz (80–100 g) per person is sufficient if the cheese is to be served as a dessert. It is advisable to provide a number of cheese knives with the platter, one for white mold cheese, one for red culture cheese, and one for blue-veined cheese.

SERVING CHEESE IN THE RIGHT SEQUENCE

Cheese ought to be enjoyed in the right sequence and the cheese is therefore best arranged clockwise on the plate, beginning with the mildest and moving through to the strongest and most piquant. If you begin by eating the strongest cheese on the platter first, the taste buds are then ruined for a delicate Brie afterward.

The logical sequence that applies to a menu with regard to the taste buds also applies as a basic rule for cheese, namely from light to heavy, from mild to piquant. The preceding cheese should in no way overpower the subsequent cheese and should enable a progression instead.

It is best to begin with a fresh, mild, slightly acidic cheese. It is not important whether the cheese is made from cow's, sheep's, or goat's milk. This should be followed by a subtle-tasting, semi-hard cheese made from cow's or sheep's milk, then a light, fruity soft cheese with exterior mold. Thereafter a ripe goat's milk cheese, and then a soft cheese with a washed rind and very distinctive aroma. Only then should the somewhat stronger and more robust red culture cheeses follow. The piquant blue- or green-veined cheeses come at the end. Hard cheeses are an exception to the rule and, depending on ripeness, they can be served with an aperitif or else after the mold cheeses. Young hard cheeses come before the varieties that have been ripened for months or years at a time. The pieces of cheese are placed on the plate with the tips to the outside as this makes it easier to cut off the rind. When should the cheese be served, however: before or after the dessert? According to experts, both are possible and correct, the sequence being based on the main course. In the classic French menu sequence the cheese comes before the dessert.

What to serve with cheese?

BREAD AND BUTTER

Bread goes with cheese, of course. Cheese specialties develop their flavor especially well when served with bread varieties that do not have a strong flavor of their own, such as baguettes or other wheat flour or combined wheat flour breads. If you have a penchant for experimenting, then here are a few suggested bread and cheese combinations that are worth a try. If the cheese is slightly salty, as is often the case with soft cheese with white mold on the rind, then it also goes well with brown or nut bread. Stronger aromatic cheeses with washed rinds are especially suited to whole wheat bread, for example, while a subtle soft cheese from the same family tastes good with onion bread. Hard cheeses or mold cheeses are good partners for robust rye bread. A ripe goat's milk cheese teams up well with nut bread, and olive bread goes very well with an aromatic alpine cheese. A robust, dark bread harmonizes well with a ripe Cheddar.

Whether you want to eat your cheese with butter is a question of personal taste. With sheep's or goat's milk cheese you should check first of all whether it goes with the butter as the fat structure of these cheeses differs from that of butter made from cow's milk.

FRUIT AND VEGETABLES

Acidic fruit or nuts are better suited to mild cheese varieties than to aromatic ones. The fruit is best eaten after the cheese, however, because it contains enzymes that break down proteins, thus making the cheese easier to digest. Pickled vegetables such as cornichons, olives, or cocktail onions need a robust cheese as a counterpart. Flavorsome fresh tomatoes, spring onions, or radishes go with almost all cheese varieties. Sweet fruit provides an interesting accompaniment to piquant mold cheeses.

PIQUANT JAMS AND CHUTNEYS

Piquant jams, a wide selection of which are available in gourmet food stores, are a great accompaniment for cheese. They are made from green or red tomatoes, pumpkin, red onions, quinces, grape must, or figs and are preserved with sugar and spices (and wine vinegar in the case of chutneys), as well as with nuts on occasion. It is worth trying a fig-mustard sauce with Camembert and other soft cheeses, or a sweet cherry jam with sheep's milk cheese, as is often the custom in the Basque region. To have cheese with dessert is a tradition in Provence, where a mild, aromatic goat's milk cream cheese is drizzled with honey and sprinkled with pine kernels.

Sophisticated: Lamb's lettuce with goat's milk cheese or blue-veined cheese farfalle with pumpkin.

Worth the indulgence: Cheese noodles with Savoy cabbage or grated alpine cheese.

Cheese in the kitchen

The different cheese varieties can be used in a multitude of ways in the kitchen. Be it as a flavoring, for baking, or for melting, cheese is a real jack-of-all-trades for the cook. Cheese thickens and flavors soups and adds an extra kick to salads. Almost every kind of cheese is suitable for baking and grating, and it simply melts into its role as the main ingredient in fondues and raclette. Unusual combinations of sweet snacks and cheese for dessert can provide a culinary highlight. Canapés and snacks using cheese are welcome at any party, while cheese adds an extra touch to sweet and savory baked goods.

Fatty cheeses are generally better suited to cooking than low fat varieties because fatty cheese has better melting properties. The cheese should not become too brown when baked, otherwise it may taste bitter.

FRESH CHEESE

Fresh cheese is suitable for making dips and spreads and also for desserts. It can be combined with butter according to taste and flavored with herbs and spices. Fresh cheese with chives served with baked potatoes is a simple but unbeatable indulgence. Diluted with cream or yogurt it makes a tasty dip for fresh, raw vegetables. Those with a sweet tooth enjoy fresh cheese combined with fresh fruit, sugar, jam, or honey as a dessert. Fresh cheese made from goat's milk may be preserved in oil, spices, and herbs, or grilled slightly and served with lamb's lettuce. Fresh cheese also makes a good party snack shaped into balls and rolled in ground paprika or ground nuts.

SOFT CHEESE

Freed of its rind and cut into slices, soft cheese is ideal for melting over baked potatoes. A quick, tasty supper can be made by wrapping soft cheese in puff pastry and baking it in the oven, or crumbing it and frying it in a skillet.

SEMI-HARD CHEESE

In the kitchen semi-hard cheese is especially suited to baked dishes. Coarsely grated or sliced, it provides a delicious, golden-yellow coating for bakes, toast, meat, or fish. Served as a cheese stick with pieces of fruit or vegetables, semi-hard cheese makes an uncomplicated finger food. It provides a quick warm snack coated in breadcrumbs and fried in the skillet, while cut into cubes it turns a salad into a filling main course. It is just as suited to cheese soufflés and pies as it is to providing a filling for sausages and pancakes.

BLUE-VEINED CHEESE

Blue-veined cheese can be puréed and used with a vinaigrette of oil and vinegar as a salad dressing for tasty salads. The milder varieties such as Fourme d'Ambert or Stilton can be used for baking over sweet-tasting vegetables (endive, celeriac), pears, or even steaks. Very mild blue-veined cheeses such as Gorgonzola can be combined with cream and mixed into warm pasta. With their intense flavor, blue-veined cheeses are also top performers when it comes to flavoring sauces.

PROCESSED CHEESE

Cut into pieces, it serves as the basis for a cheese soup as well as providing a creamy thickener and piquant flavor for sauces.

HARD CHEESE

As pieces, slices, or shavings, hard cheese can be used in the kitchen in a multitude of ways and serves as a flavoring for soups and sauces. Ground with a cheese mill, it is classically sprinkled over freshly cooked pasta. Flavorsome baked goods benefit from the addition of finely grated hard cheese. Hard cheese should be grated if it is to be used for baking as it then melts more easily and becomes nice and crispy.

Cheese and drinks

There are a number of other drinks in addition to wine that are ideally suited to many types of cheese. Beer, grape must or cider, and schnapps can be outstanding accompaniments. A neutral tasting mineral water is recommended if you want to savor the pure flavor of the cheese.

What applies to wine also applies to beer: It should complement but not overpower the flavor of the cheese. In general the slightly bitter taste of beer harmonizes well with the milky-creamy flavor components of the cheese. Mild beers with less of a hop flavor go well with creamy, mild cheese varieties and a robust, flavorsome bock beer is well suited to a robust, flavorsome cheese such as a Tilsit or a strong soft cheese with a washed rind.

Cheese and wine

"Every cheese has its favorite wine, just as everyone has their own special love" (Maurice des Ombiaux, 1868–1943, Belgian author and gastronome).

The combination of wine and cheese provides for exciting as well as new flavor experiences. In principle anything goes, provided you like it and it tastes good. Yet some rules can be helpful, even in the face of such generosity—and even with the combination of cheese and wine. A ripe, aromatic cheese can indeed overpower a

reticent wine, just as a fragrant wine quickly dominates the flavor of fresh, light cheeses. As both cheese and wine are wonderfully lively products, they undergo complex processes that alter their aroma and flavor during the ripening process, which often takes several years. Yet what applies to cheese also applies to wine: Some enchant with the charm of their youth while others reveal their quality only after a long waiting period. Both products derive from one ingredient—one from grapes, the other from milk. When correctly selected, the interaction between wine and cheese provides the connoisseur with a sensory revelation. In the end, however, it is up to each individual to decide which combination tastes best. Be it perfect harmony through the balance of the partners, be it the successful combination of contrasting flavors, or simply the accentuating of an aromatic component with wine, it is certainly worth a try.

It is a myth that red wine definitely goes with cheese. The tannins often come over as hard and bitter in the interaction with the acidity or salinity in the cheese. Fruity red wines with little tannin or mature red wines therefore cover a much larger selection of cheese varieties than young, tannin-rich wines. It is advisable to avoid robust, tannin-rich wines with ripe cheeses in particular, namely those which are already somewhat alkaline

(which especially includes cheeses with washed rinds). White wines with residual sweetness or else robust, slightly malty beers are in fact much more suitable partners.

It is not only the combination of white or red wine with cheese that provides for plenty of indulgence. There are other specialties that offer a range of surprises. For example, Champagne goes well with a fresh, mild goat's milk cheese, while cider is the perfect complement to a ripe Camembert. Calvados, which is distilled in Camembert's home region, can also be a great accompaniment. With its robust character, sherry works well even with hard cheeses from Switzerland, and the Vin Jaune from the Jura region, which is produced in a similar manner, is the classic accompaniment to the Comté cheese from the same region. Port wine and sweet dessert wines are a better enhancement for blue-veined cheeses than any dry red or white wine. What does apply as a rule of thumb is that the beverage specialty from the home region of the cheese in question is usually the best accompaniment.

The following tips may be of some help for anyone feeling somewhat reticent with regard to the cheese and wine adventure. Refined, mild cheese varieties go well with good, refined, and mild wines. Flavorsome and piquant cheese varieties, on the other hand, need full-bodied and robust wines. Salty cheese varieties should be paired with dry, acidic white wines only with care as the acid and salt can accentuate one another slightly. Semi-sweet white wines or wines with subtle acid tones are a better choice in this case. Otherwise, simply try out different combinations and enjoy those that appeal to you the best.

A blue-veined cheese such as Stilton harmonizes well with a mature port wine, the sweetness of the wine neutralizing the salty character. A classic combination with the same effect is Roquefort accompanied by the most famous of sweet Bordeaux wines, namely Sauternes. Mild blue-veined cheeses are complemented by a subtly bitter or elegantly fruity wine that has a hint of residual sweetness.

Mild semi-hard cheeses, fresh cheeses, or else young goat's milk cheeses require a fine white wine which may indeed have a trace of residual sweetness. Stronger semi-hard cheeses such as Edam or Gouda need a white wine with a certain amount of body or a touch of residual sweetness, while a bloomy, somewhat piquant Tilsit pairs very well with a mild, fruity white wine or a ripe, velvety and not too heavy red wine.

Aromatic cheeses need an expressive, aromatic wine and it is therefore no surprise that an Alsace Münster cheese is the ideal partner for a Gewürztraminer from the same region. This is a combination that also works exceptionally well with another red coated cheese, namely Livarot. Alternatives are also robust Chardonnays, Pinot Gris, or Pinot Blanc, as well as aromatic wines such as a Scheurebe. What is important is that they should not have been matured in barrels.

Fruity white wines with little acid, or a fine rosé, go well with creamy soft cheeses. Mild soft cheeses work well with a fresh, even a sparkling, white wine with balanced acids and a low alcohol content. Aromatic wines such as Gewürztraminer are recommended for more flavorsome soft cheeses.

Fresh cheeses pair well with sparkling, fresh, and even acidic white wines. The mild acids in the cheese and the robust acids of the wine balance each other out in this combination.

Mild hard cheeses harmonize very well with light red wines or uncomplicated, fruity white, or rosé wines. A robust beer can work well with aromatic semi-hard cheese varieties. Ripe, full-bodied semi-hard or hard cheeses pair better with robust red wines, however. The latter do need to be sufficiently mature. The aggressive tannins will otherwise be bitter in combination with the distinctly salty flavor components.

Mildly flavored white mold cheeses make a pleasant combination with both medium-bodied white wines and fruity, not too heavy red wines. Ripe white mold or red coated cheeses often have a distinct ammonia flavor and therefore need to be teamed with very robust wines. These can be white wines or else red wines with mild tannins.

Wine and sour milk cheeses do not make good partners. Beer, grape must, or schnapps is generally recommended for sour milk cheeses.

Interview with Markus Del Monego, World Champion Sommelier and Master of Wine

 Markus Del Monego became World Champion Sommelier in Vienna in 1998 and Master of Sake (Kiki Sakeshi) in Japan just a few months later. Together with a Frenchman, he is the only European entitled to use this significant Japanese title. In 2003 he was awarded the title of Master of Wine in London.

Markus Del Monego is the first person in the history of these competitions to carry both of the sought-after titles of World Champion Sommelier and Master of Wine simultaneously.

Do you like cheese?

Absolutely, I think cheese is one of the most fascinating foodstuffs. It is healthy and fascinating at the same time, due to its tremendous diversity of flavors. I enjoy a fresh, young goat's milk cheese with a crispy salad as an appetizer just as much as an alpine cheese from Valais that has matured over a period of years.

What would you recommend for a beginner when it comes to cheese?

Taste, taste, and taste again. At the beginning perhaps the somewhat younger and not quite so robust varieties such as white mold cheeses, for example. Young hard cheeses or semi-hard cheeses such as Gruyère or Gouda, for example, with their mild nutty flavors can also provide an easy start for beginners. An aromatic, robust Münster or an intense Roquefort are better left to the cheese connoisseurs.

Which cheese and wine combinations definitely ought to be tried once?

Roquefort together with Sauternes is a classic. The sweetness of the wine takes away the sharpness of the cheese, while the salty and slightly bitter character of the cheese offsets the sweetness of the wine. A truly classic combination. Also outstanding is a Comté with a Vin Jaune from the Jura region. The nutty flavor of the cheese harmonizes perfectly with the nutty, subtle sherry-like flavor of the wine. And anyone who likes a touch of sophistication can try a cheese with a washed rind, such as an Ami du Chambertin, together with a well-matured Chambertin Grand Cru. Fresh goat's milk cheese is just as ideally suited to a young Sauvignon Blanc, although I also like to enjoy it with a crisp German Riesling. The two different acid structures offset each other wonderfully.

Which combination would you not recommend under any circumstances?

There are quite a few, but the worst is probably blue-veined cheese with a dry, tannin-rich red wine. That just has the bitterness dancing on your tongue. A sweet wine is definitely the better choice in this instance.

What would be an alternative to wine as a cheese accompaniment?

Beer is certainly a classic beverage in this situation and it plays a role in the production of a whole range of cheese varieties. A refined distilled beverage can also work fantastically well with cheese, however. If you have ever tried a ripe, mature Gouda or an old Mimolette with a very old Cognac you can almost forget wine. Fruit schnapps can also harmonize very well with cheese. Calvados with Camembert or a youthful Gruyère with a fine, clear plum schnapps. Such combinations are truly indulgent.

FRANCE
Tour de Fromage

French cheese means a tremendous amount to gourmets all over the world. The country's oldest cheese has been about for 2,000 years; the newest ones are innovative modern creations. With over 500 varieties, there is an incredible range and variety of French cheeses—and that figure does not include the 1,000 or so different branded cheeses. In former times, cheese was sold in markets in the region where it was produced. It is still made to centuries-old recipes and methods today. The *savoir faire* of the artisanal tradition of cheese production is enhanced by the *terroir*, representing the interplay between natural conditions such as the climate, soil, and vegetation, plus the perfect herds for these conditions. The various *terroirs* and the quality of the milk are most evident in French cheeses that are made from raw, or unpasteurized, milk. Every fifth cheese produced in France comes from raw milk, and at least half of those have PDO status (Protected Designation of Origin).

Just as in other European cheese-producing countries, the industry in France is largely commercialized. The latest production methods are employed to guarantee the consistent quality of the product, even with large quantities. There are, however, still a number of small farmhouse cheese producers, whose high quality products are much loved and appreciated.

Left: Cheese, wine, and bread—the symbols of French *savoir vivre*.

THE BAGUETTE

"Typically French" —and yet the 28 in (70 cm) long loaf is less than 100 years old. French bread used to be dark and coarse, round and large, with a dense crumb and thick crust. Longer length loaves first appeared during the eighteenth century. Yeast was added to give the baguette its golden crust and a looser crumb. *Tout Paris* was enamored. However, country folk preferred their traditional broad loaves. The baguette was not accepted in the provinces until the twentieth century. A good baguette is crusty and golden on the outside; the crumb is not too white, and it reveals a springiness when pressed. The flour for artisanal baguettes is ground carefully, the dough rises slowly, and it develops its flavor during this process. A piece of the previous day's dough is retained as the starter for the next day's batch, which adds a nuttier flavor to the bread.

FIRST-CLASS QUALITY

Even though many products may share the same name, that does not necessarily mean that they all share the same quality. The best example of this is Camembert. Although numerous Camemberts are produced all over France as well as in several other countries, Camembert de Normandie is the only one that is allowed to use the AOC seal. AOC stands for Appellation d'Origine Contrôlée, the protective designation of origin, which has been in force in France since 1919. It refers to cheese produced in a defined region according to traditional, handcrafted methods. Its history goes back a long way. There is in existence a first written regulation that dates back to 1666. It was issued by the parliament of Toulouse, and applies to Roquefort. Roquefort was France's first cheese to receive the AOC, which it did in 1921. Today, 44 French cheeses carry the AOC seal. There are 41 regional specialties throughout Europe that are entitled to carry the protective designation of origin (PDO) label.

Right: Looking about at the brocante — there's one in almost every small village.

Bottom: The best sheep's cheese in the Pyrenees is made by shepherds.

NORTHWEST
Creamy under a white bloom

Northwest France is a region with lots of different types of landscape: One is Normandy with its luscious green meadows, home to the world-famous soft cheese that is made from the creamy milk of the region's cows. Normandy also produces the region's unofficial ambassador: Creamy Camembert de Normandie with its typical white bloom.

Away from the major towns and cities, the cheerful landscape of the Loire has mostly retained its rural character. The farms in the region are relatively small. Areas where the wine is particularly good because the vines grow on stony, poor soils also provide excellent living conditions for goats—as in Berry, Touraine, and Poitou. The region produces young, creamy, mild goat's cheeses that have been produced there since the eighth century and are some of the best in France.

More cheese is eaten in the extreme north than anywhere else in France. The people here love rich, tasty, well-seasoned meat dishes, seafood, and beer. Culinary influences from Flemish and French cuisine combine to create an exceptional mixture. The border region is a must for those who love hearty, aromatic cheeses.

Traveling through the nature reserves of Picardy toward Paris, you will find yourself in the rural Ile de France. This region is home to the best Brie in the country. The soft cheese is named after the Pays de Brie.

Left: Impressions of Normandy, paradise for soft cheeses.

CAMEMBERT:
FROM BUTTERY YOUTH
TO A BLOOMY PLEASURE

1 The cheese-making process begins when lactobacilli and a little rennet are added to the milk, which has been heated to 93 °F (34 °C). The raw milk is poured into metal vats, where it separates once rennet has been added. **2** The junket is cut with a special knife until it is the size of grain. This produces the curd. **3** It is ladled—*à la louche*—into small perforated molds. **4** The ladle contains a precisely specified quantity and determines how much the cheese will weigh. A Camembert usually weighs about 9 oz (250 g). **5** When the whey has drained from the curd, the cheeses are removed from the molds and stored in maturing chambers. Mold is added, and then the Camembert is left for three weeks to develop its characteristic bloom. **6** Red marks appear on the white bloom when it has achieved the optimum ripeness. The Camembert is soft and yellow on the inside.

Left: The best Calvados and cider come from the Pays d'Auge.

Bottom: The Calvados that tastes best is made from nondescript apple varieties.

THE BEST OF THE APPLE

The Normans conjure their national beverage from nondescript wrinkled, tiny apples. As with wine and grapes, mixtures of the various apple varieties are what give character to this apple wine—cider—that is later used to make Calvados. After distillation, the raw spirits for Calvados are left to mature in oak barrels for several years, and continue to improve throughout this period. The fine apple brandy is a classic digestif. It is also invaluable if your stomach wants to give up after just a few courses of a many course meal. Then it's time for the *trou normand*—the Norman hole. A glass of Calvados between courses stimulates the digestion and makes room for the cheese.

Pommeau is as old as Calvados, and is made by adding freshly pressed apple juice to the young Calvados. Pommeau has to be left to age in wooden barrels for at least 14 months. It is drunk cold as an aperitif or with an apple-based dessert.

Camembert de Normandie (PDO)

Soft cheese with a white mold rind
made from raw cow's milk
45% FDM

ORIGIN AND HISTORY

Basse-Normandie,
Département Calvados

The Camembert we know and love has only been about for a little over 200 years. The inventor is believed to have been farmer's wife Marie Harel from the village of Camembert in Normandy, who is said to have made it for the first time in 1791. Following the construction of the railway line between Paris and Alençon in 1862, however, it was also sold outside the region. In 1880 an engineer named Ridel invented the characteristic wooden box inside which the delicate cheese can travel safely and without damage. It became so famous that it was copied more than any other soft cheese. Despite its glorious history, Camembert de Normandie did not receive AOC recognition until 1983.

PRODUCTION

Rennet is added to milk to make it separate. Five ladles of curds are poured into molds at intervals of one hour. Only cheese made in this way may be called Camembert de Normandie au lait cru, *moulé à la louche* (hand ladled). Dry salt is added, and it is then left to mature. Cheese makers add a tiny amount of mold to help it form its typical white mold. It is left to mature in

rooms at a specific humidity and temperature. It is vital that the cheese is turned every 48 hours. It must be at least 21 days old before it can be offered for sale. It takes about 5 pints (2.2 l) of milk to produce one Camembert.

CHARACTERISTICS

Small cylindrical shape, measuring 4–5 in (10–12 cm) in diameter and 1 in (3 cm) thick, weight about 9 oz (250 g). There are soft red marks on the fine, grooved, white-bloomed rind of the mature cheese. The mass is white to light yellow, soft but not runny. The heart of fresh Camembert is crumbly and flaky; when ripe it is soft, elastic, and smooth. Fresh Camembert tastes slightly acidic, and when it is ripe a little fruity.

SERVING SUGGESTIONS

Sommelier's recommendation: The best time for raw milk Camembert is from mid-April until mid-November. Very ripe Camembert goes well with a hearty artisanal cider, or with a mature Calvados if served at the end of a meal. Young Camembert is happy alongside fine red wines with a fruity, ripe character and understated tannin, such as those from the Côte de Beaune, and also with mature wines from Saint-Émilion.

SPECIAL FEATURES

Genuine Camembert de Normandie is packed in typical wooden boxes. Camembert made from pasteurized milk is not entitled to carry the AOC label.

SIMILAR CHEESE VARIETIES

Calva d'Auge, a Camembert that undergoes a special affinage, is made to an old Norman tradition in the Pays d'Auge. The rind is scraped off the semi-ripe Camembert, after which it is soaked in Calvados for three to four hours. The cheese is then coated in breadcrumbs to fix the aromas. It can then be left to mature for up to three weeks. Calva d'Auge has a mature Camembert flavor, paired with the mild apple aroma of Calvados. Coeur de Camembert au Calvados is similar. This cheese tastes best with a cider or a glass of Calvados—what else?

NORMANDY— PARADISE FOR SOFT CHEESE

Even the name of this French province is reminiscent of its origins: The Normans arrived in the ninth century, and founded a strong farming culture that continues to this day. Documents dating back to 911 confirm its long tradition of cheese production. Until the eighteenth century cheese was primarily a regional food, but then Neufchâtel, Livarot, and Pont l'Evèque became known all over France—and especially in Paris.

Livarot AOC

Soft cheese with a washed rind
made from cow's milk
40% FDM

ORIGIN AND HISTORY

Basse-Normandie,
Département Calvados

Livarot is mentioned in several very old documents. Thomas Corneille included it in his *Dictionnaire Universel Géographique et Historique* in 1708. In 1877, 4.5 million Livarot cheeses matured in 200 cheese cellars. It was also known as "poor man's meat" because of its flavor and nutritional values.

PRODUCTION

The curds are cut and kneaded. After shaping, the cheese is turned several times, drained, and sprinkled with coarse salt. It is washed and turned three times a week during its four-week ripening period. The rind is brushed with a red-yellow annatto tincture, which is made from the seeds of the achiote tree. It is bound with five thin strips of paper to give it its distinctive shape. This cheese is also known as "the Colonel."

CHARACTERISTICS

Flat cylindrical cheese that comes in several sizes. It is usually 5 in (12 cm) in diameter, 2 in (5 cm) thick, weight about 12–18 oz (350–500 g). Also available as three-quarter, half, and one-quarter Livarot. Smooth, shiny, orange rind that gradually darkens. The yellow elastic mass has tiny holes. Spicy aroma; strong, spicy, dry, slightly acidic aromatic flavor.

SERVING SUGGESTIONS

Sommelier's recommendation: Livarot is delicious served with apples and pears. A young Livarot goes well with strong white wines such as Chardonnays, and also with well-matured red Burgundy, Gewürztraminer, or a strong Pinot Gris. Mature cheese goes well with expressive white wines such as Gewürztraminer, but also with Vendanges Tardives, a strong cider, or Calvados.

SIMILAR CHEESE VARIETIES

It has much in common with Mignot, which is made in the Vimoutiers region.

Pont-l'Évêque (PDO)

Soft cheese with a washed rind
made from cow's milk
45% FDM

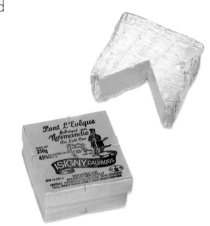

ORIGIN AND HISTORY
Basse-Normandie,
Département Calvados
This cheese may be traced back to the twelfth century, when it was first called Angelot; later, in the sixteenth century, it was changed to Augelot in reference to its place of origin, the Pays d'Auge. This was also the name which Guillaume de Lorris referred to in the thirteenth century in the *Roman de la rose*. In the seventeenth century it was given the name of the tiny village of Pont-l'Évêque.

PRODUCTION
Today, Pont-l'Évêque is usually made from pasteurized milk. The separated milk is cut, the resulting mixture of curds and whey is mixed together, and the liquid is drawn off. The rind is washed regularly in brine so that a red smear can form. The cheese matures for at least two and up to six weeks in a cellar.

CHARACTERISTICS
The square shape is typical. Pont-l'Évêque normally measures 4 in (11 cm) down the side, is 1 in (3 cm) thick, and weighs 12–14 oz (350–400 g). Other size options are the Petit (3–4 in/8.5–9.5 cm side length), the Demi, and the Grand

(7–8 in/19–21 cm side length). The mass is enclosed in a smooth, orange to gray-white rind with tiny red veins. The cheese is light and creamy, delicate, and smooth. It has a strong, decidedly rural aroma, and a taste reminiscent of hazelnuts, slightly dry to strong and savory.

SERVING SUGGESTIONS
Sommelier's recommendation: Young Pont-l'Évêque goes well with strong white wines or velvety, mature, round red wines, especially Pinot Noir. Well matured, the perfect accompaniments are expressive white wines such as Gewürztraminer, as are Vendanges Tardives or a strong cider.

SIMILAR CHEESE VARIETIES
Pavé d'Auge; Pavé du Plessis (name of the local cheese dairy), Pavé de Moyaux (named after the Moyaux region), Pavé de Trouville (after the tiny harbor town of Trouville).

Saint-Paulin

Semi-hard cheese
made from cow's milk
40–50% FDM

ORIGIN AND HISTORY
Basse-Normandie/Manche
For 100 years northern France has been
one of the most important regions in
the production of Saint-Paulin, one of
the many products that are similar to
the famous monastery cheese Port-du-
Salut. Today, Saint-Paulin is the generic
term for Trappist cheese made to the
Port-Salut recipe. In 1930, Saint-Paulin
was the first cheese made from pasteurized milk to be put on sale. However,
with a little luck it is still possible to find
small cheese dairies that sell Saint-
Paulin made from raw milk. Although
the best cheeses come from the
Mayenne, Maine, and Bretagne regions,
Saint-Paulin is now made all over
France.

PRODUCTION
The production method is similar to
that of Port-Salut. The mass is pressed,
not heated, and the ripening period is
two to three weeks.

CHARACTERISTICS
There are two sizes: 8 in (20 cm) diameter and 5 in (12 cm) diameter. Firm,
very smooth mass with irregular holes,
white interior, slightly salty, orange rind
(washed and waxed), mild, slightly
strong, pleasant flavor.

SERVING SUGGESTIONS
Sommelier's recommendation: Fruity
white wines, and also young Bordeaux
with ripe tannins.

Neufchâtel (PDO)

Soft cheese with white mold made from cow's milk 45% FDM

ORIGIN AND HISTORY

Haute Normandie, Département Seine-Maritime

Neufchâtel officially first appeared in the Abbey Saint-Amand in Rouen in 1543. According to legend, during the Hundred Years' War young girls gave the cheese to their English admirers as tokens of their affection.

PRODUCTION

It is made from raw or pasteurized milk to which rennet has been added. Sometimes lactobacilli are added. The cheese is put in linen bags and left to drain for several hours under slight pressure. The mass is injected with chopped bloom-covered cheese and stirred until the mass is homogeneous. It is placed on wooden slats in cellars and left to mature for 10 to 14 days.

CHARACTERISTICS

Neufchâtel is available in various sizes and shapes. The *carré* (square), *bondon* (cylinder), and *briquette* (brick) weigh 3½ oz (100 g); the double-*bondon* and small heart weigh 7 oz (200 g); the larger ones 21 oz (600 g). The rind has a white bloom, and the mass is soft, creamy, and slightly grainy. Mature Neufchâtel has a slightly yellow mass with red spots on the rind. The cheese smells and tastes slightly of mushrooms, and young Neufchâtel is quite strong and acidic. The mature cheese has an intense, slightly piquant flavor.

SERVING SUGGESTIONS

Neufchâtel can be eaten fresh or mature. It tastes best as an artisanal *fermier* produced between August and November. Cider goes extremely well with mature Neufchâtel. Suitable wines are Crus du Beaujolais or mature Saint-Émilion.

SIMILAR CHEESE VARIETIES

Coeur de Bray is a young Neufchâtel in the shape of a heart. The fresh cheese variants of Neufchâtel include Carré Frais and Maromme. Cream is added to Bondard, and it is left to mature for longer.

BLEUS AND PERSILLÉS

Blue-veined cheeses, collectively known as blue cheeses or *fromage à pâte persillé*, have a history of more than a thousand years. The molds range from a blue-gray to dark green, depending on the particular mold culture that is used. The most famous French blue cheeses come from mountain regions or poor areas. The best known are Bleu des Causses (Cévennes/Languedoc), Bleu d'Auvergne and Fourme d'Ambert from the Auvergne, Bleu de Gex (Haute-Jura), Bleu du Vercors-Sassenage (Vercors-Massiv), and—of course—Roquefort (Aveyron).

One of the less common blue cheeses is Bleu de Bresse, which comes from the gastronomically blessed area of Lyons. Unlike other blue cheeses, it is the actual milk that is injected with mold cultures rather than the Bleu de Bresse itself. Bleu de Termignon is produced by just five alpine dairies on the high mountain pastures about the alpine village of Termignon. Often the cheeses are sold even before they leave the maturing cellar. Bleu de Tignes or Tignard from the winter sports village of the same name is produced from goat's milk.

Pavé d'Auge

Soft cheese with a washed rind
made from cow's milk
50% FDM

ORIGIN AND HISTORY
Haute-Normandie, Département Eure
Pavé d'Auge belongs to the family of
Pont-l'Évêque, and is today a generic
term for square, soft cheeses with a
washed rind from the Pays d'Auge. As
most of the producers now specialize in
the production of Pont-l'Évêque, this
local specialty is increasingly being
forgotten.

PRODUCTION
Identical to Pont-l'Évêque, except that
it is left to ripen for longer (2–4 months)
because of its thickness. It is washed
twice a week in brine during affinage.

CHARACTERISTICS
Square cheese with a side length of
about 5 in (12 cm) and about 2 in (6 cm)
thick. It weighs 1½ lb–2 lb (700–800 g).
The rind is a yellow-orange color with
the white mold shining through in
places. It has a similar taste to Pont-
l'Évêque, but is generally stronger and
slightly more bitter.

SERVING SUGGESTIONS
Sommelier's recommendation: Strong
white wines toward Pinot Gris, oak-
ripened Chardonnays, mature red wines
with mild tannins such as Burgundy, or
wines from the southwest go well.

THE CENDRÉS

The term *cendré* applies to a large
group of soft cheeses, the rinds of
which are covered in ash. The wood
ash neutralizes some of the lactic acid
and determines the microflora.
Cheeses with ash rinds take longer to
mature, are drier, have a lower fat
content, and therefore keep better.
There are *cendrés* made from cow's
or goat's milk. These low fat cheeses
used to be made in many wine
regions as sustenance for laborers
during the grape harvest. They are
now found only rarely.

Brillat-Savarin

Soft cheese with white mold
made from cow's milk
75% FDM

ORIGIN AND HISTORY
Haute Normandie/ Seine-Maritime
The inventor of this cheese was Henri
Androuët, the well-known cheese
affineur from Paris. It is said that the
Norman specialty Excelsior inspired
him to create Brillat-Savarin in 1930.
Androuët named his creation in honor
of the renowned eighteenth-century
food writer and statesman Jean-
Anthelme Brillat-Savarin. With regard
to its reputation, Brillat-Savarin is the
best known representative of the category *triple crème*.

PRODUCTION
Typical soft cheese product made from
pasteurized cow's milk to which warm
cream is added, and then rennet to
make it separate. Matures for three to
four weeks.

CHARACTERISTICS
Flat wheel of about 5 in (12–13 cm)
diameter and over 1 in (3.5 cm) thick,
weight 14 oz–1 lb (450–500 g) or more.
The rind is white to ivory in color with
a soft flora. The mass is smooth, very
delicate, creamy, and soft. If left to
mature for a long time, red marks that
add aroma form on the rind.

SPECIAL FEATURES
As it does not mature for long and soon
loses its flavor, this cheese is best
consumed without delay.

SERVING SUGGESTIONS
When fresh it has a mild flavor, and so
goes well with fresh fruit or berries.
Sommelier's recommendation: Lots of
wines are suitable companions for this
cheese, although red wines should not
have too much tannin. Wines with a
fresh fruit, whether white or red, are
excellent choices.

JEAN-ANTHÈLME BRILLAT-SAVARIN

Brillat-Savarin was born in 1755 and grew up in Bugey, the area between Savoy and the Jura that boasts excellent cheeses and meat products. He studied law in Dijon and qualified as a lawyer, then soon made a name for himself as district court president, mayor, and commandant of the National Guard. Brillat-Savarin loved little more than cooking for his guests. However, he also had a passion for chemistry, physics, archeology, and astronomy. The bachelor Brillat-Savarin combined his passions for gastronomy and science in his famous work *Physiologie du Goût* (The Physiology of Taste) by addressing the subjects of food and drink scientifically, wittily, and with literary brilliance. In 1826, just a few weeks after the anonymous publication of his masterpiece that significantly influenced French gastronomy, Brillat-Savarin died in Saint-Denis.

Crottin de Chavignol (PDO)

Soft cheese made
from raw goat's milk
45% FDM

ORIGIN AND HISTORY

Centre, Département Cher

Goats have been grazed and cheese produced on the hills of the Berry and in the village of Chavignol near Sancerre for over 400 years. The tiny cheeses known as Crottin have been much appreciated since the early nineteenth century. Experts do not agree on how Crottin got its name. Some believe it is a reference to a small oil lamp, others to a slang word for horse dung.

PRODUCTION

Classic goat's cheese made from the raw milk of brown mountain goats. Crottin matures for at least two weeks in damp cellars and is turned frequently. The cheese is relatively dry after 20–30 days. There are cracks in the rind and often brown marks of piquant mold. The longer the cheese is left to age, the harder, drier, and stronger it becomes. About 1½ pints (75 cl) of milk are required to make a small Crottin de Chavignol.

CHARACTERISTICS

Small, round cylinder, nearly 2 in (5 cm) in diameter, 2 in (5.5 cm) thick, weight at least 2 oz (60 g). White rind with yellow-white, sometimes blue, mold; semi-hard consistency and a white, homogeneous texture. As the cheese ages it shrinks in size, the mold becomes more pronounced, and the cheese becomes hard and dry. Fresh Crottin has a faint aroma of goat, and a slightly nutty, mild, creamy flavor. As it ages it initially acquires a slight piquancy, but then an increasingly strong, mildly soapy taste.

SERVING SUGGESTIONS

The best time for Crottin de Chavignol is the spring, when grasses and herbs start to grow. It is popular grilled on small slices of baguette, served with salad, or marinated in white wine. Sommelier's recommendation: Traditionally, Crottin de Chavignol is served with Sancerre. Other Sauvignon-Blancs such as those from Pouilly-Fumé, Menetou-Salon, and Quincy are also good choices. Sancerre Rouge should be served with Crottin while it is still semi-hard and mild.

LARGE AND SMALL RELATIVES
OF CROTTIN DE CHAVIGNOL

In line with the success of Crottin, goatherds and cheese makers from Berry tried a number of variations, all of which acquired reputations and popularity of their own. They are made on the same principle as Crottin, but vary in shape, weight, and affinage. These criteria undoubtedly have an effect on the consistency and flavor. The season for this cheese lasts from spring until fall. The collective term for the tiny goat's cheeses in the shape of Crottin de Chavignol is *fromages de chèvre du Sancerrois*.

Sancerre *fermier* could be called the big brother of Crottin de Chavignol, and ripens for three weeks. It weighs 11 oz (320 g), has a delicate, typical aroma of goat, and a soft, creamy texture. Le P'tit Berrichon is Crottin's little brother. It ripens for just a week, and so is softer and milder—although it soon gains in firmness and aroma. As its name implies, Bouchon de Sancerre is shaped like a wine cork. It weighs less than 1 oz (25 g). As it is so small, it ripens comparatively quickly. Pavé du Berry takes the shape of a large rectangle and generally weighs about 9 oz (250 g). It ripens for two to three weeks, during which time it acquires a white mold that also contains a certain amount of blue mold.

The consistency remains creamy. The flavor is finer and more delicate than that of the smaller shapes.

Right: Crottin de Chavignol at various stages of ripeness.

Bottom: The French owe a debt of gratitude—to goats—for one of their most delicious families of cheeses.

Selles-sur-Cher (PDO)

Soft cheese made from raw goat's milk
45% FDM

ORIGIN AND HISTORY
Centre, Département Loir-et-Cher
Although it is believed that Selles-sur-Cher has long been made by a traditional method, it has only been known outside its home for a little over a century. The production area is limited to the central area of the Loire, with the tiny town of Selles-sur-Cher as the geographic center.

PRODUCTION
Natural acetogenic bacteria and a little rennet are added to the milk to make it separate, after which the curds are measured into forms with a ladle. Once it has drained and become firmer, a mixture of finely grated wood ash and salt is sprinkled over the top. It ripens for 21 days. The cheese is usually produced by small dairies and artisanal businesses.

CHARACTERISTICS
A cut sphere of just 4 in (10 cm) diameter, 1 in (2.5 cm) thick, and weighing 5 oz (150 g). A black-blue rind with white-gray mold envelops the pure white, dense, fine cheese. Mild aroma of goat, mild flavor, nutty, and slightly salty. It smells more strongly of goat and nuts as it ripens.

SERVING SUGGESTIONS
Selles-sur-Cher is at its best in spring and summer. It is important not to remove the rind since that is what adds the special, slightly salty-smoky note. Sommelier's recommendation: Excellent companions are Sauvignon-Blancs from the Loire, and also wines made from Chenin Blanc grapes, such as those from Vouvray. The fruity red wines of Touraine also enhance the aroma of the cheese.

SIMILAR CHEESE VARIETIES
Cœur du Berry.

Valençay (PDO)

Soft cheese made from
raw goat's milk
45% FDM

ORIGIN AND HISTORY

Centre, Département Indre

Valençay has a long tradition. It is said that it used to be shaped like a pyramid, and that its present shape is thanks to Napoleon. Following his overwhelming defeat in Egypt, Napoleon stayed at Valençay Palace. At the sight of the goat's cheese, the shape of which reminded him of the Egyptian pyramids, he became so enraged that he sliced the tip off the cheese with his sword. According to a different story, farmers simply wanted to copy the shape of the bell tower of the church of Valençay. A second name for this cheese is Levroux. However, only the name Valençay is protected by AOC.

PRODUCTION

The curds of the raw goat's milk are measured into special molds. Once the mass has hardened, it is sprinkled with fine charcoal ash and left to ripen in rooms at about 80% humidity until blue mold has formed on the soft rind. This usually takes about two weeks.

CHARACTERISTICS

The flattened pyramid shape is typical of goat's cheese specialties from Berry. Valençay has a square base with sides measuring 3 in (7 cm), and is 2 in (6 cm) thick. It weighs 8 oz (220 g), and Petit Valençay weighs 4 oz (110 g). Natural bluish soft rind, sprinkled with ash, and covered with white and blue mold. Valençay's mass is fine, consistent, and dense, and generally quite soft. Characteristic but understated, delicate aroma of goat, mild and nutty with a soft touch of blue mold.

SERVING SUGGESTIONS

It is at its best from spring to fall. Sommelier's recommendation: Recommended wines are a Quincy, Reuilly, or red Bourgueil.

GOAT'S CHEESE PARADISE

The areas of Orléans, Berry, and Touraine, which today make up the Région Centre, have largely been able to retain their historic roots and individuality. In addition to famous goat's cheeses, this region also produces some of France's best white wines (Sancerre) and red wines of charming character (Touraine).

As used to be the case in many wine-growing regions, the vintner families in Berry often kept goats to improve the revenue from wine growing. When grape phylloxera ravaged the Loire after 1870 and destroyed vast quantities of vines, farmers in Chavignol and other regions increased the size of their goat herds. Their cheeses were sold to Auxerre, Orléans, and Paris, where they soon gained a loyal following.

Right: These brightly colored goats may be seen all over France.

Left and below: Azay-le-Redeau in the Département Indre-et-Loire.

RARE GOAT'S CHEESES
FROM THE PAYS DE LA LOIRE

One particular specialty is Galette du Paludier, a round, soft goat's cheese weighing about 3 oz (90 g), from the Département Loire-Atlantique. It is made by farming families and left to ripen on a bed of algae for one to two weeks, which gives it an incomparable taste. A sparkling Muscadet is the perfect accompaniment to this cheese. The triangular Trois cornes de Vendée is made from raw goat's milk with a white mold ring, and is thickened by lactobacilli. The cheese is traditionally made in the area of the tiny town of Chaillé at the heart of the dry marsh regions in the Département Vendée. According to tradition, the curds have to rest for 20 hours before they are drained and put into molds. It is left in dry, ventilated cellars to ripen for one month. It is at its best in spring and fall—beautifully complemented by a rosé from Provence.

Pouligny-Saint-Pierre (PDO)

Semi-hard cheese made from raw goat's milk
45% FDM

ORIGIN AND HISTORY

Centre, Département Indre

Pouligny-Saint-Pierre, also known as "Tour Eiffel," originally hails from the Vallée de la Brenne, a peaceful valley with several rivers running through it. Today, Pouligny's home covers a small area with 22 communities about Pouligny-St. Pierre. There is a favorable microclimate in Berry to the west, where cherry trees, wild heather, and sweet clover thrive. This flora provides the perfect food for the typical mountain goat, which produces a nutritious and sweet-smelling milk, the flavor of which is reproduced in the cheese.

PRODUCTION

Great care is required when transferring the very finely grained curds into the mold to ensure the delicate mass does not break. When the mass is firm enough, it is salted and then placed on straw or slats in ripening cellars. After a few weeks a touch of blue mold will have developed on the rind. Pouligny-Saint-Pierre tastes best after four to five weeks.

CHARACTERISTICS

Characteristic pyramid shape, slightly blunt on top, 5 in (12.5 cm) high, 3–4 in (8–9 cm) side length at the base, 1 in (2.5 cm) at the tip. It typically weighs 9 oz (250 g). There is a smaller cheese weighing 5 oz (150 g). A natural, delicately blue rind covers the textured, pale ivory mass. Firm, smooth consistency. Elegant aroma of goat, slightly acidic, nutty—more pungent than other goat's cheeses from Berry.

SERVING SUGGESTIONS

This cheese is particularly creamy and full of flavor from May, when the goats are in the meadow. On the cheeseboard it harmonizes well with nut bread and a Pouilly-Fumé. It also goes extremely well with a not-too-sweet Côteaux de Layon.

Sainte-Maure de Touraine (PDO)

Soft cheese made
from raw goat's milk
45% FDM

ORIGIN AND HISTORY
Centre, Département Indre-et-Loire
The name is a reference to the Moors, who penetrated as far as Poitiers in the eighth century. They are accredited with being the first in central France to keep goats and produce cheese. Sainte-Maure is the best known goat's cheese with a protective designation of origin.

PRODUCTION
Some 50 dairies still produce this cheese by traditional methods. The goat's milk is poured into long molds. After it has been taken out of the mold it is lightly salted. Sometimes a straw is inserted through the middle in order to hold the fragile cheese together. If it is to be left to mature for some time, the cheese is first covered with salted, powdered charcoal before being stored in a cellar for ten days to three weeks, depending on the level of ripening desired.

CHARACTERISTICS
The characteristic bar is available in two sizes. The small version is 5 in (15 cm) long, 1½–2 in (4–5 cm) thick, and weighs 9 oz (250 g); the large one is 11–12 in (28–30 cm) long, 2–3 in (5–6 cm) thick and weighs around 1¼ lb (500 g). The *chevrefeuille* has been left for longer, has a more intense flavor, and is firmer in consistency with a dry, yellow rind. The *cendré* has been sprinkled with ash. The rind is soft and the mass a brilliant white. Firm consistency, slightly crumbly at the core, creamy under the rind. Mild flavor that becomes nuttier with a slight hint of mushroom as the cheese ages.

SERVING SUGGESTIONS
This cheese is at its best from early summer. It is ideal for serving sliced and toasted on sliced baguette or with salad. Good companions are a Sauvignon de Touraine and a red wine from Touraine.

SIMILAR CHEESE VARIETIES
Similar cheeses are available in many qualities, sizes, and origins from the region, from both artisanal and commercial production.

CHEESE IN A CHESTNUT LEAF

Very many artisanal goat's cheeses are produced in Poitou, and in particular the Vienne and Deux-Sèvres Départements. Numerous goat breeders and cheese makers develop their own variations—round or square, large or small, thick or thin, creamy or dry, mild or strong. Some cheeses are wrapped in chestnut or plantain leaves to ripen. The best known of these is Mothais sur feuille, a round, flat disk with a white, soft, slightly sticky rind, very creamy mass, and a mild flavor. Unlike other goat's cheeses, Mothais sur feuille ripens for three to four weeks in cellars with almost 100% humidity. Another chestnut leaf variety is Couhé-Vérac, a flat, square, creamy goat's cheese. Unlike Mothais, it makes much of its goat origins—something that connoisseurs truly appreciate.

Chabichou du Poitou (PDO)

Soft cheese made
from goat's milk
45% FDM

ORIGIN AND HISTORY

Poitou-Charentes/Vienne

As with Sainte-Maure, the Moors are responsible for the origins of Chabichou. Its name is derived from the Arabic word *chebi*, meaning a young goat. The appellation region forms a large circle about the town of Poitiers; it may be produced in the Haut-Poitou, including a part of the Vienne, Deux-Sèvres, and Charente Départements.

PRODUCTION

Rennet is added to make the raw, warm goat's milk coagulate in a little over half an hour. The curds are ladled into conical molds. The cheeses are left to ripen for three to four weeks and turned frequently. *Fermier* cheeses are made from raw milk, commercially produced ones usually from pasteurized milk.

CHARACTERISTICS

Blunt sphere with a lower diameter of nearly 2½ in (6 cm) and an upper one of 2 in (5 cm). The height is over 2 in (6 cm), and it weighs 5–6 oz (150–60 g). The rind is yellow-white. Depending on the level of ripeness, a gray-blue mold forms, and later a reddish one. The mass is firm, homogeneous, and snow-white. There is a moderate aroma of goat. Initially Chabichou tastes quite mild and creamy with an undertone of hazelnut. As it ripens, it becomes drier with a strong flavor of goat, and also quite tangy.

SERVING SUGGESTIONS

Chabichou is at its best during the summer months. It is an attractive addition to a summer cheese board.

Sommelier's recommendation: Suggested wines are a Sauvignon from the Haut-Poitou or a cool Gamay from the Touraine.

SIMILAR CHEESE VARIETIES

Sainte-Maure (see entry). Goat's milk cheeses similar to Chabichou de Poitou that are produced away from the protected appellation are called Chabi, and are made all over France.

Port-Salut

Semi-hard cheese made from cow's milk
50% FDM

ORIGIN AND HISTORY
Pays de la Loire/Mayenne
Port-du-Salut, an ancestor of Port-Salut, is one of France's oldest Trappist cheeses. It comes from the Trappist Abbey of Notre-Dame de Port-du-Salut (Harbor of Healing) in the parish of Entrammes. The abbey had a cheese dairy as early as 1817. From 1873 the monks took their cheese to Paris, where it quickly became popular. In 1938 the monks of Entrammes were granted the exclusive right to produce this cheese. However, as they were unable to keep up with demand, they sold the license for production to the dairy cooperative of Mayenne, where it was produced under the name of Port-Salut.

PRODUCTION
Fresh, pasteurized milk is quickly heated. The curds are cut into corn-size pieces. Half of the whey is drained off and replaced with the same amount of water. The curds and whey mix is stirred rapidly until the grains are the size of wheat. The curds are pressed for a short time before being put into molds. A second press takes place after two to four hours. The cheeses are placed in a salt bath for eight to twelve hours, and then dry for two to three days. They ripen at high humidity for about three weeks, during which time they are turned and washed regularly.

CHARACTERISTICS
Round shape of 8 in (20 cm) diameter, 1½ in (4 cm) thick, and weighing about 3 lb (1.3–1.5 kg). The natural orange-red rind envelops a smooth, ivory-colored mass with only a few holes. Mild, slightly acidic flavor, aromatic.

SERVING SUGGESTIONS
Sommelier's recommendation: Fruity white wines and young red wines from the southwest, such as Gaillac, Bordeaux, or Bergerac with a ripe tannin structure are recommended.

SPECIAL FEATURES
Throughout France, other monastery cheeses are produced to the same original recipe as for Port-du-Salut—such as Saint-Paulin, which is produced all over the country.

COW'S MILK CHEESE FROM THE LOIRE

Although the Région Centre is known for its goat's cheeses, it also produces specialties made from cow's milk. One of them is the soft cheese Olivet cendré from the town of the same name near Orléans. It is ash ripened for at least a month. The cheese has a slightly viscous mass with an ash-gray mold on the rind. A younger creation is Olivet au foin, the white surface bloom of which is covered in hay. A farmhouse soft cheese is Pithiviers au foin from the tiny town of Bondaroy. In former times, farmers produced this cheese only during times when there was plenty of milk. It was then stored in hay so there was plenty of food for the fall. Today it is available all year.

Fromage du Curé, a soft cheese with a washed rind that is made from raw cow's milk with 45% FDM, comes from the western Pays de la Loire. It is said that this cheese was first made by a priest in the Vendée. According to history, during the French Revolution a fleeing monk took it to the Pays Nantais, a region that had little to offer in the way of cheese. Fromage du Curé is shaped like a pavé (rectangular and flat), has a washed rind, a yellow, slightly fatty mass, and—similarly to Romadour—a strong, aromatic flavor. It is also known as Curé Nantais, Petit Breton, or Fromage du Pays Nantais dit du Curé.

THE MAROILLES FAMILY

The Maroilles family of cheeses is an extensive one. A diversity of shapes and sizes results in many different varieties. Smaller cheeses, for instance, need much less time to ripen through and acquire the flavor of ripeness. Vieux-Lille (also called Gris-de-Lille, Maroilles gris, or Vieux-gris-de-Lille) is a strong soft cheese. It certainly deserves its nickname of *puant macéré* ("preserved stinker"). It ripens over three to four months, during which it is repeatedly washed in salt water until the rind is wrinkled and gray. Strong Baguette Laonnaise or Baguette de Thiérache is shaped like a brick, and ripens for three to four months in damp cellars. The treatment with salt water gives it a brick-red cheese flora and a soft mass. The heart-shaped, strong red spreading cheese Coeur d'Arras is much loved in the northern Pas de Calais. The Maroilles family of cheeses also includes Rollot, Sorbais, Boulette d'Avesnes, and Dauphin.

Maroilles (PDO)

Soft cheese with a washed rind
made from cow's milk
45% FDM

ORIGIN AND HISTORY
Picardie/Aisne
This cheese goes back to the Benedictine monks of the monastery of Maroilles in the Thiérache. It has been made for over 1,000 years to a recipe that remains almost unchanged to this day. The name Maroilles comes from Maro-Ialo, the old Gallic name for the village near the monastery, and means "great clarity." The inhabitants were bound by an edict to give one-tenth of their milk to the Abbey of Maroilles on the feast day of St. John the Baptist (June 24) to be used for making cheese so that it would be ready 100 days later, on the feast day of St. Remy (October 1).

PRODUCTION
The milk from the colorful cows of the Avesnois is used both raw and pasteurized. Once it has been thickened with rennet and the whey drained off, the white mass is soaked in brine and dried for 10–14 days. It then forms a rind with a delicate, blue-white mold. The cheeses are then damp brushed or washed, and ripen for five weeks to four months. The microflora in the cellars of the Thiérache facilitate the development of the unusual covering.

CHARACTERISTICS
Shaped like a paving slab, and sold in various formats. Large: 5 in (13 cm) side length, 2 in (6 cm) in height, weight over 1½ lb (720 g); Sorbais (¾ size): a little over 1 lb (540 g); Mignon: 13 oz (380 g); Quart: 6 oz (180 g). Glossy, moist, orange to brick-red rind, soft to fatty mass with lots of tiny holes. Strong, intensive, slightly smoky smell and a strong, piquant flavor. The smaller cheeses are milder but still strong. The vieux Maroilles is particularly piquant.

SERVING SUGGESTIONS
Maroilles is an excellent ingredient in cooking. It can be eaten unripened (*blanc*), medium aged (*blondin*), or mature (*vieux*). Connoisseurs remove the rind and enjoy it with a dark Trappist beer. Sommelier's recommendation: Suitable wines are strong, rich, ripe red wines such as Cornas or Châteauneuf-du-Pape.

Rollot

Soft cheese with a washed rind
made from cow's milk
45% FDM

ORIGIN AND HISTORY
Picardie/Somme
Farmhouse cheese with a long tradition
from the village of Rollot. Louis XIV
enjoyed it on his travels through
Picardy. From then, the reputation of
this tiny, strong cheese grew and grew.

PRODUCTION
The production method is similar to that
of Maroilles. The soft cheese ripens for
one to two months in a damp cellar,
during which it is washed twice a week
in beer.

CHARACTERISTICS
A *fermier* cheese, it is a small, flat
cylinder with a diameter of about 3 in
(7–8 cm), a height of 1 in (3 cm), and
weighing 10–11 oz (280–300 g). It has
a thin, grainy, orange-red to light ocher,
moistly glistening rind, whereas the
mass is soft and of a cream color.
Commercially produced cheeses are
usually heart-shaped. Strong-aromatic,
spicy, piquant, and often quite salty.

SERVING SUGGESTIONS
A delight with a mineral Sauvignon
Blanc, but also with a fruity cider or
even a Trappist beer.

SIMILAR CHEESE VARIETIES
Guerbigny is a strong, heart-shaped
cheese with a moist-sticky mass from
the village of the same name in Picardy.
It ripens for five weeks.

TINY MASTERPIECE

Crayeux de Roncq, a red smear
cheese from the town of the same
name near Lille, is widely regarded
by connoisseurs as a tiny masterpiece. It is refined for six weeks so that
the center remains chalky (*crayeux*).
When ripened for less than that, it is
also called *carré du vinage*. The
recipe is similar to that for Maroilles. It
is square with a side length of 4 in
(10 cm), 2 in (4.5 cm) thick, and
weighs about 120 oz (300 g). The
rind is pale orange and the mass
cream color. Crayeux de Roncq has a
marked yet delicate flavor.

Mimolette

Semi-hard/hard cheese
made from cow's milk
min. 40% FDM

ORIGIN AND HISTORY
Nord-Pas-de-Calais/Nord
Mimolette (also called Boule de Lille
and Vieux-Lille) is believed to originate
from Holland. It is made in the same
way as Edam. French Mimolette gets
its own character from a long affinage
and dark-orange color. It is said to have
been General Charles de Gaulle's
favorite cheese.

PRODUCTION
Rennet and annatto are added to the
milk. The curds are pressed and
reheated. Microscopically small mites
gnaw away at the natural rind, which
enables the cheese to breathe, and the
rind is brushed regularly. Young Mimolette is offered for sale after two to three
months; *demi-vieille* has ripened for
6–8 months. The most popular is
Mimolette after 12–14 months (*vieille*)
or 18 months (*extra-vieille*). However,
a *vieux cassant* can be left to ripen for
up to 24 months.

CHARACTERISTICS
Sphere weighing 4–9 lb (2–4 kg) with a
gray, holey rind. Brilliant dark-orange
mass with a few tiny holes. Smooth to
firm, dry, and very hard and crumbly,
depending on the level of ripeness. The
young cheese has a fruity, nutty aroma
and mild flavor. When riper it is stronger
and more piquant with an almost medicinal aroma.

SERVING SUGGESTIONS
The classic companion for mature
Mimolette is a mature Bordeaux.
However, strong, sweet wines also go
extremely well with a well-ripened
Mimolette. A dark beer from Flanders,
old Pineau de Charente, or aged Cognac
is a particularly exciting accompaniment to Mimolette.

RECIPE MIMOLETTE MACÉRÉE À LA CH'TI

1 medium-age Mimolette, 1 bottle Ch'ti blonde beer, pepper

Ideally, prepare the Mimolette the day before you want to use it. First, use a sharp knife to cut a zigzag two-thirds of the way up the cheese, then remove this "lid." Scoop the cheese out of the lower part with a spoon. Place the cheese pieces in a bowl, sprinkle with freshly grated pepper, and pour over the beer. Leave in the refrigerator for 24 hours. Pour off the liquid and return the marinated Mimolette pieces to the hollowed-out shell. Replace the lid.

THE BEST PARTNERS FOR BOULETTE

The strong aroma of Boulette d'Avesne is best accompanied by the local schnapps, Genièvre. This juniper spirit was first distilled in the area of Rotterdam in Holland in the second half of the sixteenth century. It had its breakthrough in northern France in 1806, and numerous distilleries grew up about the northern Pas de Calais, only a few of which are still in existence today. Although juniper berries provide the unmistakable aroma, the basis is provided by barley, rye, and some oats. The extract is distilled three times, and then the juniper is added. Genièvre is only bottled once the spirits have been left to mature for several years.

Pavé de Roubaix

Semi-hard/hard cheese
made from cow's milk
45% FDM

ORIGIN AND HISTORY

Nord-Pas-de-Calais/Nord
Traditional hard cheese from northern
France that became an important food
in the lives of workers with the development of the textiles industry of
Roubaix. Poor people bought it while it
was still very young. As they rarely had
a cellar, it was buried in the ground
where, thanks to the natural dampness,
it was left to ripen slowly.

PRODUCTION

The curds for Roubaix are put in a long
mold to drain. The cheese is then placed
on wooden slats to ripen, during which
it is turned and brushed once a month.

CHARACTERISTICS

A somewhat irregularly shaped loaf
about 5 in (13 cm) wide, 10 in (26 cm)
long, and 3 in (8 cm) thick. It weighs
7–11 lb (3–4.5 kg). The natural rind is
light brown and very hard. The dark-
yellow mass is smooth and firm, turning
orange toward the rind. Spicy, nutty
aroma with a strong, piquant flavor.

SPECIAL FEATURES

Only a handful of cheese makers still
produce Pavé de Roubaix, and it is very
much at risk of disappearing altogether.

SERVING SUGGESTIONS

The best companion is a sweet brown
beer. Those who prefer wine would do
well to choose a Rivesaltes Tuilé or a
sweet Rasteau.

CHEESE FROM
THE CONVENT

Toward the end of the late nineteenth
century, a group of nuns opened a
convent in Belval. Like the Trappist
monks, they started to make cheese—
and used a similar method. Today,
some 40 nuns are still producing
Trappist or Trappe de Belval. They
buy the milk from farmers in the area.
In addition to their famous Trappe de
Belval, they also sell various other
cheeses and artisanal foods from
some 30 French and Belgian
convents in their shops.

La Boulette d'Avesne

Semi-hard cheese made from
pasteurized cow's milk
45% FDM

ORIGIN AND HISTORY
Nord-Pas-de-Calais/Nord
Boulette is first mentioned in old
records at the Abbey of Maroilles in
1760. For reasons of economy, the farmers used the milk that was left over from
butter making to produce cheese. Until
the Second World War the cheese was
shaped like a ball, hence the name
"Boulette."

PRODUCTION
Boulette is made from a fresh piece of
Maroilles and buttermilk. The mass is
kneaded, shaped into a ball, and
seasoned with tarragon, parsley, cloves,
pepper, and often ground paprika. It
ripens for up to nine weeks in damp
cellars, during which it is regularly
washed in beer. Annatto is added to
commercially produced cheese to give
it the red rind.

CHARACTERISTICS
Cheese shaped like a pear, with a diameter of 2–4 in (6–9 cm), measuring
around 4 in (9–10 cm) in height, and
weighing 10–13 oz (300–380 g), with
reddish rind. Soft consistency; strong,
piquant aroma, but with a delicate
flavor of herbs.

SERVING SUGGESTIONS
Most Boulettes are sold fresh and
should be consumed within a month.
They go best with rustic farmhouse
bread and a glass of dark Trappist beer
or Genièvre. Sommelier's recommendation: Good wines are a young Gamay
or Pinot Noir.

SIMILAR CHEESE VARIETIES
Boulette de Cambrai is made from
butter and Maroilles and seasoned with
tarragon, onions, and parsley, but is not
matured. It is spread on bread as fresh
cheese. Dauphin is a combination of
chopped, fresh Maroilles cheese
seasoned with tarragon, parsley, and
pepper. This cheese specialty is said to
have been named after the son of Louis
XIV, who as the crown prince (dauphin)
tried it while traveling through the
Hainaut. The cheese is shaped like a
dolphin (dauphin) and has a piquant
taste of herbs and spices.

Mont des Cats

Semi-hard cheese made from
raw cow's milk
45–50% FDM

ORIGIN AND HISTORY
Nord-Pas-de-Calais/Nord
Even before Trappist monks built an
hermitage on the peak of Mont des Cats
between Lille and Dunkirk in the mid-
seventeenth century (which later
became Mont des Cats Abbey), farmers
in the region were producing a mild
cheese that families in the north put on
bread and dipped in their breakfast
coffee. In 1890 the monks started
producing cheese with milk they
obtained from neighboring farmers. In
1995 the cheese was named part of the
culinary heritage of the Nord-Pas-de-
Calais region.

PRODUCTION
The monks produce Mont des Cats as a
rennet cheese in the style of Port-Salut.
The curds are pressed but not heated.
The cheese is left in a cool cellar for two
months, and during this time it is
washed regularly in brine with annatto.

CHARACTERISTICS
Wheel 1½ in (4 cm) thick, 10 in (25 cm)
diameter on average, and weighing up to
4½ lb (2 kg). A semi-dry, yellowish rind
surrounds the semi-hard yet soft and
creamy mass with characteristic tiny
holes. Mild, delicately nutty aroma.

SERVING SUGGESTIONS
Recommended wines are fruity white
wines, and also young red wines with a
ripe tanning structure from the south of
France, such as Côteaux du Languedoc,
Minervois, or Côtes du Roussillon.

SIMILAR CHEESE VARIETIES
Saint-Paulin, Port-du-Salut.

Bergues

Soft cheese with a washed rind
made from cow's milk
15–20% FDM

ORIGIN AND HISTORY

Nord-Pas-de-Calais/Nord

The cheese has been made in Bergues
near Dunkirk (Flanders) since the
Middle Ages. For a long time it was
believed to be an imitation of Holland's
Mimolette, but it has now been recognized as being something unique and
truly special. Although it is enjoying
quite a large popularity, it is still made
by hand.

PRODUCTION

Semi-skimmed milk from local dairy
breeds is thickened with rennet. Once
the whey has drained off and the mass
has hardened, the cheeses are placed
on slats in special raised chambers,
known as "hoofsteads," for three weeks
to two months to mature. Twice a week
they are turned and washed with beer
or brine.

CHARACTERISTICS

Round cheese, 8 in (20 cm) diameter,
nearly 2 in (4 cm) thick, and weighing
nearly 4 lb (about 1.7 kg). The thin rind
is yellow with white marks, the mass
ivory with tiny irregular holes. Mild,
piquant aroma. Pleasantly piquant
flavor with a slight undertone of yeast.

SERVING SUGGESTIONS

Recommended wines are simple
aromatic varieties such as white wines
from the Touraine, but also Chablis or
light reds such as Beaujolais. A cool
Flemish beer is also an extremely
successful companion.

SIMILAR CHEESE VARIETIES

Bergues's little brother Saint-Winoc is
now quite rare, but used to be
extremely widespread. There is only
one producer left, in Esquelbecq. The
cheese weighs 10–11 oz (300 g) and is
matured in beer.

Vieux-Boulogne

Soft/semi-hard cheese made
from raw cow's milk
45% FDM

ORIGIN AND HISTORY
Nord-Palais-de-Calais/Pas de Calais
A fairly new cheese that is made artisanally by just three producers near the
sea at Boulogne-sur-Mer.

PRODUCTION
It is made exclusively with the milk of
cows that graze near the sea. The curds
are salted, and then matured for two
months in St. Léonard beer.

CHARACTERISTICS
Square shape, 1½ in (4 cm) high, side
length 4 in (11 cm). The moist, reddish
rind is slightly grooved and encloses an
elastic mass. The cheese has a penetrating aroma. The milk smells slightly
piquant and of iodine, which is also
evident in the flavor of the young
cheese.

SERVING SUGGESTIONS
Good wines are white wines with a
mineral tone such as Vouvray, and also
demi sec. Red wines should be mature
with little tannin.

Brie de Meaux (PDO)

Soft cheese with white mold made from raw cow's milk 45% FDM

ORIGIN AND HISTORY

Ile-de-France/Seine-et-Marne

It is not known just where Brie de Meaux was created and who invented it. One thing that is certain is that it is the best known of all the Bries, and that Charles the Great and many other members of the nobility enjoyed it. It had its greatest triumph in 1814, when Talleyrand and the retailers of the Viennese Congress named it the "king of cheeses."

PRODUCTION

The curds hardly need to be cut since the whey is able to drain away from the large surface of the cheese while it is still in the mold. Affinage is generally eight weeks.

CHARACTERISTICS

Flat disk, height 1 in (2.5 cm), diameter 14–16 in (35–40 cm), weight 5½–6½ lb (2.5–3 kg). Mature Brie de Meaux has a white mold bloom with red marks or veins on the rind. The mass is straw color, creamy, and smooth, but not runny. Short ripened Brie de Meaux have a fruity-spicy note, whereas cheeses that have matured for longer smell strongly of mold and have a mildly sweet flavor.

SERVING SUGGESTIONS

A mature Brie should be eaten quickly. Bries taste best in summer, fall, and winter. Great care should be taken when transporting it in summer.

Sommelier's recommendation: Strong, rich, mature red wines. Brie goes well with varieties from Burgundy, the Rhône, and fine wines from Bordeaux, as well as with white wines that have a slightly nutty flavor. Chardonnay from the traditional growing regions is a good companion.

BRIE—POPULAR AND RESPECTABLE

The Ile-de-France is France's Brie paradise. The first documents mentioning a "fromage du pays du Brie" date back to 1217. This cheese is mentioned in the registers of the court of Champagne. It is named after the Pays de Brie, a region to the east of Paris. The various types of Brie are named after the places where they are made. Brie de Meaux comes from the town of Meaux, whereas Brie de Melun comes from the plains about Melun.

The Bries of various origins differ in the level of ripeness. Whereas Coulommiers, which is similar to Brie, can be consumed as soon as the first mold bloom appears, Brie de Meaux is fully ripened before it is served. Brie de Meaux and Brie de Melun have protected origin (PDO). Brie is also made outside France, in Germany (German Brie), the UK (Melbury), the USA, and Canada (Brie).

The characteristic shape of a Brie is the wheel (*tarte de Brie*). Smaller formats are called *petit brie*. The individual pieces are called *pointe de brie*. Brie de Melun is the heaviest: It weighs 5 ½–7 lb (2.5–3 kg), is up to 2 in (5 cm) high, and has a diameter of 13–14 in (32–36 cm). The largest Brie is Brie de Meaux with a diameter of up to 16 in (40 cm). Coulommiers is particularly small: It is a disk weighing 1 ¼ lb (500 g) with a diameter of about 6 in (14–16 cm).

Bries *fermier* are usually made from raw milk, more rarely from pasteurized milk. The production method for Brie is very similar to that of Camembert. Preripened evening milk is added to fresh milk, and then rennet is added to the two kinds of milk. The thickened milk is ladled into the molds using a round, flat ladle (*écremette*) with lots of holes. This process is repeated in five layers. While the whey is draining, the cheese is turned several times and salted twice by hand. The first salt layer is usually applied in the night within 12 hours. It is important to get the timing of this right so the rest of the whey can drain off and the formation of the rind is not damaged. When the second salt layer is applied, the mold cultures are sprinkled over the milk. It takes great skill on the part of the cheese maker to turn the large, flat cheeses as they are quite fragile and break easily. Affinage usually lasts four to eight weeks. When the Brie goes on sale, the mass should be at least half-ripened. Bries are usually mild and aromatic, although they can vary depending on the production method and range from slightly acidic to strong and piquant.

BRIE VARIETY
FROM THE DÉPARTEMENT SEINE-ET-MARNE

Strong smelling and strongly flavored Brie de Montereau is rare. It is never more than 8 in (20 cm) in diameter. One of the last local Brie specialties is Brie de Nangis. It is now made in the tradition of its place of origin near Tournan-en-Brie. It ripens for four to five weeks. Brie le Provins had already disappeared from the market when an enterprising producer rediscovered it. This Brie is at its best after ripening for four to five weeks, when the milk aroma and clear mold flavor have fully developed. Petit Morin looks like a small dome, and is produced on the banks of the river Morin. Its flavor puts it in the same category as Brie, although the addition of cream during the production process makes it somewhat milder. It matures for two to three weeks.

Brie de Melun (PDO)

Soft cheese with a white mold rind
made from raw cow's milk
45% FDM

ORIGIN AND HISTORY
Ile-de-France/Seine-et-Marne
The best Bries de Melun come from the
plains about Melun. With reddish
stripes visible through the white mold,
Brie de Melun is the most rustic variety—and one of the oldest. Its production area is closely delineated and
smaller than that of its cousin from
Meaux.

PRODUCTION
Lactobacilli are added to the milk to
make it separate. However, no mold
cultures are added to Brie de Melun. It
has quite a long ripening time (two
months), in cellars that are slightly less
damp than for other Bries.

CHARACTERISTICS
With a diameter of approximately 6 in
(14–16 cm) and weighing about 1 lb
(0.5 kg), Brie de Melun is quite small.
The rind is covered in blue-gray to light
blue-white mold that develops a red-
brown flora after a longer affinage.
Fresh, young Brie de Melun is called
"bleu" because the rind is dusted with
ash. The mass is slightly crumbly, and
the natural mold gives it a strong aroma.
Strong, slightly salty flavor.

SERVING SUGGESTIONS
Although Brie de Melun can mature for
a long time, it is much loved as a young
cheese. When overripe it becomes dry
and darker, more like Brie des Moissons,
which as a Brie of second choice used
to be given to farm laborers. As well as
the wines that are recommended for
Brie de Meaux, which also harmonize
with Brie de Melun, a wine with a delicate residual sweetness can also create
an exciting combination with mature
cheese.

Coulommiers

Soft cheese with a white mold rind
made from cow's milk
min. 40% FDM

ORIGIN AND HISTORY
Produced from Seine-et-Marne to the Meuse

Coulommiers originates from the town of the same name. Brie's "younger brother" is also closely related to Camembert. Some specialists include it in the Brie family, but it has long been regarded as an independent variety.

PRODUCTION
Coulommiers made from raw milk has to mature for two months, and for only half that if pasteurized milk is used. Most are made from pasteurized milk.

CHARACTERISTICS
Small, flat cylindrical cheese with a diameter of 5 in (13 cm) and weighing about 1¼ lb (500 g). Locals prefer their Coulommiers before it is fully ripe (*affiné à point*)—with a sour-milk core surrounded by a fresh, creamy mass.

SERVING SUGGESTIONS
A Coulommiers *fermier* is recommended since—unlike its commercially produced siblings—its aroma is highly typical of the region. Good wines to go with it are strong reds with plenty of character, such as those from Burgundy, Bordeaux, or Côtes du Rhône with a ripe tannin structure. White wines of the varieties Chenin Blanc and Pinot Gris are excellent choices.

SIMILAR CHEESE VARIETIES
Le Fougerus looks and tastes the same as Coulommiers, but is a little larger. It is also included in the Brie family. One key characteristic is a fern leaf on the surface, which both serves as decoration and adds aroma (the smell of the fern combines with that of the mold). After maturing for four weeks, the cheese develops a fresh, elastic, slightly salty mass. It is at its best from spring to fall. Strong, full-bodied red wines are good companions.

FRESH, CREAMY DELICACIES
FROM THE ILE-DE-FRANCE

Fontainebleu is a double-cream fromage frais that is thought to originate from a village near the forest of Fontainebleu. It is a mixture of cream and fresh cheese with a slightly sweet, creamy flavor. The cheese is shaped in a gauze-lined container. Served with fresh fruit or honey and nuts, it makes a wonderful dessert. Vin doux naturel is a good accompaniment. Explorateur, a creamy triple-crème with a white mold rind, is a postwar variety of a type similar to Brillat-Savarin.

Explorateur is made from milk to which crème fraîche has been added; it matures for two to three weeks. Weight 9 oz (250 g), height 2 in (6 cm), diameter 3 in (8 cm). Explorateur is smooth and creamy with a mild aroma of sour milk. It also has a slight smell of mold. Boursault is like Brie, but tastes a little sourer. Henri Boursault first made the cheese—which was named after him—in Perreux-sur-Marne after the Second World War. Cream is added to the milk, and then Boursault is left to mature in a cellar for 12 days. It is packed and left to mature for another month before it goes on sale. By that time, Boursault has developed a soft, smooth, creamy mass with a delicate white mold rind that occasionally develops a red-brown flora. This cheese is also known as Délice de Saint-Cyr, and is now produced in Limousin.

CHEESE SECRETS FROM THE ABBEY

In the Middle Ages, the art of cheese making was often introduced and refined by monks. The Trappists in particular became specialists in the craft. Cheese still provides a solid income for several abbeys that specialize in its production. Their cheeses are sometimes only known by their local names, but sometimes also as La Trappe, Le Trappiste, Fromage de Trappiste de…, Trappiste de…, or Abbaye de… . Examples are Belloc (Béarn/Basque country), Belval (Picardy), Chambarand (Isère/Dauphiné), Cîteaux (Burgundy), Echourgnac (Périgord), Mont-des-Cats or Trappe de Bailleul (Nord-Pas de Calais), or Tamié (Savoy).

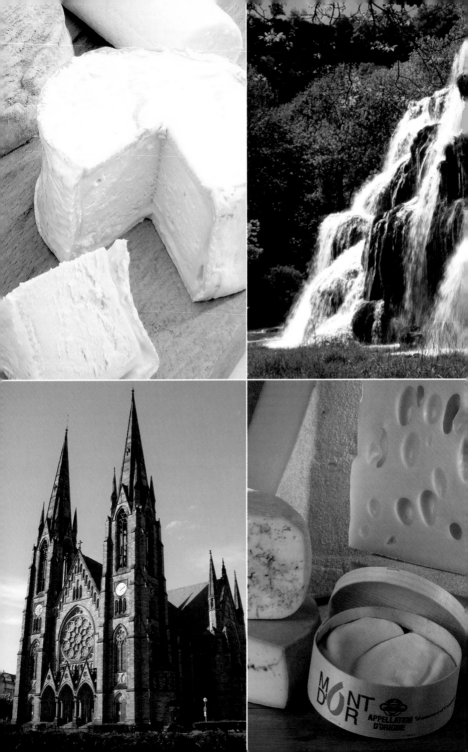

NORTHEAST
Paradise for gourmets

The northeast of France comprises the Champagne, Alsace, and Lorraine, plus the southern regions of Franche-Comté and Burgundy. The home of Champagne, the elegant and ever popular beverage, has remained true to its roots—and is the home of fabulous cheeses such as creamy Chasource and the stronger tasting Langres. Hearty food is very much appreciated here. Pork is a key item on the region's menus. In that respect, the preferences of the Champenois closely resemble those of their neighbors in Lorraine and Alsace. There, the locals are considered experts in brining and smoking, and in the production of patés and cheeses. The local Munster cheese also packs quite a punch: With an intensive bouquet, it is strong and full of character.

Further south, on the Swiss border, lies the mountain region of Franche-Comté with the regions Haute-Saône, Jura, Doubs, and Belfort. The mountains and high plains of the Jura in particular have maintained their traditions. Today, as centuries ago, the farms and tiny farming cooperatives produced smoked goods, the mysterious Vin Jaune, and delightful mountain cheese.

To the west is Burgundy—to the true gourmet the ultimate paradise. Once the realm of famous dukes, it has a long tradition of wine and cooking that has been passed on and refined for generations. And yet at its heart, Burgundy remains true to its farming roots. Burgundy has produced many exquisite delights: Excellent wines, delicious escargots, Bresse poultry, meat from the Charolais cattle, and—of course—wonderful cheeses.

Left: Northeast France is known for many traditional specialties.

Chaource (AOC)

Soft cheese with a white mold rind made from raw cow's milk
50% FDM

ORIGIN AND HISTORY
Champagne/Aube
Chaource, the creamy soft cheese from the town near Troyes of the same name, was produced in the Middle Ages. It is first mentioned in written documents that date back to 1531. Today it is also made in parts of northern Burgundy.

PRODUCTION
Coagulation takes at least 12 hours, and is effected primarily by lactobacilli. Regulations require that drainage must be both spontaneous and slow. It matures in cool cellars for three weeks (young Chaource), but it can last up to two months (fully ripe Chaource). Due to its high acid content, Chaource—unlike Camembert—does not mature through to the core, but remains slightly crumbly in the middle.

CHARACTERISTICS
Cylindrical in shape, Chaource is available in two sizes, small with a diameter of 3½ in (9 cm) and a height of 2–3 in (6–7 cm), weighing 9 oz (250 g); and large with a diameter of 4 in (11 cm) and a height of about 2 in (5–6 cm), weighing 1¼ lb (450 g). Smooth, creamy white, very fine mass. Creamy flavor with a pleasant note of sour milk. Chaource melts in the mouth! Mature Chaource smells slightly of mushrooms and cream. It also has a reddish flora on the upper rim of the rind.

SPECIAL FEATURES
Mainly produced commercially. Of the total of five Chaource producers only one cheese dairy still produces it artisanally.

SERVING SUGGESTIONS
Chaource tastes best in summer. It is excellent with a glass of Champagne, and a young Chaource goes well with a Blanc de Blanc or Brut. Champagne may be served with a riper, more mature Chaource, and rosé Champagne is also excellent. Chaource with a fine, traditionally grown Chablis is a delight. Cut into small pieces, Chaource makes a good snack to serve with an aperitif.

CHAMPAGNE AND CHEESE

Soft cheeses with a white mold rind go well with Champagne—especially if the cheeses are still young and not too ripe. The mass—which at this stage is creamy, slightly crumbly, and dense—harmonizes well with the perlage of the Champagne. One classic combination is Champagne with Brie. However, other excellent partnerships are creamy Chaource, Brillat-Savarin, and fresh Neufchâtel served with Champagne. As well as these quite delicate combinations, aged hard cheeses with more piquancy are excellent with Champagne. A glass of Champagne with a small piece of Comté is a very special treat for the taste buds. Mature Champagne can even hold its own against a strong cheese, such as a Langres or Maroilles. As is so often the case—the proof of the pudding is in the eating!

Langres (AOC)

Soft cheese with a washed rind
made from cow's milk
50% FDM

ORIGIN AND HISTORY

Champagne/Haute-Marne
This cheese specialty bears the name of
the town of Langres, 40 miles (65 km)
to the northeast of Dijon, which was an
important trading center in the Middle
Ages. Only 100 years ago, Langres was
solely produced on farms. Its history
goes back to the eighteenth century.
Even then, cheese merchants and refiners
in Langres were selling the cheese
to places as far away as Paris and
Geneva.

PRODUCTION

The sliced curd must be neither washed
nor kneaded. It is permissible to add
annatto to the brine, which is regularly
rubbed onto the cheese either with a
cloth or by hand.

CHARACTERISTICS

Cylindrical shape with a well in the
middle of the surface. This occurs
during affinage, since Langres is not
turned. There are two sizes. Large:
28 oz (800g) in weight, with a diameter
of 6–8 in (16–20 cm), and 2–3 in
(5–7 cm) in height. Small: 5 oz (150 g)
in weight, 3–3½ in (7.5–9 cm) in diameter,
and 1½–2 in (4–6 cm) in height.
Yellowish to brownish-red, moist, shiny
rind, and white mass that becomes
softer toward the center. Intensive,
typical aroma, very pleasant, characteristically
piquant flavor, sometimes
slightly acidic.

SERVING SUGGESTIONS

True connoisseurs refine Langres by
pouring a little Champagne or Marc de
Bourgogne into the well on the surface
to mature the cheese further. When this
is done, the cheese is best served with
the drinks that were used to refine it.
However, it also goes very well with a
mature, strong rosé Champagne or a
full-bodied, velvety red wine such as
Burgundy.

SIMILAR CHEESE VARIETIES

Chaumont.

Carré de l'Est

Soft cheese with a white mold / washed rind
made from cow's milk
52% FDM

ORIGIN AND HISTORY

Lorraine/Vosges

Compared with other soft cheeses with
a washed rind, Carré de l'Est is a mere
"youngster." It was first made at the end
of the 1930s to provide a long-lasting,
low-fat cheese for the summer months.
It is made almost exclusively in eastern
France.

PRODUCTION

Classic soft cheese production method:
made from unpressed and unheated
mass. The rind is washed regularly with
brine during the one-month affinage.

CHARACTERISTICS

As its name implies, the cheese is
square. Its sides are 4 in (9.5 cm) long;
it is 1 in (3 cm) high, and weighs 8 oz
(230 g). It has a dense, closed white
mold bloom with a little red smear.
Moist, elastic rind. Light-yellow, firm,
somewhat sticky mass. The young
cheese has a slightly acidic flavor, which
turns mild and aromatic, spicy, and a
little salty.

SERVING SUGGESTIONS

Place in the refrigerator to after-ripen
for a few days before consuming.
Sommelier's recommendation: Suitable
wines are whites from the Alsace, such
as Pinot Gris or Pinot Blanc; a Gris de
Toul is also a good choice. Mature Pinot
Noirs also harmonize well—as does a
glass of Mirabelle de Lorraine.

SIMILAR CHEESE VARIETIES

Le Saulxurois from the tiny Champagne
village of the same name is considered
the original Carré de l'Est. It is a soft
cheese made from unpasteurized cow's
milk, with a washed rind. Delicate,
aromatic, full-bodied flavor, sometimes
a little salty; matures for two months.
The version refined with schnapps is
known as "mirabellois."

HEARTY AND STRONG

Alsace, the smallest region of France, reaches from the Palatinate in the north to Switzerland in the south, and its landscape is a key feature of the Rhine plane. The Rhine plane adjoins the vineyards that are crowned in the west by the mountain ranges of the Vosges and form the border to the Lorraine with picturesque beauty.

Alsace is one of France's main culinary regions. Its people love eating, and love eating well, and its cuisine makes the most of the abundance from its fertile soil. It offers Alsace wines, beer and spirit, "Flammekuche," sauerkraut, foie gras, and—of course—full-bodied, lively Munster cheese, which is also a specialty on the Lorraine side.

Left: This is where the famous Munster-Géromé soft cheese is made.

Bottom: Farmhouse cheese traditions are still practiced with love in the Vosges.

RARITY FROM THE VOSGES

"Bargkass" is the name in the local dialect for "Bergkäse" (barg = Berg = mountain, and kass = Käse = cheese). Farmers in the Vosges and in the Munster valley were producing the milk for their own requirements of Bargkass or Fromage du Val St. Grégoire even 100 years ago. The cheese is made from semi-skimmed milk from the evening and full-fat milk from the next morning; the curd is pressed with heavy weights. Affinage is generally for two to three months, and a maximum of five to six. The cheese is moistened with brine once or twice a week to prevent mold from forming on the surface. It is wrapped in a light-brown natural rind, and weighs 16–17 lb (7.5–8 kg). The mass is straw colored with a soft, elastic consistency. Full-bodied flavor, slightly acidic at the end. Bargkass is only available in the region; it is still produced on a number of farms. The locals prefer to enjoy the cheese with a dark, strong, wholegrain bread and a glass of Alsace Gewürztraminer.

Munster Géromé (PDO)

Soft cheese with a washed rind
made from cow's milk
45% FDM

ORIGIN AND HISTORY
Alsace and Lorraine

The history of Munster cheese begins in the Middle Ages, on the south side of the Vosges. Benedictine monks from Italy founded a monastery there, and a small village soon grew up around it. The village was called Munster, derived from the Latin word *monasterium*, meaning monastery. The monks were expert cheese makers, and chose the best pastures in the Alsace—and shortly afterward in Lorraine. In 1285 Alsace and Lorraine together built the town of Sancti Gerardi Mare, which soon became known locally as Gérardmer, pronounced "géromé" in the local dialect. The Alsace and Lorraine monastery cheese was sold there. Now the two share the AOC: In the Alsace the exciting red smear cheese is called Munster, in Lorraine Géromé.

PRODUCTION

Made with raw (*fermier*) or pasteurized milk from Vosgienne cows. The divided curd must be neither washed nor kneaded before molding. The cheese has to be rubbed by hand every two days. Affinage usually takes two to three months, although it is about two weeks for Petit Munster.

CHARACTERISTICS

Flat, round cheese of 5–7 in (13–19 cm) height, diameter 1–3 in (2–8 cm), and weighing about 1¼ lb (450 g). Petit Munster is smaller and weighs about one quarter of that. The cheese has a smooth, moist, orange-red rind. Young Munster has a creamy, slightly crumbly consistency, and tastes fresh, nutty, and full. The rind of mature Munster is more colorful and moister, smells a little pungent, and is piquant and full of character in flavor, intensive and aromatic. The mass is soft and creamy to flowing. The alternative Munster cumé, seasoned with cumin, can sometimes be found.

SERVING SUGGESTIONS

The people of Alsace and Lorraine enjoy eating Munster-Géromé with plain boiled potatoes. Sommelier's recommendation: Suggested accompaniments are an aromatic Gewürztraminer or an Alsace beer. Munster *fermier* is at its best in summer and winter.

Bleu de Gex (PDO)

Blue cheese made from
raw cow's milk
50% FDM

ORIGIN AND HISTORY
Franche-Comté/Jura
The tradition of Bleu de Gex goes back
to the thirteenth century, when the
cheese was made in the Abbey of Saint-
Claude—albeit from goat's milk. In the
sixteenth century, its reputation spread
throughout the estates of Charles V,
who was a tremendous fan of the
specialty.

PRODUCTION
Bleu de Gex is made exclusively in the
mountains. Blue mold spores are added
to the milk. During affinage, air is
inserted into the mass with a syringe so
the blue mold develops. Matures for
about one month.

CHARACTERISTICS
The cheeses are cylindrical in shape
with a diameter of 14 in (35 cm), 3–4 in
(8–10 cm) in height, and weighing
15–19 lb (7–8 kg). The fine, dry,
yellowish rind with red marks is
covered in a layer of white, powdery
mold. White to ivory-colored, slightly
crumbly mass, blue-green marbled. Gex
is milder than other blue cheeses, with
a sweeter aroma and a delicate nutty
flavor, and tastes slightly bitter. The
other key feature of the cheese is the
special aroma of the milk: The cows
graze on lush pastures with wonderfully
aromatic vegetation.

SERVING SUGGESTIONS
Bleu de Gex made between May and
October is the best. In Jura, it is traditionally eaten with boiled potatoes. The
cheese is also excellent for fondues,
gratin dauphinois, and raclettes.
Sommelier's recommendation: The best
accompaniments are a Vin de Paille du
Jura, fine sweet wines, or a mature
tawny port.

SPECIAL FEATURES
The names Bleu de Gex, Bleu de Septmoncel, and Bleu du Haut Jura are all
permitted in the AOC and the EU-
protected designation of origin. Gex
and Septmoncel are two small towns in
Jura, just 10 miles (17 km) from
Geneva. The most frequently used
name is Bleu de Gex.

A CHEESE DAIRY IN EVERY VILLAGE

Lots of nature and woodlands, rivers, and above all cheese and wine—that's Franche Comté, a low mountain region that follows the French-Swiss border. Vast quantities of milk are produced in Franche-Comté, where the cows graze on picturesque mountain pastures and almost every village has its own cheese dairy.

Comté is the size of a wagon wheel and is made by hand, as are French Emmental, Vacherin de Mont-d'Or, and Bleu de Gex. Morbier has typical stripes of vegetable ash, and Cancaillotte, a type of cooking cheese, has been around since the thirteenth century.

Comté (PDO)

Hard cheese
made from raw cow's milk
45% FDM

ORIGIN AND HISTORY
Franche-Comté/Jura

In Franche-Comté, the tradition of producing oversize cheeses goes back more than 1,000 years. The *fruitières* (cheese or alpine dairy cooperatives) were already officially producing cheeses of quality in the twelfth and thirteenth centuries. Due to the size of the wheels, it was possible to store them during the long snowy months of winter. Today, there are still some 200 cheese dairies in Jura that produce Comté.

PRODUCTION

The milk has to come from Montbéliarde and Pie-Rouge cows, and the fresh raw milk may not be transported more than 15 miles (25 km) to the production site. The production of one whole Comté requires on average the daily production of 30 cows—about 130 gallons (500 l). The cheeses have to mature for about 4 months—a good Comté will mature for between 12 and 18 months.

CHARACTERISTICS

The large wheels are cylindrical with a slightly rounded edge. They are 3–5 in (9–13 cm) in height with a diameter of 20–30 in (50–75 cm); the weight can vary 66–120 lb (30–55 kg). The rind has a grainy golden or brown surface. Typi-cally, the mass is compact and smooth, cream-colored in winter, and dark yellow during the grazing period. The eyes in the mass vary from the size of a pea to that of a cherry. Winter Comté has a nutty flavor. Summer Comté is fruity with several aromas. Sweet aftertaste. Mature Comté is a little stronger, saltier, and more concentrated.

SPECIAL FEATURES

Comté is also known as the "king of the mountain cheeses." Next to Beaufort, Comté is one of France's most popular cheeses.

SERVING SUGGESTIONS

Comté goes extremely well with fish and seafood, and is also delicious as raclette and in fondues. Sommelier's recommen-dation: Comté harmonizes well with Cham-pagne or a dry white wine from Jura. A more mature cheese is better served with a more mature, not too heavy Burgundy.

THE FRUITIÈRES

Because the quantities of milk required for the production of a Comté, Beaufort, or Emmental are too vast to be supplied from a single pasture, farmers in the Middle Ages joined forces in small cooperatives. Only by combining their yields were they able to produce cheeses of this size, which provided essential nourishment during the long winters. More than 200 of these so-called *fruitières*, the dairy cooperatives, still produce Comté in Jura today.

TRADITIONAL VACHERIN

In the early Middle Ages, cheese made from cow's milk (*la vache* = cow) was generally called vacherin in order to distinguish it from chevrotins (*chèvre* = goat), cheeses made from goat's milk. Although the vacherins were too soft to be transported long distances, they soon acquired a reputation away from the mountain regions. Farmers produced vacherin toward the end of the grazing period, when there was no longer sufficient milk to produce the large, hard cheeses. The creamy, soft delicacies in the spruce band have centuries of tradition both on the French and on the Swiss side of the Alps.

VINJAUNE AND VIN DE PAILLE

Vin Jaune, the yellow wine made from Sauvignon blanc, and Vin Paille, straw wine, are probably the most unusual wines from Jura. Vin Jaune is produced only there. Like other dry white wines, yellow wine is fermented. It is then poured into wooden barrels without filling them to the top. After six years' aging, due to evaporation there is only about 21 fl oz (63 cl) left of every 2 pints (1 l) of wine—which equates to the capacity of a clavelin, the special bottle used for Vin Jaune. Vin de Paille is made of grapes that are left to shrink on the grapevine, and then picked individually and stored on straw, hung from wooden frames, or stored in wooden crates with ventilation holes. The grapes are pressed after two months. The must acquired this way has a very high sugar content, and fermentation takes months. The wine is then poured into oak barrels. The end product is a rich, strong, sweet nectar that is wonderful served slightly chilled with desserts or foie gras.

Right: Grapes hanging from the kitchen ceiling being dried for straw wine.

Bottom: Spruce strips add their aroma to Vacherin Mont-d'Or.

Morbier (PDO)

Semi-hard cheese made from
raw cow's milk
45% FDM

ORIGIN AND HISTORY
Franche-Comté/Doubs
Morbier is named after the Jura village of the same name, and—next to Comté—is the best-known cheese from Franche-Comté. In former times, Comté cheese dairies only produced Morbier for their own consumption.

PRODUCTION
The black-gray, horizontal stripe halfway up the cheese is characteristic. It was originally made of ash, which farmers used to cover the cheese made from morning milk to keep insects away. In the evening they wiped the ash off before then filling the cheese molds with fresh cheese made from the evening milk. Morbier still has the gray layer, although today it is made from a vegetable product. The best taste develops after ripening for three to four months.

CHARACTERISTICS
Flat cheese of approximately 3 in (8–9 cm) in height and a diameter of 10–16 in (25–40 cm); weight 11–20 lb (5–9 kg). The mass is encased in a smooth, homogeneous rind, gray or beige-orange in color. It has only a few small holes. The cut cheese reveals the ash layer as a narrow strip in the middle of the cheese. Mild, delicate flavor.

SERVING SUGGESTIONS
Red or white wine from the Arbois goes well with this cheese— generally, fresh, fruity white wines and reds with a fresh character and understated tannin structure harmonize well.

La Cancoillotte

Kochkäse/processed cheese
made from cow's milk
5–10% FDM

ORIGIN AND HISTORY
Franche-Comté/Doubs
Farmers' wives used to use the milk and whey left over from making butter and cheese to make this cheese. Its nicknames are "merde de diable" (devil's dung), "fromage fort" (strong cheese), and "tempête" (storm).

PRODUCTION
The skimmed milk is pressed, and the coagulated curd pressed into blocks. This so-called *metton* is cut again and fermented in vats at a low temperature until the hazelnut-size grains turn yellow and become pungent. The mass is then combined with water, salt, and butter, and melted over low heat until it is smooth and liquid.

CHARACTERISTICS
The consistency of this processed cheese—which is sold in pots—is somewhat sticky, while the flavor is quite plain. Cancaillotte is also available seasoned with cumin or garlic, with added butter, or flavored with white wine.

SERVING SUGGESTIONS
Sommelier's recommendation: Connoisseurs enjoy this specialty served warm with potatoes, stirred into scrambled eggs, or served cold as a spread on bread. White wine from Jura, perhaps based on Chardonnay or Savagnin, is a good accompaniment.

TIPS FOR VISITORS

Lots of cheese dairies welcome visitors. "Les routes du Comté" extends from St. Hippolyte to Montfleur, through the low mountains of Jura. The picturesque tiny villages contain the cheese dairies that produce the vast Comté cheeses. Many of them are open to visitors, and the museum in Poligny contains all the information you could wish to know about the production of Comté.

Vacherin Mont-d'Or (AOC)

Soft cheese with a white mold rind
made from raw cow's milk
45% FDM

ORIGIN AND HISTORY
Franche-Comté/Doubs
Even in the Middle Ages farmers were using the meadows in the Mont-d'Or massif for raising cattle and producing milk. The first cheese dairies appeared in the fourteenth century. Vacherin has been produced in Haut Doubs for centuries.

PRODUCTION
It is made at the beginning of fall, once the cows have been brought down from the meadows (August 15 until March 31). Only the milk from Montbéliarde and Simmental cows that graze at altitudes above 2,300 ft (700 m) is used. After demolding, the curd is bound in a strap of spruce wood and placed on spruce boards to continue ripening for at least three weeks, during which time it is turned frequently and washed with brine.

CHARACTERISTICS
Flat cheese, height about 2 in (6–7 cm), diameter 4–13 in (11–33 cm), weight 1¼–3 lb (500 g–1.3 kg). Wrinkled white to brown rind; delicate, creamy, slightly moist mass. Slightly acidic, full-bodied, mildly dry with a delicate, creamy flavor. The rind has the unmistakable aroma of spruce.

SPECIAL FEATURES
Vacherin is made in the same *fruitières* where Comté is produced in spring and summer. The Mont-d'Or massif is close to the Swiss border. For a long time, the French and the Swiss both claimed to have invented Vacherin Mont-d'Or. Agreement was finally reached with the addition of "du Haut Doubs." French Vacherin has to be made from raw milk.

SERVING SUGGESTIONS
Sommelier's recommendation: This cheese goes well with red or white wine from Jura and the Arbois, or white wine from Savoy.

SIMILAR CHEESE VARIETIES
Dairy farmers in the Abondance valley produce Vacherin d'Abondance using raw milk from Abondance cows. This Vacherin, which has a slightly higher fat content, ripens in spruce bands. Vacherin des Bauges comes from the Massif des Bauges, and is produced on only a few individual farms.

FROMAGES FORTS

In France, *fromage fort* refers to cheese specialties that are made by grating and breaking leftover bits of cheese and mixing them with liquids. Fromage fort is particularly common in wine-producing regions. It is a culinary delight that is served as an aperitif on toasted bread. It is best served accompanied by schnapps or an independent, very strong, full-bodied white wine.

Originally this cheese used to be made at home to add a little variety to the protein-poor dinner table. The chopped or grated cheese was mixed with whey, stock or milk, and wine, with schnapps or cider to stabilize it and add aroma. Salt and pepper, herbs and spices, or mustard were also added. Made from leftover goat's cheese, the specialty was called Cachat or Cacheilla. Today, fromage fort is still found in some restaurants or can be bought from cheese sellers, especially in Lyonnais (Fromage Fort du Lyonnais), Mâconnais, and Beaujolais, in the Dauphiné, higher up on Mont Ventoux (Cachet d'Entrechaux), and in the Nord-Pas-de-Calais. Fromages forts are notable for their piercing, piquant, often strong smell and flavor, and tingle slightly on the tongue. Depending on the production method, the cheese becomes creamy and mild after ripening for a long time—as for instance with Confit d'Epoisses. For Confit d'Epoisses, young Epoisses is steeped in white Burgundy with a dash of Marc de Bourgogne for about one week. The mix ferments for one week, then the liquid is drained off and replaced with fresh wine.

Fromage Fort de Béthune, made from well-matured Maroilles, is typical in northern France. The cheese mass is seasoned with parsley, tarragon, and pepper, and steeped in beer for a period of two to three months. The extremely strong, piquant cheese product with a marked aroma was the preferred snack for miners, who liked to accompany it with a glass of Genièvre.

Emmental Grand Cru (PGI)

Semi-hard cheese made from
raw cow's milk
45% FDM

ORIGIN AND HISTORY

*Franche-Comté / Rhônes-Alpes / Jura,
Savoy, Vosges*
The Jura has centuries of tradition in
the production of these famous, large
Emmental cheeses. Emmental Grand
Cru is protected throughout the EU as
a regional specialty. The production
range includes Jura, Savoy, and the
Vosges in the first line.

Swiss white wines of the Chasselas variety and white wines from Savoy are also
good choices.

PRODUCTION

Unlike Emmental français, which is
made from pasteurized milk all over
France, Emmental Grand Cru can only
be made from raw milk. As with Comté,
the curd is heated and pressed.
Emmental Grand Cru ripens for a minimum of 12 weeks.

CHARACTERISTICS

These vast cheeses are almost as
big as mill wheels. Their diameter is
30–40 in (80–100 cm), height 5–10 in
(13–25 cm), and weight 132–285 lb
(60–130 kg). Dry, ocher-colored natural rind. Smooth, elastic, ivory to pale-yellow mass; mildly sweet, fruit flavor.

SERVING SUGGESTIONS

Fruity red wines such as Pinot Noir from
southern Burgundy and red wines from
Savoy go well with Emmental.

SIMILAR CHEESE VARIETIES

The reputation enjoyed by Emmental
from Savoy goes back to the nineteenth
century, and Emmental from the mountains of Savoy was sold for much higher
prices than other Emmental cheeses.
Its production range is smaller, and
cheese of this designation may only be
produced in Savoy and Haute-Savoie.
This Emmental is also protected as a
regional specialty throughout Europe.

Soumaintrain

Soft cheese with a washed rind
made from cow's milk
50–60% FDM

ORIGIN AND HISTORY
Bourgogne/Yonne
This specialty had almost disappeared
completely until it was rediscovered 15
years ago. Today, Soumaintrain is
produced on about ten farms and by a
dairy in the vicinity of the village of
Soumaintrain (Yonne).

PRODUCTION
The production method is similar to
that of Epoisses. However, unlike
Epoisses, Soumaintrain does not ripen
in alcohol. It is left to mature for at least
three weeks and up to three months.

CHARACTERISTICS
Small cylinder with a diameter of
4–5 in (10–13 cm) and a height of about
2 in (3–4 cm). It weighs 9 oz–1 lb
(250–400 g). The fresh cheese weighs
about 1¼ lb (550 g). Similar to Epoisses
in consistency, color, and rind. Young
Soumaintrain has a fresh cheese consistency and a pleasantly sour flavor.

SERVING SUGGESTIONS
Soumaintrain is best eaten fresh. The
ideal accompaniments are wines such
as Chablis or Sauvignon de Saint-Bris.
Pinot Noir is a good choice for red wine.

ISLAND OF GOURMETS

For visitors, Burgundy has historic
buildings, romantic villages, relaxing
landscapes, and about 750 miles
(1,200 km) of waterways that cover
the whole area and are perfect for
exploring by boat. The people are
cheerful and down to earth, with an
excellent reputation—not least for their
cuisine. Connoisseurs appreciate their
famous wines, Cassis liqueur, and Kir
Royal, Dijon's famous mustard, the
juicy meat of the Charolais cattle, and
the cheese—such as creamy Epoisses
with the intensive bouquet that
matures in Marc de Bourgogne.

Saint-Florentin

Fresh cheese made from
cow's milk
45–50% FDM

ORIGIN AND HISTORY
Bourgogne/Yonne
The cheese is made in Saint-Florentin
in the Auxerrois.

PRODUCTION
Lactobacilli separation; mature cheese
is washed regularly in brine for about
two months.

CHARACTERISTICS
Fresh Saint Florent is available in jars
or bowls. Young, immature Saint-
Florentin has a smooth, white surface
with no rind. The flavor has a pleasant
touch of sour milk. As the cheese ripens,
the rind becomes light gray. The mature
cheese is round, about 5 in (12–13 cm)
in diameter, 1 in (3 cm) high, and weighs
about 12 oz to 1¼ lb (350–550 g). The
mass is creamy in color, soft, and tastes
almost pungently aromatic.

SERVING SUGGESTIONS
Saint-Florentin goes very well when
accompanied with traditionally grown
Chardonnay (unwooded).

MAMIROLLE—THE "STUDENTS'CHEESE"

Mamirolle is a brick-shaped cheese
with a washed rind. It was invented in
1935 by students of the ENIL (École
Nationale d'Industrier Laitière) in
Mamirolle, the oldest dairy college in
France, and is now the only cheese
that is made solely by students. The
students wanted Mamirolle to be a
cheese that kept well with no impair-
ment of quality, and in a small,
practical shape with the same qualities as larger, traditional cheeses.
Mamirolle is about 8 in (20 cm) long,
and 2 in (6 cm) high and wide; it
weighs between 1 lb 5 oz and 1 ½ lb
(550–600 g). It is smooth and elastic
in consistency with a very mild flavor.

Abbaye de Cîteaux

Semi-hard cheese with a washed rind
made from raw cow's milk
45% FDM

ORIGIN AND HISTORY
Bourgogne/Côte d'Or
The Abbey of Cîteaux is not far from
the famous wine resort of Nuits-Saint-
Georges. In vast, lush meadows, the
Cistercian monks keep their own Montbéliarde cows that produce rich milk
that is perfect for producing Cîteaux
cheese. This cheese is the main part of
the income of the 40 monks.

PRODUCTION
The curd is pressed in molds for about
20 hours, and then placed in a salt bath.
During the ripening period of two to
three weeks in cellars with high humidity, the cheese is washed in brine every
second day. The cheeses are then
wrapped in paper and left to ripen for a
further week.

CHARACTERISTICS
Round cheese, 1–2 in (3.5–4 cm) high,
6–7 oz (16–18 cm) in diameter, weight
2¾ lb (700 g). The elastic, yellow-red
rind encloses a soft, smooth mass. Striking, very mild, and particularly fine
aroma that is typical of the region.

SPECIAL FEATURES
The best way to procure cheese from
the Abbaye de Cîteaux is to pay it a visit.
The cheese is so popular in Burgundy
that it is only rarely found elsewhere.

SERVING SUGGESTIONS
Sommelier's recommendation: The
cheese tastes best in summer, when it
has ripened for a month. It goes very
well with the grapes from the region,
and is as good with white Burgundies as
with the region's reds. Young, fruity
wines from the Côte de Beaune and
more mature versions of Côtes de Nuits
are highly recommended.

SIMILAR CHEESE VARIETIES
Reblochon and Saint-Paulin (see entry)
are similar.

THE EPOISSES FAMILY

Ami du Chambertin, which was not invented until after the Second World War, is a cousin of Epoisses. This cheese, which comes from the famous wine village of Gevrey-Chambertin, is also refined with Marc de Bourgogne. Because of its shorter ripening time, it is milder than Epoisses, but when mature tastes equally strong and has a very soft mass. Another variation on red smear cheeses from Burgundy is Le Petit Creux. It is made by hand from raw milk. It is ripened for four weeks with dilute Marc de Bourgogne. Traditionally, a little Marc du Bourgogne is poured into the small well on the top.

The little Trou de Cru or Coeur d'Epoisses is refined with Marc and has a very fine flavor. Aisy Cendré is a young Epoisses that is also refined with Marc, but then matures for eight weeks in ashes. The circular cheese is 4–5 in (10–12 cm) in diameter and weighs 9 oz (250 g). Pierre-qui-vire is a soft cheese with red smear, and is made from raw cow's milk. This cheese has been made since 1920 by the monks of the Abbey Pierre-qui-vire (Yonne). The cheese is sometimes also refined with Chablis (Pierre-qui-vire affiné au Petit Chablis). It has a strong aroma with a marked overtone of the terrain.

Right: Pinot Noir at veraison, the coloring of the berries.

Bottom: Color and tannins are taken from the marc and skins in the must (pigeage).

Epoisses de Bourgogne (PDO)

Soft cheese with a washed rind
made from raw cow's milk
50% FDM

ORIGIN AND HISTORY

Bourgogne/Côte d'Or

Burgundy's best known cheese comes from the Auxois. In the sixteenth century, the village of Epoisses was an important base for the Cistercians. The monks began to produce cheese, and farmers in the region later perfected the production method. It is said that even Napoleon appreciated Epoisses—preferably with a Chambertin. In 1825 Brillat-Savarin called Epoisses the king of cheeses. However, production almost ground to a halt after the Second World War. The production area is relatively small, and includes part of the Départements Haute-Marne, Côte d'Or, and Yonne.

PRODUCTION

Thickening the milk with lactobacilli makes the ripe cheese very soft, and almost flowing. It is washed two to three times a week, initially with brine, and then with dilute Marc de Bourgogne. Epoisses matures for six to eight weeks.

CHARACTERISTICS

Flat cylinder in two sizes: The small Epoisses has a diameter of about 4 in (9.5–11 cm) and weighs 9–12 oz (250–350 g). The larger version has a diameter of 6½–7 in (16.5–19 cm), and weighs up to 2½ lb or so (1,100 g). The height of the two varies between 1 and 2 in (3–4.5 cm). Damp, shiny, red-brown rind; soft, elastic, almost white mass. Striking but pleasant smell, strong flavor. Very creamy; melts in the mouth.

SPECIAL FEATURES

Epoisses is one of the last French cheese classics still available today that is made by coagulation, and is offered with a washed rind.

SERVING SUGGESTIONS

Sommelier's recommendation: A young Epoisses harmonizes well with a white, dry Burgundy, whereas ripe Epoisses is a delight in combination with a mature Pinot Noir, perhaps a Nuits-Saint-Georges or a Gevrey Chambertin.

Charolais/Charolles

Soft cheese made from
raw goat's milk
45% FDM

ORIGIN AND HISTORY
Bourgogne/Saône-et-Loire
Charolais, often also called Charolles, comes from the granite plains of the county of Charolais, near Beaujolais. The region is famous for its excellent beef cattle of the same name.

PRODUCTION
Charolais can be made from goat's milk or a combination of goat's and cow's milk. Tradition has it that a Charolais cheese should be made from the milk of two goats and one cow. It is only available as farmhouse-produced *fermier* and artisanal cheese. Ideally, it matures for four weeks. The rind develops its delicate, gray-blue crust during the first two weeks.

CHARACTERISTICS
A small, barrel-shaped soft cheese, 3 in (8 cm) high and weighing 7 oz (200 g), with a natural blue or white mold rind. The mass is white and firm, and often dry. The fresh smell and slightly salty-sweet flavor are typical. The cheese can be eaten fresh, semi-aged (demi-sec), or very aged (sec). The flavor is much more piquant when it is very mature.

SPECIAL FEATURES
Producers and affineurs have applied for the designation AOC for their cheese.

SERVING SUGGESTIONS
Sommelier's recommendation: Summer and fall are the best times to enjoy this cheese. A fruity young Beaujolais goes well with a Charolais, and a Sauvignon de Saint-Bris or fresh Burgundy Chardonnay is also to be recommended.

GOAT'S CHEESE FROM BURGUNDY

It is not well known that Burgundy produces excellent goat's cheese as well as many other cheese specialties. Some of these specialties are produced by only a few producers, and sometimes only by one. Vézelay, sold today as a strictly organic product, comes from the Yonne. The small, dome-shaped goat's cheese made from raw milk was created in 1990 by the monks of the Abbaye de la Pierre-qui-vire. The same abbey also produces Chèvre fermier affine, which is based on Crottin de Chavignol. Lardu is a bacon-wrapped flat goat's cheese. Côte d'Or has Poiset au Marc, which is made in a method similar to that of Epoisses and matures for six eight weeks. Burgundy also produces a number of Tommes de chèvre, as well as various fresh and soft cheeses made from goat's milk.

Mâconnais AOC comes from southern Burgundy (Saône-et-Loire), and is also known as Chevreton de Mâcon or Cabrion de Mâcon. Over 400 rural producers ensure that this stump-shape specialty is not lost to us. It has held the French AOC since 2006. It is popular in its home region as a fresh cheese, and can be eaten within six days of being produced. After two to three weeks it has developed a beautifully homogeneous mass with a pale-blue mold rind. The same region also produces the Boutons de culotte ("trouser buttons"), tiny goat's cheeses in the shape of a cylinder that weigh just 2 oz (60 g). These may become very hard, firm, and piquant during the two weeks of their affinage.

SOUTHEAST
High Alps and Riviera

Southeast France reaches from the High Alps of Savoy in the east, along the Swiss border, and down to the French Riviera. Corsica forms the southernmost peak, and Languedoc-Roussillon delineates it to the west.

Rhône-Alpes has everything to make a gourmet's pulse race. The markets of Lyons, Saint-Etienne, Grenoble, and Valence overflow with an abundance of fruit and vegetables from the Rhône valley, with Bresse poultry and guinea fowl from the Drôme. The alpine region of Savoy produces a number of excellent cheese specialties, and it is particularly well known for its Tommes. Goat's cheese is produced in the hilly landscape about Lyons.

The Central Massif starts to the west of the Rhône-Alpes region. The fertile volcanic soils and plentiful water guarantee excellent grazing. The Auvergne is home to a wide range of excellent cheese specialties with names such as Bleu d'Auvergne.

Far down in the south, in Languedoc and Roussillon, sun and blue skies are typical of the Mediterranean lifestyle. To the east lies Provence with the Camargue, the sophisticated Côte d'Azur, the former papal residence of Avignon, and the plain of Haute-Provence with breathtaking lavender fields and the delightful Lubéron.

The regions not only produce good rosé wines but also aromatic herbs, the best olive oil, excellent honey, and air-dried sausages. The isle of Corsica is part of the southeast, and—like Provence—provides wonderful goat's cheese.

Left: France's famous cheese specialties from the south.

FIRST-GRADE CHEESE

The landscape of Savoy (French Savoie), a first-grade cheese paradise, is situated on the head of the alpine pass between France to the west and Switzerland and Italy to the east. The flora in the pastures of the Savoy Alps is completely different from that in the valley. Cheese and milk are popular ingredients in Savoy cooking, especially in the numerous vegetable gratins. Beaufort, a hard cheese the size of a millstone, is the most typical cheese from the Savoy Alps. Abondance, a hard cheese made from the milk of Savoy cows, is another typical variety. The Savoy people like to serve a Reblochon at the end of a meal. Savoy is the home of the Tomme, the semi-hard cheese of which there are numerous local variations.

GRUYÈRES

The family of French Gruyères includes the large hard cheeses from the northwest Alpine region made from curds that are heated and pressed. They are Emmental, Beaufort, and Comté. Gruyère des Bauges (Gras de Bauges) from the barren mountain pastures of the Bauges to the north of Chambér is more like Emmental.

A Gruyère de Savoie cheese is higher than Comté, but is similar to it in flavor and texture. The average weight is 88 lb (40 kg). It matures for at least 4 months, although the cheese tastes best after 8–12 months.

Abondance (PGI)

Hard cheese made from
raw cow's milk
48% FDM

ORIGIN AND HISTORY

Rhône-Alpes/Haute Savoie
This cheese was originally made in the
Abondance valley between Lake
Geneva and the Swiss Valais. The monks
of the Abbey of Abondance used the
milk from the golden-brown Abondance
cows of Burgundy. Even today, only
milk from Abondance, Tarine, and
Montbéliarde cows is used. In 1381 the
Abbey of Abondance was the official
supplier of cheese for the papal elec-
tion. On that occasion, 1,500 lb (680 kg)
of cheese was sent to the conclave of
Avignon. Abondance was the first
cheese from Savoy to be granted the
AOC, in 1990.

PRODUCTION

Production commences directly after
milking. Rennet is added to the milk to
coagulate it, and the curd is heated and
stirred. The cheese is wrapped in a cloth
and placed in a wooden mold, pressed,
and left to mature for at least 90 days.

CHARACTERISTICS

The cheeses have a diameter of
15–17 in (38–43 cm), are about 3 in
(7–8 cm) high, and weigh 15–26 lb
(7–12 kg). The edge is rounded, the rind
smooth and brown. Firm, compact,
smooth mass ranging in color from
ivory to golden. Highly aromatic with a
fruity, fine flavor and an overtone of
nuts.

SERVING SUGGESTIONS

Top-quality Abondance is made with
summer milk. It tastes best after maturing for four to six months.

Sommelier's recommendation: The fresh
white wines of Savoy go well with Abondance. Wines from the region of Lake
Geneva such as Dézaley and Epesses are
also good choices.

SPECIAL FEATURES

In addition to the plain Abondance,
there is also one that has aged for seven
months, Abondance d'hiver, a "winter
cheese," and Abondance d'alpage,
which has to be made from the milk of
cows that have grazed on a single
pasture and matures for about ten
months.

Beaufort (PDO)

Hard cheese made from
raw cow's milk
48% FDM

ORIGIN AND HISTORY
Rhône-Alpes/Savoie
Beaufort is a typical specialty of the
Savoy Alps. The AOC zone covers the
high valleys with their rough climate,
coarse peaks, and extensive pastures.
The richness of the flavor is due to the
milk of the Tarine and Abondance cows,
which graze on an abundance of plants
on the snow-free high pastures.
Although the name Beaufort has only
been known since 1865, Pliny the
Younger spoke of a similar cheese.

PRODUCTION
Production requires over 100 gallons
(400 l) of milk. Once thickened, the
curd is heated and pressed. It ripens for
at least four months at a temperature
below 59 °F (15 °C) and in humidity of
92%. During this time, it is regularly
washed with brine and brushed.

CHARACTERISTICS
Beaufort is the most aromatic of all
the Gruyère varieties. It is a wheel
of cheese 14–30 in (35–75 cm) in
diameter, 4–6 in (11–16 cm) high, and
weighing 44–154 lb (20–70 kg). The
yellow to brown rind envelops a
homogeneous mass with hardly any
holes but with fine cracks. The consistency of Beaufort is firm and smooth.

The aroma is strong, fruity, flowery, and
slightly nutty.

SERVING SUGGESTIONS
Beaufort is an important ingredient in
the traditional Fondue Savoyard, and is
delicious with rustic bread. It is excellent for gratins.
Sommelier's recommendation: The
fruity wines of Savoy go well with a
young Beaufort. Mature Beaufort also
harmonizes with the stronger wines of
the Jura, such as Chardonnay and
Savagnon.

SPECIAL FEATURES
Beaufort été is made from June to
October, and Beaufort chalet d'alpage
is made with the milk of cows that have
grazed on pastures at a minimum height
of about 5,000 ft (1,500 m).

Grataron d'Arêches

Soft cheese with a washed rind
made from raw goat's milk
45% FDM

ORIGIN AND HISTORY
Rhône-Alpes/Savoie
Grataron is a farmhouse goat's cheese
from the area about Beaufort. There are
only three cheese dairies left in the
valleys of Beaufort that still produce it.
It is the only soft goat's cheese with red
smear in the French Alps.

PRODUCTION
The mass is gently pressed and
washed regularly in brine during the
one to two months maturing period.

CHARACTERISTICS
The cheeses have a diameter of 3–4 in
(8–10 cm), are 1–2 in (3–4 cm) high,
and weigh 12 oz to 1 lb (350–400 g). A
beige to orange-pink rind envelops the
soft, rich mass, which has a few small
holes. Grataron is similar in texture to
Reblochon, whereas the flavor is reminiscent of a Tomme.

SERVING SUGGESTIONS
The fine acidity of a dry Riesling, the
freshness of a Sauvignon Blanc, and the
aroma of a delicate Traminer are perfect
accompaniments for this cheese. To
complement the wine care must be
taken with the preparation of the
cheese.

"CAIL-LÉ DOUX" SPECIALTIES

It is not easy to make goat's cheese
from soft curd (cail-lé doux), but it
gives the mass a unique creamy
consistency and a creamy flavor.
Some examples are Saint-Félicien de
Lamastre from the high plain, and
Rogeret de Lamastre from the northern
Ardèche. Rennet is added to the milk
to produce the curd, and processing
continues as soon as it thickens. The
soft curd is roughly chopped and left
to drain. The cheese then matures for
about 15 days. Rogeret matures on
damp straw, and forms a reddish
mold.

Fromage à Raclette

Semi-hard cheese made from
cow's milk
45% FDM

ORIGIN AND HISTORY

Rhône-Alpes/Haute Savoie

Although Raclette cheese originally came from the Savoy Alps, it has been made in other parts of France for some time now. The name "raclette" is derived from the French word *racler* (to scrape). Mountain farmers used to make their raclette on their isolated pastures by melting cheese over a wood fire and then scraping the melted cheese onto a plate.

PRODUCTION

Raclette with the Label Rouge quality seal is made from first-class milk, and may be produced only in certain parts of France. According to the traditional method, it must mature for at least ten weeks. The rind has a striking flora, which is produced by natural fungi.

CHARACTERISTICS

Large wheels of 10–15 lb (4.5–7 kg), about 11 oz (28–30 cm) in diameter, height 2–3 in (5–7 cm). White to pale-yellow, very firm mass with small holes; melts easily. The thin rind is golden to light brown. Mild flavor of the full milk.

SERVING SUGGESTIONS

Raclette is perfect with pickled vegetable such as gherkins, tiny onions, pumpkin, or beets, or simply in a salad with a strong vinaigrette. Sommelier's recommendation: Raclette goes best with white wines such as those from Savoy, Lake Geneva, or the Valais. The Chasselas here is a fine, restrained companion. However, rather than taking a mouthful of wine directly after the sharp gherkins, neutralize the palate first with cheese and potatoes.

Reblochon (PDO)

Semi-hard cheese with a washed rind
made from raw cow's milk
45% FDM

ORIGIN AND HISTORY

Rhône-Alpes/Haute Savoie
Made since the fourteenth century in
the mountains of the Pays de Thônes,
this cheese was used by farmers as a
form of payment for their leases. When
the landowner came to check, the farmers never milked their cows completely.
Later, they milked the cows a second
time (*reblosser*). This milk was much
creamier, with a higher fat content, and
is still used for the cheese today.

PRODUCTION

The milk comes from Abondance, Montbéliarde, and Tarine cows that graze at
altitudes of at least 1,600 ft (500 m).
Production takes place in the morning
and evening directly after the milk is
supplied. The curd is poured into molds
and gently pressed. The young cheeses
are washed several times over a period
of two weeks. Reblochon matures for
three to four weeks.

CHARACTERISTICS

Flat wheel, 5½ in (14 cm) diameter,
1 in (3.5 cm) high, weight about 1½ lb
(450–500 g). The small Reblochon, Petit
Reblochon, weighs between 8 and 10 oz
(240–280 g). Saffron yellow, encased in
a rind with a fine white bloom, mass
ivory colored, soft, and very smooth.
Flavor creamy, mild, full-bodied, and
buttery.

SERVING SUGGESTIONS

Sommelier's recommendation: Fine,
fruity white wines are perfect with young
Reblochon. Stronger wine varieties such
as Pinot Blanc and Pinot Gris work well
with a more mature cheese.

SIMILAR CHEESE VARIETIES

Chevrotin des Aravis AOC is a soft
cheese with a washed rind that is made
from goat's milk. It is round and flat,
weighs 9–12 oz (250–350 g), and tastes
best in summer and fall. The Reblochon
family also includes Tamié. Chambarand
from the Dauphiné (Departément
Isère) is made exclusively by monks in
the monastery at Chambarand using a
similar method. A white mold bloom is
hidden beneath the sticky orange rind.
The annual production of about 60 to 90
tons provides their annual income.

Tamié, Abbaye de Tamié

Semi-hard cheese made from
raw cow's milk
50% FDM

ORIGIN AND HISTORY
Rhône-Alpes/Savoie

Trappist monks in the area about
Bauges have been making cheese for
over 900 years. In 1677, in order to
perfect their cheese-making skills, they
consulted a master cheese maker from
Gruyère. Today, the cheese is the
monastery's main source of income.

PRODUCTION

Every day except Sunday, 12 monks
spend 5 hours a day turning in excess
of 1,050 gallons (4,000 l) of raw milk
from 11 farms into cheese in the
monastery's cheese dairy. The cheese
ripens for at least a month. Twice a week
the cheese is washed in brine.

CHARACTERISTICS

The large Tamié weighs 3 lb (1.5 kg),
measures 7 in (18 cm) in diameter, and
is 2 in (5 cm) high. The small one
weighs 1½ lb (600 g). Saffron-yellow
rind with a white mold bloom at the end
of the ripening period. The mass is
slightly creamy with large irregular
holes and a mild flavor. Tamié has a mild
taste.

SERVING SUGGESTIONS

The fine, creamy, nutty aromas harmonize perfectly with white wines from
Burgundy, wines of the Pinot family, and
also with mature, strong Crus from
Beaujolais or slightly stronger Chardonnays from Jura. Savoy wines are the
traditional accompaniment.

PROVENCE-ALPES-CÔTES D'AZUR

Provence consists of extremes in
landscape in a very small area. Its
cheese varieties are equally diverse.
The best known is without doubt
Banon, although there are also
countless local specialties. Haute-
Provence produces cheese made
from cow's and goat's milk; sheep's
cheeses are at home in the Rhône
delta, and goats come into their own
a little further south.

Tomme de Savoie (PGI)

Semi-hard cheese made from
raw cow's milk
48% FDM

ORIGIN AND HISTORY

Rhône-Alpes/Savoie

Tomme de Savoie is the oldest cheese variety from Savoy; its origins go back to the fourteenth century. Tomme de Savoie bears the regional protective designation of the Savoy region. When seasoned with wild-growing cumin from the region, the words "au cumin" are added to the name.

PRODUCTION

Tommes with the quality seal of the Savoy region and the EU protection of origin must be made from raw milk. The unwashed, grain-size curd is pressed for five to eight hours. Once it has been turned for the first time in the mold, the cheese is salted and then left to mature for at least six weeks.

CHARACTERISTICS

Tommes de Savoie is 7 in (18 cm) in diameter, 2 in (6 cm) high, and weighs 3½ lb (1.6 kg). The hard rind is gray in color, with red or yellow marks depending on the affinage. Semi-hard, elastic mass with a few tiny holes. Very mild, creamy flavor.

SPECIAL FEATURES

As well as Tomme de Savoie with the protected geographic designation, there are also Tommes de Savoie made from pasteurized milk; they do not bear the quality seal. The many other Tommes from Savoy are local specialties, usually made from raw milk, all with different flavors and consistencies depending on the kind of milk used, the period of maturing, and the type of pasture.

SERVING SUGGESTIONS

White Crus from the northern Rhône such as Hermitage Blanc or Condrieu harmonize well, as do stronger white wines from Savoy. A mature, not too tannin-rich Syrah wine such as St. Joseph or Crozes-Hermitage can also be an excellent companion for a Tomme.

TOMME — CHEESES FROM THE FARM

It is a typical feature of Tomme cheeses that they are made on farms. They can be made from cow's, goat's, or sheep's milk, or a combination of the three. The typical Tomme is a medium-sized, flat wheel of 2–4 ½ lb (1–2 kg), 2–3 in (5–8 cm) high, with a diameter of about 8 in (20 cm). However, Tommes can weigh up to 9 lb (4 kg). The curd is pressed lightly during production, but not heated. Tommes do not keep well. Many of the cheeses named Tomme de … (formerly *tome*) are semi-hard cheeses from Savoy. There are numerous variants, and they often differ from one town to another.

They are named after the valley, mountain, or town where they were made. It is joked that Savoy has almost as many Tommes as it has mountains and valleys. In former times, if bad weather prevented the milk from being delivered to the collection points — the *fruitières* — or if there was not enough for the production of Beaufort or other large cheeses, the farmers made

Tomme instead. The name "tome" used to be used in Savoy for any cheese that had an elastic, semi-hard mass in order to distinguish it from a Gruyère-type cheese. Later, Tommes that were produced by a particular method or that had typical features from their place of origin were given their own names. Reblochon is one example of this. Tommes de Chèvre, which may be found in the Pyrenees as well as in Savoy, are also extremely popular.

Tomme au Marc de Raisin is a mature Tomme that has been steeped in marc, the residue that is left after the fruit has been pressed to make wine. The cheese is placed in a closed container to mature for one month. During this time, the flavor of the marc penetrates it completely. The warmth causes it to start fermenting in the container, which explains why the mass has a slightly sticky consistency. Tome Alpage de la Vanoise has a red, yellow, and gray natural mold rind, which makes it easy to identify. It is produced on the high

pastures of the Vanoise. The milk of the cows that graze there contains plenty of carotene, which causes the yellow marks on the rind. Tomme du Mont-Cenis, which is made close to the Italian border, looks a lot like freshly baked bread just out of the oven. It matures for at least three months, and is made just before the cows are brought down from the mountain pastures. The *fermier* cheese Tome de Bauges (PDO) is made in the mountain region of the same name from unpasteurized cow's milk. It usually has a solid, slightly crusty rind, and it has a particularly fruity flavor. Unlike other Tommes from Savoy, it has a "blind" mass—with no holes. The milk for Bauges d'alpage has to come from a single herd. Boudane is a *fermier* cheese with a firm, fatty mass.

Handmade Tomme de Belley was being made at the beginning of the twentieth century. It is made by lactobacilli separation, and is eaten fresh after three days of drying. Tomme de Belleville is made in the Belleville valley from the milk of mountain goats. At three months, its affinage is a lot longer than for Tomme de Savoie. The Tommes de chèvre de Savoie include Tomme de Courchevel. It is made from the milk of goats that spend the summer grazing on the slopes of the famous Les trois Vallées ski region. Like Tomme de Savoie, Tomme de Lullin bears the quality mark Label Savoie, and it is subject to the same strict guidelines. It is only made in the alpine village of Lullin. The earthy gray mold that forms after a week or so and later produces the gray rind is typical of this variety. It is soft and mild and melts in the mouth. Vieille Tomme à la Pièce is a Tomme de Savoie that has matured for a very long time, and has lots of tiny holes in the rind and mass.

Bleu du Vercors-Sassenage (PDO)

Semi-hard blue cheese
made from raw cow's milk
48% FDM

ORIGIN AND HISTORY

Rhône-Alpes/Isère

As long ago as the fourteenth century, a blue cheese named Fromage de Sassenage was being produced all over Vercors. At that time, the Vercors massif was called the Montagnes de Sassenage. Until then the counts of Sassenage received the revenue from the sale of the cheese. In 1600 the agronomist Olivier de Serres made a mention of the cheese in his *Théatre d'Agriculture*, where he described the production of Bleu de Sassenage. The isolated location of the Vercors massif has helped to keep the production method traditional.

PRODUCTION

The evening milk from Montbéliarde, Abondance, and Villarde cows is heated, skimmed, and mixed with raw milk from the next morning's milking. Once it has thickened and drained, the cheese is salted and then left to continue maturing for two to three months, during which time it is turned frequently.

CHARACTERISTICS

The flat wheel of up to 12 in (30 cm) diameter and about 3 in (8 cm) height weighs 9–10 lb (4–4.5 kg). The natural

rind has a light, whitish bloom that sometimes has red to ivory-colored marks on it. Soft, full mass. Mild, subtle flavor; delicate aroma of nuts. Bleu du Vercors-Sassenage is the most Italian of French cheeses, and is a lot like a young Gorgonzola.

SERVING SUGGESTIONS

Bleu du Vercors-Sassenage melts without losing much fat, which makes it ideal for raclettes or sauces. The mild, subtle flavor of this blue cheese is excellent accompanied by a Clairette de Die. Of the international wines, fruity Riesling Auslesen go very well with this cheese, as do Scheurebe and Muscadet wines with residual sweetness.

Saint-Marcellin

Soft cheese made from
cow's or goat's milk
40% FDM

ORIGIN AND HISTORY
Rhône-Alpes/Isère
The cheese was made famous by King Ludwig XI, who once encountered a bear while out hunting. Two woodcutters rushed to his aid, offering him cheese from nearby Saint-Marcellin for fortification. To show his gratitude, he had the cheese supplied to the royal court, and it was first mentioned in records in 1461. Originally a goat's cheese, it is now usually made from cow's milk.

PRODUCTION
After draining, the cheese is salted and turned, removed from the form after two days, and placed on straw mats. It is left to dry for ten days before being removed to the ripening cellar to mature for at least a further ten days.

CHARACTERISTICS
This is a small cheese of 3 in (7 cm) diameter, 1 in (2 cm) high, and weighing 3 oz (80 g). It can be consumed at any time, from fresh to overripe. After three weeks it develops a mild, acidic, tangy flavor that intensifies as it ripens further. After five to six weeks the cheese is quite dry and tastes piquant. Rind with gray-blue mold veins.

SPECIAL FEATURES
How a Saint-Marcellin turns out will vary depending on the influence of the affineur. The producers of Saint-Marcellin have applied for AOC.

SERVING SUGGESTIONS
Sommelier's recommendation: A young Saint-Marcellin goes well with a fruity Mondeuse from Savoy, and also with a full-bodied red wine with few tannins from the Beaujolais or Rhone valley. Another excellent companion is a strong rosé, such as from Tavel. Or you could try something a little different: Aromatic white wines such as Condrieu, a white Hermitage, Gewürztraminer, or Savagnin Rosé from Jura are excellent choices.

SIMILAR CHEESE VARIETIES
Romans from the town of the same name has a similar consistency, but is a little fattier and matures for only ten days.

Rigotte de Condrieu

Soft cheese made from
raw goat's milk
45–50% FDM

ORIGIN AND HISTORY
Rhône-Alpes/Rhône
Rigottes have been popular since the nineteenth century, and particularly so in Lyonnais. The name Rigotte, like the Italian word *ricotta*, probably has its roots in the Latin for "cooked once more." Rigotte is simply the word for cheese in the local dialect.

PRODUCTION
Unlike most Rigottes, Rigotte de Condrieu is made from goat's milk. This makes it extremely popular with connoisseurs. It matures for up to three weeks.

CHARACTERISTICS
Rigotte de Condrieu is a small cylinder of 1½ in (4 cm) diameter and ½–1 in (1.5–3 cm) in height, and weighs 1 oz (30 g). It has a white to yellow mold rind, a creamy consistency, and a mild, full flavor.

SERVING SUGGESTIONS
The wines of the northern Rhône harmonize best: Condrieu needs no further recommendation, and— depending on the level of ripeness—a white Saint Joseph or Hermitage is also a good choice. Viognier from the Languedoc is another alternative.

SIMILAR CHEESE VARIETIES
Rigotte d'Echalas is a little creamier. The little Rigotte du Forez from Lyonnais and Dauphiné used to be made from goat's milk, but is now usually made from cow's milk. The soft cheeses weigh 2–3 oz (50–85 g), mature for two to three weeks, and are sometimes macerated in white wine. They taste slightly acidic but very pleasant.

SPIRITED CHEESE SPECIALTIES FROM LYONS

Wherever wine is grown and loved, it makes sense to flavor the cheese with wine. This is done during the harvest, when cheeses made from goat's and cow's milk are matured in marc, brandy, or white wine. The *arômes* are a very typical product from the city of Lyons and the surrounding wine-growing areas. Saint-Marcellin, Pélardon, Rigotte, and Picodon take on an intensive, alcoholic flavor during this treatment. Often, the affineurs of the region buy the cheese while it is still young, and aromatize it as desired. For Fromage au Marc de Raisin (Arômes au Gène de Marc, Arômes de Lyon, Arômes Lyonnais), the cheese is placed in a closed container and steeped in grape marc (skins, pips, and stalks left over after the pressing) for a month. Arômes au Vin Blanc spends two to three weeks in a closed container on small slats that are placed over the liquid. During this time, the cheese absorbs the aroma of the evaporating wine. Afterward, the consistency of the cheese is soft and moist, and the cheese has practically no rind. The cheeses weigh about 3½ oz (100 g), and have a lively, elegant flavor of alcohol.

Picodon de l'Ardèche (AOP)

Soft cheese made from raw goat's milk
45% FDM

ORIGIN AND HISTORY
Rhône-Alpes/Drôme/Ardèche
Picodon (also Picodon de la Drôme) has long been known on both sides of the Rhône as a goat's cheese. Goats were often the only milk-producing animals in the poor mountain regions of the Ardèche and Drôme. Picodon has also been known to connoisseurs outside the region since 1873. It is the only cheese that has been to space: Astronaut Jean-Jacques Favier took 14 of them with him when he traveled on board the space shuttle Columbia.

PRODUCTION
A little rennet is added to the full-fat goat's milk. The curds are then spooned into perforated molds so the whey can drain off, and dry-salted twice. The cheese is placed on slats to dry, and matures for at least 12 days. If the cheese matures for about a month and is washed during that time, the process is known as the *Dieulefit affinage*. The longer the cheese matures, the lighter it becomes. With Picodon Dieulefit, the cheese shrinks to about half its original size.

CHARACTERISTICS
Small, round wheel, diameter about 3 in (5–7 cm), height about 1 in (1.8–2.5 cm), weight 1–3½ oz (40–100 g). The rind is covered in white or blue mold. The fine,

homogeneous, white or yellow mass becomes firmer and drier as it matures. New Picodons taste fresh, milky, and slightly acidic. When mature, they are nutty and piquant to sharp and salty. Mild aroma of goat.

SPECIAL FEATURES
Picodon is called either de l'Ardèche or de la Drôme, depending on the production area. Very young Picodons are also called Pidances.

SERVING SUGGESTIONS
Picodon is often eaten as a mid-morning snack, grilled or cold in a salad. Sommelier's recommendation: Mild red wines —rosés are even better—or white wines from the Côtes du Rhône harmonize well.

SIMILAR CHEESE VARIETIES
Picodon de Cevennes is produced by a similar method—and looks similar, too.

Banon (AOC / PDO)

Soft cheese made from
raw goat's or sheep's milk
45% FDM

ORIGIN AND HISTORY
Provence
Banon is a tiny town near Forcalquier
in the Haute-Provence. According to
official documents, the homonymous
cheese was seen at fairs and on markets
in 1270.

PRODUCTION
In winter Banon is made from sheep's
milk, and in summer from goat's milk.
The drained, unmolded curd matures
for at least 15 days. The cheese is
steeped in marc, wrapped in chestnut
leaves, and tied with raffia. It is also
called Banon à la feuille ("leaf") because
it is wrapped in a chestnut leaf.

CHARACTERISTICS
The small, round cheeses are 3–3½ in
(7.5–9 cm) in diameter, and weigh
about 3½ oz (100 g). The white to yellow
mass is homogeneous and firm, yet
creamy. When the cheese is fresh, the
leaves are still soft and green. Mature
Banon can be identified as the chestnut
leaves dry and turn brown. The young
cheese tastes mild and slightly acidic;
later, it takes on the aroma of the leaves
and becomes stronger in flavor.

SERVING SUGGESTIONS
Sommelier's recommendation: A young
Banon goes well with fruity red wines
from the southern Rhône with little in
the way of tannin. Mature Banon
harmonizes well with strong white
wines such as Châteauneuf du-Pape or
marc (eau-de-vie). Rosé wine from the
Provence or a Tavel rosé also go well
with both variants.

SIMILAR CHEESE VARIETIES
Banon has much in common with Pélardon and Picodon (see entries). There is
also a variant that is turned in spices and
herbs such as crushed peppercorns or
summer savory. Cheese that has
matured in summer savory is called
Banon au poivre d'âne. It matures for at
least a month.

Brocciu (AOP)

Soft cheese made from
raw goat's and sheep's milk
40% FDM

ORIGIN AND HISTORY
Corsica
We know for sure that this cheese has a very long tradition. The name Brocciu goes back to the Corsican-Provencal word *brousser*, to hit. Brocciu (French Broccio) is similar to ricotta and was the only source of protein for the inhabitants of isolated mountain villages. Even Napoleon's mother mentioned Brocciu as an important ingredient in typical Corsican dishes.

PRODUCTION
Brocciu is made from the curds and milk of goats and sheep in the Corsican Départements Corse-du-Sud and Haute-Corse. The curds left over from the production of soft cheese are heated to about 100 °F (40 °C). Salt and full-fat goat's or sheep's milk, plus a little water, may be added. The watery mass is heated to 176–194 °F (80–90 °C), and stirred constantly. Solid white particles from the whey protein are skimmed off and transferred to traditional baskets and drained. The dry cheese is salted and matured for about 15 days, perhaps wrapped in dry leaves or turned in herbs or crushed peppercorns.

CHARACTERISTICS
A flattened sphere in shape, weight from 9 oz (250 g) to 7 lb (3 kg). Fresh Brocciu has a soft, creamy, smooth consistency and tastes delicate and fresh. When mature, the mass is hard and crumbly, the flavor strong, dry, and salty. The fresh cheese has no rind, but as it matures it develops a light-yellow to brown rind. Cheese that has matured for three weeks is called Brocciu Passu. The salted variety is called Brocciu Salitu and has to be soaked in (frequently changed) water for 24 hours before consuming.

SERVING SUGGESTIONS
Sommelier's recommendation: Fresh Brocciu only tastes really delicious in Corsica since it does not travel well. Mature Brocciu goes well with strong, mature red wines from Corsica, while fresh Brocciu is better with a local white wine.

Niolo

Soft cheese made from
raw sheep's milk
50% FDM

ORIGIN AND HISTORY
Corsica
Niolo from the mountain regions is
called Niulincu in Corsica.

PRODUCTION
The cheese is washed regularly in salt
water. It matures for three to four
months.

CHARACTERISTICS
Squares with a side length of 4 in
(10 cm), 2 in (5 cm) high, and weighing
1¼–1¾ lb (500–700 g). Niolo has a very
creamy, slightly sticky consistency. The
flavor varies from mild to piquant.

SERVING SUGGESTIONS
This cheese not only goes well with
Corsican wine, but the slightly sharper
version, for example, enters into a very
complex combination with a Riesling
Auslese with residual sweetness.

CORSICA

The French call Corsica "Ile de
Beauté"—the island of beauty. The
bush land on the inside of the island,
the Macchia, and the mountain
regions are ideal for keeping goats
and sheep. The aromatic milk
provided by the animals is the basic
ingredient for Corsican cheese—and
the famous Brocciu. The cheeses
from the north of the island are
creamier and less piquant in flavor,
whereas those from the south are
often matured for several months
before they go on sale.

OTHER CHEESE SPECIALTIES FROM CORSICA

D'Alesani, a circular, mild goat's cheese, is available all year round. Bastelicaccia, by contrast, a creamy soft cheese made from raw sheep's milk, is only available in winter. Calenzana is a piquant soft cheese made from goat's or sheep's milk that is also only available in winter. It is square in shape and weighs 10 oz–1 lb (300–400 g). Corte, a mild, circular soft cheese made from sheep's milk, comes from the area of Corte near Venaco. It is eaten as a dry or semi-dry cheese. Galéria is a very piquant, square soft cheese that is made from goat's milk. It is given a layer of salt before being left to mature for several months. Sarteno is a somewhat firmer soft cheese, made from goat's or sheep's milk or a combination of the two. This slightly flattened sphere weighs about 2–3 lb (1–1.5 kg), and tastes strong to sharp.

Tip: Domestic wines or chestnut schnapps go best with Corsican cheese specialties. Corsicans enjoy their cheese with dried figs or preserves. Cheese is often an ingredient in *suppa corsa*, a farmhouse soup made of red beans, pasta, and onions.

Brin d'Amour

Soft cheese made from
raw sheep's milk
45% FDM

ORIGIN AND HISTORY
Corsica
Brin d'Amour comes from the bushy,
almost impassable interior of Corsica. It
is also sold as Fleur du Maquis (flower
of the macchia).

PRODUCTION
Purely a *fermier* cheese. The cheese
matures for a month in a bed of oregano,
summer savory, rosemary, juniper, and
paprika.

CHARACTERISTICS
A slab with a side length of 4–5 in
(10–12 cm), about 2 in (5–6 cm) thick,
and weighing 1½ lb (700 g). Creamy
mass, tastes slightly of sour milk; delicate but characteristic flavor with
undertones of honey. Typically smells
strongly of the dried herbs of the
macchia.

SERVING SUGGESTIONS
The rind of Brin d'Amour, which tastes
strongly of dried herbs, should not be
consumed. Harmonizes well with
aromatic, spicy red wines with a fine
fruitiness, such as those of Corsica, but
also aromatic wines such as a fine
Traminer or an elegant Riesling.

RECIPE: MEL I MATO

Mel i mato is a typical Languedoc
dessert, and very easy to make.
Serves 6: 12 oz (350 g) cream
cheese, 12 oz (350 g) fresh goat's
cheese, generous cup (250 g) sugar,
⅓ cup (100 ml) lemon juice, 2 cups
(500 ml) water, ½ cup (50 g) pine
nuts, 2 tsp (50 g) honey. Method:
Combine the cheeses with sugar and
lemon juice, then add the water by
spoons and stir well. Pour into a flat
dish and refrigerate for about two
hours. Use an ice cream scoop to
place two balls on plates. Garnish
with pine nuts and a little honey.

Pélardon AOC

Soft cheese made from raw goat's milk
45% FDM

ORIGIN AND HISTORY
Hérault

These small, flat goat's milk cheeses are generally called pélardons in the Cévennes region and in the Languedoc. There are many different versions of them, and they are very easy to make.

PRODUCTION
According to AOC regulations, the thickened milk may not be frozen, and the goats must spend most of their time outdoors. *Fermier* production: Affinage of 8–12 days, ideally 3 weeks.

CHARACTERISTICS
Small, flat, round cheese weighing 2– 3½ oz (60–100 g), diameter 2–3 in (6–7 cm), height about 1 in (2–3 cm). Pélardons have hardly any rind, and they have a yellow surface that sometimes has a gray-blue bloom. Closed, white mass with a mild, aromatic flavor of nuts, and a mild smell of goat.

SERVING SUGGESTIONS
Sommelier's recommendation: Pélardon may be consumed fresh or mature. The fresh version goes well with modern, fruity white wines from the Languedoc, whereas strong, fruity rosés or Clairette de Die are excellent with mature ones.

SIMILAR CHEESE VARIETIES
Pélardon des Corbières also belongs to the family of this small, flat *fermier* goat's cheese that is made on farms from unpasteurized milk. Similar cheeses are Banon, the slightly flatter Cabécou, and Picodon.

HEXAGONAL DELIGHT

Six Pans du Lauraguais, a hexagonal soft cheese made from raw goat's milk that weighs about 5 oz (135 g), is an absolute culinary delight. Here, where the Languedoc meets the Midi-Pyrenees, the goats' diet includes aromatic herbs such as thyme, rosemary, and summer savory. The cheese tastes of the Garrigues, the bush heath of the Midi, and is at its best from spring to fall. It ripens for two to three weeks.

Brique du Forez

Soft cheese made from
raw goat's milk
50% FDM

ORIGIN AND HISTORY
Auvergne/Puy-de-Dôme
This cheese is made in the region of
Forez in the northeastern part of the
Central Massif. Traditionally, the
production region of Brique du Forez is
also the home of Fourme d'Ambert (see
entry).

PRODUCTION
The goat's milk is sometimes combined
with cow's milk. Two production methods are used in parallel. Brique du Forez
is traditionally made from rennet-based
curds, but for about 30 years now it has
also been separated with lactobacilli.

CHARACTERISTICS
The *brique* (brick) is 7 in (17 cm) long,
3 in (8 cm) wide, and 1 in (2.5 cm) high.
It weighs about 9 oz (250 g). The rind is
white with light-blue mold if it is made
just from goat's milk. When made from
both types of milk, the color moves more
toward gray.

SERVING SUGGESTIONS
Sommelier's recommendation: A Gaillac doux is the perfect companion, but
wines with a little residual sweetness
are excellent too. Red wines with little
tannin are also a very good choice.

SIMILAR CHEESE VARIETIES
Chèvreton, a little larger and made from
a combination of cow's and goat's milk,
is practically Brique du Forez's twin
brother. Brique d'Auvergne is also made
from a combination of milks, and is
particularly creamy. Another relation is
Brique d'Ardèche, made solely from
unpasteurized goat's milk. This cheese
is smaller and weighs only about 5 oz
(150 g). It matures for longer, so it
tastes slightly sharp and more intense
than Brique du Forez.

Fourme de Montbrison (PDO)

Blue cheese made from
cow's milk
50% FDM

ORIGIN AND HISTORY
Auvergne/Puy-de-Dôme
It is believed that this traditional cheese was being produced in the mountains of the Auvergne even before the ninth century. It originates from the Monts du Forez near the towns of Ambert and Montbrison.

PRODUCTION
The milk comes from cows that graze at about 2,000–5,250 ft (600–1,600 m). Rennet and mold cultures are added to the raw or pasteurized milk. The curd is salted and placed in tall, long molds to drain. When dry, the cheeses are removed and holes are pierced in them with a long needle; this is where the mold develops. They have to mature for at least four weeks before they can be sold.

CHARACTERISTICS
Slender, tall cylinder. It is 7½ in (19 cm) high with a diameter of 5 in (13 cm), and weighs about 4½ lb (2 kg). The fine, dry, gray to yellow rind is covered in a multicolored surface mold. The mass has a light, regular blue grain with a soft, smooth consistency. Creamy mild, fruity flavor with a light undertone of mushrooms.

SPECIAL FEATURES
The rare handmade versions are usually to be found in the market in Ambert. Following a long affinage, they have a complex, piquant flavor. Fourmes differ depending on where they are produced. Fourme de Montbrison has a slightly softer, milder mass and less marbling; the rind is red-orange. Fourme d'Ambert has more mold in the mass, and there is a light bloom on the rind.

SERVING SUGGESTIONS
Fourme d'Ambert is usually scooped out of the tall cylinder. Sommelier's recommendation: Sweet choices such as Sauternes, Barsac, Loupiac, and Cadillac are ideal. Sweet German or Austrian wines are also good choices. Red wines should have very mature tannins, and the wine itself should be strong and opulent.

Gaperon

Semi-hard cheese made from
raw cow's milk
40% FDM

ORIGIN AND HISTORY
Auvergne/Puy-de-Dôme
The name probably comes from the
local word for buttermilk—*gape*—
because Gaperon was originally made
from leftovers. Fresh milk was added to
the leftover buttermilk, with garlic and
pepper added for flavor, to make the
cheese.

PRODUCTION
A little buttermilk is added to full-fat or
semi-skimmed milk. The pressed,
unheated mass is seasoned with garlic
and pepper. It matures for one to two
months.

CHARACTERISTICS
Gaperon is shaped like a dome with a
height and diameter of 3½ in (9 cm),
and weighs about 10 oz (300 g). Hard,
dry natural rind, elastic mass with a
piquancy from the added garlic and
pepper. Gaperon is often wrapped in
raffia, which is reminiscent of the
method used by farmers in bygone days
to hang the cheese near the fire to dry.

SERVING SUGGESTIONS
Sommelier's recommendation: Aromatic white wines or fruity, red wines
that are not too powerful and have an
understated tannin structure.

THE PASTURES OF
THE AUVERGNE

The Auvergne is a volcanic region,
3,300 ft (1,000 m) above sea level,
with nutrient-rich soils and lots of
rivers. It is well known for its luscious
vegetation and the many aromatic
plants that add an incomparable
aroma to the milk and cheese that are
produced here.
The strong cattle of the Aubrac and
Salers breeds provide relatively little
milk, but the milk they do produce has
a high fat content. Cattle and sheep
graze on high mountain pastures from
spring until fall.

Saint-Nectaire (PDO)

Semi-hard cheese made from
cow's milk
45% FDM

ORIGIN AND HISTORY
Auvergne/Puy-de-Dôme
This cheese owes its name and reputation to Field Marshal Henri de Sennecterre or Senneterre, who first served it at King Louis XIV's table in the seventeenth century.

PRODUCTION
The curd is pressed several times. It matures for at least three weeks, traditionally on rye straw, in natural cellars in the region of Clermont-Ferrand.

CHARACTERISTICS
Saint-Nectaire is flat, 2 in (5 cm) high, with a diameter of 8 in (21 cm) and weighing 4 lb (1.7 kg). The smaller version, Petit Saint-Nectaire, weighs about 1½ lb (600 g). Yellow marks develop on the gray or sand-colored rind of the cheese. The creamy, elastic mass tastes slightly musty and rustic, but is surprisingly mild. It smells of Champagne and rye straw.

SPECIAL FEATURES
Saint-Nectaire is made twice a day as a *fermier* cheese—once using the morning milk, and the second time with the evening milk. This cheese is found mainly in the area about the small town of Besse-en-Chandresse.

SERVING SUGGESTIONS
Sommelier's recommendation: Saint-Nectaire tastes best after five to eight weeks. Suitable wines with the young cheese are light, fruity red wines such as Beaujolais-Villages, or white wines with a nutty flavor. Mature, round red wines with a mild tannin or a mature white wine such as a premier cru from Burgundy are excellent with the more mature cheese.

SIMILAR CHEESE VARIETIES
The red smear cheeses Pavin, a semi-hard cheese, and Murol are very similar in flavor to Petit Saint-Nectaire. Chambérat is a specialty in the Bourbonnais, and is made primarily in the region of Montluçon and Chambon.

Bleu d'Auvergne (PDO)

Blue cheese made from
cow's milk
50% FDM

ORIGIN AND HISTORY
Auvergne/Cantal
Its milk comes from Aubrac and Salers cows. The drained cheese is injected so that the mold can develop. The smaller cheeses mature in ventilated cellars for three weeks, while larger ones over 2 lb (1 kg) mature for at least four weeks. The typical blue-green mold forms after about three weeks.

CHARACTERISTICS
Shape of a flat cylinder. The large cheeses have a diameter of about 8 in (20 cm), are 3–4 in (8–10 cm) high, and weigh 4½–6½ lb (2–3 kg). The smaller variants weigh 12 oz–2 lb (350 g–1 kg). Brushed, very thin rind sprinkled with blue-gray spots. Ivory mass with blue-gray veins. The piquant, nutty, strong flavor and spicy aroma are typical.

SERVING SUGGESTIONS
This versatile all-rounder adds an original touch to all sorts of dishes such as soufflés, salads, pies, and crêpes. It goes well with nuts and raw mushrooms. It is mixed with a little butter and served on canapés as an aperitif. Sommelier's recommendation: Sweet wines such as those from Gaillac or Montbazillac are excellent choices, as are sweet white Bordeaux. Care should be taken when combining with red wines since a strong tannin will create bitterness between the cheese and wine. A mature Gaillac or another strong, mature red wine from the southwest is a good choice.

SIMILAR CHEESE VARIETIES
A statue in Laqueuille commemorates Antoine Roussel, the farmer's son who is regarded as the inventor of Bleu de Laqueuille (Département Puy-de-Dôme). Like Fourme d'Ambert, it develops a particularly mild, fruity aroma. Another local blue variant is Bleu de Thiézac.

Cantal (PDO)

Semi-hard cheese made from cow's milk
45% FDM

ORIGIN AND HISTORY

Auvergne/Cantal

Pliny the Elder mentioned Cantal in his *Naturalis historia* (Natural History), saying it was extremely popular with the Romans about 200 BC. Cantal is considered one of France's oldest cheeses—and is presumably one of the oldest in the world.

PRODUCTION

Cantal is made using milk from Salers cows. One special feature is that it is pressed several times: 180–220 lb (80–100 kg) of the cut, drained curd is placed under a special large press. The compact, flat mass is cut and pressed again. The mass is then left to rest for eight hours, after which it is chopped and salted. The cheese mass is placed in cylindrical metal molds, and pressed three or four more times over the next two days. Once removed from the molds, the cheeses are left to mature for at least 30 days at 33–53 °F (10–12 °C) in damp cellars, where they are turned and brushed two or three times a week. After four weeks the cheese is white and fresh (Cantal jeune). Cantal entre deux matures for two to six months; an affinage of more than six months produces Cantal vieux.

CHARACTERISTICS

Large cylinder, 14–17 lb (36–42 cm) in diameter, 18 in (45 cm) high, and weighing about 95 lb (43 kg). Petit Cantal weighs 44 lb (20 kg), Cantalet only 22 lb (10 kg). The cheese has a thick, dry rind that is initially grayish-white, then turns golden to brown-orange as it matures. Cantal is an original, natural cheese with a mild, fresh flavor that becomes stronger as the cheese ages.

SERVING SUGGESTIONS

Cantal goes very well with fresh fruit. Sommelier's recommendation: The strong character of this cheese is perfectly complemented by strong, mature white wines with little acid, and by mature, opulent red wines with a little tannin or wines with a delicate residual sweetness. Combining it with a fine Riesling Spätlese with a residual sweetness or a mature Auslese results in a very special experience.

Salers (PDO)

Semi-hard cheese made from
raw cow's milk
45% FDM

ORIGIN AND HISTORY

Auvergne/Cantal

Salers comes from the same region as
Cantal, but may only be produced
during the grazing period from 1 May to
31 October. It gets its name from a
pretty medieval town between Aurillac
and Mauriac. The first written records
of this cheese, which is also known as
Fourme de Salers or Cantal de Salers,
date back to the Middle Ages.

PRODUCTION

Salers may only be made from the raw
milk from Salers cows, and may only be
produced on farms. It is made by some
100 *producteurs fermiers*. Rennet is
added to the milk directly after milking,
and it is then further processed. Like
Cantal, the cheese is pressed twice, but
must mature for at least three months.
Very often, it is left to develop for
12–18 months.

CHARACTERISTICS

The cheeses are cylindrical and vary
in size. The diameter is about 15–19 in
(38–48 cm) and the weight 66–110 lb
(30–50 kg). The thick rind of Salers is
naturally dry. Salers that has matured
for a long time has a thick, dark rind
with reddish spots.

The mass is initially firm and smooth,
but becomes crumbly as it matures.
Fresh mountain herbs add an unmistakable aroma to the milk of the Salers
cows. Young Salers is aromatic, slightly
acidic, and has a mildly bitter undertone. The flavor becomes stronger and
more piquant.

SERVING SUGGESTIONS

Salers goes well with apples, grapes, or
walnuts. A piece of Salers is a particular delight on a cheeseboard. Wines that
are served with Salers should have a
delicate fruitiness so as not to overpower the fine aroma of the cheese.
Understated red wines, such as those
from the Beaujolais or from the Loire,
are ideal. Very mature Salers goes well
with stronger, velvety red wines with
understated tannins. Thanks to its long
shelf-life, Salers can be enjoyed all year
round.

SOUTHWEST
Paradise for connoisseurs

The Midi-Pyrenees region in southwest France between the Atlantic and the Mediterranean adjoins Spain to the south, Aquitaine to the west, Languedoc-Roussillon to the east, and Auvergne and Limousin to the north. The eight Départements Ariège, Aveyron, Gers, Haute-Garonne, Hautes-Pyrénées, Lot, Tarn, and Tarn-et-Garonne—with the notable exception of Hautes-Pyrénées—all owe their names to various rivers, large and small. This region is notable for its magnificent landscapes.

To the north on the foothills of the Central Massif are the Aubrac or Causses hills, high limestone plains formed by water. Every summer the shepherds take their flocks up to the summer pastures. Transhumance (the seasonal migration between mountain and valley of livestock and those who tend them) has centuries of tradition. Aubrac cows find the best food on the mountain pastures of the Aubrac and the windswept high plains of the Causses. Their milk produces famous cheeses such as Laguiole and Bleu de Causses. The little town of Laguiole, where the famous knives come from, is situated in the heart of the Département Aveyron. The basaltic plateaus of the Aveyron offer vast grazing pastures and mysterious caves. This is also the home of Roquefort, the "son of the mountains and of the wind."

The Pyrenees to the south form a natural border with Spain. Wonderful mountain cheeses are made on the high mountain pastures. The Pays-Basque is in Aquitaine and the Département Pyrénées-Atlantique, which reaches up as far as northeast Spain. This is where wonderful sheep's cheeses with centuries of tradition are made.

Left: These breathtaking landscapes are a paradise for connoisseurs.

Rocamadour (PDO)

Soft cheese made from
raw goat's milk
45% FDM

ORIGIN AND HISTORY

Midi-Pyrénées/Lot
This cheese is also called Cabécou de
Rocamadour (little goat's cheese from
Rocamadour). A contract dating back
to 1451 stated that farmers were to pay
their taxes in Rocamadour cheeses.
This goat's cheese was named after the
medieval town of Rocamadour, which is
situated in the heart of the production
area as well as on the Way of Saint
James.

PRODUCTION

The raw milk for Rocamadour must
come from Alpine or Saanen goats.
Thickening and drainage are carried out
over 36 hours. Salt is kneaded into the
mass. The cheese is left to mature for at
least 12 days, but usually up to 4 weeks.

CHARACTERISTICS

Small disk weighing about 1 oz (35 g),
2 in (6 cm) in diameter, and less than
1 in (1.6 cm) high. White-yellow, velvety
smooth rind, turning ivory color after a
long affinage, with light-blue mold
bloom. Rocamadour is a relatively moist
cheese. The soft, creamy mass is white
to ivory. The mild aroma of goat's milk
is typical, and becomes more marked as
the cheese matures.

SERVING SUGGESTIONS

Sommelier's recommendation: Wines
from the southwest, such as those from
Pessac-Léognan or Bordeaux, and dry
Jurançon, are excellent with Rocamadour.

SIMILAR CHEESE VARIETIES

The small, soft goat's milk cheeses
called Cabécou in the local language are
similar to Rocamadour, but slightly
thicker with a more marked flavor. They
mature quickly and keep well, and the
flavor improves during that time. The
soft, aromatic goat's-milk mass usually
matures for two to four weeks. Cabé-
cous are only available from June to
September.
Cabécou d'Autan, which is at its best
after maturing for 15 days, comes from
the Tarn. Picadou is a mature Cabécou
that matures in plum schnapps in a
closed container, and is extremely
piquant.

Bleu des Causses (PDO)

Blue cheese made from
cow's milk
45% FDM

ORIGIN AND HISTORY
Midi-Pyrénées/Aveyron
There have been causses—small artisanal cheese dairies—on the high limestone plains of the Central Massif for
centuries. Cheese makers have long
known that cheese matures particularly
well in natural caves, and that the
climate is beneficial for the formation of
mold. The region's cheese used to be
made from a mixture of sheep's and
cow's milk. When Roquefort received
the AOC in 1925, the cheese makers had
to decide on one kind of milk: They
opted for cow's milk.

PRODUCTION
Once the cheeses have drained and
dried, they are injected with *Penicillium roqueforti*, then salted, brushed,
and pierced with needles so that the
mold can develop in the channels. The
cheese matures for three to six months
in natural caves on the north side of the
limestone massif. Cold, damp air flows
through the caves, allowing the cheese
to blossom and turn mild.

CHARACTERISTICS
Bleu des Causses is a mild cow's milk
version of Roquefort. It is shaped like a
cylinder, has a diameter of 8 in (20 cm),
is 3–4 in (8–10 cm) high, and weighs

5½–6½ lb (2.5–3 kg). The softly melting
mass is slightly crumbly with holes, but
is still easy to cut. In summer the mass
is ivory color, whereas it is white and
slightly moist in winter. Both varieties
have fine blue veins.
Also typical: Strong, piquant, but mild
flavor, nutty and intensive, pleasantly
strong aroma.

SERVING SUGGESTIONS
Bleu des Causses is used as a filling for
omelets or crêpes, with pasta or potatoes. It goes well with barbecued meat
or in a sauce. Sommelier's recommendation: Strong red wines such as mature
Comas are good. However, if served raw,
sweet white wines are better. A Muscat
de Beaumes de Venise is an excellent
option with the mature cheese.

Laguiole (PDO)

Semi-hard cheese made from
raw cow's milk
45% FDM

ORIGIN AND HISTORY
Midi-Pyrénées/Aveyron
The Aubrac region is well known for its cheese made from milk of the Aubrac cow. Laguiole is thought to date back to the fourth century B.C. It is believed that local shepherds (*buronniers*) later shared their knowledge of cheese making with the monks of the monastery of Abrac.

PRODUCTION
The traditional methods used by the old cheese makers, the *cantalès*, were retained for the production of Laguiole. The shaped curd matures under a press. The pressed curd is then cut, salted, and pressed again. The cheese has to mature for at least 4 months, but it is often left for up to 12 months.

CHARACTERISTICS
Laguiole is shaped like a tall cylinder (*fourme*), 16 in (40 cm) in diameter, 16 in (40 cm) high, and weighing 110 lb (50 kg). The rind is extremely thick, and the color varies according to the age of the cheese, from white and light orange to mid-brown. The mass is smooth, ivory to straw color, and has a smooth yet firm consistency. Laguiole smells slightly milky, and tastes strong to rustic, slightly acidic, and a little dry.

SPECIAL FEATURES
The best cheese is made on the mountain pastures using traditional methods. A few dairies that produce Laguiole on the high plain of Aubrac still remain.

SERVING SUGGESTIONS
Sommelier's recommendation: The cheese is particularly tasty from January to April. It goes with fruity red wines, such as those from Beaujolais or the southern Rhône, or strong white wines such as Châteauneuf du Pape blanc. Austrian or German wines with a fine residual sweetness are a pleasant alternative.

SIMILAR CHEESE VARIETIES
Laguiole is a close relative of Salers and Cantal.

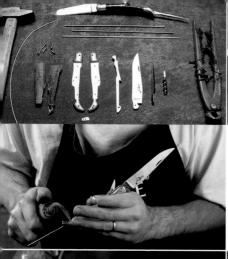

1. Everything the cutler needs.
2. Every knife is made by hand.
3. Blade, spine, shaft, and handle are connected using brass pins.
4. The handle is traditionally made from the horns of Aubrac cattle.
5. The finished knife fits beautifully into the hand.

LAGUIOLE,
FRANCE'S FAVORITE KNIFE

Any self-respecting French person will have at least one Laguiole (pronounced "layole") knife. Early in the nineteenth century, the town's blacksmiths developed a simple knife for daily use by the farmers and shepherds of Aubrac. They used a rustic blade from Navarra in the Basque country (many people from Aubrac spent the winter working in Spain), and a handle made from the horns of Aubrac cattle. Pierre Jean Calmels was the first to trade in Laguiole knives, in 1829.

Today, genuine Laguiole knives from France are available all over France and in upmarket stores all over the world. Every year, the 90 skilled staff in the small works in Laguiole produce 200,000 knives—performing every step in the process themselves. Every single knife is put together by hand and the blade is adjusted and refinished until it meets all the standard for perfection.

Roquefort (PDO)

Blue cheese made from raw sheep's milk
52% FDM

ORIGIN AND HISTORY
Midi-Pyrénées/Aveyron

Charlemagne declared Roquefort his favorite cheese, and in April 1411 Charles IV signed a charter giving the inhabitants of Roquefort "the privilege to mature the cheese as it has always been done in the caves of the afore-mentioned village." The former province of Rouergue is the home of Roquefort. The milk for the production of Roquefort traditionally comes from the Département Aveyron and the adjoining Départements Aude, Gard, Hérault, Lozère, and Tarn. However, the cheese matures exclusively in the caves of Roquefort-sur-Soulzon.

CHARACTERISTICS

The Roquefort cylinder is twice as wide as it is high: It is 7–8 in (19–20 cm) in diameter and weighs 5½–6½ lb (2.5–3 kg). The younger the cheese, the whiter its mass with fewer traces of mold. The older the cheese, the more ivory colored the mass and the more pronounced the mold. The mass is slightly crumbly. The high fat content of 52% adds a particular melt to the cheese. When perfectly mature, the flavor is tasty, piquant, salty, very inten-sive, and strong.

SERVING SUGGESTIONS

When storing Roquefort, fluctuations in temperature should be avoided. Roquefort is ideal for making sauces, canapés, salads, soufflés, and pies. Piquant Roquefort blends beautifully with the mild sweetness of a pear. An absolute classic is the combination of Roquefort with a glass of sweet Sauternes. The cheese enters into a seductive combination with Vin doux Naturel of the south, and especially with Muscat de Rivesaltes from Roussillon. Roquefort may be consumed at any time of year.

Moulis

Semi-hard cheese made from
raw cow's milk
45% FDM

ORIGIN AND HISTORY
Midi-Pyrénées/Ariège
This large Tomme originates from the
Pyrenean village of the same name.

PRODUCTION
During the affinage of one to three
months, the cheese is initially washed
in salt water every two days, then
brushed and turned regularly.

CHARACTERISTICS
The dry brown rind conceals an elastic,
straw-colored mass with lots of holes.
The flavor is penetrating and strong.

SERVING SUGGESTIONS
In its homeland, this cheese is often
combined with cherry preserve. It goes
well with a red wine from the southwest, such as an Iroulégy.

Pérail

Soft cheese made from
raw sheep's milk
48% FDM

ORIGIN AND HISTORY
Midi-Pyrénées/Aveyron
Pérail comes from the same home as
Roquefort. Findings of old, perforated
clay pots indicate that Pérail has long
been made in the region. As almost the
entire production of sheep's milk from
the region is used for making Roquefort, Pérail almost disappeared
completely. Thanks to a number of dedicated producers, it has been saved.

PRODUCTION
It matures for at least eight days, but the
longer it is left, the more the flavor
develops.

CHARACTERISTICS
Round, flat cheese weighing about 5 oz
(130 g). Rind with fine, natural mold;
smooth, white mass. Very mild flavor.

SPECIAL FEATURES
The producers have applied for AOC for
their cheese.

SERVING SUGGESTIONS
Sommelier's recommendation: Pérail
harmonizes as well with Côtes du Rhône
Blanc as with white wines from
Bordeaux, and also enters into a pleas-
ant association with fruity red wines.

SHEEP'S CHEESE FROM THE PYRENEES

The Pyrenees and the Basque country
are a sheep's cheese region par
excellence. Although modern commu-
nications and technology have made
the shepherds' lives easier, they still
spend many months in isolation on
their mountain pastures at altitudes
over 3,300 ft (1,000 m). For Ossau-
Iraty, the shepherds stop milking their
animals in August. This keeps the
sheep healthy, which in turn guarantees regular cheese production. A
herd of 400 animals will produce
some 200 cheeses each season.
Sheep's cheese from the Pyrenees is of
the very best quality, and in the
Basque country it is greatly appreciated with a small dish of cherry
preserve.

Tomme noire des Pyrénées (PGI)

Hard cheese made from
cow's milk
50% FDM

ORIGIN AND HISTORY
Midi-Pyrénées/Ariège
Tomme noire was being produced in the Saint-Girons region even in the twelfth century. Until the nineteenth century, the cheese was best known in its home area, but now it is found all over France.

PRODUCTION
Rennet and lactobacilli are added to the pasteurized milk. Once thickened, the curd is cut and the whey partly drained. The mass is put into perforated molds for drainage to complete. The cheese is then dry-salted. After maturing for three weeks, it is covered in black plastic wrap.

CHARACTERISTICS
The black rind is typical of cylindrical Tomme noire, being 8 in (21 cm) in diameter, about 4 in (9–10 cm) in height, and weighing 9–10 lb (4–4.5 kg). The soft, elastic mass has regular holes. Its yellow-rinded brother has had its own name since 1999: Tomme dorée des Pyrénées.

SERVING SUGGESTIONS
The young cheese harmonizes well with the dry white wines of the Jurancon, whereas the mature version is very happy with a sweet Jurancon. Mature red wines from the southwest with little tannin are a good alternative.

COW'S MILK CHEESE FROM THE PYRENEES

Bethmale from raw milk is one of the mildest cow's milk cheeses of the Pyrenees. This firm cheese is shaped like a large wheel, weighs 8–13 lb (3.5–6 kg), and has a fat content in dry mass of 50%. The mass is pressed, then washed and turned regularly during the two to three months maturing period. Bethmale is also made from sheep's and goat's milk, or from a mixture of goat's and cow's milk.

ROQUEFORT
THE MOLD SUPERSTAR

The star of the blue cheeses owes its existence to a prehistoric natural catastrophe. The north-western edge of the steep chalky mountain called Cambalou, between Millau and St. Affrique, collapsed, turning it into a gigantic mound of rubble. The massive rocks wedged together, creating vertical faults and fissures known as *fleurines*. They linked the natural cellars with the outside world, and provided a constant supply of fresh air.

This is an ingenious ventilation system that maintains a constant low temperature and humidity of 95%—ideal conditions for a very special mold, *Penicillium roqueforti*, to expand on the cave walls.

But where did the cheese come from? Cambalou is situated at the foot of the barren Causse de Larsac, a windswept chalky plain. Gnarled shrubs and wild herbs survived here—as did sheep. Flocks of Lacaune sheep graze on the little food that is available, which adds a fine piquancy to their milk—and the resulting cheese.

Shepherds were tending their flocks in this bleak region in the New Stone Age. According to a legend, a young shepherd put the cheese from his lunch in a cave and then forgot about it. When he returned a while later, he found that the cheese—which had originally been white—was marbled with a blue-green mold. He tried it and found it tasted much better than before. According to Pliny the Elder, the Romans were huge fans of the cheese, and centuries later Roquefort became the favorite cheese of Charlemagne.

In the fifteenth century the inhabitants of Roquefort-su-Soulzon, the village at the foot of Cambalou, decided to ripen cheese from other regions in their cellars and then sell it on. The cheese became well known and popular, but—as invariably happens in such cases—attempts were soon made to imitate it. However, it was to be another 100 years before Roquefort was made a protected brand. Roquefort enjoyed a surprising surge in popularity in the mid-nineteenth century.

Penicillium roqueforti germinating on rye bread.

The very special flavor of Roquefort is due to the use of raw sheep's milk.

Cheese dairies from miles about bought sheep's cheese, partly from the Pyrenees, and even from as far afield as Corsica. To prevent the cheese from running the risk of being diluted with cow's milk, the French government allocated it the Appellation d'Origine Contrôllée in 1921 — the very first time it had been awarded to a cheese.

THE PRODUCTION OF ROQUEFORT

The raw sheep's milk is injected with minuscule quantities of spores while it is still in the dairies. In order to encourage the growth of these spores, big loaves of rye bread are placed inside the Cambalou cave. Large quantities of green-tinged mold hairs develop on the bread after three months, which are then dried and powdered so they can later be added to the milk or junket to encourage the growth of mold. Rennet is then added to the warm milk to make it separate. The cheese is turned five times while it drains. The shaped and salted cheeses are then placed in the maturing cellar. Before they are placed on the long rows of wooden frames, they are

pierced with a nail board so air can circulate freely through the channels made and allow the mold to develop. The mold growth has to be stopped after a month. The cheeses are then wrapped individually in foil and stored further down in cooler parts of the caves. The Roquefort is left there to mature for at least three more months. Some qualities spend up to a year in the maturing cellar, and particularly exquisite ones even longer.

Exquisite cheeses are stored for a year and longer.

The cheese and cellar master for the cooperative checks the level of ripeness of every single cheese.

Ossau-Iraty (PDO)

Semi-hard cheese made from
raw sheep's milk
50% FDM

ORIGIN AND HISTORY
Aquitaine/Pyrénées Atlantiques
The Roman writer Martial mentioned
the Pyrenean cheese from Toulouse
market as long ago as the first century.
In the fourteenth century, sheep's
cheese was a popular trading commodity, and the shepherds' main source of
income. There have always been large
herds of Manech and Basco Béarnaise
sheep in the valley and high pastures of
the western Pyrenees to provide the
milk for this cheese. Ossau-Iraty is a
clever synthesis of the various cheese
types from the Pyrenees.

PRODUCTION
Only a few cheeses are still made traditionally from raw milk. The cheese is
dried and rubbed regularly for three
months. The Petit Ossau-Iraty matures
for at least 60 days.

CHARACTERISTICS
Shaped like a slightly convex cylinder,
diameter 10 in (26 cm), height 5–6 in
(12–14 cm). It usually weighs 9–11 lb
(4–5 kg), although a *fermier* cheese
can easily weigh up to 15 lb (7 kg). Petit
Ossau-Iraty weighs 4–7 lb (2–3 kg).
Firm, orange-yellow to gray rind;
smooth, white mass with a few holes.
The consistency is firm and smooth,

sometimes hard. Delicate to nutty, plant-like flavor; slight aroma of sheep's milk.

SERVING SUGGESTIONS
This sheep's cheese is at its best in
November and December. It goes well
with the white wines from its home:
Strong structured red wines and tasty
wines with character, such as Jurançon,
Madiran, and Irouléguy.

SIMILAR CHEESE VARIETIES
As recently as 20 years ago, the popular and best known sheep's cheese from
the Basque country, Etorki, was made
to the AOC requirements for Ossau-
Iraty. Today, the Fromagerie des
Chaumes in Mauleon (part of the
Bongrain Group) still make it by the
traditional methods used by Basque
shepherds and with milk from local
sheep. Etorki resembles Ossau-Iraty in
taste and appearance.

Belloc, Abbaye de Belloc

Semi-hard cheese made from
raw sheep's milk
50% FDM

ORIGIN AND HISTORY
Auitaine/Pyrénées-Atlantique
The Benedictine Abbaye de Belloc close
to the Spanish border has been in existence since 1875. Abbaye de Belloc is an
unusual monastery cheese in that it is
one of the few to be made from sheep's
milk, and it has a very high fat content.

PRODUCTION
Farms in the surrounding area supply
the milk of the Manech sheep to the
convent of Notre Dame de Belloc. The
cheese is placed in brine and matures
for 6–12 months.

CHARACTERISTICS
Small cheese of 10 in (25 cm) diameter,
4 in (11 cm) high, and weighing 11 lb
(5 kg). A rich, firm mass awaits beneath
the gray to light-brown rind. The cheese
is fruity, full bodied, and strong.

SERVING SUGGESTIONS
This extremely pleasant sheep's cheese
goes well with a mature, strong red wine
from Bordeaux.

Bouton d'Oc

Soft cheese made from
raw goat's milk
45% FDM

ORIGIN AND HISTORY
Midi-Pyrénées/Tarn
Bouton d'Oc comes from the area of
Toulouse.

PRODUCTION
Strictly *fermier* production. The small
cheeses mature for at least ten days,
but may be left for up to several weeks.

CHARACTERISTICS
Small, aperitif cheese in the shape of a
pear, weight about 33 lb (15 g). The
1–1½ in (3–4 cm) high minis are sold by
the dozen. The taste ranges from pleasantly mild to penetrating and piquant,
depending on the affinage and type of
milk used.

SERVING SUGGESTIONS
Served as a young cheese with an aperitif, Bouton d'Oc goes very well with
sparkling wines. If it is served a little
maturer, then white wines from the
Languedoc and mature red wines, for
instance from the Minervois, make
pleasant companions.

Ardi-Gasna

Firm semi-hard cheese made from
raw sheep's milk
50% FDM

ORIGIN AND HISTORY
Aquitaine/Pyrénées-Atlantique
In the Basque language, sheep is *ardi*
and cheese *gasna*—so the origins of the
name cannot be explained more clearly.

PRODUCTION
The slightly pressed cheese is mature
after two to three months and ready for
consumption. However, it can mature
for up to two years.

CHARACTERISTICS
Small Tomme 7½ in (19 cm) diameter,
3 in (7 cm) thick, and weighing about
6½ lb (3 kg); the *fermier* variety is a
little larger and heavier. Yellow and
orange rind encases the firm, compact,
light-golden mass, which has a few
irregular holes. Very pleasant, full, and
round flavor.

SERVING SUGGESTIONS
In its home, this cheese is often eaten
with black cherry preserve. It goes well
with a red wine from the deepest southwest, such as Iroulégy. The cheese is
also a delight when served with a
mature Bordeaux.

THE NETHERLANDS
Paradise for semi-hard cheese

Cheese-making traditions go back centuries in the Netherlands. Cheese has been one of the country's main export products since the Middle Ages. The typical varieties, such as Gouda, Edam, and Maasdam, are not only some of the world's most popular cheeses, but also the most frequently imitated. The important role played by cheese for this country is determined largely by the landscape and climate, both of which are ideal for the dairy industry. Farmers have always had to dig ditches, construct dykes, and build windmills to protect the land below sea level from flooding. The interplay between water, soil, sea, and climate provides the perfect conditions for dairy cattle. Even in the Middle Ages, the many waterways and the proximity to the North Sea made it easy to transport the products. Excavations indicate that there was a form of dairy industry in this area 2,000 years ago. The region's trade in cheese and butter flourished in the Middle Ages, and exports became one of the main sources of revenue. By the seventeenth century, Holland was exporting its semi-hard cheese to almost every country in Europe. Today, over half the Dutch cheese production is exported. Without doubt, the no. 1 cheese is Gouda. However, other specialties such as Bauernkäse— farmhouse cheese—and goat's and sheep's cheese have become increasingly important. The range on offer in this paradise of semi-hard cheeses is indeed far more comprehensive than you would at first think; there are over 80 varieties at different stages of maturity.

Left: The juicy grass is like manna for Dutch cows.

DUTCH CHEESE MARKETS—A COLORFUL SPECTACLE

Although cheese production and marketing have long been updated and now use the latest technology, a number of traditional cheese markets still remain. They are a popular tourist attraction, and take place from early April until the end of September. In Edam, the familiar Edam balls dominate the weekly cheese market on Wednesdays. Thursday is the day for the cheese market in Gouda. Early in the morning the yellow wheels are carted into the medieval town center. Gouda's cheese market is more than a tourist attraction; farmers from all over the southern Netherlands take this opportunity to sell their homemade cheese to bulk buyers—after it has been weighed.

Numerous visitors frequent the country's most famous cheese market, in Alkmaar. This traditional spectacle always takes place on Fridays, right in the historic town center. Getting there involves a lovely stroll through the pretty lanes of the old town, past the

Right: Some things never change—Edam's cheese market takes place on Wednesdays.

Bottom: A treat for tourists: Cheese carriers almost run as they cart their produce to the scales.

OTHER DUTCH CHEESES

Although the Dutch cheese landscape consists primarily of semi-hard Gouda- and Edam-type cheeses, the addition of herbs and spices increases the range and variety. As well as cloves and cumin, these include nettles, kitchen herbs, garlic, paprika, pepper, mustard, and chopped walnuts. For the health conscious, there are varieties with reduced salt made by adding less salt during the production process. The flavor is correspondingly delicate and mild. Dutch specialties also include cheese made from goat's and ewe's milk. Gouda made from goat's cheese in particular has acquired a tremendous following in recent years. Soft and semi-hard cheese made from goat's milk is usually still young when taken to market, often shaped by hand or with additions such as blue mold, nettles, or garlic. Sheep's milk is used mainly for semi-hard cheese in wheels of between 14 oz and 9 lb (400 g to 4 kg), and is left to mature for seven to ten weeks. These cheeses have a finely grained, light texture with no holes. Flavors range from mild to savory.

houses with their old gabled roofs. In view of the tremendous demand, it is well worth getting to the huge cheese scales in good time. These were set up in a converted chapel in the sixteenth century. Market activities commence as the bells in the tower chime at 10 o'clock. Solemn-faced sellers and potential buyers stride through the "cheese streets," taking small samples from a cheese here and a cheese there and examining them with nose, palate, and fingers before—after noisy and apparently endless haggling—finally sealing the sale with a firm handshake. Members of the highly traditional guild of cheese makers, clad in white suits and brightly colored straw hats, then trot to the scales carrying the cheeses on long wooden sleds. A visit to the cheese museum, where visitors can learn much about the country's cheese production, is the perfect conclusion to the market experience.

Boerenkaas (TSG)

Semi-hard and hard cheese
made from raw milk
30–48% FDM

ORIGIN AND HISTORY

To this day, the age-old craft of cheese making is still practiced by traditional methods on some 350 farms in the Netherlands. Boerenkaas (farmhouse cheese), greatly prized by cheese connoisseurs, is made during the cattle's grazing period from spring to autumn. The name "Boerenkaas" may be used only for products that are made on the farm from raw milk by traditional methods, primarily from the farm's own dairy cattle. Raw milk must be processed as quickly as possible.

PRODUCTION

The individual farmhouse cheeses may be made as Gouda (Goudse Boerenkaas), Leiden (Leidse Boerenkaas), and Edam (Edamer Boerenkaas). Boerenkaas may be made from goat's milk (*van geitenmelk*), sheep's milk (*van schapenmelk*), or buffalo milk (*van buffelmelk*).

For example, for farmhouse Gouda: Early in the morning, just after milking, the chilled evening milk is combined with the still-warm morning milk, poured into stainless steel-lined cheese tubs, and heated to 84 °F (29 °C) before adding lactobacillus and rennet. When thickened, the cheese maker cuts the curds with a special knife, and the whey that is then released is let off through a tap at the bottom of the tub. In the next stage hot water is added to the curd. The grainy mass draws together, and more whey is drained off. After being left to rest for a short time, the cheese mixture is scooped out of the vat in a linen cloth and, while still wet, kneaded into wooden molds by hand. Before or during the pressing stage, a casein stamp with the name "Boerenkaas" is applied to the cheese, sometimes with the addition of the type of milk.

The mold is closed with a perfectly fitting lid and placed under a cheese press, where it remains for four to six hours. Afterward, the cheese maker removes the young cheese from the mold and places it in a (not too) cool saline bath. This is where the rind and typical flavor of the cheese gradually develop. After the young farmhouse Gouda has floated in the brine for a few days, it is taken to the cheese store, where the temperature and humidity are carefully regulated.

The actual maturing process begins while the cheese is left to rest on wooden shelves. During the several months of this stage, the cheese has to be turned and checked regularly. A breathable plastic material is rubbed into it several times in order to protect the rind against mold. How long the cheese will take to mature depends on other ingredients. Farmhouse Gouda has five different levels of maturity and flavor.

Farmhouse Gouda that matures for about five weeks is considered young. After maturing for at least two months, it is *jong belegen* (young), after four months *belegen* (aged), after seven months *extra belegen* (very aged), and after ten months *oud* (old). There are marked differences in the flavors at the various levels of maturity. The creamy mild aroma of a young cheese gradually turns into the hearty delight of an aged Gouda. The longer the cheese matures, the more intensive the taste experience. Old Boerenkaas is extremely strong and full bodied.

CHARACTERISTICS

The weight and dimensions of the cheese may vary greatly, depending on whether the Boerenkaas is made the Gouda way (flat cylinder with rounded edges), the Leiden way (flat cylinder with square corners), or the Edam way (a spherical or loaf shape). The rinds also vary: Gouda and Edam varieties have a white-yellow rind and the Leiden type has a red one. In all varieties the cheese has a coating on the outside. The consistency ranges from firm to malleable and smooth to hard and cuttable. As a general rule, the cheese should be three to four times its diameter in height, and weigh about 5–66 lb (2.5–30 kg). A wheel 4 in (10 cm) high and 16 in (40 cm) in diameter weighs about 26 lb (12 kg).

PIKANTJE VAN ANTJE

Pikantje van Antje is a Gouda that is guaranteed to have matured for four months, and is the shared Gouda trademark of all Dutch cheese producers. It is hearty and full flavored, and with its excellent melting properties it is a veritable all-rounder in the kitchen. Pikantje may be identified by its red, white, and blue label with the Frau Antje logo that covers the whole surface of the 24–26 lb (11–12 kg) wheels.

Gouda

Semi-hard cheese made from
pasteurized cow's milk
48% FDM

ORIGIN AND HISTORY

Totaling well above 50% of the country's entire cheese production, Gouda is one of the most popular of all cheeses. It was named after the town of the same name, not far from Rotterdam. It is believed that farmers in the region were already producing a similar cheese in the sixth century. Thanks to extensive trade associations, the recipe was spread throughout Europe in the Middle Ages, and soon it was being imitated all over the world.

PRODUCTION

Gouda is a rennet cheese, and today it is mostly made in state-of-the-art cheese dairies to standardized production methods. The steps in industrial production are largely the same as the old farming principles (see Boerenkaas). The maturing period varies tremendously, and can be more than a year—by which time the standard product is a genuine specialty. There are six levels of maturity for Gouda: Young Gouda matures for four to twelve weeks, aged Gouda for three to six months, very aged Gouda for six to eight months, old Gouda for eight to twelve months, and extra-aged Gouda—also known as Brokkelkaas (crumbly cheese)—for over a year.

CHARACTERISTICS

Gouda is available in wheels or blocks. The appearance and texture change during the maturing process; wheels become smaller, the center (pâte or paste), darker and firmer. Wheels with a waxed, usually yellow (young Gouda) or black rind (old Gouda) weigh on average between 5–33 lb (2.5–15 kg). A large proportion of Gouda is sold in vacuum-matured blocks. Young Gouda is firm to cut, smooth and silky in consistency and has small round holes. The cheese gives in when pressed with a thumb. By contrast, old Gouda is so hard and crumbly that it is almost impossible to slice. The mild, creamy aroma of young Gouda becomes sharper as the cheese ages; old Gouda is strong and full bodied in flavor.

Connoisseurs particularly appreciate extra-aged Gouda, also known as "Brokkelkaas," which can mature for up to two years.

SERVING SUGGESTIONS

Young Gouda is delicious on bread, in salads, and with all kinds of cold dishes. Aged Gouda is ideal for hot dishes where good melting and delicate seasoning are required. Old Gouda is best eaten alone in small pieces, but it is also very good to grate and an excellent tasty ingredient for all kinds of dishes.

Sommelier's recommendation: Young Gouda goes best with bottom-fermented beers with a mild bitter note, strong white wines from Burgundy, varieties such as Pinot Blanc and Pinot Gris, and also Chardonnay (not oaked), white Bordeaux wines, and young, fruity red wines with little tannin.

A medium Gouda harmonizes well with more mature wines. Here too, strong whites are excellent; reds can be a little stronger but without too much tannin after maturity.

Old Gouda is perfect with mature wines such as Riesling Auslese, Traminer, or Muscatel varieties with a residual sweetness.

However, the traditional combination is a complex, mature wine from Bordeaux, especially from the Médoc or its famous appellations, and from the Libournais with Saint-Emilion, Pomerol, and other associated labels.

FRAU ANTJE WITH REAL DUTCH CHEESE

When the pretty blonde lady with the white lace cap says "cheese," she means Dutch cheese. For over 40 years the lady called Antje has played the part of the friendly taster of an agrarian product that could not be more Dutch.

The *Kaasmeisje* (cheese lady) was the symbol of the dairy industry in The Netherlands by the 1950s. In the UK she advertised "Real Dutch Cheese" and in France "Fromage de Hollande."

Edam

Semi-hard cheese made from
pasteurized cow's milk
40% FDM

ORIGIN AND HISTORY
Edam, the Netherlands' second traditional variety, is just as well known as
Gouda. It was soon exported into other
European countries. It gets its name
from the harbor town of Edam on the
Ijsselmeer, north of Amsterdam. Today
it is made all over the country—and the
world. The focus is shifting back to
traditional farmhouse production with
the protected Boerenkaas.

PRODUCTION
Edam is now made from skimmed or
semi-skimmed pasteurized milk.
Because it has a reduced fat content,
Edam is drier than Gouda. It usually
matures for between four weeks and
four months, sometimes even longer. It
keeps extremely well.

CHARACTERISTICS
Ball-shape, diameter about 5 in (13 cm),
weight 3–6 lb (1.5–2.5 kg); loaf-shaped
blocks weighing 6–11 lb (2.5–5 kg).
Both are covered in red or yellow paraffin wax. Farmhouse Edam has a light-
yellow to medium-brown natural rind.
The texture of young Edam is smooth
and elastic with only a few holes, and it
is mild and slightly sweet or nutty in
flavor and aroma. As the cheese ages, it
becomes firmer in consistency and

stronger in flavor. Old Edam usually has
a black coating.

SPECIAL FEATURES
There are countless Edam varieties—
with added herbs, pepper, and cumin;
made with vegetarian rennet, or
vacuum matured. Dutch Mimolette or
Commissiekaas, a mature Edam
colored with carrot juice, is only rarely
found outside the country.

SERVING SUGGESTIONS
Ideal in sandwiches and hot or cold
dishes. Sommelier's recommendation:
Young Edam likes dry white wines with
a fine fruitiness and ripeness, and
velvety red wines with little tannin,
such as Pinot Noir and fruity Dornfelder.

Maasdam (Leerdam)

Semi-hard cheese made from
pasteurized cow's milk
45% FDM

ORIGIN AND HISTORY

Maasdam cheese was not produced until the late 1980s, and it is an excellent example of the innovative spirit of the cheese industry of the Netherlands. The story of its success is unique since it quickly reached the second position in the list of Dutch cheese exports. Its popularity is due to the fact that it combines the best characteristics of Gouda and Emmental. Leerdam is the most important Maasdam-style cheese, and also Europe's best-selling variety.

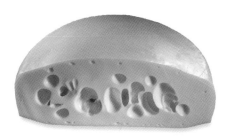

PRODUCTION

Maasdam is generally made in the same way as Gouda. However, other acid starters are used (including lactbacilli), and the propionic acid bacteria added to the milk cause the cheese to rise like dough during the (minimum) 42-day ripening period, thereby creating the characteristic large holes—about 1 in (2–3 cm) in diameter.

CHARACTERISTICS

Round, flat cylindrical wheels, diameter about 12 in (30 cm), weight 13–26 lb (6–12 kg); smooth, light rind and yellow paraffin wax or plastic coating. Smooth straw-colored texture with large shiny holes. Nutty, slightly sweet flavor with a fruity background. It has a much lower salt content than Gouda and Edam.

SERVING SUGGESTIONS

Sommelier's recommendation: Fruity, dry white wines with fine mineral and elegant tones in addition to their fruitiness, such as Franconian Silvaner, Gutedel from the Markgräfler Land or Chasselas from the Valais or Vaud, Muscatel sur lie from the Loire, Soave Classico from northern Italy, and white wines from Rueda in Spain. Grüner Veltliner from Austria is worth a try. Of red wines, wines with little tannin but plenty of fruit, Beaujolais, Pinot Noir, Valpolicella, Bardolino, and lighter Merlots are all good accompaniments.

Leidenkaas (PDO)

Semi-hard cheese made from
cow's milk
40% min. FDM

ORIGIN AND HISTORY

This cumin cheese used to be made on
lots of farms around Leiden. Today,
there are only about 20 of them left,
producing several thousand cheeses by
hand every year. They are identified by
a label showing the town's coat of arms
with its crossed keys.

PRODUCTION

The farm-produced varieties are made
with semi-skimmed cow's milk (usually
raw), which has to be left in the cellar
for a few days first to pre-ripen so the
cream can form. Cumin (and sometimes
anise) is added to the curds. The treatment of the curds and the pressing—for
up to 24 hours—make Leiden cheese
firm and dry. Red dye is brushed on the
rind. The cheese is also made commercially from pasteurized milk; this variety has an FDM of 20 or 40%.

CHARACTERISTICS

Flat, round wheels with a sharp bottom
edge and rounded top edge, diameter
12–16 in (30–40 cm), height 4 in
(10 cm), weight 18–22 lb (8–10 kg).
The orange rind is firm or very firm
with a red wax coating. Light to
medium-yellow paste with an even,
dry to firm consistency with no holes;
cumin seeds throughout, adding a

touch of spiciness to the otherwise
mild cheese.

SPECIAL FEATURES

Sailors took the recipe for Leidenkaas
to Norway in the early seventeenth
century, where it was also marked with
the crossed keys (*nøkkel*) and so
became known as Nøkkelost.

SERVING SUGGESTIONS

Thanks to its low fat content, Leiden
cheese is ideal for cheese lovers who
like a cheese that is both low in fat and
tasty. Sommelier's recommendation: A
strong Gewürztraminer is just right.
Bottom-fermented beer, Genever
(Dutch gin), and Acquavit are the traditional companions.

SIMILAR CHEESE VARIETIES

Nøkkelost (Norway), Friesekaas (the
Netherlands); see entries.

Friesekaas

Semi-hard cheese made from
cow's milk
40% FDM

ORIGIN AND HISTORY
Friesekaas, or Friesian clove cheese,
has a similar history to that of Leiden
cheese.

PRODUCTION
Even though Friesekaas is a relative of
Gouda, its manufacture (from raw or
pasteurized cow's milk) differs from the
usual production process. The addition
of fresh buttermilk (instead of acid
starters) is characteristic. There are
two varieties of this often skimmed
cheese (when skimmed it has 20% FDM
and is called Friese Nagelkaas). Once
the curd has been separated from the
whey, the curd is cut to make it drier
and finer. This is when the cloves are
added. The curd is placed into cheese
molds and pressed for several hours.
Then the cheeses are dipped briefly in
hot water before going back under the
press for several more hours. The full,
piquant flavor develops after a fairly
long maturing process. This is sold
solely as an aged cheese—that is, after
six months.

CHARACTERISTICS
Large wheels, height normally 4 in
(10 cm), diameter 16 cm (40 cm),
weight up to 44 lb (20 kg). Natural rind,
not very elastic, very firm, usually with
a colored wax or plastic suspension on
the outside. Yellow to greeny-yellow
semi-hard, smooth cheese. The cloves,
often combined with cumin, give it a
distinctive flavor.

SPECIAL FEATURES
There are versions of Friesekaas with
added spices, such as Kruidkaas (with
cumin) and Nagelkaas (with cloves).

SERVING SUGGESTIONS
Friesekaas is usually served on bread,
eaten by itself, or used for gratins.
Sommelier's recommendation: Strong
Muscatels and Gewürztraminer, or
bottom-fermented beer or Genever.

Kernhem

Semi-hard cheese made from
cow's milk
60% FDM

ORIGIN AND HISTORY

This new cheese is actually the result of a coincidence. Under normal circumstances, it would have been an Edam. However, as the weather was quite damp at the time and the cheese maker was unable to control the humidity in her maturing cellar, on one occasion it turned out slightly flat rather than round in shape; furthermore, the corynebacteria (red smear culture) present in the moist air were activated, settled on the unfinished rind, and turned it orange-red. The result was a mild, creamy cheese with a distinctive note. The NIZO, the Netherlands Institute of Dairy Research in Ede, developed its own controlled production process. The cheese was named Kernhem after the estate where the institute was located at the time.

PRODUCTION

In some respects, its production is similar to that of Edam, but it requires a high level of care during the four-week maturing process: The cheeses have to be rubbed with a special culture at regular intervals to prevent the mold from overdeveloping. It matures in damp cellars at about 60 °F (15 °C).

CHARACTERISTICS

Flat, round wheels, height about 2 in (5–6 cm), diameter 10 in (25 cm), weight about 4–6 lb (1.6–2.5 kg). Orange rind with a surface flora similar to that of Saint-Paulin or Reblochon, yellow-red, very smooth, almost creamy texture with tiny holes. Flavor creamy-aromatic to piquant; strong smell. The rind is not suitable for eating.

SERVING SUGGESTIONS

Kernhem is considered a classic dessert cheese. It goes well with fruity white wines with a fine, dry character, with aromatic varieties such as Scheurebe, Traminer, or Muscatel, and with strong Pinot Gris, but less well with reds. With regard to beer, a top-fermented beer is to be preferred.

Kanterkomijnekaas (PDO)

Hard cheese made from
cow's milk
20–44% min. FDM

ORIGIN AND HISTORY

The traditional word *Kanter* is a reference to the angular shape of the cheese, which has a sharp overhang from the sides to the bottom. Farmers in Friesland and the Westerkwartier used to sell their cheese in local markets.

The Friesians were exporting their cheese to England and Germany by 1532. The soils in this rural, relatively unspoilt area came from eroded peat bogs and fens, and 80% is used for grazing cattle. The grass is extremely nutritious. The modern production method differs only slightly from the original one.

PRODUCTION

Kanterkaas may be enriched with cloves (Kanternagelkaas) and/or cumin (Kanterkomijnekaas). The milk is skimmed, quickly pasteurized, and processed into half-fat cheese. The milk separates at about 86 °F (30 °C) with the addition of animal rennet, and a mixed culture of suitable lactobacilli provides acidification. Cumin or cloves are added to the washed curd. The curd is ground or cut, salted, and then poured into pressing vats to acquire the desired shape and rind. The cheese is next placed in brine. It matures for four weeks to over a year.

CHARACTERISTICS

Smooth, closed rind; flat cylindrical shape, 7–19 lb (3–8.5 kg) in weight. The rind can be left as it is, or finished with a colorless or yellow coating. Close texture, sometimes a few holes. Kanterkaas is ivory colored or yellow to yellow-green throughout. Piquant to spicy in flavor. The addition of cloves or cumin gives it an aromatic component. The cheese is firm to hard in consistency.

SERVING SUGGESTIONS:

Sommelier's recommendation: Aromatic grape varieties like Gewürztraminer, Muscatel, Scheurebe, and Torrontes go very well with this cheese. Bottom-fermented beer or Genever are also popular classics.

BELGIUM
Interesting specialties

Belgium has a highly traditional, if still quite young, history of cheese making, with its own interesting specialties.

However, most Belgian cheeses are not well known beyond the country's borders. A variety of influences on the recipes are notable, varying according to the particular region. In the Flemish part of the country, cheese making is traditionally orientated toward the Netherlands, whereas proximity to France is evident in Wallonia. Until the twentieth century, farming was still at the heart of agricultural production in Wallonia.

However, declining cereal prices forced the farmers to rethink. More attention was paid to raising cattle, and the first major dairies were set up around 1900—although initially almost exclusively for the production of butter. Cheese production increased consistently in the 1950s and, as in so many other countries, great importance was attached to standard varieties and large quantities. In Belgium these were mainly Saint-Paulin and Gouda-type cheeses.

Following the rediscovery in the 1960s of a number of old recipes used in farms and monasteries, several committed cheese producers set about giving varieties such as Remoudou, Brusselse Kaas, Rubens, Postel, Maredsous, and Beauvoorde a new lease of life—albeit on a small scale. Apart from Herve, which is now protected by the EU, the most famous cheese of Belgian origin is Limburg, although this has now been more or less forgotten in its homeland.

Left: Knight's castle Vêves-Celles in Wallonia.

OTHER BELGIAN CHEESES

The Belgians' great preference for red smear cheeses becomes evident when you consider that in addition to Herve and its variant, Remoudou, there is a whole range of other cheeses of this type. These include Rubens, a semi-hard cheese with a waxed rind and made from cow's milk, which has almost completely disappeared from the market. The recipe for it was preserved by a small dairy. Rubens—which weighs about 7 lb (3 kg)—is indeed named after the famous Flemish artist. Another variety that has regained popularity is the soft cheese Maredsous, named after the monks of the same name, which—like the Postel monastery cheese—is a member of the extensive family of Trappist cheeses. It has a slightly smoky undertone to it. Beauvoorde is a semi-hard cheese with a mild aroma and spicy smell, and was developed by the publican Arthur Djes at the beginning of the twentieth century. The wheels weigh between 7 and 14 lb (3–6 kg), and are now produced by a leading dairy. The typical Belgian cheese varieties include a number of remarkable fresh and whey cheeses (Plattekaas); Chevagne is a large-holed goat's cheese that combines the nutty flavor of Maasdam with the aroma of goat's milk.

MUSSELS, HAM, AND CHIPS

Belgian's cuisine and gastronomy are quite rightly famous: The tiny kingdom is certainly up with the giants in this sector. The restaurants along the Belgian coast are famed for their fish and mussels dishes. Those who try the fish stew Waterzooi or mussels in white wine will find both delicacies equally memorable.

Pommes frites—chips—are also much loved. It is said that the inventors were the fishermen of Liège; on bad days when they caught little, they chipped up the potatoes and threw them into hot oil so they had something to eat. Belgians are proud of their "pommes frites" and regard Germany's "Pommes," America's "French fries," the Dutch "Patat," and England's "chips" as extremely poor imitations of their national dish. Belgian's delightful chocolates, biscuits, and waffles must also be tried on a visit to Brussels or Liège.

A THOUSAND YEARS OF BREWING TRADITION

Although the Belgians love their wine, beer is their particular favourite. There are hundreds of types, some of which are among the best in the world. The Trappist monasteries such as Chimay, Orval, Rochefort, and Westmalle all made their names with their brews. Anyone who orders a beer in Brussels, Liège, or Antwerp will be rewarded with a questioning look from the waiter. You will have to be a little more specific. Of course, not all beers will taste the same to the typical Pils drinker, because pretty much everything that is brewed can be called beer in Belgium. That is why there are also exotic varieties such as cherry and peach beer. Brewing laws like Germany's purity law do not exist, and corn or rice is often used as a substitute for barley. And yet the Belgians take their beer very seriously, and will choose a variety to suit their mood at the time—or even the weather. Whereas only six brewing methods are used in Germany, there are almost 200 in Belgium. Every village has its own beer, every beer its own glass. The monastery beers have always been the classics. To gain a comprehensive understanding of Belgian beer, visit the café Mieder Lambik in Brussels (Savoiestraat) and ask for the beer menu. You will be presented with a leather-bound book—and then have the problem of choosing from almost 1,000 options.

Right: To the Belgians beer is both food and luxury—and, above all, lifestyle.

Bottom: Fabulous mussels dishes are served all along the Belgian coast.

Passendale

Semi-soft cheese made from
cow's milk
50% FDM

ORIGIN AND HISTORY

Passendale was named after a village in
Flanders. Although it is quite a young
Belgian cheese, it has achieved a certain
level of fame beyond the country's
borders.

PRODUCTION

Passendale is made to an old monastery
recipe that has been passed down
through the centuries, and it bears quite
a resemblance to Dutch semi-hard
cheese. It is still made by hand from
pasteurized cow's milk, so no two
wheels are the same. It matures under
a blue-mold rind at moderate humidity
for about 45 days.

CHARACTERISTICS

Passendale's most striking feature is its
shape: it resembles a farmhouse loaf,
and it weighs 8 or even 13 lb (3.5–6 kg).
Very hard, brown crust with a slight
white mold (hard rind), light-yellow
semi-hard, smooth texture with typically small, irregular holes. Mild, spicy
aroma and full-bodied, slightly spicy
flavor. Young Passendale tastes mild
and creamy. As it matures it gains in
aroma and piquancy.

SERVING SUGGESTIONS

Passendale tastes best on bread, but
may also be used for gratins. Fruity,
half-dry white wines (Riesling, Kerner)
and rosé wines from the south of France
go well with it, as does a light beer.

Brusselse Kaas

Soft cheese made from
cow's milk
up to 2% FDM

ORIGIN AND HISTORY
Brusselse Kaas (Fromage de Bruxelles in French) is one of the most typical Belgian cheeses, and it is also known as Hettekaas or Hettkees (hard cheese). It has been made on farms for centuries, and commercially since the 1960s. This cheese remains popular all over Belgium.

PRODUCTION
Brusselse Kaas is made from pasteurized and skimmed milk, in two stages. The curd is cut and acidified, then pressed and dried slightly in sacks before being ground, salted, and poured into molds. When the cheese is firm enough, it is left to mature for at least two months. During this time it is washed regularly in saline, and then smeared with a special culture (local bacterial cultures that are also used to make Lambiek beer). Finally, the mature cheeses are washed to remove all traces of the smear.

CHARACTERISTICS
Round, flattened wheels, diameter about 6 in (15 cm), weight about 2 lb (950 g–1 kg). The wheels are cut into portions of 5–6 oz (150–160 g). Smooth and light on the outside with a slightly shiny yellow rind. Whitish texture with a moist, slightly crumbly consistency and no holes. Mildly piquant, dry, citrusy, and salty in flavor. Brusselse Kaas is usually sold wrapped in film or waxed paper.

SERVING SUGGESTIONS
The cheese is usually eaten as it is on bread, and tastes best with Lambiek beer or a dry, youngish Riesling.

Herve (PDO)

Soft cheese made from
cow's milk
45% FDM

ORIGIN AND HISTORY

Fromage de Herve, known simply as Herve after the region of the same name in Wallonia in eastern Belgium, is the country's most famous cheese. Its history may be traced back to the seventh century. The cheese experienced a tremendous upsurge at the time of Charles V, when it became a popular barter object with farmers who were not allowed to export grain at the time. Sales expanded to Germany and Austria in the eighteenth century, and later to France.

PRODUCTION

This red smear cheese is made from pasteurized cow's milk (from raw milk in farmhouse production), and is similar to Limburg and Romadur. The cheese is shaped into bars, and when it has achieved the required level of firmness it goes to be salted, being turned regularly. It stays with the producer or goes to the affineur (specialist in the curing and maturing of cheeses) to mature, which takes between two and three months. It is stored at about 59 °F (15 °C) in high humidity, and smeared regularly with a special salt solution based on a local bacterium culture (*Bacterium linens*).

CHARACTERISTICS

Either in brick-shape loaves 4 in (10 cm) long, 2 in (4.5 cm) wide, and 1 in (3 cm) high, with a weight of 7 oz (200 g); or in cubes with a side length of 3 in (7.5 cm) and a weight of 14 oz (400 g) or a side length of 2 in (5.5 cm) and a weight of 7 oz (200 g). The thin red to orange-brown, shiny, moist rind is protected by foil or waxed paper. Light-yellow, soft to slightly firm, smooth texture, almost entirely without holes. Whereas the rind is sharp and spicy in flavor, the flavor of the cheese ranges from slightly sweet to strong and a little salty, depending on the age.

SPECIAL FEATURES

There is also a double-cream version of Herve. A more piquant—both in flavor and smell—and particularly intense version of Herve is Remoudou (also Remoudoux, Remedou, or Le Piquant). Some specialists believe the name comes from the Wallonian word *remoud* (after milking), whereas others say it comes from the German word *Rahm*, meaning cream. These cheeses are bigger than Herve and take longer to mature—which gives the bacteria on the surface the chance to develop a distinctly pungent aroma. This explains Remoudou's nickname of "stinky cheese."

SERVING SUGGESTIONS
Both Herve and Remoudou taste best as they are; there are no particular uses for them in cooking. Top-fermented Trappist beer goes well with them, but so does beer brewed from wheat. Aromatic Muscatel and strong, low acid Gewürztraminer wines also make good accompaniments. Wines with a residual sweetness are highly recommended too. It is more difficult to team red wines with this cheese, but cider with a residual sweetness is another excellent choice.

SIMILAR CHEESE VARIETIES
Limburg and Romadur (Germany), Pont l'Éveque (France).

OTHER CHEESES FROM WALLONIA

Lots of goat's cheeses that are made from raw milk come from small artisanal dairies all over the area. They are usually shaped by hand and offered as fresh cheese. Ripe goat's cheese has a natural rind or is dipped in ash, seasoned with herbs and pepper, or wrapped in bacon. The Crottins, Bûchettes, and Tommes are some of the mature, strong cheese varieties. Less well known but no less appealing are the sheep's cheeses that some shepherds make themselves from raw milk.

Classic Trappist cheeses are Orval, Chimay, and Rochefort or La Val Dieu.

Fine, softly acidic wines of the Sauvignon Blanc or Riesling grape go well with young goat's cheeses.

Maturer goat's cheese needs a stronger partner—by all means Riesling with a touch of residual sweetness, or Sauvignon Blanc with an intensive minerality such as Pouilly-Fumé. The varieties that mature in bacon go well with a fresh bottom-fermented beer, and also with an oaked Chardonnay.

Chimay

Semi-hard cheese made from
cow's milk
45% FDM

ORIGIN AND HISTORY
Cattle have always been farmed in the
area of Chimay in the province of Hainaut, which is full of woods, rivers, and
meadows. The Trappist monks of
Scourmont first started producing this
cheese in 1876, and left it in the
monastery's cellar vaults to mature.

PRODUCTION
Typical monastery cheese, paste
pressed but not heated, natural rind. It
matures in the monastery cellars for
four weeks.

CHARACTERISTICS
Wheel of 8 in (21 cm) diameter, weight
5 lb (2.2 kg), ochre-colored natural rind;
creamy texture; fresh, smooth, mild
flavor.

SPECIAL FEATURES
For Chimay à la bière, the rind is
washed several times with Chimay
Trappist beer. This cheese tastes
slightly of hops. Suggested drink:
Chimay Trappist beer.

Kachkéis

Kochkäse made from
cow's milk
40% FDM, or 0% FDM (fat-free)

ORIGIN AND HISTORY

Kachkéis is a traditionally made Luxemburg specialty cheese. It is believed that Spanish troops brought the recipe to Luxemburg in the seventeenth century. The Luxemburgers even dedicated the song of Kochkäse, the "Madelon," to it, and it gives the Luxemburg comic book hero Superjhemp his special powers.

PRODUCTION

Once the milk has been thickened with lactobacillus cultures, it is left to curdle slowly. The curd is heated, ground, and pressed to remove as much of the whey as possible. The dry curd is left to mature for three to five days. During this stage, the cheese is sold on for users to cook themselves. The next stage in the production of a spread—whether at home or in the dairy—is the gentle simmering of the pre-ripened cheese in a double-boiler; depending on the recipe, it is flavored with salt and pepper, herbs, garlic, or mustard, and finished with white wine or butter.

CHARACTERISTICS

Kachkéis is very sticky in consistency. As a spread, the various flavors are sold in cups. The uncooked cheese for finishing at home is sold in rolls or blocks. It is notable for its mild, creamy flavor, which varies depending on the seasoning and finish.

SERVING SUGGESTIONS

Traditionally, the Luxemburgers enjoy Kachkéis spread on farmhouse bread with a thick layer of mustard on top or underneath, and possibly some butter, accompanied by a glass of white wine from the Luxemburg Moselle.

GERMANY
Infinite variety

Germany is Europe's biggest consumer of cheese, producing hundreds of different varieties. Bavaria and Baden-Württemberg in the south, and Lower Saxony, Schleswig-Holstein, and Mecklenburg-Vorpommern in the north, rank among the main producing regions. However, central and eastern parts of Germany are also home to numerous cheese dairies.

Official German cheese regulations differentiate between standard cheeses and so-called free varieties of cheese, which may vary in terms of composition and production method. Standard cheese types must conform to strict manufacturing regulations.

Nowadays, most German cheese manufacturers produce a variety of different cheeses and are constantly introducing new kinds to their range. However, many of these products are spin-offs of popular European cheeses. In contrast to France, very few traditional cheeses are produced between the North Sea coast and the Allgäu.

The dairy industry in Germany is traditionally populated by medium-sized enterprises and, despite efforts to concentrate production, there are still more independent dairies and cheese factories here than in most other countries. Small farm-based and organic cheese producers tend to offer varieties of cheese with a strong regional character or rely on their organic provenance. They have, for the past 25 years, provided an interesting "alternative" cheese culture. Although the majority of cheeses are made from cow's milk, ewe's and goat's milk cheeses are growing in popularity. The range of farm cheeses available from independent producers is formidable and provides a welcome addition to the essential mass-produced cheeses.

Left: The Victory Column, affectionately known to Berliners as Goldelse (Golden Elsa).

"ADOPTED" GERMAN CHEESES —
GOUDA, EDAM, CAMEMBERT, & CO.

Dutch cheeses such as Gouda and Edam, and Swiss-style cheeses like Maasdam, are especially popular in Germany. Since their designation of origin is not protected by law, they may be manufactured and sold in Germany under the same name. This is similarly true of Cheddar (and frequently Cheshire) cheese and Trappist cheese, as well as of soft Camembert- and Brie-style cheeses, Feta cheese (which originates in Greece) and the so-called *pasta filata* family of cheeses (e.g. Mozzarella). In 1999, the *pasta filata* cheeses became the latest group to be officially adopted as a member of the German cheese family under the German Cheese Regulations. In terms of production methods, shape, taste, appearance, and texture, these cheeses are virtually no different from the originals. They are sold either under the name of the particular variety or under an individual brand name.

Butterkäse

A semi-hard
cow's milk cheese
40–60% FDM

ORIGINS AND HISTORY
Butterkäse is one of Germany's oldest cheeses and is not associated with any specific region.

PRODUCTION
This cow's milk cheese is manufactured in much the same way as other semi-hard cheeses. The type of Butterkäse found in most shops is the foil-ripened version, whereas the more traditional variety with its yellowish-brown rind has become much less common and is only found as a locally manufactured product. It matures in three weeks.

CHARACTERISTICS
This loaf- or wheel-shape cheese comes in all sorts of sizes, varying in weight 9 oz–44 lb (250 g to 20 kg). Usually foil-ripened, the cheese comes without a rind. Delicate yellow in color with a few small holes, it is ideal for slicing. The mass-produced version is firmer in texture. It has a creamy, mild, and buttery—occasionally slightly acidic—flavor.

SERVING SUGGESTIONS
In the past it was often nicknamed the "lady's cheese" or Damenkäse because of its mild flavor and virtual lack of aroma. It is particularly popular in Germany as a breakfast or supper cheese. Sommelier's recommendation: Butterkäse goes well with light, sparkling white wines such as Gutedel, Silvaner, and Müller-Thurgau, not to mention fresh Rieslings, young reds with a low tannin content, or Export-type beers and lagers.

THE NORTH
Partial to stronger flavors

With its ideal climatic and agricultural conditions for cattle and dairy farming, cheese production has always played a significant role in northern Germany. The dairy industry is in the hands of relatively large businesses running comparatively large herds of animals. In Schleswig-Holstein each farm has, on average, more than 50 cows, but most of the farms remain family-run concerns. Northern Germans prefer their cheeses a little stronger than their southern German compatriots, as is evident from local specialties such as the aromatic Wilstermarschkäse, one of Germany's oldest cheeses. Tilsit cheese is a specialty of the Baltic region. A regional specialty of Vorpommern (West Pomerania) is Boddenkäse, a pungent, aromatic cow's milk cheese made on the island of Rügen.

DELICATE SPREAD

Processed cheeses and other soft cheese preparations are produced in all parts of Germany. Available in a variety of forms, sizes, and packaging—and with a choice of fat content—these cheeses may be firm for ease of slicing or come in spreadable form. The flavor and aroma are determined partly by the type of cheese, and partly by the addition of a range of aromatic ingredients such as mushrooms, ham, herbs, and walnuts. If the cheese is layered or wrapped in herbs or other ingredients, it produces the contrast of a soft-textured cheese with a piquant aroma. There is an unlimited choice of processed cheeses, which are usually sold under a brand name.

Left: Northern Germany, where heaven joins with the sea.

Wilstermarschkäse

Semi-hard cheese
made from cow's milk
30–50% FDM

ORIGINS AND HISTORY

Schleswig-Holstein

Wilstermarsch cheese takes its name from a fertile stretch of land along the river Elbe near Hamburg. It belongs to the Tilsiter family of cheeses and was described for the first time in 1821. Although this type of cheese is not very widespread, it has a loyal following of enthusiasts.

PRODUCTION

This type of cheese is produced in much the same way as Tilsiter cheese. However, the milk is left to curdle for longer, which gives the finished cheese a softer texture. Its characteristic flavor results from its being matured in special cheese-ripening foil. The maturing process takes approximately five weeks.

CHARACTERISTICS

This square- or loaf-shape cheese is available in various sizes. Sometimes it is shaped in the form of a wheel (height 4 in (10cm), diameter 12 in (30 cm), weighing up to 9 lb (4 kg) in block form or about 13 lb (6 kg) in wheel form. The cheese does not have a rind and is sealed in a coat of protective wax. Beneath this wax covering is a smooth, pale-yellow cheese of semi-soft consis-tency, punctuated by tiny, evenly spaced holes. It has a dry, slightly fruity taste with a mildly spicy tinge.

SERVING SUGGESTIONS

Wilstermarsch cheese is popular as a table cheese, but it is also used as a cooking ingredient and is good for grating. Sommelier's recommendation: The traditional accompaniment in northern Germany is a refreshing, Pilsner-style beer. Alternatively, dry white wines—particularly Burgunder and robust, late harvest Burgundy wines with a good body—also go well with this cheese.

Steinbuscher cheese

Semi-soft cheese made from
cow's milk
30–50% FDM

ORIGINS AND HISTORY

Mecklenburg-Vorpommern /
northern Germany

Steinbuscher cheese is one of the oldest
German cheeses and has been about
since 1860. During the last war and the
days of the GDR, it was one of the most
popular cheeses produced by the Meck-
lenburg cheese-making establishments, but during the past few decades
this cheese has dwindled in popularity
to some extent. Steinbuscher is another
member of the Tilsiter cheese group.

PRODUCTION

Lactic acid and rennet are added to the
milk to produce the curd, which is then
crumbled, salted, and placed in a mold
and left to mature for at least three
weeks. Thanks to its small size, the
cheese ripens quickly, developing quite
a pungent flavor after just a short time.

CHARACTERISTICS

Small, flat blocks, often square in shape
measuring 4 x 4 x 3 in (11 x 11 x 8 cm),
weighing 7 oz–2 lb (200–1,000 g) or
more. Yellowish-brown or reddish rind,
with a little reddish-brown smear and,
in some cases, a slight covering of mold
on the surface. The cheese has a smooth
texture and is pale to golden yellow in
color with very few holes. Young cheese
is lighter in the center. It is mild to
piquant in flavor with a spicy aroma and
a pronounced smell.

SERVING SUGGESTIONS

Sommelier's recommendation: Steinbuscher goes well with hearty country-
style bread and is best accompanied by
fresh, fruity, youthful, and aromatic
white wines; fruity reds, low in tannins,
provide a pleasant alternative.

FARM CHEESE MADE FROM RAW MILK

Cheese has been produced on farms in Schleswig-Holstein for a very long time. As far back as 1578 cheese production on a significant scale was taking place at Gut Behl farm near Plön. Present-day ecological considerations have led to a revival of this ancient tradition in some of the smaller farm-based cheese dairies, and Schleswig-Holstein has therefore remained an important center of cheese making. Since the so-called Cheese Route was established at the beginning of 2000, the number of participating members has risen to 38, most of which make local farm cheese by hand—including delicious cow's milk, sheep's milk, and goat's milk cheeses, many of which are made from untreated milk. The Backensholz Rohmilchkäserei (cheese dairy) is based in the small village of Oster-Ohrstedt near Husum. This organic farm specializes in products made from raw milk, all of which are made from the farm's own milk. Its first product was launched in 1991: A farm cheese resembling Esrom, with a piquant flavor. The other cheese varieties produced by Backensholz—such as Husum cheese, Deich cheese, and Fabro, a creamy dessert cheese—also have a robust yet elegant flavor.

German Tilsiter cheese

Semi-hard cheese made from
cow's milk
30–60% FDM

ORIGINS AND HISTORY
Northern Germany

Tilsiter is named after the former East Prussian town of Tilsit on the river Memel, where it is thought to have been accidentally produced early in the nineteenth century by Dutch cheese makers. They were actually trying to produce Gouda or Edam cheese, but they failed in their attempt and Tilsiter cheese was born instead. This cheese quickly became very popular all over the Baltic region and ultimately across Europe. There are numerous versions of this type. In Germany it is generally produced in the north of the country.

PRODUCTION

Tilsiter cheese is usually made from pasteurized milk, although a handful of small farm cheese-making establishments do still use untreated milk. Since the cheese curd is not subject to much pressing, small irregular holes form during the ripening process and run through the whole block of cheese. The whey is squeezed out by the cheese's own weight. During the first two months of ripening, the cheese is rubbed regularly with red smear cultures to encourage the formation of a rind. On the naturally ripened versions, instead it is washed and brushed regularly to pro-

mote the formation of the crusty rind. Tilsiter cheese is also available with added herbs, pepper, or caraway seeds. It ripens in two to five months, but ideally it is left to mature over a longer period. Old Tilsiter cheeses are left to ripen for up to one year.

CHARACTERISTICS

Generally sold in the shape of a loaf, but occasionally found in wheel form, usually 3–4 lb (1.5–2 kg) in weight. It has a thin, dry rind with a yellow-beige crust, sometimes with a light covering of mold. Tilsiter may also be ripened in wax or foil. It is elastic in texture and has numerous tiny irregular holes. It varies in flavor from mildly pungent to slightly spicy.

SERVING SUGGESTIONS

This cheese is often eaten after just four weeks. Dry white wines, full-bodied reds, and beer make excellent companions to Tilsiter cheese.

CENTRAL GERMANY
The heartland of sour-milk cheese

Cheese manufacturing in Germany's central and eastern states is strongly influenced by neighboring regions on the one hand, and by the production of international specialties and newly developed varieties on the other. In both these areas cheese making is of far less economic significance than it is in northern or southern parts of the country. Saxony-Anhalt is regarded as the heartland of typical German sour-milk cheese. Saxony, which is primarily a producer of soft and semi-hard cheeses, is home to Altenburger Ziegenkäse (Altenburg goat's cheese), one of the four German cheese varieties to have a protected designation of origin. Another of Saxony's cheeses, which enjoys something of an international reputation, is Milbenkäse, the surface of which is covered with layers of brown mite colonies. Cheese production in Hesse focuses mainly on the manufacture of sour-milk cheese and Kochkäse, as well as on various standard products. Hesse likewise boasts a cheese specialty with its own protected designation of origin—Odenwald Frühstückskäse. After Bavaria and Lower Saxony, North Rhine-Westphalia occupies third place in terms of milk production, although its dairy industry is mainly devoted to producing milk for drinking and fresh milk products. There is less emphasis on cheese manufacture, which tends to concentrate mainly on semi-hard cheese—by far the most popular type of cheese in North Rhine-Westphalia. Even so, this state can also boast a traditional culinary specialty of its own: Original Nieheimer cheese.

Left: Central Germany—lush forests, wild crags, and medieval towns.

Odenwald Frühstückskäse

Soft cheese made from
cow's milk
10% FDM

ORIGINS AND HISTORY
Southern part of Hessian Odenwald
Odenwald Frühstückskäse (breakfast cheese) may only be made from Odenwald milk. It must be manufactured in the Odenwald region of southern Hesse according to a traditional recipe. It gets its name from the old custom of eating this cheese for breakfast after the early morning milking session. Nowadays the only place making this cheese is a small private dairy in Hüttenthal.

PRODUCTION
Odenwald Frühstückskäse is pasteurized, skimmed, and pre-ripened with bacteria cultures producing lactic acid. Next, calf's rennet is added to coagulate the milk and turn it into curd, a process that takes 30 minutes, after which the cheese is turned. This procedure is repeated three times. Finally, the cheese is washed in brine, then left for 12 hours in a pre-ripening room. During this time yeast colonization takes place on the surface of the cheese, a reaction that ensures the deacidification necessary for the actual two-week ripening process.

CHARACTERISTICS
Cylindrical in shape, similar to Camembert, weighing nearly 4 oz (100 g). Smeared, brownish-yellow rind. Ivory-colored or yellowish cheese of soft consistency, with occasional holes. It has a strong to pungent flavor, is robust and aromatic, and is somewhat similar to sour-milk cheese.

SPECIAL FEATURES
Although Odenwald Frühstückskäse is often served as "Handkäse mit Musik" (cheese marinated in oil and vinegar, and served with onions), it differs from Harzer cheese, which is made from sour-milk low fat curd cheese, in so far as it is a handmade red smear cheese that has more in common with Weinkäse or Münster cheeses.

SERVING SUGGESTIONS
In its native area this cheese is often used as the strong-flavored basis of the specialty known as "Handkäse mit Musik." Ideally, it should be accompanied by a beer or a local Hessian apple wine.

Harz cheese

Sour-milk cheese made from
cow's milk
less than 10% FDM

ORIGINS AND HISTORY
*Lower Saxony, Hesse, Thuringia,
Saxony-Anhalt, Saxony*
This cheese was first produced
commercially in the Harz region during
the late eighteenth century.

PRODUCTION
The cheese is made by mixing sour-milk
curd cheese (occasionally with casein)
with cooking salt and ripening salts, and
shaping the mass after a few hours into
small round loaves. These are then
ripened with yellow and red smear
bacteria cultures. Harz cheese ripens
in just one or two days.

CHARACTERISTICS
It is sold in small balls, often packed
together in rolls consisting of four to five
individual balls, weighing about 1 oz
(25 g). Harz cheese has no rind, but a
golden yellow surface. The cheese itself
is yellowish although it may be whiter
near the center if it is not fully ripened.
Harz cheese may vary from mild to sharp
and spicy in flavor, with an unmistakable
aroma and a pungent smell.

SERVING SUGGESTIONS
Harz cheese tastes best when served as
part of the specialty known as "Handkäse mit Musik." Sommeliers' recommendation: Ideal beverages include
beer and apple wine, as well as German
white wines such as a dry, fresh Riesling
or a full-bodied Kerner wine.

HANDKÄS' MIT MUSIK

The Harz region is famous for its large
variety of sour-milk cheeses, which
began to materialize in the early nineteenth century when many of the region's
farmers took up dairy farming. Cheese
specialties such as "Handkäse mit
Musik" (cheese with "music") and
Spundekäs (a spicy mixture of fresh
cheese, curd cheese, and sour cream)
are still very popular in Hesse.
"Handkäse mit Musik" consists of small
and well-ripened sour-milk cheeses
(Korbkäse) cut into thick slices, mixed
with onion rings, and steeped in a mari-
nade of oil, vinegar, caraway seeds,
and pepper. It is excellent served with
wholemeal bread and accompanied by
beer or apple wine.

PROBABLY THE BEST CHEESE SHOP
IN THE WORLD

Anyone visiting Dresden will quickly become aware of the special features of this city. One of Dresden's truly special attractions and, at the same time, a unique treasure in dairying history may be found in the new part of town situated on the opposite bank of the Elbe: Pfund's Dairy, probably the best dairy and cheese shop in the world. This national treasure, built about 1900 and protected by a conservation order, has been saved from falling into complete neglect and completely restored. It is now not only a tourist attraction but a truly remarkable cheese shop. Its extensive range of specialties—which include cheeses made from untreated milk, imported from all over the world—is worthy of a cosmopolitan city. Its historic ceramic display case contains international cheeses made from cow's, ewe's, and goat's milk, and cheeses manufactured in Saxony as well as favorite classics from all over eastern Germany. It also stocks a significant selection of raw-milk specialty cheeses from France.

Würchwitzer Milbenkäse

Hard cheese made from
cow's and goat's milk
1% fat FDM

ORIGINS AND HISTORY

Although the tradition of Milbenkäse (mite cheese) production largely died out in the Altenburg region following the Second World War, a few families in the rural village of Würchwitz still continue the practice. One of these is the family of Helmut Pöschel, the only producer permitted to sell this cheese. Milbenkäse is known to have been produced in Würchwitz for over 500 years and has been made in the Altenburg region for over 1,000 years.

PRODUCTION

This type of cheese may be made from goat's, cow's, or sheep's milk. It is turned into curd by the addition of rennet. This is then poured into a sack and the whey is pressed out of the mass. It is seasoned with caraway, salt, and elderberry blossom. The curd is shaped by hand into small bars or balls and left to dry for two days, before being placed in a wooden chest with cheese mites. As the mites nibble at the cheese, their saliva softens it and the enzymes thereby released work their way into the cheese, killing off any mold that may be present. Thanks to the antiseptic action of the saliva enzymes, the cheese has a virtually unlimited shelf life. It ripens for approximately three months, although

black Milbenkäse should be left to ripen in the chest for one to two years.

CHARACTERISTICS

This cheese is available in 2 oz (50 g) bars or balls, as well as in the form of a so-called "Holunderbirne." It has a hard, brown rind. Young cheeses (3 months) have a waxy consistency but may quickly go hard and crumbly. Amber-colored, strong-flavored cheese with a slightly bitter note.

SPECIAL FEATURES

Consuming the rind may help alleviate allergic reaction to domestic dust mites.

SERVING SUGGESTIONS

Würchwitzer Milbenkäsebutter and Bummler Butter are two tasty snacks comprising butter mixed with fresh pieces of cheese. Sommelier's recommendation: Sweet wines, such as Spätlese or Auslese.

Original Nieheimer cheese

Sour-milk cheese made from
cow's milk
1% FDM

ORIGINS AND HISTORY
Nieheim, Höxter district in eastern
Westphalia-Lippe
A newspaper article extolling Nieheimer
cheese was published in 1858. The area
surrounding the town of Nieheim has a
long history of cheese making. The
hedgerows (a fence of hazel shrubs and
willow branches) surrounding the fields
in the region were home to many delicious herbs, which were eaten by the
cows who produced correspondingly
aromatic milk. Wild hops likewise grew
in these hedgerows, and they were once
used to wrap the cheese for drying.
Nieheimer cheese is consequently sometimes known as "hop cheese." Nowadays
this specialty cheese is produced locally
by only two cheese-making firms.

PRODUCTION
Dry, low-fat sour milk curd cheese is
finely ground and left to ripen for three
to five days. At the appropriate
moment, the ripening process is halted
by the addition of salt to the low fat
curds before the cheese is turned into
"Handkäse" with salt, caraway, and
water. The cheese becomes firmer and
harder the longer it is stored. It may
become so hard that it is suitable for
grating (which is why it is known locally
as grating cheese).

CHARACTERISTICS
Small, round, golden-yellow medal-
lions, each weighing about 1 oz (35 g).
Tasty, sharp, and spicy with a distinct
caraway aroma. Nieheimer cheese will
keep for several weeks.

SPECIAL FEATURES
Nieheimer cheese was one of the deciding factors for the choice of Nieheim as
a venue for the German Cheese Market.
Every two years the town plays host to
a market that presents farmhouse
cheeses sourced from all over Europe.
Nieheimer cheese is also represented
on the Slow Food "Ark of Taste."

SERVING SUGGESTIONS
Sommelier's recommendation: The best
accompaniment is a glass of local beer.
However, if wine is preferred, aromatic
varieties with a delicate, sweet flavor—
for example a Gewürztraminer Spätlese—also go well with this cheese.

Altenburger Ziegenkäse (PDO)

Soft cheese made from cow's and goat's milk
45% FDM

ORIGINS AND HISTORY
Saxony, Thuringia
This traditional Thuringian specialty, which has been granted a protected designation of origin, dates back to the middle of the nineteenth century, when it was produced exclusively on individual farms. After 1900, Altenburger Ziegenkäse (Altenburg goat's cheese) began to be produced by dairies on a much larger scale and reached a peak of popularity. During the days of the GDR, production dropped dramatically and only began to increase again after reunification.

PRODUCTION
The milk used in Altenburger Ziegenkäse comes from the surrounding countryside. It is first separated according to the type of milk, then cooled, filtered, homogenized, and pasteurized. Goat's milk (a prescribed minimum of 15%) and cow's milk are then combined. It is made into cheese in a continuous process. A pinch of caraway is added to the finely cut curd before it is placed in the molds. The disks are then dry-salted, and they ripen in eight to ten days. During this period, a fine white mold develops on the surface, similar to that found on Camembert—which it resembles in

many respects. The ripening period lasts for eight to ten days.

CHARACTERISTICS
It is produced in flat disks, crescents, or flat rounds. Weight varies from 4½ oz (125 g) for crescents to 9 oz (250 g) for disks and over 3 lb (1.5 kg) for rounds. The thin natural rind has a covering of white mold. The cheese itself is yellowish in color with virtually no holes and is a little drier and firmer than Camembert. It has a mild and delicate flavor and a delicious aroma of goat's milk.

SERVING SUGGESTIONS
Sommelier's recommendation: This cheese specialty is excellently complemented by aromatic Sauvignon Blancs and fresh Rieslings, as well as by wines with a suggestion of residual sweetness and fruity, aromatic reds.

SOUTHERN GERMANY
Quality and tradition

The tradition of cheese making in southern Germany dates back to the Middle Ages, since when the excellent reputation of Bavarian and Baden-Württemberg cheeses has extended far beyond national borders. One of the reasons for this is the high quality of the milk. Also significant is the fact that cheese producers continue to set great store by preserving traditional recipes and skills. Apart from the major manufacturers, there is also a large number of small and medium-sized cheese factories. The Allgäu region, which lies partly in Bavaria and partly in Baden-Württemberg, is generally seen as Germany's "cheese kitchen." This region of green meadows, gentle hills, and high mountains encompasses numerous alpine farms that produce the famous Allgäu mountain cheese, to name but one example. Furthermore, many of the big German cheese manufacturers have their processing plants in the Allgäu or in neighboring Swabia. The most successful varieties on the market include Allgäuer Emmentaler; specialty cheeses designed for melting; soft cheeses with white, blue, or red mold; Limburger, Romadur, and Weißlacker. For centuries, cheese was made in monasteries all over Old and Upper Bavaria and some of today's recipes date back to those times. The preference in Old and Upper Bavaria is for strong, aromatic cheeses such as Limburger and Romadur. The central mountain regions of Hohenlohe, Franconia, and the Upper Palatinate are similarly known for some notable specialties.

Left: In southern Germany people enjoy their comforts, including hearty food.

Allgäuer Emmentaler (PDO)

Hard cheese made from
raw cow's milk
45% FDM

ORIGINS AND HISTORY
Allgäu

In 1821, the master dairyman Josef Aurel
Stadler brought two Swiss dairymen to
Weiler to work as "development assis-
tants." Although round, hard cheese had
been produced in the area for centuries,
the results had never been altogether
satisfactory. It was a further six years
before the efforts of the two cheese
makers culminated in the continuous
production of the cheese in Gunzes-
rieder Tal. Not until 1840 was a top-class
cheese developed. The introduction of
Swiss-style maturing rooms played a
major role in improving quality.

PRODUCTION

Allgäuer Emmentaler is made in the
same way as Swiss Emmentaler,
although its ripening period of three
months is somewhat shorter. During this
time the cheese will spend at least four
weeks maturing at a minimum temperature of 68 °F (20 °C) in a ripening cellar.

CHARACTERISTICS

Round loaves, diameter 28–33 in
(70–85 cm), height 6–10 in (15–25 cm),
weight 132–290 lb (60–130 kg). It is also
available in blocks 26 x 26 x 6 in (66 x
66 x 16 cm) of at least 88 lb (40 kg). It
has a smooth, waxed, golden-yellow
natural rind, a supple texture, and holes
the size of cherry pits. It is slightly
aromatic with nutty undertones, and its
taste becomes sharper with age. Large
and elongated holes denote a mild
flavor, while small, round holes indicate
a full-bodied, strong-tasting cheese.

SERVING SUGGESTIONS

Sommelier's recommendation: Full-
bodied white wines such as a Württem-
berg Kerner, an Austrian Grüner
Veltliner, or a Soave Classico from
Veneto make excellent accompaniments. Aromatic, fruity red wines such
as a Baden Spätburgunder, Beaujolais, or
Bardolino complement this cheese too.

SIMILAR CHEESE VARIETIES

Hard, Emmentaler-style cheeses are
also made from pasteurized milk. Most
of these foil-ripened cheeses are stored
for a shorter period, have a milder
flavor, and are less typical.

Allgäuer Bergkäse (PDO)

Hard cheese made from raw cow's milk
45% FDM

ORIGINS AND HISTORY

Allgäu

This Allgäu mountain cheese may be produced only in the Allgäu Alp areas of Lindau district about Lake Constance, Oberallgäu, Ostallgäu, Unterallgäu, and Ravensburg, as well as in Kaufbeuren, Kempten, and Memmingen—and only from milk produced in these areas. Mountain cheese was initially produced in the Allgäu alpine pastures. As the number of local cheese dairies increased about 1820, cheese making moved down from the mountains and into the valleys. By 1840, important cheese-making dairies had sprung up all over the region.

PRODUCTION

The evening milk is skimmed the next morning and mixed with the morning milk. The milk is warmed and rennet is added. The curd is cut into pea- to hazel-nut-sized pieces, which are reheated to 122 °F (50 °C) and stirred. Finally, the cheese is removed from the vat with a cloth and pressed over the course of 24 hours with an increasing pressure of 2–4 lb per lb of cheese (5–8 kg per kg), being turned three times in the process. The next morning the cheese is immersed in a salt bath for at least one day, after which it is left to mature for two months in a cellar at a temperature of 60 °F (16 °C). During this time it is washed in brine and turned two or three times a week. After a further month of maturing at 54 °F (12 °C), it will have reached its peak of maturity for consumption. The minimum age for Allgäuer Bergkäse is four months, but it may be stored for up to one year.

CHARACTERISTICS

Wheels with a diameter of 16–35 in (40–90 cm), 3–4 in (8–10 cm) thick, weight 33–110 lb (15–50 kg). The rind is dark yellow to brownish. Dense, smooth, and pale yellow cheese with small, pea-sized air bubbles. Typical nutty flavor and delicate, milky aroma.

SERVING SUGGESTIONS

Sommelier's recommendation: It is an important ingredient in the preparation of cheese Spätzle. It is best eaten with full-bodied, aromatic wines such as Müller-Thurgau and Gewürztraminer.

TASTY REDS

The Germans have rediscovered their love of red bacterial rind cheeses. Limburger and its close relatives—such as the somewhat milder and smaller Romadur, Münster cheese (a traditional variety of Alsace-style cheese produced in the Black Forest), and Weinkäse (small blocks of cheese with a particularly mild taste)—are regarded as the classics of the group, which are known rather unappetizingly as red smear cheeses. More recently, they have come to be classified in somewhat more delicate terms as red bacterial rind cheeses. They are so called thanks to the special method by which they are produced. Prior to ripening, this soft cheese is washed in brine and smeared with a fungal culture to promote the growth of a red bacterial rind, forming a moist and slightly oily surface. Since the bacterial culture requires oxygen to grow, it is not smeared or sprayed on until after the cheese has been shaped and salted. The desired aroma is produced by bacterial enzymes breaking down proteins on the surface of the cheese. The development of the eventual aroma is strongly dependent on the moisture content of the cheese surface. The moister the cheese, the stronger its typical flavor. The growth of red bacterial cultures may be further stimulated by adding organisms such as yeast. The presence of *Bacteria linens* itself produces pigments (carotene) that give the rind its color. Modern, industrially produced cheeses with red bacterial rinds differ in flavor and appearance from the classic cheeses. They are milder yet piquant at the same time, and have a creamy consistency and an attractive appearance.

Obazda

Cheese product made from
Camembert and spices
45% FDM

ORIGINS AND HISTORY
Bavaria
The history of Bavarian Obazda is closely entwined with that of the Bavarian beer garden. Camembert and Brie first began to be produced in Germany about the same time as beer gardens began to spring up throughout the country. It was the Eisenreich family, landlords of the Bräustüberl in Weihenstephan near Munich, that were first accredited with the invention of this Bavarian specialty. They hit upon the idea of using up the remains of fairly strong Camembert by mixing it with butter and adding onions and spices to the mixture. Obazda or Obatzter (in Franconia this specialty is known as Gerupfter) soon became popular in Bavarian beer gardens and, at the same time, provided people with a cheap snack. This cheese product is now inextricably associated with beer gardens and has become a classic on the Bavarian snack menu. It is made on an industrial scale only in Bavaria.

PRODUCTION
The cheese mixture consists of 30–60% Camembert and/or Brie, with Romadur and/or Limburger cheese if desired, fresh cheese, butter, spices and spice extracts, onions, and salt. Cream and casein may also be added to Obazda, if wished. The addition of cream makes the Obazda more digestible and easier to spread. A little beer may also be used in the making of Obazda to help improve the flavor. Traditional methods dictate that no preserving or thickening agent may be used in its manufacture. Caraway and paprika are the spices used to round off the flavor.

CHARACTERISTICS
Hearty, piquant flavor, soft and spreadable.

SERVING SUGGESTIONS
Sommelier's recommendation: Obazda is best enjoyed with an aromatic light beer, fresh pretzels or hearty rustic-style bread, and radishes.

Romadur

Soft cheese made from
cow's milk
45% FDM

ORIGINS AND HISTORY
Mainly Bavaria
No one knows for sure where the name
of this cheese originated. Some experts
suggest it derives from the French word
remoudre (to milk again). A piquant
Herve cheese known as Remoudou was
indeed popular in Belgium. Like
Limburger cheese, Romadur was introduced to the Allgäu in 1830 by Karl
Hirnbein.

PRODUCTION
Starter cultures and rennet are added
to the milk and the curd produced is cut
into hazelnut-size pieces (somewhat
smaller than in the case of Limburger
cheese) and placed in molds without
being reheated. After being turned
several times, the cheese is placed in a
salt bath for 12–16 hours. After this, it
is stored at a temperature of 57 °F
(14 °C) and over 90% relative humidity
for 14 days. During this period the
cheese is smeared with *Bacteria
linens*.

CHARACTERISTICS
Romadur is a soft cheese with a red
bacterial rind. It is usually produced
in brick form weighing about 4 oz
(100–25 g). It is rindless and its treatment with red bacteria gives it a yellow
or red surface. The washed rind hides a
compact, soft cheese of fine creamy
consistency. Its taste may vary from
mild to sharp, but it is somewhat milder
than Limburger cheese.

SERVING SUGGESTIONS
Ideally, Romadur should be served with
a mature Gewürztraminer.

Edelpilzkäse

Semi-soft cheese made from
cow's milk
45%, 50%, and 60% FDM

ORIGINS AND HISTORY
Bavaria
Many of the cheeses made in Bavaria
and other German cheese-producing
regions are based on recipes that
imitate foreign neighbors. This is true,
for instance, of German Edelpilzkäse
(noble fungus cheese), a blue-veined
cheese that is very similar to Roquefort.
Unlike Roquefort, it is made not from
raw ewe's milk but pasteurized cow's
milk. However, regulations do permit
ewe's milk, or a combination of the two,
to be used in the production of this
cheese.

PRODUCTION
Edelpilzkäse, which bears considerable
similarity with Roquefort and Danish
Blue, has characteristic blue-green
veins of mold created by injecting the
cheese with air canals and adding mold
cultures (*Penicillium roqueforti*
only). The cheese reaches its peak of
maturity after a ripening period of at
least five weeks, when the mold on the
rind is seen to "bloom."

CHARACTERISTICS
Round wheels, diameter about 7 in
(17 cm), weighing 4–11 lb (2–5 kg).
Rindless cheese with a pale whitish
surface, packed in protective foil. The

cheese is creamy yet also crumbly, with
well-defined blue-green veins. This
cheese has a distinctive aroma with the
characteristic overtones of blue-green
mold. Its taste becomes more intense as
it matures.

SERVING SUGGESTIONS
Sommelier's recommendation: Appropriate wines to accompany the young
cheese include Spätlese and Auslese
wines, as well as full-bodied fruity
wines, low in tannins. The more mature
cheese goes best with port wines,
robust sweet wines, or dessert wines,
such as Sauternes and Tokaji Aszu.

FRESH CHEESES FROM GERMANY

Fresh cheese and the popular Quark (a curd cheese, also known in Bavaria as Topfen), are products that are closely related to one another in terms of the way they are produced. Curd cheese is available in all fat-content categories but is most commonly found as a low fat version. Numerous varieties are produced by different manufacturers, offering a choice of consistency, with a range of extra ingredients and even the addition of cream. One of the coarser versions, originally produced in the USA, is cottage cheese. Another type of German curd cheese is Schichtkäse or layered cheese, a somewhat firmer version of curd cheese. It owes its name to the way individual layers are piled on top of one another during production. In the case of fresh cheese and fresh cheese preparations, there is an even greater variety available on the market. These cheeses can be either creamy in consistency (in some cases frothy) or have a semi-soft texture. The taste, packaging and shape, ingredients, and fat content depend entirely on consumer preference.

CREAMY BLUE-VEINED CHEESES FOR BEGINNERS

German cheese factories are constantly at pains to develop ever more new varieties of cheese and innovative products. They have been particularly successful in this respect with the types of blue-veined soft cheeses that have been on the market since the late 1950s. These were originally conceived as a type of Gorgonzola. Despite their distinctive blue-cheese flavor, they are considerably milder than their traditional role models, and newcomers to blue cheese can acquire a taste for this type of cheese on a gradual basis. The fine, white Camembert-type mold that forms on the surface of the cheese is also helpful in this respect. The group of white mold cheeses known as white-blue cheese is also available in a large variety of shapes and sizes, with fat contents ranging up to 70% FDM. This type of cheese is creamy and aromatic and sometimes has a strong piquant flavor. It ripens in just two to three weeks.

Weißlacker (Bierkäse)

Semi-hard cheese made from
pasteurized cow's milk
40% FDM

ORIGINS AND HISTORY
Bavaria

Weißlacker is often referred to by its
alternative name of Bavarian Bierkäse.
It is a classic if somewhat neglected
Bavarian specialty. In former times it
was popular in the Allgäu as a white
cheese designed for spreading, and was
then produced in a flat shape. It was
invented in 1874 by Josef and Anton
Kramer, two brothers from Wertach.
Starting with a traditional brick cheese,
they increased the salt and fat content
so that it would keep longer. In 1876, the
Kramers were granted a 15-year royal
patent for their cheese.

PRODUCTION

Milk for this cheese comes from alpine
farms situated over 2,600 ft (800 m)
above sea level. After the rennet has
been added, the curd is carefully cut
into walnut-sized pieces and scooped
out onto tables after two to three hours.
After turning, the cheese is immersed
in a 20% salt bath for two days. The
cheese spends six weeks in a warm
room, where it is rubbed twice a week
with salt. Finally, it is left to ripen for
nine months in cold storage. Production is tricky and not without risk.

CHARACTERISTICS

In the form of a cube, approximately
5 in (12.5 cm) long, weighing about 4 lb
(1.7–2 kg), and often packaged in small
pieces of up to 2 oz (60 g) each. This
cheese is practically rindless, with a
watery coating. It is white, crumbly, and
a little greasy but not sticky. It is sharp
to strong in taste, full-bodied, and
substantial with a very intensive aroma.

SPECIAL FEATURES

Weißlacker is represented in the Slow
Food "Ark of Taste."

SERVING SUGGESTIONS

Weißlacker is traditionally eaten as a
snack cut into small chunks on buttered
bread and accompanied by fresh
radishes and a pinch of pepper. Its salty
flavor produces a great thirst for beer,
so it is wise to have adequate supplies
of cold, light beer to hand.

Limburger

Soft cheese made from
cow's milk
20–50% FDM

ORIGINS AND HISTORY
Bavaria

Limburger cheese is named after the Belgian town and district of Limburg, where it is also known as Herve cheese (see entry). In 1830 Karl Hirnbein introduced this cheese to the Allgäu. He employed two Belgian brothers by the name of Groesjan to produce this soft cheese. The Allgäu version of Limburger cheese has become a popular German cheese. It grew in importance to such an extent that for a long period of time the price of Limburger cheese, like that of Emmentaler, formed part of the equation in calculating the price of milk. Limburger is also known as brick or block cheese.

PRODUCTION
This cheese is very difficult to produce since it is very sensitive to the surrounding external conditions during its preparation and ripening period. During the first ten days it is frequently washed with a special red bacterial solution that promotes a reddish growth on the moist rind. After approximately two weeks of ripening in conditions of high humidity, it is ready for consumption. The higher the cheese's fat content, the softer the cheese and the stronger the taste.

CHARACTERISTICS
Small blocks or bricks, varying in height, breadth, and length. This red smear cheese is usually sold in packs weighing around 7–18 oz (200–500 g). It is a rindless cheese with a yellow or red surface color. The cheese is compact and smooth in texture with a firm white center, becoming light yellow toward the edges. It is soft and creamy and has an aromatic, spicy flavor. The quality of Limburger suffers if it is allowed to become soft and runny and the rind goes oily. This cheese is best eaten when its texture is still firm and slightly elastic.

SERVING SUGGESTIONS
Limburger makes a delicious snack marinated in vinegar and served with onions. It is a good companion to all types of bread when served with beer or dry white wines.

SWITZERLAND
Centuries of cheese-making tradition

Switzerland consists of three main regions: the Jura, the Alps, and the Swiss midland. About 80% of the cultivated area is unsuitable for farming and is used instead as grazing land for livestock. Dairy farming is older than the country itself. A thriving cheese trade existed with Italy as early as the fifteenth century, when mules were used to transport wheels of cheese across the Alps, returning with spices, wine, and rice. Switzerland has an international reputation for its cheese varieties. Worldwide, cheese makers have benefited from Swiss expertise in the production of Emmentaler cheese.

Switzerland produces a vast variety of different types of cheese. Approximately one third of all its cheeses are exported abroad. Emmentaler, Gruyère, and Sbrinz—as well as Appenzeller and Tête de Moine—are among the country's most famous cheeses, both at home and abroad. Switzerland also produces creamy soft cheese, mild Tommes, and aromatic red smear cheese.

Swiss cheese production is a decentralized affair. About two-thirds of its cheeses are made in small, family-run cheese dairies that are supplied with deliveries of fresh milk from local farms. The cows that produce the milk are not allowed to eat silage fodder.

Switzerland has its own AOC cheese specialties with protected designations of origin. On account of Switzerland's unique position in terms of European trade, these are not (yet) recognized on a European level. Switzerland has ensured, however, that its AOC and IGP products conform to European standards.

Left: View of the Wooden Bridge in Lucerne.

Berner Alpkäse AOC

Hard cheese made from
raw cow's milk
50% FDM

ORIGINS AND HISTORY

Bernese Oberland

Cheese has been produced among the alps of the Bernese Oberland since the fifteenth century. It was traditionally consumed as a young alpine cheese or as a Hobelkäse (grating cheese), which had been stored and matured for several years. Berner Alpkäse and Hobelkäse may be produced only during the summer months while the cows are grazing on the high pastures and on only one of the 560 alps in the Bernese Oberland.

PRODUCTION

Each day the fresh milk is turned into cheese in a copper vat heated over a wood fire. After the milk has been coagulated by the addition of natural rennet and special bacterial cultures, the curd/whey mixture is cut and heated to about 127 °F (53 °C) under constant stirring. After being pressed, the cheese is placed in a salt bath for 24 hours, after which the wheels of cheese are matured in a ripening room, where they are regularly rubbed with salt and a smear. When winter comes, the young Alpkäse is moved to a central cheese-ripening storehouse. There it is stored and tended for a further six to twelve months in conditions of at least 70% humidity and at a temperature of about

54 °F (12 °C). Hobelkäse is made exclusively from cheeses that have been matured for an extra-long period (*surchoix*) and have remained on the alp the whole time. The rind smear is completely removed before the wheels of cheese are left to mature for at least a further 12 months in a ripening room kept at a constant temperature.

CHARACTERISTICS

The wheels are 9–18 in (28–48 cm) in diameter and weigh 11–31 lb (5–14 kg). Alpkäse has a dry rind with a small amount of smear. Its tasty flavor develops and becomes more pronounced with age. Because the milk is processed in an open vat over a wood fire, the resulting cheese has a smoky note. Thanks to its long maturing period, Hobelkäse is an extra-hard cheese with a dry, smooth rind. Two- to three-year-old cheeses are said to be fully developed in terms of the true, spicy Hobelkäse character.

NOT EVERY ALPINE CHEESE IS AN ALPKÄSE

Bergkäse, or mountain cheese, is produced throughout the year by local village dairies in mountain valleys. In other words, it is also produced in the winter when the cows are in their cattle sheds, being fed with hay. Pasteurized milk is used in Bergkäse in some cases. Alpkäse, on the other hand, is produced only in summer, when it is made on site up in the grazing pastures. The cows are left to roam freely, grazing among the lush, rich alpine meadows. The fresh, aromatic alpine herbs and flowers lend a unique flavor to the raw milk, which is often still warm from the cow and has to be transported only a short distance before it can be turned into cheese—more often than not in the traditional manner in a copper vat over a wood fire. Each alp produces milk with a typically individual flavor since the herbs and flowers that grow in the alpine pastures differ from one alp to another. The wood fire over which the cheese is warmed, as well as the individual expertise of the cheese makers, produce different nuances in taste and flavor. Alpkäse comes in many different sizes, colors, and shapes and with varying degrees of ripeness and hardness. These range from semi-hard cheese to an extra-hard version that has been left to mature over an extra-long period and is designed for grating, crumbling, or shaving. With tastes ranging from pleasantly mild to sharp and spicy, Alpkäse has something to appeal to everyone. Over half the cheeses produced in the Swiss mountains carry the AOC seal, which guarantees their geographic origin. Alpkäse is very versatile, but it works best with companions from its own region, such as full-bodied wines, crusty bread, potatoes, nuts, or pears.

Right: During the summer months, delicious Alpkäse is produced up on the high alpine pastures.

Below: A cow grazes in a lush alpine meadow filled with an abundance of aromatic flowers and grasses.

Alpen Tilsiter

Semi-hard cheese made from
raw cow's milk
45% FDM

ORIGINS AND HISTORY
Thurgau, St. Gallen
In 1893, Otto Wartmann brought the recipe for this cheese from Tilsit in East Prussia back to his native Thurgau, enhancing it with the addition of alpine herbs and local wine.

PRODUCTION
Once the cheese is made, the wheels of Tilsiter are placed in cool, damp cellars to ripen for four to six months, during which they are turned on a daily basis and rubbed regularly with a mixture of alpine herbs and Müller-Thurgau white wine.

CHARACTERISTICS
Flat, round wheels with a grayish-black rind and with a diameter of 10–12 in (25–30 cm), about 3 in (8 cm) high and weighing 9–10 lb (4–4.5 kg). The cheese is ivory to pale yellow in color with small round holes. It has a delicately spicy taste.

SERVING SUGGESTIONS
In its native region it is often accompanied by a locally produced apple wine. A red late harvest Burgunder also makes a good partner for this cheese.

ST. GALLEN KLOSTER-KÄSE — SMALL AND DELICIOUS

St. Gallen Klosterkäse is produced in a handful of artisanal cheese dairies in the cantons of St. Gallen and Appenzell. It is one of Switzerland's most popular cheeses. This cow's milk cheese has a smeared, brownish-yellow rind and is smooth and elastic. It is allowed to mature for 10 to 14 weeks, during which St. Gallen Klosterkäse develops a distinctive and well-rounded aroma. A Riesling-Sylvaner from eastern Switzerland is the classic accompaniment, but a velvety Pinot Noir also makes a good partner.

Appenzeller

Semi-hard cheese made from
raw cow's milk
Minimum 48% FDM

ORIGINS AND HISTORY

*Canton of Appenzell and parts of the
St. Gallen and Thurgau cantons*

In northeastern Switzerland lies the
tranquil canton of Appenzell, which is
characterized by meadows and lush
pastures. The first recorded mention of
Appenzell cheese was 700 years ago.
During the Middle Ages the monks from
the monastery at St. Gallen acquired a
taste for this spicy specialty, which they
received in the form of tithes from
Appenzell farmers. Today, the cheese is
produced by more than 70 dairies.

PRODUCTION

Appenzeller cheese is made from raw
milk produced by cows that have fed
exclusively on grass and hay. Some of
the milk is skimmed, mixed with whole
milk, and coagulated with lactic acid
bacterial cultures and rennet. The corn-
sized curd is heated under constant stirring until the desired degree of firmness
is reached, then placed in a mold. Next,
the cheese is washed in brine and left
to ripen in conditions of 90% humidity
and at a temperature of 57–59 °F
(14–15 °C). During this period, a herbal
brine—the recipe for which remains a
strictly guarded secret—is applied
regularly to the rind as it cures. The
maturing time is at least three months.

CHARACTERISTICS

Round wheels with a diameter of
12–13 in (30–33 cm), 3–4 in (7–9 cm)
thick, and with a weight of 14–16 lb
(6.4–7.4 kg). Appenzeller's natural
brushed rind is yellow to reddish-brown
in color. Inside, it is ivory to pale yellow
with pea-sized holes. This cheese
comes in several categories of maturity:
Appenzeller Classic has a full, fruity
flavor and ripens for at least three
months. Surchoix, a stronger, tangier
version, matures for four months, while
Appenzeller Extra, a very strong
cheese, has a guaranteed age of six
months or more.

SERVING SUGGESTIONS

Sommelier's recommendation: Gutedel/
Chasselas, Müller-Thurgau / Riesling-
Sylvaner, as well as a Johannisberg du
Valais all make good partners, while
fitting reds include a smooth Walliser
Pinot Noir and a typical Cornalin.

Emmentaler AOC

Hard cheese made from
raw cow's milk
45% FDM

ORIGINS AND HISTORY
Canton of Bern
Emmentaler cheese gets its name from the Emme valley and its origins date back to the thirteenth century. Family farms were normally passed on to the youngest son, while the older brothers were given a cash payment only. Many of them worked as cowherds in the cheese-making business. After the first cheese dairies were established in the valleys about 1815, cheese production spread across the entire Swiss midland.

PRODUCTION
The milk for this cheese is supplied by cows fed exclusively on grasses and hay. The milk is heated with the addition of bacterial cultures and natural rennet. A cheese harp is used to cut the curd into small pieces, and the curd/whey mixture is heated to 126–129 °F (52–54 °C) under constant stirring. The cheese is then transferred to a mold and pressed under an increasing hydraulic pressure for about 20 hours. The wheels are next placed in a salt bath for two days. They then remain in a cool cellar for 5 to 20 days at a temperature of 54–61 °F (12–16 °C), before being moved to a warm ripening room at a temperature of 66–75 °F (19–24 °C), where they remain for a further six to eight weeks.

Young Emmentaler is ready for sale at four months; Emmentaler Extra, Surchoix, or Reserve ripen for at least eight months. Cave-aged Emmentaler cheese matures for a minimum of 12 months and spends 6 months ripening in a cave.

CHARACTERISTICS
Large wheels weighing 165–220 lb (75–100 kg). Fine, supple texture with walnut-sized holes. Winter-produced cheese tends to be ivory in color whereas summer cheese is pale yellow. The cheese has a nutty, fruity flavor that becomes sharper and spicier with age.

SERVING SUGGESTIONS
Emmentaler tastes delicious with dark, nutty, or fruity types of bread. Full-bodied, mature red wines such as Dôle and Pinot Noir, as well as white wines such as Humagne Blanche, Malvoisie, and Ermitage du Valais make good companions to this cheese.

Le Gruyère AOC

Hard cheese made from
raw cow's milk
49% FDM

ORIGINS AND HISTORY
Western Switzerland
In 1115 a charter granted the first count
of Gruyère the right to all the cheese
that was produced in the mountains of
the Gruyère region. During the Middle
Ages, Gruyère cheese was exported to
Vevey and Geneva, and later to Lyons,
Paris, and Italy. From 1860 it was even
being exported to the English and
Dutch colonies in India.

PRODUCTION
The milk is poured into copper vats with
starter cultures and natural rennet. The
curd is heated to 131 °F (55 °C), then
pressed in a form under high pressure.
Finally it is transferred to a salt bath for
24 hours before being stored in a cellar
at 55–57 °F (13–14 °C). Young Gruyère
is matured for four to five months and
mature Gruyère Reserve is kept for up
to 12 months. During the first ten days,
the wheels of cheese are turned each
day and washed in brine; thereafter this
treatment occurs only twice a week.

CHARACTERISTICS
Wheels with an oily, brownish grainy
rind. These vary in size from 4-5 in
(9.5–12 cm) in thickness, 22–25 in
(55–65 cm) in diameter, and weigh
55–88 lb (25–40 kg). This fine, firm

cheese is slightly crumbly and ivory
colored. Its fruity flavors and aromas
vary depending on where it is produced
and reveal a salty note. A well-aged
Gruyère has a sharper and spicier taste.

SPECIAL FEATURES
Gruyère Alpage is produced only in the
summer months on the high alpine
pastures of the Alps and Jura.

SERVING SUGGESTIONS
In Switzerland, Le Gruyère is one of the
most popular cheeses used for cheese
fondue. However, it also makes an
excellent ingredient for use in gratin
dishes, baked savory dishes, and cheese
soufflés. Fairly fruity wines such as
Fendant, or a red wine such as Dôle,
work well with young Gruyère. A
mature Gruyère is best accompanied by
robust whites such as Malvoisie du
Valais or mature reds, such as Merlot or
Cabernet-Sauvignon.

Glarner Schabziger

Sour milk cheese made from
cow's milk
3% FDM

ORIGINS AND HISTORY
Graubünden/Glarnerland
Glarner Schabziger cheese is thought to
be Switzerland's oldest cheese product.
Historical records show that Schabziger
cheese was produced in the Glarner
Alps as long as 1,000 years ago. The date
of April 24th 1463 is regarded as particularly significant as it was on this day
that a law was passed stating that all
producers of Ziger were obliged to
observe certain quality regulations and
supply their products with a seal of
origin. Glarnerland was once home to a
large number of Ziger producers, but
nowadays the only manufacturer is
Geska AG in Glarus. The Swiss affectionately refer to the truncated cone-
shaped cheese as "Zigerstöggli."

PRODUCTION
The production of Glarner Schabziger
is unusual as very few cheeses nowdays
are produced by the process of heat-
acid precipitation. Natural lactic acid is
added to fresh, skimmed cow's milk.
As the milk is heated to over 194 °F
(90 °C), the milk curdles. The curd is
separated from the whey and transferred to fermentation containers while
still at hand temperature. Here it undergoes an initial period of fermentation
and ripening for 4 to 12 weeks. The raw
curd is then transported to Glarus,
where it is ground into powder, mixed
with salt, and stored in silos for three to
eight months. A further period of
fermentation and maturation follows.
The cheese is then finely ground and
mixed with blue fenugreek that gives it
its color. Modern machinery presses the
cheese into molds that shape it into its
traditional *stöckli* form.

CHARACTERISTICS
Truncated cone, dry, coarse-grained,
green-tinged rind, and hard, dry
texture. It has a unique and piquant
taste with slightly tart undertones and
a very pungent smell.

SERVING SUGGESTIONS
Schabziger is an excellent grating
cheese, used for flavoring and enrich-
ing various dishes. It is often served with
Gschwelten (a warm potato dish) or
mixed with butter and spread on bread.

Tête de Moine AOC

Semi-hard cheese made from
raw cow's milk
51% FDM

ORIGINS AND HISTORY
Swiss Jura

Tête de Moine has over 800 years of tradition. The first mention of this cheese was in 1192, when it was used as a form of payment. It has been known as Tête de Moine (monk's head) since 1790. It is unclear whether this is a reference to the similarity between the "shaven" cheese and a monk's tonsure or whether it is a reference to the storage of cheese "per monk's head." Monks were evicted from the monastery during the French Revolution but cheese continued to be produced in the former abbey's cheese dairies.

PRODUCTION

Tête de Moine is now produced in nine dairies. The evening milk is mixed with the next morning's milk. Rennet is added and the resulting mass is heated again before being pressed into molds to form small cylinder-shape wheels. The cheese continues to be pressed and turned until the whey has drained off. The cheese is then immersed in brine for 12 hours. The young cheese is placed on pine boards to mature for three to four months in cool, humid cellars. They are brushed with a mixture of saline and bacteria culture so that they form a smear on their rind.

CHARACTERISTICS

Cylindrical rounds, 4–6 in (10–15 cm) in diameter. They must be at least 70% and at most 100% of the diameter in height and weigh 25–32 oz (700–900 g). The cheese has a firm brown rind and its color varies, depending on season, from ivory (in winter) to a rich yellow (in summer). It has a supple consistency and melts easily on the tongue. Tête de Moine has a clean and aromatic flavor.

SERVING SUGGESTIONS

Tête de Moine is shaved into very thin slices—ideally by means of a device known as a *girolle*. The cheese is pared into wafer-thin rosettes, which allows the full flavor of the cheese to develop. It makes the perfect starter to serve with an aperitif or as part of a cheese board. Wine tip: Oeil de Perdrix, Pinot Noir, and Dôle Blanche. A punchy Chasselas from the Dézaley region with its mineral overtones also works very well.

Tomme Vaudoise

Soft cheese made from
cow's milk
45% FDM

ORIGINS AND HISTORY

French-speaking Switzerland (Waadt, Geneva)

Production of Tommes is believed to have begun during the seventeenth century, when it was made in alpine chalets in the Vallée de Joux region. It provided small cheese dairies with a solution for times when the milk yield was low. The first occurrence of the name "Tomme Vaudoise" was recorded in 1902. During the seventeenth century this cheese was produced only in summer in alpine dairies situated in the Swiss Jura. It soon became so popular that people began making it in the village dairies down in the valleys.

PRODUCTION

Typical soft cheese production method, using raw or pasteurized milk. Maturation takes seven to ten days. Tomme Vaudoise is made from raw milk delivered twice a day to the dairy. The cows are fed primarily on grass and hay. The milk is turned into cheese, placed into molds, and left to drain for five to eight hours without pressing. After salting or immersion in a salt bath for fifteen to sixty minutes, the rounds of cheese are matured for seven to fourteen days. The small wheels are turned regularly until reaching the desired degree of ripeness.

CHARACTERISTICS

Flattish wheels with a diameter of about 3 in (8 cm) and weighing approximately 3½ oz (100 g). A delicate, white crusty rind with a dusting of white mold. Soft to runny consistency, and mild, slightly milky taste that becomes sharper with age.

SERVING SUGGESTIONS

A very young Tomme may be paired with white wines such as Gutedel and Chardonnay. Riper specimens may also be teamed with red wines such as Salvagnin (Spätburgunder/Gamay).

Vacherin Fribourgeois AOC

Semi-hard cheese made from
raw cow's milk
48% FDM

ORIGINS AND HISTORY
Freiburgerland
The word *vacherin* is said to stem from the Latin *vaccarinus* (little cowherd). In the alpine meadows, it was the young boys' job to help milking and tending the cows. While the adults concentrated on producing the giant Gruyère, the young cowherds' task would be to make the smaller Vacherin cheeses. In earlier times, Vacherin was traditionally produced in the alpine pastures, but by the early nineteenth century production had begun to spread to the village cheese dairies down in the valley.

PRODUCTION
Vacherin Fribourgeois is made with raw milk, natural rennet, a little salt, and lactic acid cultures. Like Gruyère, this cheese matures at a high temperature, which is why they are both often accommodated in the same ripening cellar. The two types originate, after all, in the same region. The young Select version is ripened for 12 weeks, while the Extra variety takes 17 weeks to mature.

CHARACTERISTICS
Round wheels, about 13 in (33 cm) in diameter, 2–4 in (6–9 cm) thick, weighing 15–17 lb (7–7.5 kg). It has a reddish-brown, natural rind, while on the inside it is pale yellow to ivory colored with a fine, smooth, satiny consistency. It is a good melting cheese with small round holes and slits. It is fairly strong and creamy. Vacherin Fribourgeois Alpage is traditionally made in the summer months up in the mountain dairies.

SERVING SUGGESTIONS
Vacherin Fribourgeois is the only semi-hard cheese that melts at a temperature of about 122 °F (50 °C) and needs just the addition of water, making it an ideal fondue cheese.

Vacherin Mont d'Or AOC

Soft cheese made from
cow's milk
50% FDM

ORIGINS AND HISTORY

Waadtländer Jura and Jura foothills
Vacherin Mont d'Or is a specialty cheese
from the Jura region, where it is
produced in the traditional manner by
local cheese makers. The peak of Mont
d'Or is on the French side of the Jura,
but the cows graze on both the Swiss
and French sides. The cheese's AOC
category is shared between France (see
entry) and Switzerland.

PRODUCTION

Following considerable problems
toward the end of the 1980s, the Swiss
no longer make this cheese from raw
milk but rely instead on thermized milk,
to which lactic acid cultures are added.
The gentle thermization process allows
the milk to retain all its natural qualities
while ensuring improved bacteriological conditions. Under AOC regulations,
the use of pasteurized milk is forbid-
den. Traditionally, Vacherin Mont d'Or
is produced only between October and
April. About 15 cheese dairies are
involved in the production of Swiss
Vacherin and about a dozen affineurs
mature the cheese in their cellars.

CHARACTERISTICS

It has a soft, wavy rind and is amber to
reddish-brown in color and covered
with a dusting of white mold. The small
wheels are marketed in round pine
boxes. The cheeses are 1–2 in (3–5 cm)
in thickness with a diameter of 4–13 in
(10–32 cm), and a weight of 14 oz–7 lb
(400 g–3 kg). The ivory-colored paste
is thick and creamy and has a mild, delicate flavor tinged with a hint of pine
bark. It is aged for about one month.

SERVING SUGGESTIONS

Vacherin Mont d'Or is regarded as a
typical dessert cheese or may be served
warm from the oven. It goes well with
potatoes cooked in their skins and may
be eaten with white bread, like a mini-
fondue. The warm cheese combines
very well with Swiss white wines.
Served ripe and in its natural state, it
works well with punchy white wines
from the Wallis region, such as Petite
Arvine, Humagne Blanche, or even a
Heida. If you prefer a red wine, a mature
Pinot Noir also makes a good partner.

SAUERKÄSE AND BLODERKÄSE

The area where Sauermilchkäse (cheese produced from milk that has been curdled by natural souring) is produced is limited to Liechtenstein and parts of the canton of St. Gallen. In Switzerland it is also known as Bloderkäse or Sauerkäse. Farmers from Obertoggenburg, Werdenberg, and the principality of Liechtenstein paid their taxes to the princes, abbots, and governors in the form of "Surchäs" or "Bloderchäs." Historical records of deliveries to the St. Gallen monastery make specific mention of deliveries of "Labkäse"—cheese made with the addition of rennet. It is assumed, therefore, that the remainder of the cheeses listed consisted of Bloderkäse. The name "Bloderkäse" or "Ploderkäse" is mainly used in Toggenburg, where the naturally curdled milk is known as "Bloder" (or "Ploder") in local dialect.

Bloderkäse and Sauerkäse are low fat cheeses which have been produced from cow's milk that has curdled from natural souring without the addition of rennet. The skimmed milk is thickened by means of lactic acid bacterial cultures. The curds are cut, then heated to 113 °F (45 °C). Sometimes a little whole milk, herbs, or spices are added. The cheese is then transferred by hand into molds before being pressed and, in some cases, lightly salted. Bloderkäse is consumed within three weeks of production. It is white in color and fairly soft, porous but without air bubble holes. It has a comparatively neutral flavor and a slightly acidic taste. Sauerkäse is the big brother of Bloderkäse and must spend at least 60 days in ripening. During this time it is brushed regularly with hot water. This treatment encourages the breakdown of milk proteins, which form a type of shiny, yellow rind. The white, smooth interior of Sauerkäse is harder than that of its smaller cousin. It has a very pronounced flavor with a typically distinctive tinge of ammonia.

Bündner Bergkäse

Semi-hard cheese made from
raw cow's milk
45% FDM

ORIGINS AND HISTORY
Graubünden
The alpine meadows situated high in
the Graubünden region are lush with
grasses, flowers, and herbs, all of which
lend a special quality to the milk
produced here.

PRODUCTION
About 500 mountain farms supply
alpine milk to the 13 alpine dairies situated at over 3,300 ft (1,000 m) that
produce this Bündner mountain cheese
specialty. After three months of being
ripened and cared for, the wheels are
brought down into the valley, where the
cheese is stored for a further period
before being marketed. Depending on
the type of cheese, the degree of
ripeness varies from four weeks to nine
months ("Extra" quality cheeses).

CHARACTERISTICS
The wheels weigh about 11 lb (5 kg).
Young, two to four month old Bündner
Bergkäse has a mild, almost velvety
taste, while the nine month old "Extra"
version is aromatic and spicy. This pale,
satiny cheese melts easily on the tongue
and is enveloped in a natural, brown to
reddish rind.

SPECIAL FEATURES
The producers of this cheese market
their Bündner Bergkäse jointly under
the brand name of Piz Bever, after the
10,500 ft (3,200 m) mountain of that
name in the canton of Graubünden.

SERVING SUGGESTIONS
Bündner Bergkäse lends itself perfectly
to warm dishes—it is used in gratins
and cheese-based dishes, but is also a
popular dessert cheese. Excellent
white wine partners include aromatic
Riesling-Sylvaners from eastern
Switzerland and fruity Grauburgun-
ders. A good red wine to drink with this
cheese would be a mature Bündner
Blauburgunder.

Sbrinz AOC

Hard cheese made from
raw cow's milk
45% FDM

ORIGINS AND HISTORY
Central Switzerland
This hard cheese is produced in central Switzerland using traditional methods. As early as the sixteenth century, Sbrinz cheese was being taken to the large central produce market in Brienz to be exported. Historical records show that the Italians named the cheese after the trading centre of Brienz, a name that eventually evolved into "Sbrinz." It was also known in Switzerland as Spalenkäse.

PRODUCTION
The curd is heated to a temperature of 129–135 °F (54–57 °C). The cheese is pressed, then placed in molds, turned several times, and pressed again until it has finished draining. The finished wheel is next plunged in a salt bath for 18 days, before being matured in a dry state for several weeks and "sweated" at a temperature of 64 °F (18 °C). During this time, the cheese loses much of its fat and water content. Finally, it is transferred to a cool ripening room, where it is stored vertically and left to age. Sbrinz must mature for a minimum of 16 months, 12 of which must be spent within the legally designated place of origin. Its traditional method of production in a copper vat and the use of traditional bacterial cultures contribute to Sbrinz's distinctive flavor.

CHARACTERISTICS
Round wheels, 17–26 in (45–65 cm) in diameter, weight 55–100 lb (25–45 kg). It has a rich, spicy, and aromatic flavor, and is very hard, dry, and crumbly in texture. The older the cheese, the more aromatic and spicier its bouquet. It is also marketed in the form of pre-shaven curly rolls of wafer-thin cheese.

SERVING SUGGESTIONS
Sbrinz lends itself to shaving, grating, or breaking into so-called "Möcklis" with a special almond-shaped knife. These thin shavings of cheese are popular served as carpaccio—that is, as a garnish on wafer-thin slices of Bündnerfleisch and sprinkled with vinaigrette. This salty cheese should be accompanied by wines with residual sugar such as Amigne Flétrie or Spätlese and Auslese wines. Alternatively, a well-aged Sbrinz goes well with a robust red such as a Ticino Merlot.

FRESH GOAT'S CHEESE FROM TICINO

Goat farming and the production of goat's cheese have for centuries played an important economic and cultural role in the mountain regions of Ticino. Today the number of goats in the canton exceeds 10,000, a figure that represents 20% of the total number of goats farmed in Switzerland. Two types of goat's cheese are produced in Ticino: Büscium da carva and Robiola. In Ticino dialect *Büscium* means "stopper," and the shape of this cheese does indeed resemble the cork of a bottle laid in oil. The name first appeared in 1920, but the traditions of fresh goat's cheese production in the region date back much further. The small rounds of goat's cheese are produced from full-fat, untreated milk or thermized milk. After pressing, the fresh cheese is hung up in bags to allow the whey to drain off. It takes 24 hours for the curds to form, and the cheese is ready for consumption just one day later. The geographical area of Büscium da carva production encompasses the canton of Ticino and Val de Mesolcina in the canton of Graubünden.

L'Etivaz AOC

Hard cheese made from
raw milk
min. 49% FDM

ORIGINS AND HISTORY
Alpes Vaudoise / Lake Geneva
Etivaz cheese is made only during the
summer months. It is from this that the
cheese gets its name, a derivation of the
French word *estivage*, meaning
"summer grazing"—the cows spend the
summer grazing on the high alpine
pastures. L'Etivaz is also the name of a
village in the area, in which the ripening cellars are situated. In the early
1930s, several producers in the region
joined together in a cooperative to
improve the quality and coordinate the
marketing of their cheese. The first
cheese cellars in L'Etivaz could accom-
modate 3,200 wheels of cheese; nowadays the maturing cellars in the village
have room for 20,000 cheeses.

PRODUCTION
This hard cheese is only made from May
to September. It is produced in approximately 130 mountain cheese dairies
(chalets) by small, local cheese producers. L'Etivaz is traditionally made in
copper vats over an open wood fire.
Once a week, after being pressed and
drained, the wheels are taken down into
the valley, where they are stored in the
ripening cellars of L'Etivaz. Here they
are regularly turned and brushed with
brine. The aging process takes at least

135 days. Quality cheeses for export are
left to ripen for as long as 18 months.

CHARACTERISTICS
Round wheels weighing 22–84 lb
(10–38 kg) with a diameter of 12–26 in
(30–65 cm). The rind is brownish in
color, while the inside of the cheese is
yellowish or ivory colored and fine, firm,
and supple in consistency. It is a clean-
tasting, aromatic cheese with a slightly
fruity flavor incorporating a touch of
hazelnut and a hint of smoke.

SERVING SUGGESTIONS
It is ideal for fondue and other hot
dishes, but tastes equally good served
cold. Recommended wines: Local wines
(e.g. Spätburgunder). There is also a
protected origin wine from L'Etivaz
itself. Chasselas wines from the Waadt-
land, such as Dézaley, Saint-Saphorin,
Epesses, and Aigle also make delicious
partners.

Raclette du Valais AOC

Semi-hard cheese made from
raw cow's milk
50% FDM

ORIGINS AND HISTORY
Valais
Sometime during the sixteenth century,
someone in the Valais region had the
clever idea of placing a block of cheese
over a wood fire and scraping (French
racler) the molten cheese off its
surface. Since 1874 this melting Valais
cheese has been known as Raclette.

PRODUCTION
The curdled milk is pre-pressed, then
placed in wooden molds and pressed
for at least six hours. It is salted either
by immersion in brine or dry, by hand.
The rind smear is encouraged to
develop by means of natural rind smear
cultures present in the dairy. The
cheese is then aged on pine boards.

CHARACTERISTICS
Round wheels, measuring 11–12 in
(29–31 cm) in diameter and weighing
11–12 lb (4.8–5.2 kg). The natural rind
is orangey brown in color and slightly
oily. The cheese has a homogeneous,
creamy consistency with a small
number of pea-sized holes.

SERVING SUGGESTIONS
Thanks to its outstanding melting qualities, Raclette du Valais is ideally used
in a Raclette dish, but it also lends itself

to gratins. In the Valais region the wheel
of cheese is halved and the cut surface
placed near to the source of heat. As the
cheese melts, the molten surface is
scraped off with the blade of a knife onto
a warm plate. It is delicious served with
a dry local white wine such as a
Fendant, as well as with other white
wine specialties such as Johannisberg,
Malvoisie, and Petite Arvine.

SIMILAR CHEESE VARIETIES
Raclette Suisse is also made in several
other cantons north of the Alps, using
cultures of special lactic acid producing
bacteria. These cultures ensure opti-
mal ripening and the melting properties desired. Raclette Suisse is
marketed both in wheels and square
blocks. The fat content must be at least
45% FDM. It has a mild, slightly acidic
flavor and becomes more aromatic with
age. Ideally, it should be consumed
when it is three months old.

HOT TIP: FONDUE AND RACLETTE

In the Middle Ages "Bratchäs" was the name the Swiss gave to cheese that was melted over an open fire and then scraped off the surface with a knife. When making classic Raclette, allow 7 oz (200 g) of Raclette cheese and 9 oz (250 g) of potatoes cooked in their skins per person. Serve with a selection of gherkins, mixed pickles, and silver onions. Depending on personal preferences, other accompaniments can include corn-on-the-cob, salami, or ham. The molten cheese is sprinkled with paprika and pepper. Cheese fondue, Switzerland's national dish, is traditionally prepared in a *caquelon* (a heatproof ceramic pot). It is usually a combination of two sorts of cheese. Popular types include Gruyère and Vacherin Fribourgeois (half-and-half, Fondue fribourgeois), or — in the case of Neuchâtel cheese fondue — Emmentaler and Gruyère. Appenzeller is a good choice if a stronger-flavored fondue is preferred.

NEUCHÂTEL CHEESE FONDUE
Serves 4

7 oz (200 g) Emmentaler
1 lb (400 g) Gruyère
1 clove of garlic
1 ⅓ cups (300 ml) dry white wine
1 tsp lemon juice
1 heaped tsp cornstarch
1 measure of Kirsch
nutmeg, pepper
2 lb (1 kg) bread (baguette, cut into cubes)

Preparation:
Coarsely grate the cheeses, rub the inside of the fondue pot with the garlic, pour in the wine, and heat slowly on the hob. Add the lemon juice, then the cheese. Heat slowly and bring the mixture to simmer, stirring constantly. Dissolve the cornstarch in the Kirsch and add to the fondue as soon as it turns creamy. Season with a little nutmeg and freshly grated pepper. Serve with bread cubes.

AUSTRIA

A mountain cheese paradise

The history of Austrian cheese goes back to the time of the Celts, who settled in the Alps during the first millennium BC, bringing with them their knowledge of cattle and alpine farming. From the ninth century on, monasteries came to play an important role in the development of cheese production. The end of the eighteenth century saw the emergence of the first dairy cooperatives and the transfer of mountain cheese production to the valleys.

After Austria joined the EU, cheese production increased dramatically and a large number of interesting new cheese varieties were developed. Yet despite the introduction of various ewe's milk and goat's milk cheeses—not to mention the wide range of domestically produced fresh and soft cheeses—it is still the traditional mountain cheeses that form the heart of Austria's cheese diversity.

Austria's landscape differs dramatically from region to region. The Vorarlberg, the most westerly Austrian province, remains the heartland of Bergkäse and Alpkäse production. Graukäse and Schottenkäse have been produced in the Tyrolean mountains for a very long time. Nowadays, the Tyrol is famed for its aromatic hard cheeses. About three-quarters of Austria's Bierkäse and a third of its Emmentaler come from the Salzburg region. Its delicious goat's cheese is also famous. Top of the list in terms of Austrian dairy farming, however, is Upper Austria, where about half of all Austria's milk is produced and numerous large cheese factories have been established. The monasteries of Upper Austria as well as small, local farms continue to produce cheese using old, traditional methods.

Left: Ideal conditions for good mountain cheese: Alpine pastures, like these in the Zillertal, are rich in herbs.

Gailtaler Almkäse (PDO)

Hard cheese made from
raw cow's milk
45% FDM

ORIGINS AND HISTORY
Gailtal, Carinthia
There is a long tradition of cheese making in the Gailtal. The first evidence of cheese being made in the alpine pastures about the Gailtal and Lesachtal dates from the fourteenth century. A protected origin cheese, Gailtaler Almkäse is produced in situ from raw milk collected in the pastures and processed by 14 alpine dairies.

PRODUCTION
Only raw cow's milk—and in certain cases raw goat's milk (up to a maximum 10%)—is used for the cheese. Each morning and evening the cows are brought back from the pastures to the milking sheds to be milked. The fresh evening's milk is cooled and transferred into round containers called *Stotzen* in a ripening room. The milk begins to curdle naturally overnight. The next morning it is placed in the vat and mixed with fresh morning milk, heated to 90 °F (32 °C) and inoculated with rennet. The curdled milk is then cut into lentil-sized pieces. The curds are stirred and heated until the correct consistency is reached, before being scooped out of the vat and placed in cheese forms. The curd is pressed slowly and the freshly made cheese is immersed in a salt bath for two

days, where it develops a natural rind. Finally the Gailtaler cheese is left to mature for at least seven weeks, though usually longer, in a ripening room.

CHARACTERISTICS
Round wheels weighing 1–77 lb (0.5–35 kg) with a hard, dry, yellow, natural rind. The cheese is smooth and yellowish in color and supple in texture, with a few small, regular holes. It is a full-flavored cheese with a slightly spicy and aromatic taste.

SERVING SUGGESTIONS
Sommelier's recommendation: Gailtaler Almkäse goes well with white wines such as a Grüner Veltliner, a mature Riesling, or a white Burgunder. Suitable red companions include Pinot Noir and Zweigelt.

SIMILAR CHEESE VARIETIES
Mondseer.

ALPKÄSE AND BERGKÄSE
MADE FROM AROMATIC PASTURE MILK

The production of Alpkäse and Bergkäse (alpine cheese) is an important element in the survival of family-run farms. About 60% of all Austrian Bergkäse comes from the Vorarlberg region, but other areas—such as the Tyrol, Styria, Salzburg, and Carinthia—produce equally delicious alpine cheeses of their own.

Alpkäse is produced only during the summer months in small alpine dairies high up among the pastures. Bergkäse, on the other hand, is produced all year round in modern cheese dairies down in the valleys. Cheese that is made from milk taken fresh from the cows and produced in situ up in the alpine pastures is known as Alpkäse, while any cheese produced from milk collected from surrounding mountain regions and taken to dairies in the valley for processing is called Bergkäse. All traditional types of Alpkäse and Bergkäse must be made from milk taken from cows fed exclusively on alpine grasses. During the summer, the cows graze solely on grasses and scented alpine herbs; in winter they are fed on hay. The farmers—many of whom are committed to organic farming—abhor the idea of feeding their livestock on fermenting silage fodder and, in so doing, ensure that their milk is of the highest quality.

In the case of Alpkäse and Bergkäse, their aromatic, spicy flavor intensifies the longer they are aged, a process that is very labour-intensive. Any cheese enthusiast should make a point of sampling a genuine Bergkäse at its different levels of maturity (3, 4, 6, 10, and 12 months), for at each stage there is the prospect of delicious discoveries in terms of diversity of aromas and flavors. Austria produces many types of Bergkäse, Alpkäse, and Almkäse, which also vary widely in aroma and flavor. Young, often mild-flavored cheeses are ideally partnered by some of Austria's fine white wines. Grüner Veltliner from the country's wine-growing region, Wachauer Rieslings, Sauvignon Blanc from Styria, and Burgunder wines from Burgenland make perfect partners for this type of cheese, while equally suitable are fruity reds made from Blaufränkisch, Zweigelt, and Pinot Noir grapes. Some of the mature, somewhat tart types of cheese go well with more complex white wines, even ones with residual sugar. Fine wines, such as a Smaragd wine from the Wachau region; or complex, sweet varieties like Ruster Ausbruch, Auslese, or Trockenbeerenauslese wines from Burgenland also make excellent companions. Full-bodied, complex, and mature reds, especially Burgenland specialties, work extremely well with some of Austria's sharper cheese specialties.

Pinzgauer Bierkäse (PDO)

Semi-hard cheese made from
cow's milk
15% FDM

ORIGINS AND HISTORY
Pinzgau/Salzburger Land
The first recorded mention of this cheese is in 1650. Pinzgakas, as it is locally known, was born out of necessity. Since the milk's cream was used to make valuable butter, this cheese was made from the leftover skimmed milk. In order to make the cheese more palatable, it was wrapped in beer-soaked linen cloths while it was being matured. Due to this procedure, the name Bierkäse (beer cheese) was given to the cheese. The fact that its piquant, full-flavored taste also produces a mighty thirst for beer is pure coincidence.

PRODUCTION
Pasteurized milk is partially skimmed before it is processed. The cheese matures for six to eight weeks, although in special cases it may be left for up to three months—during which time the natural rind is treated with red smear bacteria.

CHARACTERISTICS
Wheels or blocks of cheese, weighing 3–9 lb (1.5–4 kg). It has a reddish-brown, natural rind, is pale yellow in color, and has a smooth texture with an even spread of holes. More piquant and full-flavored as it ages.

SERVING SUGGESTIONS
This cheese makes the perfect snack, served simply with bread, butter, salt and pepper, and a glass of fresh beer. Bierkäse is also an essential ingredient in various regional specialties such as Pinzgauer Kasnocken and Kaspressknödel.

STYRIA—MURTALER STEIRERKÄS

This semi-hard Kochkäse was originally produced by farmers for their own use. It is made from matured low fat curd cheese, to which spices (caraway and pepper), cooking salt, emulsifying salts, and milk are added. This gives Murtaler Steirerkäs its typical full-bodied, spicy flavor. Butter may also be added for additional richness.

Tiroler Alpkäse (PDO)

Hard cheese made from
raw cow's milk
45% FDM

ORIGINS AND HISTORY
Tirol
A document in the Tyrolean Land Archives dating from 1544 attests to the traditional production of a regional cheese with good keeping qualities. Pastures used for dairy farming and the production of cheese are situated up to 8,200 ft (2,500 m) above sea level. In the Tyrol uplands to the west of Innsbruck the cheese is known as Alpkäse, and in the lowlands as Almkäse.

PRODUCTION
This cheese is produced only during the summer when the cows are grazing on the alpine pastures. The evening milk is placed in shallow wooden containers and then skimmed the next morning. It is mixed with fresh morning milk, inoculated with bacterial cultures, and induced to coagulate by the addition of natural calf's rennet. The curd is cut into pea-size grains by dairymen using a cheese harp and then "cooked," whereby the curd/whey mixture is heated to 122–129 °F (50–54 °C) under constant stirring. Once the desired consistency is achieved, the curd is removed from the vat, then shaped and pressed. After one to two days in a salt bath, the cheese is removed and left to mature in relatively humid conditions

for a period of four and a half to six months. During this time, the cheese is washed in brine to which a red smear culture may be added. Some varieties of cheese also have a dry smear.

CHARACTERISTICS
The wheels of cheese weigh between 66–132 lb (30–60 kg). The rind is firm, yellow to brownish in color, and without cracks. It is sometimes covered with a thin dried-on smear. The cheese is firm to supple in texture, is a uniform ivory to light yellow in color, and has a few pea- to cherry-size holes. The alpine vegetation, the altitude, and the exclusive diet of grass and herbs that the cows have consumed all combine to impart a special flavor to the milk used in the production of this cheese. It has a punchy, aromatic, and piquant taste.

SERVING SUGGESTIONS
Sommelier's recommendation: White wines make the best partners, with aromatic Grüner Veltliner topping the list. Wines with a delicate residual sweetness are also very suitable.

Tiroler Graukäse (PDO)

Sour-milk cheese made from
cow's milk
2% fat absolute

ORIGINS AND HISTORY
The production of this cheese has been
a significant element in Tyrolean peasant gastronomy for many centuries. It
was very simple to produce and
provided a logical use for the skimmed
milk left over from butter making.
Numerous farm recipes list Graukäse
as one of their main ingredients. It owes
its name to the cheese's bluish/gray-
green rind, which is sometimes shot
through with veins of gray mold.

PRODUCTION
Tyrolean Graukäse is made from
skimmed raw or pasteurized milk. It
coagulates due to natural souring without the addition of rennet. The cheese
ripens in approximately two weeks from
the outside inward, which may result in
the outer edges being a little dry. When
mature, the cheese is fatty toward the
inside with occasional unmatured
pieces of curd. Young Graukäse is
usually rather coarse-grained and crumbly. The riper the cheese, the smoother
and juicier its texture. It remains yellow
and fatty at the center.

CHARACTERISTICS
Small wheels or bars of cheese weighing 2–9 lb (1–4 kg). The cheese has a
thin, bluish-gray to grayish-green rind

with occasional cracks and mold veins
on the surface. The inside is gray to
gray-green and marbled, with a white
center and a dry, crumbly consistency.
After two weeks of ripening, its flavor is
tart, spicy, and lightly acidic. Graukäse
differs from region to region: In the
Upper Inn valley it is fatty and well
matured, while in the Lower Inn valley
it is curd-like and matures very slowly.

SERVING SUGGESTIONS
Graukäse is traditionally consumed
with a sour garnish. In other words, the
Graukäse is sliced, garnished with onion
rings, and seasoned and marinated in
salt, pepper, vinegar, and oil. It is served
with country-style bread and freshly
poured beer.

SIMILAR CHEESE VARIETIES
Schottenkäse is a piquant, coarse-
grained hard cheese made from whey
and buttermilk and marketed in different sizes of rounds.

Tiroler Bergkäse (PDO)

Firm semi-hard cheese made from
pasteurized cow's milk
45% FDM

ORIGINS AND HISTORY

The first evidence of Bergkäse production in the Austrian Tyrol dates back to about 1840. Its storage capacity and reliability in terms of safe food hygiene meant that it could be transported to places far away from the valleys of the Tyrol, where the cheese was produced.

PRODUCTION

Tyrolean Bergkäse is made from raw milk from cows fed mainly on grasses and hay. The milk, which is free from any trace of silage fodder, is turned into cheese in much the same way as Alpkäse/Almkäse, except for the fact that it is not pre-ripened with lactic acid bacteria.

CHARACTERISTICS

A round wheel, weighing at least 26 lb (12 kg), with a smeared, dried rind, varying in color between brownish-yellow and brown. This is a firm cheese with a supple, satiny texture. It is ivory to pale yellow in color with a small number of pea-size holes. The taste varies from mild to slightly piquant.

SERVING SUGGESTIONS

Grüner Veltliner wines, as well as Wachauer Rieslings, Sauvignon Blanc from Styria, and Burgunder-type wines combine well with this cheese. Fruity reds made from Blaufränkisch, Zweigelt, or Pinot Noir grapes also work well with young Bergkäse. Riper, stronger-flavored cheeses may also be paired with more complex white wines or ones with residual sugar.

EWE'S MILK CHEESE FROM LOWER AUSTRIA

Fresh ewe's milk cheese forms an integral part of every wine tavern's *Heurigenjause* (hearty cold snack). Mostviertler Schofkas was originally produced for domestic consumption. It is eaten with a layer of chives, seasoned with salt and pepper, and accompanied by a glass of pear juice. Waldviertler Selchkäse is a smoked semi-hard ewe's milk cheese.

Vorarlberger Alpkäse (PDO)

Hard cheese made from
raw cow's milk
45% FDM

ORIGINS AND HISTORY
*Vorarlberg/Alpine and Vorsäß/Maisäß
regions*
A substantial amount of alpine milk
production goes into the making of
Alpkäse and has done so since the eighteenth century, when it acquired its
name. The finished cheeses are brought
down into the valley when the cows are
taken down from the high pastures in
September.

PRODUCTION
Vorarlberger Alpkäse is produced only
over a short period in the summer
(three to four months) and is made into
cheese in situ up in the high alpine
pastures. The evening's milk is poured
straight into small shallow wooden
containers or tubs. The following day
the milk is skimmed by hand, then
mixed with the next morning's whole
milk before being placed in a copper
vat. Lactic acid producing cultures and
rennet are added. The curd is heated
and pressed and the cheese is washed
regularly with brine to encourage the
development of a good rind. Alpkäse is
left to mature for three to six months.

CHARACTERISTICS
The cheese is ivory in color and supple
in texture with pea-size holes. It has an
aromatic, slightly spicy taste, which
grows stronger with age.

SERVING SUGGESTIONS
This cheese works best with white
wines that are not too acidic. Grüner
Veltliner, Weißburgunder, Grauburgunder, and Chardonnay all combine very
well with it. The most suitable reds are
fruity wines that are low in tannins.

SALZBURGER LAND CHEESE MADE FROM ALPINE PASTURE MILK

The aromatic grasses and herbs give
the milk, and ultimately the cheese, its
unique flavor. Flachgauer Heumilchkäse from Flachgau takes several
months to mature. Tennengauer
Heumilchkäse from Adnet in Tennengau, famous for its marble quarries, is
ripened naturally in ancient cave
cellars.

Vorarlberger Bergkäse (PDO)

Hard cheese made from
raw cow's milk
45% FDM

ORIGINS AND HISTORY
Milk production, followed later by cheese making, was first underway in the Vorarlberg region during the fourteenth century as the population in that area began to increase. By the middle of the eighteenth century, cheese production had reached such proportions that the local population could not consume it all, whereupon it was exported, primarily to Italy. In 1921, the Vorarlberg alpine dairies and farmers formed a marketing cooperative that still markets Bergkäse to this day. The raw milk comes exclusively from producers and farmers in the Bregenzerwald, Kleinwalsertal, Großwalsertal, Laiblachtal (Pfänderstock), and Rheintal areas.

PRODUCTION
This cheese is made exclusively from alpine pasture milk. Milk is delivered at least once a day to the cheese dairy, where it is processed straight away. The raw milk is partially skimmed and coagulated, using a combination of natural rennet, a lactic acid, and a whey culture. The curd is heated and pressed, after which the wheels are soaked in brine for two to three days. The cheeses are left to age in a ripening cellar in conditions of relatively high humidity for three to

six months. The wheels are regularly brushed with brine to encourage the development of their typical rind and taste.

CHARACTERISTICS
The cheese comes in wheels that are 4–5 in (10–12 cm) thick and weigh 18–77 lb (8–35 kg). The rind is smeared or dried on, brownish-yellow to brown, and grainy. The cheese is supple with a matt or shiny finish and varies between ivory or pale yellow in color. It has small, evenly distributed round holes. Its flavor ranges from aromatic to spicily piquant, and its taste recalls the flora of the Vorarlberg's alpine pastures.

SERVING SUGGESTIONS
Wachauer Grüner Veltliner wines or even Smaragd make good partners, while a mature St. Laurent from Burgenland or the Styrian spa region also goes well with this cheese.

ITALY

Much more than just Parmesan

Italy has a long tradition of cheese making. Even ancient Roman town houses had their own cheese kitchens. While the Teutons were only familiar with soft or sour-milk cheese, the Romans were adept at producing hard cheese. The milk's natural souring process was accelerated by adding juice from the bark of fig trees, as well as thistle seeds, wine vinegar, and the herb known as yellow bedstraw.

"Here, on the green leafage, we have ripe apples, mealy chestnuts and a wealth of tangy cheeses," writes Virgil in one of his pastoral poems. Cheese was a staple food amongst the peasant population and formed part of a Roman legionary's rations, along with grain and a pint (0.5 l) of wine. A fresco in Issogne Castle in the Aosta valley illustrates that several different cheese varieties were on sale in Italy as early as the fourteenth century. There is a nineteenth-century record of the composer Gioachino Rossini thanking Marquis Antonio Busca in a letter for sending him two Gorgonzola cheeses: "These cheeses are better than all the crosses, orders, and ribbons liberally bestowed on me by the different princely houses of Europe," wrote Rossini.

The range of Italian cheeses is extremely varied and complex. There are countless local variations, with different names for each type of cheese. Several types of cheese may even be grouped together under one collective name, according to production, maturing time, and place of origin. The dividing lines between soft, semi-hard, and hard cheeses are often indistinct. Also, some soft or semi-hard cheeses may turn into hard ones, suitable for grating.

Left: One of the most famous buildings in the world: The Leaning Tower of Pisa.

RICOTTA—ROMAN IN ORIGIN, AND NOW KNOWN ALL OVER THE WORLD

Originating in Rome, Ricotta long ago went on to conquer the whole of Italy and the rest of the world. It was originally made from sheep's milk, but has for a long time been made from cow's milk, which is more plentiful. Cow's milk Ricotta (Ricotta Vaccina) is generally a little softer than sheep's milk Ricotta (Ricotta Pecorina).

Ricotta is usually consumed when it is fresh. In some areas it is eaten mixed with whole milk or cream. Fresh Ricotta quickly turns sour if it is not kept refrigerated. Mature Ricotta is good for grating over pasta and other hearty dishes.

Salted Ricotta is traditional in the hot south. The fact that it is salted means that it keeps longer. The maturing period is longer; in the case of salted Ricotta it is 60 days. Known as Ricotta Salata, it may also be used as a hard cheese. In Sicily Ricotta is dried in the sun (Ricotta Secca) and used for grating.

Some regions produce a smoked or baked Ricotta. Ricotta Affumicata Carnica is very popular in Friaul, Venice, and Trentino. Drained and unsalted Ricotta is smoked over a beechwood fire and develops a sweet, aromatic flavor. The difficulties involved in storing fresh Ricotta led to the development in Sardinia of smoked sheep's milk Ricotta, called Ricotta Affumicata Sarda. It is heavily salted to begin with in order to slow down the aging process. It has a spicily piquant flavor. Smoked Ricotta is also produced in the Ossola valley, in this case over a juniper wood fire. Ricotta Ossolana is grated, mixed with butter and cream, and served on warm salted potatoes with chopped chives. It has an intensely aromatic flavor. Apulia is home to Ricotta Forte, which is somewhat similar to Bruss cheese. The Ricotta is salted and mixed with cream before fermentation. The resulting firm cream with its full-bodied, piquant flavor is eaten with bread or pasta. In Sicily someone hit upon the idea of baking Ricotta to make it last longer. Nowadays, Sicilians are fond of Ricotta Infornata as a dessert, mixed with sugar, sultanas, candied fruits, or chocolate drops. It has a delicate, sweet flavor.

GRAPPA

Grappa, a fragrant brandy made from Italian grapes, prides itself on a brilliant career. In the past Grappa distillers were obliged to trudge from one vineyard to another in order to distill a warming winter drink for the vineyard owners in situ. Nowadays demanding connoisseurs are willing to travel long distances to visit the famous Grappa distilleries. Outstanding Grappa is brewed in Piedmont and Friuli-Julian Veneto. However, Lombardy, the Aosta valley, Veneto, Trentino, and the southern Tyrol also feature amongst the main producers. If a bottle of Grappa is simply labeled "Italian Grappa," it is usually a blend from different regions of Italy. In Friuli, a Grappa produced from the marc of the single-varietal, high yield Picolit grape is regarded as an exceptional treat. Young brandies are best appreciated slightly cooled and drunk from long stemmed glasses. Older Grappa is best drunk at a temperature of 60–64 °F (16–18 °C) from a brandy goblet.

NORTHERN ITALY
The high Alps and the Mediterranean

Few travel destinations offer as much diversity as the countryside between the high Alps and the Mediterranean, with cultural cities like Venice, Verona, Ravenna, Bologna, and Milan. From the hiker's paradise of the southern Tyrol, the land descends to the vast flood plains of the river Po. Narrow streets wind their way up to the remote heights of the gigantic rocky peaks of the Dolomites. The tranquil region of Piedmont, along Lago di Garda and Lago Maggiore, is very close to the Swiss border. Upper Italy offers cheese specialties from both the high mountains and from the vast plains.

The southern Tyrol and Trentino are best known for regional Almkäse and Bergkäse specialties, while Venetia and Friuli are home to delicious cheeses, such as Montasio, Pressato, and Asiago.

Lombardy is one of Italy's cheese paradises. A large proportion of Grana Padano, which is often seen as a rival of Parmeggiano Reggiano, is produced in Vala Padano in the Po valley. Creamy delicacies such as Stracchino and Mascarpone are also produced here, as are Bagoss, Bitto and Branzi, Taleggio, and Provolone.

To the west of Lombardy lies the province of Piedmont, which is famous for its wines and cheeses. This region's cheese specialties are made from cow's, goat's, and sheep's milk. A large number of DOP cheeses also originate from here. Fontina, a delicate cheese, and many other mountain cheeses such as Toma, Tomini, and Caprino are produced in the Aosta valley, while the Emilia-Romagna region is home to the king of Italian cheeses, Parmegiano Reggiano. The region also produces some delicious soft cheeses.

Left: Wine and fine cheese—northern Italy is a great favorite with gastronomes.

Fontina (PDO)

Semi-hard cheese made from
raw cow's milk
45% FDM

ORIGINS AND HISTORY
Aosta valley
Fontina cheese is inseparably linked
with the Aosta valley. This cheese was
already being produced in the Middle
Ages, and the first recorded mention of
its present name was in 1717.

PRODUCTION
The red spotted cows that produce the
milk for this cheese are grazed only on
the high pastures. Two batches of
cheese are made every day, each from a
single milking. The curd is heated and
pressed for 12 hours. For the first three
months the wheels of cheese, stored on
pine boards, are turned on a daily basis
and alternately salted or brushed with
brine. They are matured for four to five
months in rock caves, tunnels, and
former bunkers as well as in an old
copper mine that accommodates about
22,000 wheels of cheese.

CHARACTERISTICS
Cylindrical wheels with a slightly con-
cave edge, measuring 3–4 in (7–10 cm)
in height, with a diameter of 12–18 in
(30–45 cm), and a weight of 18–40 lb
(8–18 kg). The rind is soft and elastic,
and is colored light brown or orange.
The interior of the cheese is a rich straw
yellow in color and has just a few small
holes. It has a delicate, mild flavor.
Young Fontina has a milky taste and a
summery aroma that recalls the alpine
pastures. Older Fontinas have a subtle,
nutty flavor.

SERVING SUGGESTIONS
Mature Fontinas, in particular, melt
easily and are consequently favorites for
fondues and often used in creamy cheese
dishes and as cheese toppings. Fonduta
Valdostana is a popular dish made from
Fontina cheese, milk, and egg yolk.
Young Fontina also makes a delicious
table cheese. Sommelier's recommendation: Fontina-based cheese dishes
combine well with red wines from the
Piedmont region, such as Barbera
d'Alba. Young Fontina cheese goes well
with Arneis wines and wines from the
Val d'Aosta region.

SIMILAR CHEESE VARIETIES
The spicy Toma di Gressoney cheese is
produced in a similar way to Fontina.
Only a handful of alpine farmers still
produce this specialty during the
summer months. This semi-fat cheese
has its own unique, salty, and piquant
flavor. Only 1,000 to 1,500 wheels of this
cheese are produced in one year.

Bra (PDO)

Semi-hard/hard cheese made
from cow's milk with some
ewe's and goat's milk
32% FDM

ORIGINS AND HISTORY
Cuneo, Turin

Although this cheese gets its name from
the town of Bra in the Cuneo region, it
has never been made there. Its origins
date back to when it formed part of the
staple diet of shepherds. Nowadays,
apart from Bra d'alpeggio, the majority
of Bra cheese is produced in small
dairies down in the valley.

PRODUCTION

Small amounts of ewe's and goat's milk
are added to skimmed cow's milk. Traditionally the curd has to be cut twice so
that the whey drains off more effi-
ciently. The cheese mass is then
pressed into molds and salted for
several days. Soft Bra (*tenero*) takes
up to 45 days to mature, while the hard
version of Bra (*duro*) takes up to a year.

CHARACTERISTICS

Cylindrical wheels with a diameter of
85–105 in (30–40 cm). They measure
3–4 in (7–9 cm) in height, and weigh
13–18 kg (6–8 kg). Bra Tenero: Soft to
semi-soft on the inside, this cheese has
a few small holes. It varies in color from
white to ivory. The pale-gray rind is
smooth and uniform with a pleasant
aroma, slightly piquant and spicy. Bra
Duro: This cheese is brownish in color,
tending toward yellow ochre with a few
small holes. Its hard, thick rind is straw
colored. Bra Duro has a slightly spicy,
piquant, and intensive flavor.

SERVING SUGGESTIONS

Bra is traditionally served as a table
cheese, while older specimens may be
used for grating. Sommeliere's recommendation: Duro deserves a mature
Piedmontese red wine, for example one
made from Barbera or Nebbiolo grapes.
Tenero combines well with fresh, young
Piedmontese wines, such as a fruity
Barbera d'Alba or a modern Dolcetto.

SPECIAL FEATURES

With a bit of luck, you may come across
small firms in Cuneo province that
still produce Furmai Marçet ("rotten
cheese") using old traditional methods.
Imperfect wheels of Bra cheese have
deep holes drilled into them, into which
fresh milk is poured. The cheese is then
left to mature at room temperature for
about three months, during which time
it develops a piquant flavor.

Castelmagno (PDO)

Semi-hard cheese made from
cow's milk
at least 34% FDM

ORIGINS AND HISTORY
Cuneo

A document dated 1277 refers to Castelmagno as a form of rental payment. During the 1960s production dwindled considerably as an increasing number of rural farmers moved into the towns to earn more money. Meanwhile, Castelmagno has staged something of a comeback, not only in the major Italian cities but also in Paris and New York. This rare type of cheese may only be made in three mountain villages, which together make up the district of Castelmagno.

PRODUCTION

The evening's milk is left overnight in wooden or stone containers, then mixed next day with the fresh morning milk. Occasionally some partially skimmed sheep's or goat's milk is added to the mix. The curd is separated into large clumps, which are laid on a cloth and hung from a hook for 20 hours to drain off the whey. The cheesy mass, still in its cloth, is then placed for three to four days in a container to pre-ripen before eventually being cut into small pieces, salted, transferred into molds, and pressed. After several applications of dry salt, the young cheese is left to mature for two months in cool damp cellars or rock caves. If Castelmagno is left to age for longer, it will spontaneously develop a covering of mold after five months.

CHARACTERISTICS

Cylindrical cheese measuring about 6–10 in (15–25 cm) in height and diameter and weighing 4–15 lb (2–7 kg). Young Castelmagno is pearly white to ivory colored, with a dense, dry consistency. Its reddish-yellow rind is thin, smooth, and elastic. The cheese is creamy and mild with a slightly salty taste. Older cheese has a rough ochre-colored rind, while the inside is ochre-yellow in color with a light marbling effect of blue-green veins of mold. It has a full, spicy, and piquant flavor.

SERVING SUGGESTIONS

Although this cheese should be eaten while fresh, its aroma does not reach its full potential until after the mold has developed. Sommelier's recommendation: Mature reds with a robust body and mild tannins, such as Barbaresco, Barolo and Nebbiolo d'Alba, or Moscato d'Asti.

Gorgonzola (PDO)

Soft cheese made from
cow's milk, with interior mold
48% FDM

ORIGINS AND HISTORY

Cuneo, Novara, Vercelli, Bergamo,
Brescia, Como, Cremona, Lodi,
Milan, Pavia

The first recorded mention of this type
of blue-veined cheese dates back to the
twelfth century. Legend has it that an
absent-minded cheese maker left a sack
of curds hanging from a nail to drain
and forgot all about it. To cover up his
mistake, he added more fresh curds.
When the cheese was ready, he discovered that it had been invaded by green
mold—and tasted it. Although it gets
its name from the small Lombardy town
of Gorgonzola, the majority of Gorgonzola production takes place in the two
Piedmontese provinces of Novara and
Vercelli.

PRODUCTION

The cheese is produced from a combination of curds from two milking
sessions: The curds from the evening's
milk is combined with curds made from
warm, fresh milk. Mixing the two lots of
curds in this way encourages the
growth of bacteria. Small cavities are
formed, in which the mold develops. To
increase the circulation of air, the
cheese is also penetrated with long
probes. Gorgonzola is matured for two
to four months.

CHARACTERISTICS

Tall cylinders, weighing about 13–29 lb
(6–13 kg), with a height of 6–8 in
(16–20 cm) and a diameter of 10–12 in
(25–30 cm). They have a rough, moist
rind, which becomes reddish with age.
The compact, white to yellow interior is
full of greenish-blue striations. The
most traditional form of Gorgonzola is
the *piccante* version, although only
10% of overall production is devoted to
this strong cheese. During the post-war
years Gorgonzola Dolce, a creamier,
milder and more buttery version, has
taken the lead as the most popular form.

SERVING SUGGESTIONS

Sommelier's recommendation: Ven-
demmia Tardiva, Ramandolo, a sweet
Picolit, and even Moscato d'Asti all
make excellent companions to this
cheese. Beerenauslese or Sauternais
wines also work well. Caution must be
exercised in the case of red wines as the
bitter elements of the mold can impart
a bitter taste to the tannins.

CREAM CHEESE THAT PACKS A POWERFUL PUNCH

In some poorer areas people often used their leftover cheese to make this blended cheese with its powerful aroma. The number of local cheese varieties is as great as the number of variations in spelling: Brus, Bruzzu, Bruz or Bross, for example. In *El nuevo Gribaud*, a dictionary of Piedmontese, this cheese specialty is described as "cheese moistened in schnapps." Small pieces of ripe cheese are soaked in milk and whey, or mixed with milk, cream, or Ricotta. The fermentation process is interrupted at intervals by adding small amounts of high proof alcohol. It takes the cream cheese three months to one year to mature. Depending on the type of cheese used, its color varies between very white (Raccoverano) and gray (Castelmagno). It has a provocative smell and is piquant to spicy in flavor. Ideally this cheese should be accompanied by whatever type of drink has been used in the dish, or, alternatively, by a robust red wine such as Barbaresco, Nebbiolo d'Alba, or Rossese di Dolceaqua.

Piedmont is home to other similar cream cheeses—for example Cachat, produced in Cuneo from leftover goat's cheese, and Sargnòn from Biella. In Liguria Bruzzu is made entirely from leftover Ricotta. Trento's particular specialty is called Pestolato, and it is made by grinding the cheese in a mortar before it is fermented and finally mixed with schnapps.

OTHER CHEESES FROM THE AOSTA VALLEY

In the Aosta valley, cheese is known in the local patois as *fromazdo*. In former times Valle d'Aosta Fromazdo (PDO), a classic alpine cheese made from raw, skimmed cow's milk, was known as *fromazdo meigro* or low fat cheese. It can be made out in a fresco dating back to 1480 at the castle of Issogne, which portrays a cheese maker's shop.

The process of turning cow's milk into hard cheese usually involves the addition of a little goat's milk, and occasionally a few herbs. The cheese is gently pressed into its wooden mold, rubbed with dry salt or immersed in brine, and left to ripen in a cellar for two to ten months. Depending on height, 1–2 in (5–20 cm), and diameter, 6–12 in (15–30 cm), the wheels of cheese weigh between 2 lb and 15 lb (1–7 kg). The rind is fairly thick and yellowish-gray in color, while on the inside the cheese is compact with a sprinkling of small holes. Young cheese is white, becoming straw yellow as it matures. It smells of milk and alpine herbs. When fresh, this cheese has a semi-sweet flavor that becomes more intense, with a hint of saltiness, as it matures. Reblec, another alpine cheese delicacy, is a fresh cheese to which cream is sometimes added (Reblec de Crama). It is shaped into small portions that can be eaten just 12 hours after production.

Murazzano (PDO)

Fresh cheese made from
sheep's and cow's milk
50–62% FDM

ORIGINS AND HISTORY

Cuneo

Murazzano is produced in a region that
encompasses 43 towns in the Langhe
region of Cuneo, where it was originally
made by the Ligurians. The main center
of production is Murazzano. The cheese
is traditionally produced from the Alta
Langa breed of sheep. Murazzano is one
of the most famous members of Piedmont's Robiola family of cheeses.

PRODUCTION

Murazzano is mainly produced in small
cooperative dairies. It must contain a
minimum of 60% pure sheep's milk.
Murazzano made entirely from sheep's
milk has a fat content of at least 53%.
The cheese is dry salted. Ripening takes
seven to ten days, but some cheeses are
matured for longer—up to two months.
During this period they have to be
washed daily with lukewarm water.

CHARACTERISTICS

The cylindrical rounds have a narrow
edge 1–2 in (3–4 cm) thick. They are
4–6 in (10–15 cm) in diameter and
weigh 11 oz–1 lb (300–400 g). Fresh
cheese is milky white on the outside,
while maturer cheeses have a yellowish
patina. The interior is always milky
white, occasionally with a few irregular
air bubbles. Murazzano has a fine, delicate, and pleasant aroma of fresh
sheep's milk, which may become a little
bitter in maturer cheeses.

SPECIAL FEATURES

Murazzano is sometimes used as the
main ingredient in a specialty known as
Bruss, to which schnapps is added after
about a week. This secondary fermentation turns what started off as a mild,
soft cheese into a strong, piquant, and
tart specialty.

SERVING SUGGESTIONS

Sommelier's recommendation: Murraz-
zano makes an ideal accompaniment to
Cugna, a fruit preserve made from the
must of Moscato grapes, to which late
summer fruits and vegetables are
added. Good wines to drink with this
cheese include sweet varieties, such as
Moscato d'Asti.

Raschera (PDO)

Semi-hard cheese, made
from cow's milk
32% FDM

ORIGINS AND HISTORY
Cuneo
This cheese is named after Lago
Raschera in the Valli Monregalesi,
where it was originally produced. Its
square shape makes it particularly good
for transporting on the backs of mules.

PRODUCTION
A single day's milk is collected, heated
to 82–86 °F (28–30 °C) and coagulated
with rennet. It is permissible to add
some milk from sheep or goats. The curd
is stirred with a spatula-style device.
Once the liquid has drained off, the curd
is placed in a cloth and pressed for ten
minutes. The curd is cut a second time
into granules and pressed manually in
muslin, using weights, for one day
(circular cheeses) or five days (rectangular cheeses). The cheese is then dry
salted for several days, during which
time the surface is punctured with holes
so that the salt can penetrate more
easily. The ripening time varies between
three weeks and three months.

CHARACTERISTICS
Circular, cylindrical wheels, about 3–4 in
(7–9 cm) thick, diameter of 14–16 in
(35–40 cm), and a weight of 15–20 lb
(7–9 kg). Alternatively, the cheese may
be quadrangular in shape, measuring

16 in (40 cm) on one side, with a height
of 5–6 in (12–15 cm) and weighing
18–22 lb (8–10 kg). Its smooth, reddish-
gray rind occasionally displays yellow
highlights or red patches, which become
even more pronounced as the cheese
matures. Beneath the rind the cheese is
white to ivory colored and riddled with
small, irregular holes. Its flavor is fine
and delicate, becoming slightly piquant
with age.

SPECIAL FEATURES
Raschera is made in the Cuneo region
in ten mountain villages, situated at an
altitude of at least 2,950 ft (900 m). This
earns it the right to include the words
d'alpeggio (alpine cheese) in its name.

SERVING SUGGESTIONS
Sommelier's recommendation: Young
Raschera goes well with Piedmont white
wines, such as Gavi or Arneis from the
Langhe region. Maturer cheeses deserve
wines with more body, such as a cask-
aged, mature Chardonnay or a Nebbiolo.

Robiola di Roccaverano (PDO)

Fresh/soft cheese made from
cow's, goat's, and/or
ewe's milk
50% FDM

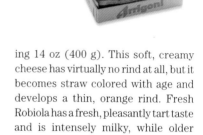

ORIGINS AND HISTORY

Alessandria, Asti

It is said that the ancient Romans made Robiola cheese according to the recipe that is used to this day. Robiola is the name given to a range of mostly small, circular cheeses from northern Italy, in particular from Lombardy and Piedmont. Its name probably derives from the Latin word *rubium*, meaning "red" —its rind develops an orange-red color as it matures. Robiola di Roccaverano comes from the region about the small town of Roccaverano in the Piedmont.

PRODUCTION

Robiola di Roccaverano is made from a combination of cows' and sheep's or goat's milk. The proportion of cow's milk must be less than 85%. Alternatively pure goat's or ewe's milk may be used. The milk is coagulated with the aid of lactic acid bacteria and rennet. The natural ripening process takes at least 3–14 days at a temperature of 59–68 °F (15–20 °C). This process can be accelerated by wrapping the cheese in Savoy cabbage leaves (Robiola Incavolata).

CHARACTERISTICS

Flat squares, 4–6 in (10–14 cm) in diameter, about 2 in (4–5 cm) thick, weighing 14 oz (400 g). This soft, creamy cheese has virtually no rind at all, but it becomes straw colored with age and develops a thin, orange rind. Fresh Robiola has a fresh, pleasantly tart taste and is intensely milky, while older cheeses have a more intense, fuller flavor.

SPECIAL FEATURES

The tastiest Robiola, rare though it is, is made entirely from goat's milk. Robiola del Becco is a much prized goat's milk specialty. This cheese is only produced from October to November.

SERVING SUGGESTIONS

Once Robiola has matured for at least two weeks, it can be preserved in oil with herbs and spices. Fresh Robiola goes well with complex white wines such as Gavi or Chardonnay. A full-bodied Pinot Bianco, Pinot Grigio, and Sauvignon Blanc also combine well with this cheese. Older Robiola cheeses demand wines with aromatic character such as Muscatels or Gewürztraminer.

ROBIOLA—PLEASURE OF A SPECIAL KIND

Whereas Piedmontese Robiola di Roccaverano consists of a mild fresh cheese without a rind, made from a combination of cows', sheep's, and goat's milk, Robiola from Lombardy has a thin rind and consists usually only of cow's milk. Robiola is available in well-stocked supermarkets or from farmers' markets. It has a delicate, aromatic flavor and goes well with bread, pasta, risotto, and polenta dishes. Sweet, fresh, and very fatty, Robiola d'Alba is made entirely of cow's milk and generally eaten fresh. Robiola d'Alba alle Ortiche is a Robiola cheese from Alba that has been stored for a few days under a layer of finely chopped nettles. The smaller Robiola delle Valsassina is a kind of mini-Taleggio from Valsassina that ripens more quickly. The name Robiola delle Langhe encompasses a variety of briefly ripened, sweet and milky, almost runny fresh cheeses that come from the Langhe region. Robiola di Vesime is made from goat's milk and is matured wrapped in various types of leaves. A few farms where this specialty is still produced exist in and about the village of Vesime.

Toma Piemontese (PDO)

Semi-hard cheese
made from cow's milk
35% FDM

ORIGINS AND HISTORY
Alessandria, Asti, Biella, Cuneo,
Novara, Turin, Vercelli
There is a long tradition of Toma cheese
in the alpine regions and in Piedmont.
Since the 1990s, Toma Piemontese has
been the only Toma with protected
origin status.

PRODUCTION
Toma Piemontese is made entirely from
either full-cream or skimmed cow's
milk. The curd is warmed to 113–118°F
(45–48°C), then pressed and dry salted.
The cheeses are matured in traditional
caves or special rooms. Cheeses weighing under 13 lb (6 kg) are ripened for at
least 15 days, while heavier cheeses are
left to mature for at least 60 days. It is
not uncommon for some cheeses to age
for up to a year. Toma Piemontese is
often stored under a layer of alpine
grasses and herbs.

CHARACTERISTICS
Toma generally takes the form of a squat
cylinder with a slightly domed top and
bottom. It is 2–5 in (6–12 cm) in height,
measures 6–14 in (15–35 cm) in diameter, and weighs between 4 and 18 lb
(1.8–8 kg). The color of its smooth, elastic rind varies in the case of whole-milk
Toma from straw yellow to reddish-

brown. Inside, the cheese is ivory white
with small, regular holes. Toma made
from full-cream milk is mildly sweet and
pleasantly delicate. Semi-fat Toma
made from skimmed milk has a harder
rind, reddish-brown to straw yellow in
color. Its ivory-white interior is full of
tiny holes. It has a pleasant smell and a
strong and aromatic taste.

SPECIAL FEATURES
Under its protected designation of
origin, Toma Piemontese encompasses
all similar, local Toma cheeses from the
Piedmont region.

SERVING SUGGESTIONS
Sommelier's recommendation: Ideal as
a table cheese or for cooking purposes,
Toma works very well with robust white
wines, such as cask-aged Chardonnay
from the Langhe region. Mature red
wines like Barolo and Barbaresco likewise combine well.

Bitto della Valtellina (PDO)

Hard cheese made from
cow's or goat's milk
45% FDM

ORIGINS AND HISTORY
Sondrio, Bergamo

The river Bitto, a tributary of the Adda, flows through the Valtellina valley. To this day goats are an integral part of the landscape among the alpine pastures of this region. The first recorded mention of Bitto cheese dates back to the seventeenth century. Centuries before this, a similar cheese was used as a form of rent payment.

PRODUCTION

About 70 alpine chalet dairies specialize in the production of Bitto cheese. A small quantity of goat's milk (maximum 10%) is added to the cow's milk to enrich the flavor. The curd is heated, pressed, and salted. Young Bitto ripens in 70 days, medium-mature cheeses are stored for three to six months, while older Bitto is left for between one and three years—if not longer.

CHARACTERISTICS

These wheel-shape cheeses 12–20 in (30–50 cm) in diameter and measuring 3–5 in (8–12 cm) in thickness, weigh 33–55 lb (15–25 kg). The rind becomes darker with age. The inside of the cheese is white to straw yellow in color and has a few air bubbles. Fresh Bitto tastes mild and delicate; more mature cheeses have a distinctive, stronger flavor.

SPECIAL FEATURES

Bitto cheese with its unique flavor is still produced in the artisanal manner, making it a real rarity.

SERVING SUGGESTIONS

Young Bitto is widely used in culinary dishes such as pizzoccheri, a typical local pasta dish from the Valtellina, and in polenta. Mature Bitto may be used for grating. Sommelier's recommendation: Serve this cheese with full-bodied, mature Valtellina wines, such as Grumello. A well-aged Sfursat makes a good partner with mature Bitto cheese.

Crescenza

Fresh/soft cheese
made from cow's milk
48% FDM

ORIGINS AND HISTORY
Milan
The name of this cheese probably derives from the Latin word *carsenza* (flat bread). One of its qualities is that it continues to ferment and rise if it is stored in a warm temperature. Crescenza is also known locally as Stracchino (see entry).

PRODUCTION
After being stirred twice, the curd is placed in forms to drain, then left to dry for several hours before finally being plunged into a salt bath. Crescenza normally ripens in five to ten days. If left to mature for several weeks, the cheese develops a grayish skin *(passito)*.

CHARACTERISTICS
This cheese has a square shape with sides 7–8 in (18–20 cm) long. It weighs up to 4 lb (2 kg), and is 2–3 in (4–5 cm) thick. The soft, paste-like surface conceals a milky white interior with a soft, buttery consistency. Its fresh, creamy, and very delicate flavor may sometimes have sweetish or slightly bitter overtones. Winter-made Crescenza is very soft, almost runny; while summer versions are firm, almost dense.

SERVING SUGGESTIONS
Sommelier's recommendation: White Piedmontese wines, for example Arneis from the Langhe region or Gavi, make pleasant companions. It also combines well with a fine Prosecco.

PIEDMONT
AN ALPINE
CELEBRITY

One of Piedmont's oldest and most famous cheeses is Bettelmatt della Valdossola. Made from cow's milk, this cheese is only produced between July and September when the herds are grazing at altitudes of over 6,560 ft (2,000 m) on the fresh pastures high up in the Val Formazzo. Bettelmatt is similar to—and often mistaken for—Fontina cheese from the Aosta valley. Aged for three to four months, this circular cheese is 4–6 in (10–15 cm) thick with a diameter of 12–16 in (30–40 cm). It has a reddish rind, and its buttery interior is straw yellow with pronounced holes.

Formai de Mut (PDO)

Semi-hard cheese
made from cow's milk
44% FDM

ORIGINS AND HISTORY
Bergamo, Upper Brembana valley
The Alta Valle Brembana provides the perfect environment for Bruna Alpina cows, which provide the milk for this type of cheese. The name is derived from local dialect, in which *formai* means cheese and *mut* means alpine pasture.

PRODUCTION
The milk is processed straight after milking. The curd is cut very finely, then heated and stirred once more. It next undergoes initial salting and pressing. Once it has dried off, the cheese is salted several times over the course of a one- to two-week period, either dry or in brine. Young Formai de Mut matures for 40 to 45 days, while older cheeses can be stored for over six months.

CHARACTERISTICS
Cylindrical wheels with a diameter of 12–16 in (30–40 cm) and weighing 18–24 lb (8–12 kg). The thin, straw-yellow rind develops a grayish tinge in older cheeses. Beneath the rind the cheese is ivory colored, dense, and elastic with a large number of holes. It has a delicate taste reflecting the herbs and flowers of the mountain pastures.

SERVING SUGGESTIONS
Formai de Mut is traditionally eaten with polenta. Sommelier's recommendation: With younger, fresh cheese it is best to drink a white wine such as a Franciacorta. An older cheese combines well with mature red wines such as Franciacorta Rosso or Valcalepio Rosso.

TIRAMISÙ

Not only has Tiramisù become something of a cult throughout the whole of Italy, but every Italian region lays claim to having invented this famous dessert, and the number of variations on the original recipe is correspondingly high. The main distinctions tend to focus on the question of which alcoholic drink goes into the dish. Whether flavored with Cognac, Marsala, Amaretto, whisky, rum, or coffee liqueur, Tiramisù tastes delicious with all kinds of alcohol.

Ingredients: 5 tbs sugar, 7 fl oz (200 ml) cream, 4 egg yolks, 1 lb 2 oz (500 g) Mascarpone, 7 oz (200 g) sponge fingers, 4 tbs very strong Espresso, 4 tbs Amaretto, cocoa powder.

Add 1 tablespoon of sugar to the cream. Whisk until stiff and mix the egg yolks to a cream with the remaining sugar. Stir the Mascarpone into the egg yolk mixture a spoonful at a time, then add the cream a little more slowly. Line a flat tin with the sponge fingers. Combine the Espresso and Amaretto and sprinkle carefully over the fingers. Spread a layer of cream on top, then another layer of biscuits, sprinkling with the Espresso–Amaretto mixture. Spread the remaining cream over the top. Sprinkle with cocoa powder and refrigerate for at least one hour.

Mascarpone

Fresh cheese made from
cow's milk cream
min. 60% FDM

ORIGINS AND HISTORY
Lodi, Abiategrasso
The name is derived from the word
mascerpa, which in the local patois
means Ricotta or cottage cheese.

PRODUCTION
Pasteurized cream from the milk of
cows is heated and induced to curdle by
the addition of citric acid or wine vinegar. Once it has cooled, the curd is left
to settle for several hours before it is
separated from the whey. After a
further period of resting, the remaining
whey is drained off. The Mascarpone is
ready to eat within 24 hours. It is not
salted or matured.

CHARACTERISTICS
Creamy and soft, and white in color,
Marscapone has a fresh and buttery
taste, occasionally with slightly tart
overtones.

SPECIAL FEATURES
This is Italy's cheese with the highest fat
content. Since Mascarpone is made
with the cream of the milk rather than
the milk itself, it cannot technically be
classified as a "proper" cheese.

SERVING SUGGESTIONS
Mascarpone is used to give numerous
dishes a more intensive flavor than
cream alone could do. Mascarpone helps
flat mushrooms, for example, to develop
their full aroma. Sweetened with liqueur
or sugar, Mascarpone makes a delicious
dessert. It is an essential ingredient in
Tiramisù and Torta di Gorgonzola
(Gorgonzola stuffed with Mascarpone).

Grana Padano (PDO)

Hard cheese made from
raw cow's milk
32% FDM

ORIGINS AND HISTORY

The history of Grana Padano (*grana* meaning grainy) may be traced back to the tenth century. Nowadays it is made in the Po valley (*planura padana*), parts of Piedmont, Veneto, and Emilia-Romagna. The center of production is in Lombardy, however.

PRODUCTION

Grana Padano is made all year. The milk from the morning and evening milking of the same day is left to stand for several hours. The morning milk is skimmed and the curd heated to 127–131 °F (53–5 °C). Once the mass becomes elastic, the curd is divided into two forms, in which they drain for two days. They then are immersed in salt water for four weeks before the cheese is left to mature for at least six months—but usually for one to two years—at a constant temperature of 64–68 °F (18–20 °C) to produce a hard cheese.

CHARACTERISTICS

The cylindrical and slightly convex, domed cheese wheels have a diameter of 14–18 in (35–45 cm), are 7–10 in (18–25 cm) high, and weigh 52–88 lb (24–40 kg). The oily, dark or golden-yellow rinds enclose a hard, crumbly cheese that is white to straw yellow in color. Young cheese (*fresco*) has a delicious, delicate flavor while *vecchio* has a fairly sweet, strong taste.

SPECIAL FEATURES

Approximately 50,000 tonnes of Grana Padano are produced each year. It takes 2 gallons of milk to produce 1 lb (17 l for 1 kg) of cheese.

SERVING SUGGESTIONS

This hard, granular cheese splits into small pieces and splinters when cut with an almond-shape knife specially designed for hard cheese. It is generally regarded as a table cheese, but it can also be used for grating or cooking. Sommelier's recommendation: White wines, such as Pinot Grigio or Chardonnay, Lugana, or Bianca di Custoza, make good partners for young cheese, while older versions combine well with full-bodied, mature red wines with moderate tannins. Slightly sweet wines also work well as these take away the salty character of riper cheeses.

Provolone Valpadana (PDO)

Stretched-curd style cheese
(*pasta filata*) made from
cow's milk
45% FDM

ORIGINS AND HISTORY

Brescia, Cremona, Padova, Piacenza,
Rovigo, Verona, Vicenza, Bergamo,
Mantova, Milan, Trento

This cheese, southern Italian in style, is
said to have been introduced during the
Austrian occupation of northern Italy.
Its name is derived from the Neapolitan
word *prova* (meaning "globe shape").
The *prova* was plunged into boiling
water to check whether the cheese had
reached the stage at which it formed
strings.

PRODUCTION

A mild Provolone is made by adding
calf's rennet to the milk. A sharper
cheese is created by the addition of
lamb's or kid's rennet. Young Provolone
ripens within one to two months,
although larger specimens may be
stored for up to a year. The cheeses are
covered with a thin coating of paraffin
to prevent them from drying out. They
are often tied with twine and hung up
to age. A smoked version of Provolone
is also available.

CHARACTERISTICS

Provolone Valpadana can come in a variety of forms: In a large sausage shape
(*salame*), small balls (*mandarino*),
pear shapes (*pera*), or as a truncated
cone. The weight varies depending on
the shape of the cheese, ranging from
2 lb to well over 60 lb (1–30 kg). The rind
is thin and shiny, golden yellow, or
yellowish-brown in color. The interior of
the cheese is cream or straw yellow
colored and the texture of the sliced
cheese is compact and smooth—or, in
the case of well-aged Provolone, somewhat flaky. Young Provolone is mild in
flavor and slightly sweet. After four
months the cheese becomes buttery
and spicy, and a six-month-old cheese
is full flavored and piquant.

SERVING SUGGESTIONS

Sommelier's recommendation: Young
Provolone is complemented by fresh
white wines from northern Italy. A
mature cheese also goes well with
mature red wines from northern Italy.
Smoked Provolone is delicious served
with youthful, cask-aged white wines
with distinct woody notes.

Quartirolo Lombardo (PDO)

Soft cheese made from
cow's milk
46% FDM

ORIGINS AND HISTORY

*Bergamo, Brescia, Como, Cremona,
Lodi, Milan, Pavia, Varese*

Until the early twentieth century the term *quartirolo* referred to a Lombardy cheese that was made entirely from a special type of aromatic milk produced by cows grazing on *herba quartirola*— in other words the last growth of new grass and herbs on the pastures following the third mowing. This cheese was especially popular in Milan, where it was known as Stracchino di Milano.

PRODUCTION

Today Quartirolo is produced throughout the year, but the best version is still the cheese produced in fall. The milk is partially or wholly skimmed, and after coagulation it is cut in two phases. The curd is transferred to rectangular molds, salted, and left to mature for 5 to 30 days.

CHARACTERISTICS

The cheeses are flat, rectangular blocks which measure 7 x 9 in (18 x 22 cm), 2–3 in (4–8 cm) in thickness, and weigh 3–8 lb (1.5–3.5 kg). Young Quartirolo has a white to straw-yellow rind and is creamy, fresh, and slightly acidic. An older Quartirolo is more supple and aromatic. It is also slightly bitter and the rind develops a brownish tinge, which conceals a firm, dense cheese. In the past Quartirolo was generally eaten after a few weeks of maturation (Quartirolo Maturo), but the current trend is to eat it fresh after just a few days (Quartirolo a Pasta Tenera).

SERVING SUGGESTIONS

Sommelier's recommendation: Pasta Tenera cheeses go best with fresh white wines, while Maturo versions demand robust, mature white wines or smooth reds with moderate tannins.

Taleggio (PDO)

Semi-hard cheese,
with red smear,
made from cow's milk
48% FDM

ORIGINS AND HISTORY

*Bergamo, Brescia, Como, Cremona,
Lodi, Milan, Pavia, Treviso, Novara*
This cheese, one of Italy's few red smear
cheeses, has been produced in the
Taleggio valley near Bergamo for many
centuries. It was first mentioned in old
documents about 1200.

PRODUCTION

Taleggio is usually made from pasteurized whole cow's milk to which rennet
is added. The curd is cut in two stages
and placed in cloths to drain before
being transferred to molds. Taleggio is
generally left to age for at least 40 days
in cool, humid conditions.

CHARACTERISTICS

A flat, more or less square slab, measuring 7 x 9 in (19 x 22 cm). It is usually
about 2 in (4 cm) thick and weighs
4–5 lb (1.7–2.2 kg). Its thin, soft rind
with its pinkish-yellow color—often
mottled with mold—conceals a homogeneous cheese, fine, soft, and supple
in texture with a friable core. It has a
slightly tangy taste that becomes
sharper and more piquant as it ages.

SPECIAL FEATURES

Variations in microclimate and the quality of milk used mean that a mountain-
made Taleggio (Taleggio di Montagna)
will taste different from one produced
in the valley (Taleggio di Planura).

SERVING SUGGESTIONS

Sommelier's recommendation: Taleggio
goes well with hot polenta or ripe pears,
especially if it is accompanied by
Gewürztraminer or Muscatel. Oltrepo-
Pavese wines also make pleasant
companions to "raw" Taleggio. Robust,
cask-aged, mature white wines and
rounded, velvety reds also make excellent partners for this famous Italian
cheese.

SIMILAR CHEESE VARIETIES

Robiola delle Valsassina is almost a
mini-version of Taleggio. Only half its
size, Robiola is better at absorbing the
salt and maturing all the way through.
Erborinato di Artavaggio, a semi-hard
cheese with green veining, is likewise
similar.

STRACCHINO—MILK FROM TIRED COWS

Stracchino used to be the collective name for a large variety of flat, square-shape cheeses that had undergone longish maturing periods and resembled Taleggio or Quartirolo. The name Stracchino likewise crops up in the names of other Lombardy cheeses, such as Stracchino di Gorgonzola. Stracchino originally referred to cheese made in the autumn from the milk of cows on their way back from their alpine pastures down to the valley, where they would arrive tired and exhausted (*strach*). Milk from these cows produced Stracchino, which was especially soft and creamy. Today the production area for this delicate fresh cheese encompasses the whole of Lombardy and parts of the Po valley. A Stracchino is rectangular or square in shape, measuring up to 10 in (25 cm) across, and 1–2 in (3–5 cm) thick. Soft and buttery in texture, Stracchino melts on the tongue and possesses a mild, sweetish flavor. In Lombardy Stracchino cheese forms part of every festive meal.

CHEESE FROM LIGURIA

The Ligurian Riviera, impregnated with the scent of herbs and flowers, may not produce a vast variety of cheeses, but it does nevertheless boast some delicious cheeses made from cow's, sheep's, and goat's milk. Its barren landscape means that livestock farming does not play much of a role in Liguria. One of its better-known cow's milk cheeses is Formaggio d'Alpeggio di Triora, a hard, sweetish cheese that has matured for 3–12 months and been produced up in the high alpine pastures during the summer months. It is also worth sampling some of Liguria's numerous small goat's cheeses (Caprini), which are marketed as fresh cheese, matured for one or two but no more than six weeks—either natural or marinated in herbs and oil, or even sprinkled with spices. In the area about Genoa, you can buy a creamy mixture, marketed in small plastic tubs, which is known by the unusual name of Prescinseûa. It is a yogurt-style cheese that is spread on bread. Mixed with a nut sauce, it is also served with pasta dishes.

OTHER CHEESES FROM VENETO

Morlacco is a typical, if rare, cheese from the Grappa mountain range. It is made from skimmed, untreated milk. The curd is heated and placed in molds, after which it is dry salted and left to ripen for about two weeks. If you are lucky, you will find this slightly tart cheese during the summer, when the cows are up in the alpine pastures. Pressato, a traditional hard cheese, is still made by a handful of small dairies in the Belluno valley. It gets its name from the pressing of the curd. It is still made in the traditional, ancient manner: The curd from almost completely skimmed milk is pressed, then the cheese wheels, weighing between 20 and 30 lb (9–14 kg), are ripened for one to three months. The cheese has a pleasantly mild, slightly sweet flavor. This Pressato should not be confused with Asiago Pressato.

Valtellina Casera (PDO)

Hard cheese made from
raw cow's milk
34% FDM

ORIGINS AND HISTORY

As a consequence of its remote location, the Valtellina valley has a unique microclimate. The cheeses traditionally produced here have histories stretching far back into the past. It was here toward the end of the eighteenth century that a sort of alpine version of Bitto was first made, a cheese that was larger and would keep longer than any of the cheeses hitherto produced. Valtellina Casera may be made only up in the alpine pastures near Sondrio, the provincial capital of Valtellina.

PRODUCTION

This cheese is produced in the same way as Bitto. It is matured for at least 60 days.

CHARACTERISTICS

Round loaf-shape cheeses weighing 15–26 lb (7–12 kg), with a diameter of 12–18 in (30–45 cm) and a height of 3–4 in (8–10 cm). It has a sweet and intense flavor, and a typical aroma of nuts and dried fruits. Both fresh and mature Valtellina are welcome additions to a meal.

SERVING SUGGESTIONS

Sommelier's recommendation: Young Valtellina goes well with full-bodied white wines, while the maturer cheese is to be enjoyed in combination with mature red wines, which possess a smooth quality—Sfursat for example.

Stelvio or Stilfser cheese (PDO)

Semi-hard cheese, made from cow's milk 50% FDM

ORIGINS AND HISTORY

Stelvio or Stilfser is a typical cheese made from natural milk produced among the pastures about the Stilfser-joch mountain. The pure quality of the milk, its authenticity, and the tradition in its area of origin have earned it protected origin status, the only cheese in southern Tyrol to enjoy this mark of distinction. Its authorized producer is Milkon/Mila in Bolzano, a dairy cooperative that is supplied by 5,000 mountain farms.

PRODUCTION

Traditionally, the surface of Stelvio cheese is washed twice a week with a weak saline solution. During the first two to three weeks of maturation, local microflora is added to the saline solution. These bacterial cultures give the cheese its characteristic rind color as well as other organoleptic features. The maturing time lasts altogether for two months.

CHARACTERISTICS

The cheeses weigh 18–22 lb (8–10 kg) and are 3–4 in (8–10 cm) thick with a diameter of 14–15 in (36–8 cm). The yellow-orange to orange-brown rind encloses a compact, pliable, soft interior that is pale straw yellow in color with irregular, small to medium-sized holes. It has a strong aroma and a spicy, robust taste.

SERVING SUGGESTIONS

Sommelier's recommendation: Local wines from the southern Tyrol make perfect companions for this cheese, although a young cheese may work better with a Pinot Bianco, Pinot Grigio, or chilled red Vernatsch. An older cheese would combine well with a Gewürztraminer, a robust Chardonnay, or a ripe Pinot Nero.

Montasio (PDO)

Semi-hard to hard cheese
made from cow's milk
40% FDM

ORIGINS AND HISTORY
Friuli, Julian Veneto, the provinces
Belluno, Treviso, sometimes Padua
and Venice
Montasio's history stretches back to the
thirteenth century, when it was
produced by the Benedictine monks of
Moggio in the Carnian Alps. Montasio is
one of several similar cheeses produced
in the Carnian Alps, which is why it used
to be known simply as Carnia.

PRODUCTION
The evening's milk is partially skimmed,
then mixed with milk from the following
morning. In all other respects the
production method is the same as for
other hard cheeses. The flavor is influenced not only by the grass and flowers
on which the cows graze, but also by
special cultures, with which the milk is
inoculated. The curd is heated and
pressed. Young Montasio (Fresco)
matures for two to four months, medium
mature Montasio (Mezzano) for five to
ten months, and an aged Montasio
(Stagionato) for at least ten months.

CHARACTERISTICS
The cheese is cylindrical in form, with a
12–16 in (30–40 cm) diameter, 2–4 in
(6–10 cm) thick, and weighs 13–18 lb
(6–8 kg). Young Montasio is mild with a
sweetish, milky taste, while the mature
cheese is full of flavor and stronger. It is
compact and pale yellow, with characteristic, homogeneous holes and a
smooth, elastic rind. It becomes grainy
and crumbly as it ages, while the rind
dries and darkens with maturity.

SERVING SUGGESTIONS
Young Montasio makes an excellent
starter served with dried fruit, nuts, or
one of the wide variety of pears grown
throughout the region. Mature Montasio makes a good grating cheese.
Sommelier's recommendation: A white
wine such as a Friaul or Sauvignon
Collio or a good Prosecco goes well with
young Montasio. Mature cheese should
be accompanied by a mature red Friaul.
Raboso Passito makes a surprising
companion to Montasio Stagionato.

SIMILAR CHEESE VARIETIES
Latteria Friulani is made in a similar way
to Montasio. Because its texture is
coarser grained, it retains rather more
moisture. Latterias vary in taste depending on where the milk is produced,
thanks to the variations in microflora
between one pasture and another.

Asiago (PDO)

Semi-hard/hard cheese
made from cow's milk
44% FDM (Asiago Pressato)

ORIGINS AND HISTORY

Vicenza, Trento, parts of Padua and Treviso

Sheep, which produced the milk for Asiago cheese, were grazing on the Asiago plateau (province of Vicenza) as far back as the year 1000. The protected origin status refers to Asiago d'Allevo and the less mature Asiago Pressato, two variations that differ in terms of their production method. Meanwhile, the quantity of Pressato produced is four times higher than d'Allevo.

PRODUCTION

The milk comes from the black spotted or brown variety of alpine cows. Asiago d'Allevo is made from partially skimmed milk taken from two milking sessions. After it is curdled, the heated curd is pressed for several days in special wooden forms without bases (*fascere*) before being plunged in a salt bath, then stored in the ripening room. Asiago d'Allevo Mezzano matures for six months, Vecchio for a year, and Stravecchio—an extra mature version—for up to two years. Whole milk is used to make Asiago Pressato. The curds are salted, reheated over a lower temperature, and then pressed. The curds are cut, scooped into the mold, and pressed a second time. The maturing time is considerably shorter—just 20 to 40 days.

CHARACTERISTICS

Asiago d'Allevo is a wheel-form cheese, 4–8 in (9–12 cm) thick with a diameter of 12–14 in (30–36 cm), and weighing 18–26 lb (8–12 kg). Its smooth, elastic rind conceals a golden-yellow, compact interior with a few holes that becomes harder and grainier with age. Fresh Asiago has a delicate milky taste, which grows stronger, spicier, piquant, and very aromatic as it matures. Asiago Pressato is slightly thicker and heavier 24–33 lb (11–15 kg). It has a smooth, straw-yellow rind with a white interior and a smattering of large, irregular holes. It tastes fresh and slightly sweet.

SERVING SUGGESTIONS

Younger Asiago goes well with white or rosé wines, while more mature cheese is better accompanied by mature, regional red wines.

Monte Veronese (PDO)

Semi-hard cheese made from
raw cow's milk
44% FDM or
35% FDM (d'Allevo)

ORIGINS AND HISTORY
Verona
Monte Veronese is one of Italy's oldest
alpine cheeses, and has been made by
local shepherds for many centuries. The
milk comes from cows grazing on the
high south-sloping pastures of Monti
Lessini, where the cows can be left to
graze in the alpine meadows for longer
than in some other alpine regions.

PRODUCTION
This hard cheese is produced in the usual
way by heating and pressing the curd.
There are two types of Monte Veronese
available: One made with full-cream milk
with a higher fat content, which ripens
for a maximum of two months; and the
traditional Monte Veronese d'Allevo,
which is made from partially skimmed
milk. The lower fat version may be
matured for six months to two years.

CHARACTERISTICS
The flat wheels of cheese measure
10–14 in (25–36 cm) in diameter, are
2–4 in (6–11 cm) thick, and weigh
13–20 lb (6–9 kg). The longer they
mature, the harder, drier, and darker
the rind. The cheese is straw yellow on
the inside with small, irregular holes. It
is a spicy, full-flavored cheese with a
slightly piquant taste.

SPECIAL FEATURES
Monte Veronese's unique qualities are
a result of the special soil and climate
conditions in the mountains about
Verona. The limited area of production,
the use of unpasteurized milk, and
traditional processing methods all
combine to make this an extremely
interesting cheese.

SERVING SUGGESTIONS
This is a classic semi-hard cheese,
commonly served with polenta.
Sommelier's recommendation: A young
Monte Veronese combines perfectly
with white wines such as Lugana from
the Lake Garda region, or even a classic, complex Soave. A medium-mature
cheese works well with fruitier red
Valpolicella and Bardolino wines. A
well-matured Ripasso or—even
better—a mature Amarone is guaranteed to go down well with a ripe, aged
cheese.

Parmigiano Reggiano (PDO)

Hard cheese made from
cow's milk
32% FDM

ORIGINS AND HISTORY
Modena, Parma, Reggio Emilia,
Mantova, Bologna

Parmigiano already enjoyed great popularity in Parma in the thirteenth century. The poet Francesco Maria Grapaldi put the following words into the mouth of Parmensis Caseus: "I am the noble fruit of the milk of Parma." Its name is based on a combination of the names of the provinces of Parma and Reggio Emilia. The same cheese was known as Reggiano in Reggio Emilia and as Parmigiano in Parma. In 1934 producers agreed to market their *Grana tipico* under the common name of Parmigiano Reggiano—also known as Parmesan.

PRODUCTION
Partially skimmed milk from the evening's milking is mixed with full-cream milk from the following morning's milking. The milk may come only from cows fed on fresh grass or hay from within the designated zone. It is heated to 108 °F (33 °C), then coagulated through the addition of rennet. The curd is broken up into small pieces and the temperature raised until the cheese and whey separate. The compacted curd is placed in muslin, transferred to a mold, and lightly pressed. The wheels remain in brine for several weeks, after which they are left to dry. Maturing takes one year, during which time the cheese is turned and washed at regular intervals. Its stages of maturity are young or *fresco* (one year), mature or *vecchio* (two years), and extra mature or *stravecchio* (three years).

CHARACTERISTICS
This cheese comes in circular, golden yellow, thick, slightly convex loaves, weighing 53–66 lb (24–30 kg). The oiled rind varies in color from dark to golden yellow. Inside, it is straw yellow with a grainy texture and has tiny air holes, which occasionally hold a residual "teardrop" of whey. It has a strong flavor with delicate nutty overtones.

SERVING SUGGESTIONS
Sommelier's recommendation: An extra mature Parmigiano combines very well with a glass of vintage Champagne. Its traditional partner is Lambrusco. Younger cheeses fare better with drier Lambruscos, while mature Parmesan can be paired with sweeter wines.

CENTRAL ITALY
Rome, Tuscany, Umbria

Central Italy is characterized by picturesque, medieval villages, and towns: Tuscany with its cultural gems of Florence and Siena, vast beaches, and—last but not least—Rome. It also comprises the green heart of Umbria, the region of Lazio, and the peaceful mountain villages of Le Marche. Abruzzo offers the cleanest beaches in Italy. The local cuisine among the cypress-covered hillsides of Tuscany is both simple and wholesome. The olive oil is particularly excellent and, combined with fresh herbs, imparts its unique flavor to meat and vegetable dishes. The range of regional cheeses includes some delicious sheep's milk specialties, with Pecorino topping the list.

The two regions of Umbria and Le Marche are well known for their art treasures and the beauty of the landscape. They also produce fresh cheeses made from cow's and sheep's milk, although these remain largely unknown outside the region. Instead, it is black and white truffles, olive oil, wine, and the highest quality meat that have earned this region its culinary reputation.

Neighbouring Lazio is a region of stunning scenery, delightful towns, and the Eternal City of Rome. The most famous dairy products from this region are named after the capital: Ricotta Romana and Pecorino Romano. Regional cuisine in Abruzzo and Molise tends to be solid and hearty. Fish is the predominant dish along the coast, while meat usually dominates the menu further inland. For a long time, these regions remained cut off from the rest of the world by high mountain ranges, a situation that has contributed to the survival of old traditions.

Left: Central Italy—a region of peaceful mountain villages and unspoilt nature.

Pecorino Toscano (PDO)

Hard cheese made from
sheep's milk
45% FDM

ORIGINS AND HISTORY

Arezzo, Pisa, Massa Carrara,
Livorno, Grosseto, Florence, Prato,
Lucca, Pistoia, Siena, Terni, Perugia,
Viterbo

This Pecorino was first produced in the
Maremma valley and in the hills about
Siena and Pisa. Pecorino Toscano is the
only Tuscan cheese with protected
origin status. Production extends to
parts of Umbria and Lazio. In Tuscany
itself and further south, this cheese is
also known as *cacio*, a later form of the
Latin word *caseus*, meaning cheese.

PRODUCTION

Pasteurized or raw milk may be used to
make this cheese. Some producers use
plant rennet. The production method
varies depending on the type of
Pecorino required—young or mature. If
the cheese is to be sold young, the curd
is cut correspondingly coarsely. When
making the more mature version, the
curds undergo additional heating. A
soft, young cheese ripens for at least 20
days. The more mature varieties are
stored for four to six months.

CHARACTERISTICS

Cylindrical rounds with a diameter of
6–9 in (15–22 cm) in, 3–4 in (7–11 cm)
in thickness, and with a weight of 2–8 lb
(1–3.5 kg). Fresh Pecorino is pale
yellow in color with a similar rind. It is
compact with a few small holes. In older
Pecorino, the color of the rind and
cheese becomes straw yellow, and it
develops a harder texture. Even after a
lengthy maturing period, Pecorino
Toscano retains a mild, full-flavored,
and sweet taste.

SERVING SUGGESTIONS

Sommelier's recommendation: A good
Tuscan wine is the best choice. Baked
Pecorino is a delicious regional
specialty that goes well with some of
the modern IGT wines of Tuscany. This
peppery delicacy, marinated in honey,
is excellent when paired with a glass of
Vinsanto. Young cheese combines well
with Tuscan white wine such as Pomino
or Vernaccia di San Gimignano. A
mature Pecorino demands a mature,
rich red wine such as Brunello di
Montalcino, and an extra mature variety works well with Vinsanto.

Casciotta d'Urbino (PDO)

Soft cheese made from
cow's or sheep's milk
45% FDM

ORIGINS AND HISTORY
Pesaro, Urbino
Casciotta d'Urbino is the only one of
many Casciotta varieties with a
protected designation of origin.
Michelangelo himself was a great fan of
Casciotta. Rents from his numerous
farm holdings were paid to him in the
form of this cheese. His favorite variety
was the cheese produced during the
spring, when the grass is at its tender-
est.

PRODUCTION
Caciotta or Casciotta is produced all
year. It is made mainly from sheep's milk
(70%), mixed with cow's milk. The
sheep's milk must come from specific
breeds of sheep. The milk must be coagulated at milking temperature. Maturing time is 15–30 days.

CHARACTERISTICS
Small, cylindrical wheels with a 5–6 in
(12–16 cm) diameter, measuring 2–3 in
(5–7 cm) in thickness, and a weight of
2–3 lb (0.8–1.2 kg). The thin rind
conceals a dense, white to straw-yellow,
crumbly interior with few holes. It is
mild in flavor with a pleasantly milky
aroma.

SPECIAL FEATURES
The word *caciotta* is derived from *cacio*
and from the Latin word *caseus*, which
in central Italy is the term given to a
small circle of cheese weighing up to
2 lb (1 kg). The cheese can be either
fresh or mature. It is usually made with
sheep's milk or a combination of sheep's
and cow's milk. Occasionally it is made
from pure buffalo or pure cow's milk. In
a region dominated by sheep farming,
the fresh, delicate taste of Caciotta
makes it a popular alternative to some
of the more mature and strongly favored
sheep's cheeses. A large number of local
Caciotta cheeses are produced in
Tuscany, Umbria, Le Marche, and Lazio.

SERVING SUGGESTIONS
Sommelier's recommendation: Choose
a modern, robust, and complex Orvieto
to accompany a younger cheese, while
mature Umbrian reds will go better with
older cheeses.

Ricotta Romana (PDO)

Fresh cheese made from the
whey of sheep's milk
50% FDM

ORIGINS AND HISTORY

Campagna romana

Ricotta Romana—a delicate, sweet cheese that is produced in the countryside about Rome—is one of the best known types of Ricotta and now enjoys protected origin status. Researchers believe that Ricotta was about even before the birth of Christ. Evidence suggests that it used to be sweetened with honey, and that it was the cheese referred to by the Roman statesman Marcus Porcius Cato (born 234 BC) in his work *De Agricultura*. The word *ricotta* means "cooked again"—the first time milk is heated to induce curdling, and the second time it is "cooked" to make cheese from the whey. Ricotta Romana may be made only from milk produced by the Siciliana, Comisana, and Sarda breeds of sheep, and production is limited to the period between November and June.

PRODUCTION

Ricotta is made from the whey of Pecorino Romano, which has been curdled by the addition of lemon or vinegar so that the milk proteins form a soft curd. The solids thus produced are scooped out and placed in a sieve. Once the Ricotta has drained and cooled, it is ready to eat immediately. Ricotta is usually marketed as a fresh product.

CHARACTERISTICS

Typically a truncated cone-shape product, many variations of which are available. The weight can range from 10 oz (300 g) up to 4 lb (2 kg). The cheese has a thin, flat rind, concealing a soft, ivory-colored cheese. It has an underlying fresh, sweet taste that is pleasantly milky and leaves a creamy flavor on the tongue. An unsalted version of Ricotta, Ricotta tipo dolce, is available, as well as Ricotta salata, a salted version, and Ricotta tipo forte, a matured and salted variety. Extra matured Ricotta is firm (Ricotta secca) and suitable for grating.

SERVING SUGGESTIONS

Sommelier's recommendation: Freshly made Ricotta is incorporated in a variety of filled pasta dishes such as ravioli, but it also tastes delicious just on its own. White wines work best with Ricotta, fresh white wines with Ricotta tipo dolce, and more complex ones with Ricotta salata or Ricotta tipo forte.

MORE CHEESE SPECIALTIES FROM CENTRAL ITALY

Caciotta Romana from the Lazio region belongs to the extended family of sheep's cheeses, even though some producers use a combination of sheep's and cow's milk. There are many different varieties of the small, soft *caciotta* cheeses in central Italy, most of them weighing less than 2 lb (1 kg). Caciotta may be consumed fresh or *semistagionato* (semi-matured). Once dried, the cheese is plunged in brine and left to ripen for about 14 days or, occasionally, up to 2 months. Abruzzo and Molise is the home of Caciocavallo di Agnone, a stretched-curd-type cheese made from cow's milk that can ripen for three months to three years. The pear-shape cheeses are tied together in twos. Young cheeses have a sweet and creamy flavor; older cheeses develop a stronger taste. Caciofiore is a typical fresh cheese from central Italy. Plant rennet from artichokes is used to coagulate the milk. In Abruzzo saffron is sometimes used to give color to this cheese. Scamorza cheese from the Abruzzo and Molise is also well known, and Basilicata from southern Italy produces a noteworthy version of this pear-shape fresh cheese too. Presumably the name—in a similar way to Motarella—is derived from the word *scamozzare* (to cut off the head). Scamorza cheese is often smoked. These sweet, creamy, and delicate *pasta-filata*-style cheeses usually mature in just a few days.

SOUTHERN ITALY
Greeks, Romans, and Normans

Landscapes of magical beauty, towns reverberating with sheer *joie de vivre*, magnificent historical landmarks ranging from Greek temples, the ruins of Roman towns and Norman castles, to sumptuous Baroque buildings—Italy's southernmost regions offer an impressive array of cultural experiences and culinary highlights.

The hot climate of Campania and its restless capital of Naples do perfect justice to the refreshing slightly sweet/sour flavor and distinctly milky taste of buffalo Mozzarella cheese. Other delicious cheeses, such as Provolone and Caciocavallo, also originate in Campania. In Apulia, Calabria, and Basilicata people live off the sea, wheat, and olive trees. The climate is too hot for lush vegetation or large-scale cattle farming. Goats and sheep, however, contend better with the sparse pastures, which explains the large amount of sheep's and goat's cheese produced in this part of the country.

In terms of its cuisine, the sunny island of Sicily has been influenced by centuries of being invaded by a succession of conquerors. The island is home to a large number of cows, which supply the milk for Sicily's famous Ragusano. Sicilians generally enjoy their Pecorino with a chunk of country-style bread, sprinkled with olive oil and accompanied by a few onions, tomatoes, olives, and, of course, a glass of wine. However, the true home of Pecorini—at least according to Sardinians—is Sardinia, the "island of shepherds." It is true that conditions here are perfect for the production of Pecorino Romano, so much so that only a small proportion of Pecorino Romano is still produced in its original home of Lazio.

Left: The impressive diversity of southern Italy.

Mozzarella di Bufala (PDO)

Stretched-curd / *pasta filata*
cheese made from buffalo milk
52% FDM

ORIGINS AND HISTORY

Caserta, Salerno, Frosinone, Latina,
Naples, Benevento, Rome

A cheese called Mozza was mentioned as early as the fourth century. The name Mozzarella comes from the word *mozzare* (to cut off), because the individual portions of cheese were cut off from the kneaded mass. Mozzarella di Bufala is made exclusively from milk supplied by black water buffalo. Buffalo have been kept in Italy since the sixteenth century and were used as draught animals in marshy river areas. Nowadays, buffalo rearing is mainly confined to southern Italy. Only Mozzarella di Bufala Campana is allowed to carry the protected origin designation.

PRODUCTION

The buffalo milk has to curdle, drain, and then dry. The curd is coarsely cut before near-boiling water is poured over the crumbly mass. It is kneaded and stirred until the steaming mass takes on a rubbery and supple consistency. The cheese must be so pliable that it can be drawn into long threads without breaking. The cheese maker cuts off sections of cheese, each weighing about 9 lb (4 kg)—the Italian *mozzatura* means "cutting off." These portions are shaped into balls or twisted into plaits, then cooled.

CHARACTERISTICS

Mozzarella comes in a variety of shapes, ranging from small, bite-size nuggets, balls, and plaits to large cheese braids. Individual weight varies correspondingly, from 1–20 oz (30–600 g). The cheese is porcelain white in color, elastic, and slightly granular to melting in consistency. When sliced the inner cheese reveals a flaky structure and is said to "weep," whereby a whitish whey oozes from the cheese. It has a pleasant, slightly tart, refreshing flavor.

SPECIAL FEATURES

Mozzarella is sometimes smoked over dried wheat stalks, foliage, or wood, in which case it is known as Mozzarella di bufala afumifacata.

SERVING SUGGESTIONS

Mozzarella is at its best when freshest and when not refrigerated. Sommelier's recommendation: It is ideally combined with a fine white wine that does not contain too much acid.

MOZZARELLA — CONQUERING THE WORLD

Mozzarella is best consumed when it is at its freshest. If refrigerated it will keep for several days preserved in whey. Before advances in technology succeeded in extending the cheese's storage capacity by preserving it in brine and vacuum-sealing it in plastic, it was only the inhabitants of Campania and Apulia that were able to enjoy Mozzarella. Increased demand has now led to Mozzarella being made from a combination of cow's and buffalo milk, or entirely from cow's milk. This is the case not only in Italy but also in the USA, Australia, and throughout Europe. In Italy this type of cow's milk cheese is known as *fior di latte* (flower of the milk). It is produced in the same way as Mozzarella and may be marketed in balls or in egg- or pear-shape portions. It has a fat content of 44% FDM. It resembles Mozzarella in consistency: White cheese with a fibrous structure composed of many layers, which become visible once you slice into it. It has a light, white, smooth, and shiny rind; it weighs 2–35 oz (50–1,000 g), and it has a mild, slightly acidic flavor. The category of *pasta filata* cheeses includes other Italian specialty cheeses, such as Provolone, Provatura, and Caciocavallo. In southern Italy extra-mature and consequently hard *pasta filata* cheeses are often used for grating.

Canestrato Pugliese (PDO)

Hard cheese made from
sheep's milk
45% FDM

ORIGINS AND HISTORY
Foggia
Even a work as old as Homer's *Odyssey*
contains references to the production
method used to make this type of
sheep's cheese. Polyphemus's technique of drying the curd in woven rush
(*canestri*) baskets is still used to this
day.

PRODUCTION
Only milk from the Gentile di Puglia
breed of sheep, which are descended
from Merino sheep, may be used for this
cheese. It is produced from December
to May. The curd is gently heated, then
transferred to rush baskets to drain
before being pressed by hand and
rinsed with hot whey. After draining,
the cheeses are dry salted with sea salt
and left to mature in cool, dry conditions for at least three months—in some
cases up to one year. During this period
the rind is brushed regularly with olive
oil or vinegar.

CHARACTERISTICS
The wheels, 4–6 in (10–14 cm) thick,
can vary in size and weight—the weight
of a wheel can be 15–30 lb (7–14 kg).
The surface of the cheese is characteristically marked with the imprint of the
pattern transferred from the woven
rush basket. The cheese is the color of
straw, with a firm consistency, and has
a strong, piquant flavor.

SPECIAL FEATURES
The majority of cheeses are matured in
a basket made from a particular type of
Apulian reed, the distinctive, sweet
aroma of which blends with the cheese.

SERVING SUGGESTIONS
Recommended wines include a Salice
Salentino Riserva, a rosé or red Castel
del Monte, a mature Negroamaro, or
any other robust wine from southern
Italy.

SIMILAR CHEESE VARIETIES
In bygone days shepherds from Apulia
used to move their herds to the Abruzzo
during the summer months to take
advantage of the pastures there. In
doing so they introduced their own
particular method of cheese making to
the region. For this reason cheeses such
as Pecorino Abruzzese and Incanes-
trato foggiano di Castel del Monte, a
typical Pecorino from Castel del Monte,
are similar to Canestrato Pugliese.

Caciocavallo Silano (PDO)

Stretched-curd cheese (*pasta filata*)
made from cow's milk
44% FDM

ORIGINS AND HISTORY

Crotone, Catanzaro, Cosenza, Avellino, Benevento, Caserta, Naples, Isernia, Campobasso, Bari Taranto, Brindisi, Matera, Potenza

This cheese was originally produced on the mountainous Sila plateau. The tradition of tying the cheeses together and suspending them *a cavallo*, or straddling a horizontal pole, may well be the origin of the name. Caciocavallo Silano is the only Caciocavallo with a protected designation of origin.

PRODUCTION

The cheese is produced in the same way as *pasta filata* cheese. The maturing time is three or six to twelve months. The cheeses are strung together in pairs to ripen and suspended from special frames (*a cavallo*). Their taste may be mild or quite strong, depending on age and on whether goat or calf rennet is chosen.

CHARACTERISTICS

This cheese can be shaped like an irregular figure of eight or like a pear, elongated, or round with a short neck. An individual cheese weighs in the region of 4 lb (2 kg). Beneath its thin, smooth rind is a smooth, compact, white or straw-yellow cheese which is notable for its full flavor. Young cheese is mild

and sweet, while older cheese is rather stronger and piquant.

SERVING SUGGESTIONS

The best way to bring out the full flavor and aroma of this cheese is to grill or cook it in a skillet with olive oil and herbs. Sommelier's recommendation: Mature Negoramaro or Nero d'Avola wines make the best companions to cheese produced in this way.

SPECIAL FEATURES

An élite version of this cheese is Caciocavallo made from the milk of the rare Podolica breed of cow (Caciocavallo Podolico). These cows graze on succulent, aromatic grasses. The cows of this breed are limited in number and their milk is of exceptional quality. Since Podolica cows yield milk only when they have calves, this type of cheese is produced only between spring and summer.

SARDINIA AND SICILY

Pecorino—the cheese with a thousand faces

This famous family of hard sheep's milk cheese, which is found in a thousand different variations, is regarded as the oldest of all Italian cheeses.

There is ample evidence that Pecorino was being consumed by the Sabinians (Lazio) some 2,000 years ago. Legend has it that Romulus fortified himself with a Pecorino made from ewe's and goat's milk when he founded Rome. A report written in the first century BC by Lucius Moderatus Columella gives a very detailed account of the production of a salted Pecorino. The Italian word *pecora* means "milking ewe," hence the Italian collective name Pecorino for all sheep's milk cheeses. Pecorini are produced all over Italy—they can be fresh, mature, mild, or piquant. They vary in size and shape, and differ in the type of milk used and in the manner in which they are produced. A true Pecorino, however, is always made from sheep's milk. It is produced mainly in central and southern Italy, Sardinia, and Sicily—in other words wherever large herds of sheep are found. Some types of Pecorino have protected origin status: Pecorino Romano (Lazio, Tuscany, Sardinia), Pecorino Sardo (Sardinia), Pecorino Siciliano (Sicily), and Pecorino Toscana (Tuscany).

Left: Sardinia and Sicily—the essence of *la dolce vita*.

ADDICTIVE BREAD

In Roman and southern Italian cuisine Pecorino is used as a grating cheese, but it is equally popular served with an aperitif. The aperitif takes on a distinctively Sardinian character if pieces of Pecorino are served with Pane Carasau, a wafer-thin, crispy flat bread. It tastes delicious all on its own, simply broken up into large pieces, but is even better served with generous circles of Pane Carasau, warmed in the oven, piled loosely on top of one another on a plate, then sprinkled with rosemary and a little coarsely ground sea salt, and drizzled with olive oil. Beware, though: Pane Carasau can become addictive. Once you begin to nibble, it is difficult to stop. Sardinian wine specialties, such as Torbato Spumante or a red Cannonau di Sardegna, are the perfect partners to serve with this dish.

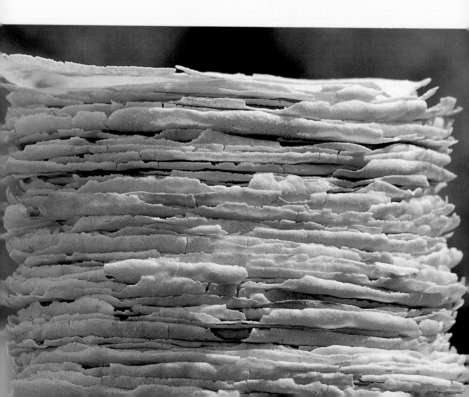

Pecorino Romano (PDO)

Hard cheese made from sheep's milk
45% FDM

ORIGINS AND HISTORY
Rome, Rieti, Viterbo, Latina, Grosseto, Cagliari, Nuoro, Oristano, Sassari
Despite the fact that the rural countryside near Rome was once the heart of mass-produced Pecorino Romano, it is now largely produced on the island of Sardinia, where millions of sheep continue to graze in what is a largely unspoilt natural environment. It is here that a regular Pecorino industry has blossomed, thanks to the efforts of some astute Roman and Neapolitan entrepreneurs.

PRODUCTION
Pecorino is produced from November to June. The evening's milk is mixed with fresh milk from the following morning. Immediately upon delivery, it is heated to induce curdling and inoculated with milk ferments. Lamb's rennet is then added. The curd is cut into grain-size pieces and heated to 118 °F (48 °C). The whey is drained off and the cheesy mass is transferred to a cylindrical form and pressed. The cheese wheels spend two months in passing through several phases, during which they are salted by hand by their own salt masters. Pecorino is finally left to mature for five months, during which time it is brushed regularly with brine.

CHARACTERISTICS
This cheese is a tall cylinder with a diameter of 10–14 in (25–35 cm). It is 8–14 in (20–35 cm) in height, 48–73 lb (22–33 kg) in weight. The outside of this cheese is covered with an intensely straw-yellow rind, or with dark-brown colored rind if it has been treated with a protective layer of fat. The cheese has a compact, grainy consistency and is white to straw colored. It is a pleasant-smelling cheese with a characteristic and distinctive aroma and a piquant, slightly sharp, and salty taste.

SERVING SUGGESTIONS
Fave Pecorino is a popular snack served in Rome to accompany an aperitif. It consists of Pecorino broken into small pieces and served with fresh fava (broad) beans and a little salt. Romans like to complement this dish with a glass of red Cerveteri from the Lazio region. Sommelier's recommendation: A fairly robust type of white wine, which—if the Pecorino is a mature one—may well have distinct residual sugar. A mature red wine, low in tannins, may also be chosen.

Pecorino Sardo (PDO)

Hard cheese made from
sheep's milk
35–40% FDM

ORIGINS AND HISTORY
Cagliari, Nuoro, Oristano, Sassari
Pecorino Sardo is a typical island
Pecorino of which Sardinians are justi-
fiably proud. It has a history that
stretches back to ancient times. It was
formerly known as Semicotto (semi-
cooked) on account of the fact that as
soon as the cheeses were ready, they
were plunged into boiling whey to
improve their keeping qualities.
Pecorino Sardo was the last of Sardinia's
three sheep's milk cheeses to be
awarded protected origin status.

PRODUCTION
The milk for Pecorino Sardo comes
from Sardinian sheep. As mentioned
above, the finished cheeses are plunged
briefly into boiling whey. There are two
types of this cheese: The mild version
(*dolce*) matures for 20 to 60 days, while
the stronger version (*maturo*) is left to
ripen for two to six months. If it is
intended for use as a grating cheese, it
matures for as long as 12 months. The
mature type may also be smoked,
which gives it an even more pronounced
taste.

CHARACTERISTICS
Young Pecorino Sardo measures 6–7 in
(15–18 cm) in diameter, is 2–4 in

(6–10 cm) thick, and weighs 4–5 lb
(1.7–2.3 kg). The thin, smooth rind is
white to straw yellow in color and
conceals a firm, compact cheese with a
delicate, aromatic flavor. On average,
Sardo Maturo cheese is usually a little
heavier (up to 9 lb/4 kg). As the cheese
ages, the rind becomes thicker and
takes on a brownish tinge, while the
cheese becomes firmer. A cheese that
has been left to ripen for about eight
months will develop a spicier, stronger
note.

SERVING SUGGESTIONS
Sommelier's recommendation: A
Vermentino di Sardegna would make an
excellent partner for a young Pecorino,
while a mature, velvety Cannonau di
Sardegna would combine well with a
more mature cheese.

Fiore Sardo (PDO)

Hard cheese made from
sheep's milk
40% FDM

ORIGINS AND HISTORY
Cagliari, Nuoro, Oristano, Sassari
This Pecorino cheese has a long history.
Fiore Sardo—"flower of Sardinia"—
probably owes its name to the ancient
custom of using wild thistles to coagulate the milk for the cheese. Fiore Sardo
used to be the only cheese known
beyond the island's shores. Great quantities were brought by merchants from
Naples, Genoa, and Livorno.

PRODUCTION
The milk for this cheese comes from
Sardinian sheep. As soon as the curds
have been placed in the molds that give
the cheese its characteristic, flattened
cylindrical shape, hot water is briefly
poured over them to make the rinds
thicker and more resistant. The fresh
cheese is initially left to dry for a while
over an open fire, which leaves it lightly
smoked. The cheeses are then matured
for up to six months in cellars. During
this period they are regularly rubbed
with olive oil, sometimes mixed with a
little mutton fat. This procedure
prevents the rind from drying out, stops
molds from forming on the surface, and
prevents the cheese from losing any of
its weight. Fiore Sardo is one of the last
Italian cheeses to have its rind
protected by this natural method.

CHARACTERISTICS
The shape of Fiore Sardo resembles
somewhat two thick, truncated cones,
the bases of which have been placed
end to end. A cheese with a diameter of
5–8 in (12–20 cm), measuring 5–6 in
(12–15 cm) in height, and with a weight
of 3–9 lb (1.5–4 kg). Depending on its
level of maturity, the rind is deep yellow
to dark brown in color and conceals a
firm, fresh, white to whitish-yellow
cheese. It has a characteristic, piquant
taste with the full flavor of sheep's milk,
a taste that becomes stronger with age.

SERVING SUGGESTIONS
Young cheese makes an excellent table
cheese, and the mature version is often
used for grating. Wines such as
Vermentino go well with younger
cheeses, while a mature Cannonau di
Sardegna would make a good companion for a stronger-flavored, older
cheese.

Pecorino Siciliano (PDO)

Hard cheese made from
sheep's milk
48% FDM

ORIGINS AND HISTORY

All sheep's cheese made in Sicily is known by the collective name of Pecorino Siciliano. This official designation does, however, cover numerous individual specialties that the Sicilians call by a host of different names, depending on the animals' fodder, the maturing time, and the season. And yet the cheese always remains the same: Legendary and steeped in tradition, a cheese, which—to quote one enthusiast—"like a true Sicilian is a blend of one, none, and a hundred thousand qualities."

PRODUCTION

Sicilian Pecorino is produced from October to June. It matures for at least four months and, occasionally, up to two years.

CHARACTERISTICS

The cheeses are cylinders with flattened sides that can weigh 9–33 lb (4–15 kg). Depending on how long it has matured, the color of the rind varies from yellowish-white to brown. The cheese has a firm consistency. Winter-produced Pecorino Siciliano is grayish-white, while cheeses produced in spring and summer are pale yellowish in color with just a few small holes. It has a pronounced, characteristic aroma and a hearty, spicy flavor.

SPECIAL FEATURES

There is also a spicy version of this cheese with peppercorns, known as Pipatu (peppered cheese). Other versions include Maiorchino and Marzulinu, which refer to fresh, unsalted cheese produced in spring. Mild young Pecorino Siciliano is known as Musciu, and as soon as it has been salted it is called Primu Sali.

SERVING SUGGESTIONS

Pecorino Siciliano is used for grating in Sicilian dishes and as a table cheese. Sommelier's recommendation: Young Pecorino combines beautifully with Sicilian white wines such as Cataratto or Inzolia. Mature Pecorino is best served with a Nero d'Avola, while the aromatic complexity of an extra-mature Pecorino will be better appreciated if partnered by a mature, well-rounded Marsala.

Ragusano (PDO)

Pasta filata/stretched-curd
cheese made from cow's milk
44% FDM

ORIGINS AND HISTORY

This cheese takes its name from the province of Ragusano where it is made. It belongs to the group of Caciocavallo cheeses, those circular *pasta filata* cheeses that are bound up with twine. Because of its appearance, it is also known in Sicily as Caciocavallo, Provolone, or Scaluni (step). When referring to a devious person, Sicilians say that he has "four faces like a Cacio-cavallo." Ragusano does indeed have four faces, in the form of four sides. Its rectangular shape distinguishes it from the familiar Caciocavallo cheese, which is usually circular in shape.

PRODUCTION

Ragusano is produced in the same way as classic *pasta filata* cheese. It takes three months to mature and is some-times left for up to one year. It is suspended strung up in pairs over a frame and occasionally smoked over a straw fire.

CHARACTERISTICS

Ragusano is produced in blocks with rounded edges 6–7 in x 17–20 in (15–18 cm x 43–53 cm) and weighs 13–26 lb (6–12 kg). The rind of young cheese is yellow to golden yellow in color, while older Ragusanos have a dark-brown rind that conceals a compact white to straw-yellow interior with a few holes. A six-month-old Ragusano has a mild, delicate taste. Older cheeses develop a spicier, piquant flavor. Because of their size, the blocks of cheese take a long time to ripen, which gives Ragusano its characteristically piquant flavor. Smoked Ragusano has a delicately smoked aroma.

SERVING SUGGESTIONS

Sommelier's recommendation: Sicilian white wines compliment young Ragu-sano beautifully, while older cheese combines very well with smooth, full-flavored reds—Nero d'Avola, for exam-ple. The smoked version of Ragusano should be accompanied by a dry Marsala or a cask-aged Sicilian Chardonnay.

SPAIN
Diversity at its finest

Cheese production in Spain has a tradition going back thousands of years. Archaeologists have unearthed equipment from the Iron and Bronze Ages clearly indicative of cheese production. Cheese has always been a staple food in Spain and, despite the not insignificant cattle farming in the north of the country, the bulk of Spanish cheese has always been made from sheep's and goat's milk—often in small family enterprises and according to centuries-old traditions. Spanish sheep's and goat's milk cheeses provide a special taste experience and are often robust and intense, but may be mellow and mild.

The diversity of cheeses is as varied as the landscape. There are over 120 delicious varieties available and almost every province has its own specialties. They range from fresh cheese to ripe cheeses, cheeses curdled with rennet and with lactic acid, to cheeses with different shapes, colors and sizes, with engraved rinds and wonderful graphic decoration, with moldy rind, or else smoked, spiced, or preserved in oil. Twenty-six of them carry the EU's protective designation of origin.

Left: Almost every province in Spain produces its own cheese specialty.

MIXED MILK CHEESE

About half of Spanish cheeses are made from mixed milk comprising cow's, goat's, and/or sheep's milk. The cow's milk provides the necessary quantity, the basic flavor, and the acidification, while the goat's milk gives an attractive white color and a slightly piquant and/or sour taste. The sheep's milk improves the flavor, consistency, aroma, and fat content of the cheese.

Three different types of mixed milk cheeses have been defined by the producers and the Spanish Ministry of Agriculture in order to be able to guarantee specific quality standards: Hispánico is made solely from sheep's (min. 30%) and cow's milk (min. 50%) with a fat content of 45% FDM. Ibérico is a three-milk cheese: It has to contain at least 50% cow's milk, at least 30% goat's milk, and at least 10% sheep's milk. Ibérico's fat content is also 45% FDM. Mesta has to be made from at least 75% sheep's milk, at least 15% cow's milk, and, optionally, up to a maximum of 5% goat's milk. The high proportion of sheep's milk means a fat content of 50% FDM. Ibérico is the most commonly produced and most widely consumed cheese in Spain.

TAPAS — SPOILT FOR CHOICE

How about a couple of almonds or olives, a piece of cheese, sausage, or air-dried ham? Or a little deep-fried seafood, tiny peppers, fried ceps, spinach croquettes, tender lettuce hearts, or tortillas? The range of tasty delicacies that start off or even replace a meal in Spain is almost unlimited. They are served cold, hot, simple, or sophisticated; fried, steamed, marinated, boiled, braised, or preserved. The main thing is that they can simply be enjoyed at the bar in the company of friends and with a glass of good wine. The precise origins of the tapas culture in Spain are a subject for dispute among experts. In Castile reference is often made to the Castilian King Alfonso X as the originator of small portions because he was advised by his doctor to exercise restraint when it came to food. The Andalusians are convinced that the tapas culture originates from Andalusia, it being an age-old custom in the sunny south to enjoy a glass of sherry out in the open together with a choice of little delicacies on a small plate (*tapa*). Then again, perhaps it was the Moors who brought the tapas culture to Andalusia from their homeland, where small appetizers are still considered a sign of hospitality today.

Top: Many Spanish cheeses are made from a combination of different types of milk.

Right and below: The choice of tapas is almost unlimited.

Ibérico

Semi-hard/hard cheese
made from mixed milk
45–50% FDM

Juan Manuel Sanz/© ICEX

ORIGINS AND HISTORY

The best known and also the most significant of the three types of mixed milk cheeses in terms of quantity is Ibérico. It comes closest to the classic definition of a mixed milk cheese and its flavor qualities also make it a success. Ibérico can be produced in all regions of Spain and the producers are primarily the large dairies.

PRODUCTION

A distinction is made between four stages of ripeness: Young (25 to 30 days), semi-ripe (50 to 60 days), ripe (three months), and old (six months). Once it has finished ripening, the cheese is covered with a paraffin or plastic layer to make sure that it does not dry out and that it retains its weight.

CHARACTERISTICS

Cylindrical in shape, similar to Manchego, measuring 6 in (15 cm) in height, with a diameter of 12 in (30 cm), and weight of 7–9 lb (3–4 kg). The color of the rind varies according to the stage of ripeness: White or light yellow with young cheeses, brown for ripe, and dark brown for an old Ibérico. The color of the cheese also changes according to ripeness, from an ivory color with the young cheese to straw yellow with an old cheese. A semi-ripe Ibérico tastes fresh and mild, the cheese becoming stronger and more piquant as it ripens. The cow's milk gives the cheese its volume and slight acidity, while the goat's milk makes it slightly piquant, and the sheep's milk gives it its buttery quality and aroma.

SERVING SUGGESTIONS

In Spain Iberico is often eaten as a dessert together with Membrillo (quince jelly). Sommelier's recommendation: Ibérico is well suited to red wines from the Valdepeñas DO. When served with quince jelly it also harmonizes well with a traditional, fortified sweet wine such as a Muscatel or a liqueur wine from Carinena.

Queso de Tetilla (PDO)

Semi-hard cheese made from
cow's milk
45% FDM

ORIGINS AND HISTORY
Tetilla may be produced throughout
Galicia even though the province of La
Coruña and parts of the neighboring
provinces of Pontevedra and Lugo are
the original homeland of the "little teat."
Tetilla is also known as Queso de Perilla,
Queso de Teta, Queso de Teta de Vaca,
and Queso Gallego de Teta.

PRODUCTION
Tetilla is produced by both small family
enterprises and large dairies using raw
or pasteurized, full-cream cow's milk.
The milk comes from Rubia Gallega
cows—a traditional, regional breed—
as well as from Friesian cows, both of
which are specially fed on autumn-flow-
ering beet in the winter. The milk is
heated and rennet added before the
curds are carefully squeezed, salted,
and shaped. Tetilla ripens very briefly
for at least 7 days, but usually for 15–20,
in a cool place that is not too damp.

CHARACTERISTICS
Cone shape, bulging outward or inward,
similar to a teat. The diameter at the
base measures 3½–4 in (9–15 cm),
height 4–6 in (10–15 cm), weight about
2–3 lb (0.75–1.5 kg). It has a thin, yellow
rind, and a compact, soft, creamy, and
elastic texture with a straw-yellow to
ivory-colored tinge and a few irregular
holes. Tetilla has a mild, creamy taste
with the characteristic aroma of beet
blossom, slightly acidic and pleasantly
fatty on the palate.

SPECIAL FEATURES
Tetilla and other handcraft cheese varieties from the region can still be bought
in corner shops in Santiago de
Compostela, the destination at the end
of the road to Santiago.

SERVING SUGGESTIONS
In Spain Tetilla is often eaten cut into
cubes and served with a little quince
jelly or paste. It goes well with fruity
white wines from Rías Baixas or reds
from Rioja. A red wine from the relatively new Valdeorras DO provides an
interesting alternative. In Galicia, incidentally, wine is often drunk from tazas,
which are small porcelain bowls.

Queso do Cebreiro (PDO)

Fresh cheese made from
cow's milk
45–60% FDM

ORIGINS AND HISTORY

Cebreiro has been prized by connoisseurs since the eighteenth century. It is a rustic cheese originating from the high Piedrafita and Becerreá mountain passes in the province of Lugo, where it is produced by hand in small quantities only. The best place to find it is at the Galician markets.

PRODUCTION

Cebreiro is usually made solely from cow's milk, but up to 40% goat's milk may be added in certain instances. The cow's milk comes from the Rubia Gallea, Pardo Alpina, and Frisona breeds. Cebreiro is available as a fresh cheese or slightly ripened.

CHARACTERISTICS

Its distinctive shape is reminiscent of a mushroom or a squashed chef's hat. Its typical features are its thin rind and its soft, creamy texture. The consistency of the cheese is similar to that of curd cheese, but it is drier and more compact, and has a slightly grainy bite. It has a fresh, subtle, slightly acidic flavor. The weight of the cheese can vary, 1–4½ lb (0.5–2 kg), depending on the producer. Cebreiro has an average diameter of around 4–5 in (10–13 cm) on the underside, with the upper surface reaching 6–7 in (16–17 cm), and a height of about 1–2 in (2–5 cm).

SERVING SUGGESTIONS

Cebreiro goes very well with the rye bread typical of the region. Buttery Cebreiro with a classic Cava is a special culinary experience worth trying.

Arzúa-Ulloa (PDO)

Soft cheese made from
cow's milk
45–8% FDM

Juan Manuel Sanz/© ICEX

ORIGINS AND HISTORY

This cheese also goes by the names Queso de Ulloa, Queixo do Pais (country cheese), Queso de Patela, and Queso Gallego. It has a long tradition in Galicia and is especially popular in the region from which it originates (near Arzúa and Ulloa), but has also acquired many fans outside its area of origin.

PRODUCTION

The milk used comes from the Rubia Gallega breed, which produces thick, fatty, sweet milk. Its production is similar to that of Tetilla, but Arzúa and Ulloa ripen for somewhat longer, namely 15 days at least.

CHARACTERISTICS

This small, flat cheese weighs ½–4½ lb (0.3–2 kg), but generally about 2 lb (1 kg). It has a smooth, deep-yellow rind, compact, elastic and soft, ivory-colored texture. The mild, buttery, slightly acidic flavor is similar to that of Tetilla, but with a stronger aroma due to the longer ripening period.

SERVING SUGGESTIONS

This country cheese is suited to young, flowery white wines from Galicia, especially those from the Rias Baixas DO.

LA RIOJA

Queso Camerano is produced in the Sierra de Cameros, between La Rioja and Soria, close to the border with Castile-Léon. This small, soft, goat's milk fresh cheese ripens in straw baskets that allow the whey to drain off. It is especially tangy but keeps for no more than about ten days. It is served as a dessert together with quince bread or mountain honey.

BLUE-VEINED DELICACIES

In the past there used to be numerous picones, cheeses that ripened in damp, natural, caves, thus developing their characteristic blue mold. Today the designation Picón is reserved for those blue-veined cheeses made from raw milk that ripen in the natural caves of the Liébanas region (Cantabria), particularly in the villages of Bejes and Tresviso. Picón Bejes-Tresviso (PDO) is made by hand using a traditional method from mixed raw milk comprising cow's, goat's, and sheep's milk. Picón has to ripen in natural caves for at least three months. The cylinder-shape cheeses weigh about 3–9 lb (1.5–4 kg) and have a fat content of 45–50% FDM. The slightly sticky, damp rind covers a soft, somewhat crumbly cheese with veins of mold running through it, and with a distinct, penetrating flavor and a pleasant moldy aroma. It can happen that the rind has an orange-colored mold and the cheese a slightly unpleasant smell. Connoisseurs are familiar with this and simply remove the rind.

Queso de Valdeón (PGI) comes from the Valdeón valley in the southern foothills of the Picos de Europa. This area, forming part of Castile-León, is remote and surrounded by high mountain passes. For many centuries cattle breeding constituted the main source of income for the residents of this secluded, hidden region. Cheese has been produced here and ripened in the mountain caves since time immemorial. Today the milk from the cows grazing on the fertile pastures throughout the valley is delivered to Posada. The highly aromatic, fatty (50% FDM), blue-veined cheese is produced according to traditional methods and ripened in the natural caves over a period of months. The cylinder-shape cheese has a diameter of about 10 in (25 cm) and measures 5 in (12 cm) in height. It can weigh as much as 9 lb (4 kg). Slightly damp, sticky, brown-colored rind. White-colored cheese with a dense network of blue mold veins running through it.

The Pedro Ximénez grape is sweet and the sherry made from it is ideal for serving with blue-veined cheese.

Piquant, aromatically intense but not too strong a flavor. Slightly crumbly, melting but firm cheese. Gamonedo (PDO) also originates from the Picos de Europa nature reserve, but has very different qualities. Its production area is located in the foothills to the northwest. Gamonedo is made from mixed milk comprising cow's, goat's, and sheep's milk. The valleys from which the milk comes are wide and sunny, making the animal feed especially aromatic, and this affects the flavor of the milk and the cheese. Gamonedo ripens for two months, has a fat content of 45–50% FDM, and weighs 3–11 lb (1.5–5 kg). The squeezing of the curds means that the texture is more compact than is the case with Cabrales. Ripening takes place in a select number of damp cellars, meaning that the blue mold marbling is significantly less. The cheese is smoked slightly during the first month of ripening, making the rind thicker and drier. The flavor is slightly acidic and milky with a touch of smoke aroma, and the texture is slightly grainy and either hard or semi-hard, depending on the stage of ripeness. The mild, piquant flavor of Gamonedo with its slight hazelnut finish makes it very well suited to a sweet sherry, a Muscatel, or to a sweet Málaga wine.

The youngest member of the blue-veined cheese family is La Peral. Created by the owner of a small cheese dairy in La Peral on the central Asturias coast, it is now being produced by the fourth generation. A soft cheese made from cow's milk, the addition of cream whey from sheep's milk gives it an added aroma and makes it resemble a ripe cheese, even though it is stored for just six weeks. The cylinder-shape cheese weighs about 2–7 lb (1–3 kg) and has a fat content of 48–50% FDM. The rind is damp and slightly sticky, with a soft, pale, almost white, and only slightly marbled cheese underneath that has a pleasantly acidic, slightly piquant and cream-like taste.

Blue-veined cheeses are highly revered in the world of upmarket gastronomy.

San Simón

Hard cheese made from
cow's milk
45% FDM

ORIGINS AND HISTORY

Produced according to traditional methods in the western foothills of the Cantabrian Cordillera, namely the Villalba region of the Lugo province, San Simón is a cheese with a long shelf life. It bears the name of its place of origin, but is sometimes also known as Queso de San Simón de la Cuesta.

PRODUCTION

San Simón's characteristic shape comes from its being pressed into a pear-shape mold. San Simón is squeezed by hand so that the whey is able to drain off, and then blanched in water. Thereafter it has to ripen for at least three weeks before being lightly smoked over birch wood. Despite its short ripening period, the extraction of much of the liquid means that San Simón has a fully developed flavor. It keeps for up to two years.

CHARACTERISTICS

Pear shape with a flattened underside, weight about 2 lb (1 kg). The smoking means that the cheese has a closed, wax-like, firm, hard rind that is copper-brown in color. San Simón is characterized by its unmistakably strong flavor and intense, tangy, smoky aroma. The ivory-colored cheese is hard and compact.

SERVING SUGGESTIONS

A somewhat fruity red wine from Galicia, from the Monterrei DO, for example, goes well with this cheese.

Beyos

Soft cheese made from
cow's and goat's milk
45–50% FDM

ORIGINS AND HISTORY

It is difficult to imagine that anyone would want to live in the imposing Los Beyos canyon between León and Asturias. The steep, towering cliffs leave little room for crops or pastures, and yet goats and cows manage to get by living in the inaccessible landscape surrounding the villages of Amieva and Ponga. This is also home to Beyos, an age-old specialty also known as Queso de los Beyos or Beyusco.

PRODUCTION

The cheese is produced using hand-crafted methods and used to be made from goat's milk only in the past. The milk was left to curdle gradually by the fireside, with the whey then being drained off slowly before the cheese was salted by hand and placed in a damp larder. There the white to orange-colored mold formed on the rind. Today a cooperative has taken over the ancient means of producing this fine cheese, which ripens for at least two weeks and is eaten young.

CHARACTERISTICS

Beyos comes in small cylinders of about 1 lb (500 g) in weight. Natural, yellow- to orange-colored rind with slight gray, irregular mold. The pale, white cheese

Juan Manuel Sanz/© ICEX

has a fine, creamy consistency and a distinct, acidic aroma.

SERVING SUGGESTIONS

A red wine from the Cariñena DO is recommended to accompany this cheese.

Afuega'l pitu del Aramo

Soft cheese made from
cow's milk
45–8% FDM

ORIGINS AND HISTORY

Afuega'l pitu is an ancient cheese variety and probably the oldest in Spain. In the Asturian language (Bable) *afuega'l pitu* means "to stick in your throat" or "to suffocate the chicken," which is understandable once you become familiar with the consistency of this cheese. Legend has it that in the past a piece of the shaped cheese mixture was fed to a chicken to test. If it had reached the right consistency the chicken choked on the piece, an experience that the poor creature did not always survive.

PRODUCTION

The milk is curdled using natural lactobacilli, a process that takes place at a low temperature over a long period of time. The shaping and squeezing is done by hand using a cloth. A natural, white mold forms during the ripening, which takes at least one week.

CHARACTERISTICS

The cheese has an irregular, spherical shape due to its being squeezed in a cloth. It weighs about 1 lb (500 g). Fatty, grainy, and soft cheese that is white to yellow in color. Fresh, mild, slightly sour taste with a touch of mushroom. The fresh cheese has practically no rind at all, with a thin surface mold forming after a week.

SERVING SUGGESTIONS

Asturias and Cantabria are not wine areas, but they do produce a wonderful, slightly bitter apple wine known as Sidra, which is a must for trying with this cheese. If you are looking for a wine as such, then a ripe, red Rioja is best, although the fresh cheese also harmonizes well with a fruity white wine from the Rueda DO.

SIMILAR CHEESE VARIETIES

One version of this cheese is known as Rojo del Aramo, produced by mixing the curds with ground paprika to give the subsequent cheese product a strong flavor. There are other varieties that are smoked and spiced.

Cabrales (PDO)

Blue-veined cheese made from
raw cow's, sheep's, and goat's milk
about 50% FDM

ORIGINS AND HISTORY

Picos de Europa

Cabras is the most well known of the cheeses from Asturias. The production area comprises three small villages in the municipality of Arenas de Cabrales. It is the only cheese produced here and is made by hand using raw milk only.

PRODUCTION

The *cabraliegos* (cheese producers) swear by the combination of the three types of milk. Cow's milk provides the acidity, the goat's milk the piquant flavor, and the sheep's milk the butteriness and aroma. The curds are broken up into pieces the size of hazelnuts, pressed into cylindrical molds, salted, and dried for one to two weeks in a cool, well-ventilated place. It is turned regularly until it achieves a dense, compact texture and a thin rind has formed. The cheeses ripen for three to six months in limestone caves or cellars with high humidity and at 39–46 °F (4–8 °C). A complex biochemical process involving the bacteria, yeasts, and molds produces a cheese marbled with mold veins after about three to eight weeks, or sometimes after as long as six months. The cheeses are turned and cleaned several times during the ripening process. The ripe Cabrales used to be wrapped in chestnut leaves but EU regulations now require that embossed aluminum foil be used.

CHARACTERISTICS

Cylindrical shape, 7–12 in (18–30 cm) in diameter, 2–9 lb (1–4 kg) in weight, 3–5 in (7–13 cm) in height. Slightly sticky, yellow-brown rind. The cheese has a buttery, firm, and creamy consistency with blue-green mold veins running through it. Distinct aromatic flavor, full bodied, pleasantly piquant, and salty. Depending on the time of the year, the cheese can comprise a larger proportion of cow's, goat's, or sheep's milk and varies in flavor.

SPECIAL FEATURES

Cabrales is produced in over 80 small cheese dairies with around 550,000 lb (265,000 kg) being made annually. The best Cabrales are to be found at the region's weekly markets or at the famous Arenas de Cabrales cheese market on the last Sunday in August.

Quesucos de Liébana (PDO)

Fresh/soft cheese made from
cow's milk
45–50% FDM

Juan Manuel Sanz/© ICEX

ORIGINS AND HISTORY

These small, simple, mild cheeses (*quesuco* means "small cheese" in Cantabrian Spain) used to be made by the shepherds themselves. The remote locations of the villages in the Liébana have led to slight variations in the recipe from dairy to dairy. The cheese is largely made from cow's milk but sometimes also from a combination with sheep's and/or goat's milk.

PRODUCTION

Pasteurized milk is curdled using rennet. The young cheeses ripen for at least two weeks, but 20 to 30 days is common practice. They usually have large holes as they are squeezed only slightly.

CHARACTERISTICS

Small, flat, cylindrical cheese weighing about 1 lb (500 g). Authentic, unadulterated milk flavor. The unsmoked varieties have a mild, buttery aroma. The smoked cheese tastes more acidic and riper.

SERVING SUGGESTIONS

Quesucos have a distinct lactic finish. A sweet wine such as an Oloroso sherry is therefore better suited to the unsmoked varieties, and a Malaga or Pedro Ximenés to the smoked type.

SIMILAR CHEESE VARIETIES

Quésucos are also available as cream cheese following the correspondingly short ripening period. They are then grainy and melt in your mouth. This variety is known as de Pido. These milky and very fatty cheeses with a buttery aroma have a complex, distinct flavor. Aliva from the region where the Deva rises was originally a goat's milk cheese, but it is produced today largely from cow's milk and smoked with juniper wood. The soft but firm cheese is slightly compact with a mildly acidic, fatty flavor and a slightly smoky finish.

Queso de Cantabria (PDO)

Semi-hard cheese made from
cow's milk
45% FDM

ORIGINS AND HISTORY

Cantabria originates from the Cistercian monastery of Cóbreces, where the monks still produce these cow's milk cheeses today. It is also produced in numerous small to medium-size cheese dairies and family enterprises using traditional methods. Prior to being awarded designation of protected origin, the cheese was also renowned as a cream cheese (Queso de Nata).

PRODUCTION

Produced in Cantabria with its evergreen pastures and extensive woods of beech trees, oaks, chestnut trees, and chestnuts providing ideal feeding for dairy cows. The very aromatic milk from the Friesian breed forms the basis of Cantabria cheese production. After curdling, the mixture is heated, squeezed, and then placed in a cylindrical container for the whey to drain off. The cheese is then left to rest in brine for 24 hours. Cantabria ripens for a short period only, but for a minimum of 15 days.

CHARACTERISTICS

Cylindrical or rectangular in shape, weight 1–7 lb (0.5–3 kg). Soft and very creamy cheese with a distinctive, melt-in-the-mouth creamy aroma. Sweet to slightly acidic in taste, buttery but light, mild, and fresh.

SERVING SUGGESTIONS

Cantabria harmonizes very well with jam or honey and is usually served as a dessert. It therefore goes well with a full-bodied Muscatel wine.

A DIFFERENT CHEESE IN EVERY VALLEY

Asturias and the neighboring region of Cantabria are true cheese strongholds. Asturias is home to many small, cylindrical goat's milk cheeses produced largely from curdled milk, with similar cheeses also being produced in the León mountains. The Valle del Pas in Cantabria has always been renowned for its milk products and the region is famous for its cheesecake as well as for its cheese. With the exception of Cabrales, which is produced in larger quantities, all of the cheeses made according to handcraft methods are available in small quantities only, in keeping with the motto "one valley, one cheese." Even in Spain these cheeses are to be found in specialist stores only, but they are worth looking for. Often, as is the case with Picón Bejes-Tresviso, it is a question of whom you know if you want to be able to get your hands on these specialties, because the bulk of the production is bought up in advance by restaurants.

SHEEP'S MILK CHEESE SPECIALTIES

The Basque region is home to Gaztazarra (meaning "old cheese" in the Basque language), Quemón, and Picañoñ cheeses, which owe their names to their characteristically sharp taste. In the case of Gaztazarra, the fresh cheese mixture is added to a somewhat older cheese as a starter and a small amount of Pacharán (sloe liqueur) is also added. Gaztazarra is similar to Tupí and, once ready for eating, still retains its liqueur flavor. Andalusia also has two characteristic sheep's milk cheeses, which are produced in very small quantities, namely Calahorra (Granada) from the northern slopes of the Sierra Nevada, and Grazalema from the village of the same name situated in the Cádiz mountains at an altitude of over 3,200 ft (1,000 m).

Curd cheese made from sheep's milk, Cuajada, is eaten throughout Spain fresh and unsalted, as a snack between meals, or as a dessert with sugar, honey, or jam. It has a grainy consistency, is slightly floury on the tongue, and is pleasantly sweet to the taste. In the Basque region this sheep's milk curd cheese is known as Gaztanbera and in supermarkets it is often available as an industrially produced version usually made from cow's milk. A number of cheese dairies in the Basque region and in Navarra have specialized in the production of authentic Cuajada made from sheep's milk and supply the fresh cheeses in small clay or glass jars.

PACHARÁN — SLOE INDULGENCE

In Navarra the grandmothers on the farms used to produce a very particular specialty by picking the blue-black fruit from the blackthorn bushes at regular intervals in the late summer and carefully preserving them in aniseed schnapps. A cinnamon stick and a few coffee beans were also added on occasion. This mixture was then placed on a south-facing window sill and, after two to four months of infusion, it produced a very palatable liqueur known as Pacharán (sloes are called *pacharánes* or *endrinas* in Spanish). It is not for nothing that it is so popular with the Navarrese: It tastes good and is said to help prevent heart attacks and arteriosclerosis. Having acquired fans throughout Spain, this Navarrese specialty is now available as industrially produced Pacharán with 25–30% vol. Demand has now grown to such an extent that the sloes growing wild in Navarra are no longer sufficient and blackthorn is now being specially planted as well as sloes being imported. A Pacharán tastes best well chilled as a digestif or as a mixed drink with orange or pineapple juice. Ice cubes should not come near a Pacharán.

Idiazábal (PDO)

Hard cheese made from
raw sheep's milk
45% FDM

Juan Manuel Sanz/© ICEX

ORIGINS AND HISTORY
Navarra, Basque region
Idiazábal is named after the town of the same name in the Basque province of Guipúzkoa. It is considered the most popular sheep's milk cheese from Spain's Basque region. Free roaming herds of shaggy Lacha sheep (Basque: Latxa) are still to be found in the Basque region, although much of the sheep breeding is now centered on the surrounding mountain farms (*caseríos*).

PRODUCTION
Only the untreated, aromatic milk of the Lacha sheep is used to produce Idiazábal. The curds are cut into pieces the size of rice grains, reheated, and pressed into a cylindrical mold for 12 to 18 hours. After being salted the cheese ripens for at least two months, but usually three to five, in humid cellars. The ripened cheese is also available in a smoked version. The cheese is smoked with hawthorn or cherry wood, giving it a distinctive aroma. Larger enterprises often use oak or beech wood for smoking.

CHARACTERISTICS
Usually cylindrical in shape, diameter 4–12 in (10–30 cm), height 3–5 in (8–12 cm), weight 2–5½ lb (1–2.5 kg).

Unsmoked: Yellowy rind, beige to pale-yellow cheese, slight aroma of hay, strong, intense, full-bodied, slightly piquant but not sharp taste. Smoked: Copper-brown rind, compact, dry, brittle but mellow cheese with a brown edge. The flavor of smoked Idiazábal is somewhat drier and stronger, with a pleasant aroma. Its special traits derive from the type of wood used.

SERVING SUGGESTIONS
Keeps for a long time and a good cheese for grating over pasta or rice dishes. A smoked Idiazábal harmonizes well with a rounded, mature, and robust Rioja Reserva or Gran Reserva, as well as with an opulent red wine from Priorat.

Roncal (PDO)

Hard cheese made from
sheep's milk
50% FDM

ORIGINS AND HISTORY

Roncal's production area, the Basque-speaking Roncal valley, is situated in the northeast of Navarra. Its unspoilt landscape makes it one of the most awe-inspiring valleys in the western Pyrenees. The statutory requirements allow it to be produced in seven villages of the Roncal valley only: Uztárroz, Isaba, Urzainqui, Roncal, Garde, Vidángoz, and Burgui. Sheep breeding and cheese production in this region may be traced back to the thirteenth century. Roncal cheese is closely related to the centuries-old history of changing pastures that sees the shepherds leaving the valley in the southern Navarra, where the herds spend the winter, and returning to the high pastures of the Pyrenees in the summer. In 1981 Roncal became the first Spanish cheese to be allocated designation of origin.

PRODUCTION

Milk from Lacha or Aragón sheep is used. The sheep yield little milk but their good forage means that it is of the highest quality, with high fat content and very aromatic. The cheese is processed in small family enterprises or in Roncal's cooperative dairy, based on the usual method for producing alpine cheeses (see Idiazábal) between December and July. After being salted, the cheese ripens for four months in natural caves ventilated by the fresh, humid mountain air from the north.

CHARACTERISTICS

Cylindrical shape, 2–8 lb (1–3.5 kg) in weight. Thick, usually yellow to brown rind, white to ivory-colored cheese with a compact, hard, and porous consistency and no holes. Mildly spicy, strong, slightly piquant, and buttery flavor, with straw, dried fruit, and mushroom aromas. Roncal is similar to Idiazábal in terms of shape and size.

SERVING SUGGESTIONS

Pimientos del Piquillo, grilled peppers that are then skinned and marinated, are served filled with Roncal, for example as tapas. Roncal is of course suited to a mature Navarra red wine.

Queso Zamorano (PDO)

Hard cheese made from
sheep's milk
45% FDM

ORIGINS AND HISTORY
Zamora

Zamorano originates from the heart of historic Castile and it is to the northern Castilian plateau what Manchego is to the south. It is produced by about 14 small to medium-size cheese dairies.

PRODUCTION
Made from raw or pasteurized sheep's milk from the Churra or Castellana breeds, two breeds that are ideally suited to the raw extremes of the continental climate. After curdling, the curds are cut up and reheated before the mixture is pressed into special molds and salted. The cheese then ripens for at least three months—often for a year or longer. The cheese is washed and turned several times during this period. Cheeses made from raw milk using traditional handcraft methods carry the guideline designation "Artesano."

CHARACTERISTICS
Cylindrical in shape, up to 9 in (24 cm) in diameter, 6 in (14 cm) in height, weight 4½–7 lb (2–3 kg). The hard, yellowy to dark-brown rind has a stylized zigzag pattern on the sides. This compact cheese is ivory to pale yellow in color depending on the stage of ripening, with tiny, uniform holes. Its distinctive, strong, spicy taste develops piquant nuances as it ripens further.

SERVING SUGGESTIONS
Some cheese dairies place Zamorano in olive oil in order to intensify its aroma. A white wine from the region, such as a Malvasia from the Toro DO, for example, or a red wine from Ribera del Duero, makes an outstanding complement to the piquant aroma. In its home region it is often enjoyed with other local specialties such as the famous Pata Negra ham.

SIMILAR CHEESE VARIETIES
The Castellano sheep's milk cheese also comes from Castile-León where eight provinces in the region are entitled to produce it. It is made from the milk of the Castile sheep.

Queso Manchego (PDO)

Hard cheese made from
sheep's milk
50% FDM

ORIGINS AND HISTORY

Manchego is Spain's most prominent and best known sheep's milk cheese. Its extensive production area encompasses the vast, dry highlands at an altitude of over 2,00 ft (600 m) south of Madrid. The climate here is characterized by raw, cold winters and long, dry summers.

PRODUCTION

The milk of the Manchega sheep is indispensable. The climatic conditions make the milk fatty, aromatic, and slightly acidic. After curdling, the curds are reheated, pressed into molds over a number of hours, and then salted. The ripening then takes place in cool rooms at 75–85% humidity and takes two (*fresco*) to six (*curado*) months depending on the stage of ripeness. A very old Manchego (*añejo*) ripens for up to two years and is extra hard.

CHARACTERISTICS

Cylindrical cheese: Diameter 3½–9 in (9–22 cm), height 3–5 in (7–12 cm), weight 3–8 lb (1–3.5 kg). Hard, straw-yellow to dark brown rind with a zigzag pattern on the sides. The upper surface and underside have a characteristic flower imprint. Firm, compact cheese that is white to cream in color with lots of small holes. The cheese is elastic in the case of a fresh Manchego, firm with a middle-aged cheese, and hard for an old cheese. Depending on the ripening stage, the flavor ranges from fresh and elegant to slightly piquant-salty and spicy-aromatic. A pleasant sheep's milk aroma with a trace of hay and rust.

SERVING SUGGESTIONS

Manchego goes well with a Manzanilla sherry. In Spain it is often eaten with quince jelly, figs, grapes, or apples. Crispy, farmhouse bread is especially well suited to the strong Manchego, as is a full-bodied, robust, and mature red wine from the up-and-coming La Mancha DO.

SIMILAR CHEESE VARIETIES

Somewhat less expensive Manchego-type cheeses are made from a combination of cow's and goat's milk. These are also very palatable but may not use the protected Manchego name.

La Serena (PDO)

Semi-hard cheese made from
raw sheep's milk
50% FDM

Juan Manuel Sanz/© ICEX

ORIGINS AND HISTORY

Its production area is the La Serena region in the southeast of Extremadura. The Serena valley also used to be known as "Spain's Siberia" due to its remoteness. The cheese here derives from the traditions of the roaming shepherds. The semi-soft La Serena sheep's milk cheese specialty is also produced according to the method handed down through the generations. The milk required is supplied by over 1,000 livestock farmers. La Serena is one of Spain's most sought after but also most expensive cheeses.

PRODUCTION

Only milk from Merino sheep is used. These sheep used to spend the winter in the *dehesa*, the grasslands of Extremadura with their centuries-old holm and cork oaks. Today they still feed on the fresh, sweet grasses, acorns, clover, leguminous plants, and fragrant wild herbs, giving the milk a unique quality. Merino sheep provide very little milk but it is very fatty, a total of about ¾ pint (0.35 l) per day. The whole day's produce from 15 Merino sheep is required to make about 2 lb (1 kg) of cheese. This sheep's milk specialty is produced between the fall and the spring only, when the moderate rainfall

and the mild climate transform the sun-dried ground into luxuriant grasslands. For the cheese-making process the raw milk is curdled using vegetable rennet, which since time immemorial has been obtained from the stamen of the Spanish artichoke, a form of thistle that blossoms from the late spring to the start of summer. The flowers are cut and dried before the stamens are removed, and soaked in cold or lukewarm water for half a day. The stamens are then ground with a pestle and mortar before being mixed with water again. A small pinch of this vegetable rennet ferment curdles about 2½ gallons (10 l) of milk. The curd is squeezed gently several times, turned, and carefully pressed so that the whey drains off. After being salted, the cheese is placed on shelves of poplar or oak wood, where it has to be turned daily to ensure that it ripens and "sweats" properly. The ripening takes at least 60 days.

CHARACTERISTICS

Flattish, round disks of cheese with a height of 1½–3 in (4–8 cm), diameter 7–9 in (18–24 cm), weighing 2–4½ lb (1–2 kg). Straw-colored, smooth, waxy rind; firm, compact, creamy, soft cheese with tiny, irregular holes. Soft to delicate melting consistency. Distinct, unmistakable flavor that can be described as pleasantly creamy, fatty, and intensely aromatic. Slightly bitter and acidic nuances due to the use of vegetable rennet.

SERVING SUGGESTIONS
White wines from Extremadura (Ribera del Guadina DO) are a first-rate accompaniment to La Serena and to Torta del Casar, or a fruity Albariño from Galicia.

SIMILAR CHEESE VARIETIES
The famous Torta del Casar (PDO), which is unique in the whole of Spain, also comes from Extremadura. This cheese is produced primarily in the small town of Casar de Cáceres and its surrounds. The creamy, soft specialty is also made from the raw milk of Merino sheep using vegetable rennet, and its production is similar to that of Queso de la Serena. The result is a cheese that looks like Serena on the outside but is very soft, viscous, and highly aromatic on the inside. The producers make only 13,000–18,000 lb (6,000–8,000 kg) of Torta del Casar a year and this cheese is therefore correspondingly rare and expensive. In order to enjoy Torta del Casar properly, you need to cut a round hole in the upper surface of the cheese using a knife and remove the rind from this area. The cheese is then spooned out of this opening. It is preferably eaten with toasted bread.

SHEEP'S MILK CHEESES FROM CASTILE-LEÓN

Burgos, a fresh cheese made from sheep's milk, was originally produced in the villages around Burgos and sold by the farmers in the local markets. Today Burgos is produced all over Spain but its features have nevertheless remained unchanged. The cheese is shaped like a truncated cone and weighs around 2–7 lb (1–3 kg). The white, moist cheese has a sweet, full cream taste and is barely salted. To the north of Burgos is Bureba, a wild mountainous area making up part of the foothills of the Cantabrian mountains, where a cheese similar to Burgos is produced, one that ripens for much longer. Like Burgos, Villalón used to be an important trading center where the shepherds from Tierra de Campos brought their cheeses to the market every week. The sheep's milk cheese Villalón (also known as Pata de Mulo, which means "mule hoof") takes its name from this market town. The cheese is shaped by hand by rolling the curds out on a cloth and pressing them with the cloth. Villalón has a cylindrical, pipe-like shape. Its wrinkled rind covers a compact, dry cheese with an acidic and slightly salty taste.

COW'S MILK CHEESES FROM ASTURIAS AND CANTABRIA

The cylinder-shape, piquant, and finely grained Peñamellera is produced in the Campo de Caso region (Asturias) using a handcraft method and very fatty, thick milk. It is a delicate, soft cheese made from cow's milk and with a washed rind. It is rolled using a special wooden rolling pin for several days in order to remove the whey. In its home region it is often served with biscuits and honey.

The Cantabrian soft cow's milk cheese Las Garmillas used to be called Pasiego. It has been produced in the Pas valley and in the province of Santander for household consumption since time immemorial. Its delicate nature and the fact that it does not keep for long almost led to production coming to a halt, however. Garmillas is shaped like a thin, uneven pancake. It has a thin rind bearing the imprints of the *cerbellanes*, the thin plant stems on which the cheese dries. A distinctive, sweet taste, mild but strong, fatty and aromatic.

EXTREMADURA — EXQUISITE SHEEP'S AND GOAT'S MILK CHEESES

In the Middle Ages Extremadura, on the border with Portugal, was almost uninhabited. Today the region is home to 15% of Spain's goat and sheep population. It therefore comes as no surprise that the area produces very appealing, exceptionally exquisite cheese specialties made from goat's and sheep's milk. You can sample them at the renowned cheese fair (Feria del Queso) which is held in Trujillo at the end of April. Other typical specialties from Extremadura, which enjoy protected origin, include honey (Miel de Villuercas-Ibores DO), ground paprika made from smoked paprika (Pimentón de la Vera DO), and Pata Negra ham.

Ibores (PDO)

Semi-hard cheese made from
raw goat's milk
50% FDM

ORIGINS AND HISTORY

This goat's milk cheese specialty originates from the Ibores und Almonte
areas in the northeast of the province
of Cáceres. In these wild, almost uninhabited mountain regions the goats
have pastures with aromatic herbs such
as thyme or rosemary as well as rock-
roses and holm oaks. The milk from the
Serrana, Verata, or Retinta goat breeds
is extremely rich and aromatic.

PRODUCTION

Ibores may only be made from raw milk.
The milk is curdled using both natural
lactobacilli and rennet. The goatherds
often still make Ibores by hand, then
sell it to affineurs in the markets in
Trujillo or Plasencia, who let it ripen for
about two months before selling it. The
rind is rubbed with olive oil. Red Ibores
is made by rubbing the cheese with olive
oil once it is ripe and then rolling it in
ground paprika.

CHARACTERISTICS

Cylindrical cheese, 2–3½ in (5–9 cm) in
height, 4–6 in (11–15 cm) in diameter,
weight about 2–2½ lb (0.75–1.2 kg). The
rind ranges from a pale or waxy color to
dark ochre or reddish-orange. Moist,
airy, and semi-soft to semi-hard cheese
with a few uneven holes. Ibores has an
acidic taste with a strong yogurt and
smoked herb aroma. Melts like butter
on the tongue.

SERVING SUGGESTIONS

Ibores goes well with a mature red wine
from the Ribera del Duero DO. The
paprika version harmonizes with a
Sauvignon Blanc from Rueda or
Penedes.

SIMILAR CHEESE VARIETIES

There is a whole range of goat's milk
cheeses from Extremadura that are
similar to Ibores, such as Quesailla—
which the goatherds produce in very
small quantities mainly in winter and
spring. It comes from the region south
of Badajoz, on the Portuguese border.

ANDALUSIA—SHERRY

It was in about the thirteenth or fourteenth century that Andalusian seafarers discovered that Andalusian wine could be kept for very long periods of time if a little spirits were added. Hence sherry was born. Sherry owes its popularity in England to Sir Francis Drake, who attacked Cádiz in 1587 and promptly rounded up the 2,900 sherry barrels stored at the harbor in order to take them back to England. It was the English that gave the noble beverage the name "sherry," being unable to pronounce the original Arab name *Xeris* (which is what the Arabs called the town of Jerez) correctly. A wine bearing the designation sherry has to come from the triangle comprising the towns of Jerez de la Frontera, Sanlúcar de Barrameda, and El Puerto de Santa María in the province of Cádiz. Of the sherry grapes in this region 95% are Palomino Fino, the sweeter Pedro Ximénez and Muscatel varieties also being grown.

Sherry is made by fortifying the white wine made from the Palomino grape with spirits, this combination then being placed in oak barrels. It spends its first year in the dark, damp, and cool Bodega cellars. During this time a yeast layer develops on the young wine, the composition of which later determines the quality of sherry which the wine will ultimately turn into. After six to eight months the cellar master is able to check the quality of the wine with a first tasting. He does this using a Venencia, a narrow, silver beaker with a long handle, to remove some of the wine from each barrel, and then checks its color, clarity, smell, and taste. Wines with particularly appealing yeast growth become sherry Fino with its characteristic spicy and slightly bitter almond nuances. Wines without a yeast layer become Oloroso, in which case they are fortified with more spirits in order to halt the yeast activity, and the sherry is left in the barrel to mature into an aromatic and full-bodied end product. An Amontillado is a Fino that has matured further after the yeast has died off.

Sweet sherries are produced by adding sweet wines made from the Pedro Ximinéz or Muscatel grape to an Oloroso or an Amontillado. Sherries are traditionally matured according to the solera method. The barrels with the oldest wines (soleras) lie right at the bottom of the rows of barrels stacked on top of one another. The cellar master removes wine from them and replaces it with the same quantity of wine from the barrels above until, ultimately, all—including the uppermost barrels—are infused with younger wine. The maturation period of sherry is at least three years before it is made available for sale, but the majority of sherries mature for much longer.

CATALONIA—
REVIVING OLD TRADITIONS

Catalonia is home to the characteristic Mató, the name of the soft, mild mixture obtained by curdling goat's milk with vegetable rennet (Herbacol). Catalonia has a long tradition of goat's milk cheeses, and the tradition is being revived by the increasing number of young people moving to the country from the towns. Mató is an unsalted fresh cheese shaped like a truncated cone (the curd is poured into cone-shape ceramic molds), which is produced and eaten on the same day—as a dessert or a snack with sugar, honey (mel i mató), aniseed, dried fruit, or jam. If Mató is sold as a ripened cheese, it is slightly salted to make it keep longer and drained more thoroughly. The cheese is compact and very moist, and has a consistency similar to that of gelatin. It comes in a variety of shapes, the most common being the semi-circular, rounded Matós produced by the natural draining of the curd in cotton or linen cloths.

Garrotxa or Pell Florida

Fresh/soft cheese made from
raw goat's milk
50% FDM

Juan Manuel Sanz/© ICEX

ORIGINS AND HISTORY

Production has been taken up again, thanks to a small cooperative of goatherds from La Garrotxa, an area near Girona in the Pyrenees. The ripened goat's milk fresh cheese is now being produced again throughout Catalonia by cheese dairies using hand-craft methods. The name "Pell Florida" means "moldy skin." Garrotxa has undergone a particular renaissance due to young people opting to move from the towns to the country so they are able to live on their own produce.

PRODUCTION

The goat's milk is curdled using lacto-bacilli. The cheese used to be shaped in old clay molds. The mold (*Penicillium glaucum*) develops on the rind by itself, thanks to the humid climate with its high rainfall. The ripening period is at least three weeks.

CHARACTERISTICS

This slightly rounded, cylindrical cheese weighs 2–3 lb (1–1.5 kg). Velvety rind that is colored blue-gray by the mold. Soft, creamy cheese that melts like butter on the tongue. Very mild, milky, fresh flavor with hazelnut nuances and fresh mushroom aromas are what characterize this cheese.

SERVING SUGGESTIONS

In Catalonia the cheese is usually eaten together with the sausages typical to the region: Salchichón de Vic, a hard sausage, or Bufitarra, a boiled sausage, to both of which a red wine from the Priorat DO is well suited.

SIMILAR CHEESE VARIETIES

The new cheese creation called Montsec is very similar to Garrotxa. This is a cheese that was developed in the 1990s in a form of commune in the Sierra del Montsec (Lérida). Montsec ripens in damp caves. Ash is rubbed into the rind during the ripening process, allowing a layer of gray mold and yeast to form. If the moldy rind is sprinkled with ash, the cheese is known as Cendrar.

Tronchón

Semi-hard cheese made from
sheep's and goat's milk
45–50% FDM

Juan Manuel Sanz/© ICEX

ORIGINS AND HISTORY

*Catalonia, Aragón, Valencia, Teruel,
Castellón, Tarragona.*

Its production area extends from
Aragón via southern Catalonia to the
north of the Valencia region. Tronchón
is a tiny village to the southeast of
Teruel, and enjoys a reputation for
producing good cheeses in a rural, inaccessible, and mountainous area with an
extreme climate. There have been
combined herds of sheep and goats here
for centuries. Even Sancho Panza,
squire of Don Quixote de la Mancha,
sang the praises of the cheese from
Tronchón. The attractive shape and its
lovely plant and animal motifs also
contributed to its spreading beyond the
Tronchón region.

PRODUCTION

The curds are pressed into wooden
molds, the insides of which are decorated with animal and plant motifs.
They ripen for a minimum of 45 days,
often for up to several months.

CHARACTERISTICS

Characteristic cylindrical shape with a
depression in the middle of the upper
surface; weighs 2–5½ lb (1–2.5 kg). Soft,
buttery cheese, mild but distinctive
taste, pleasant aroma of butter and hay.

Pale, straw-yellow rind, ivory-colored,
compact cheese.

SERVING SUGGESTIONS

A well-ripened Tronchón may be cut
into cubes and fried. It goes well with a
red wine from a region such as the
Campo de Borja DO or a fresh rosé from
the Somontano DO.

SIMILAR CHEESE VARIETIES

The goat's milk fresh cheese Cassoleta
originates from Nucía (Valencia
province). It is produced in Levante by
handcraft dairies using mixed milk.
Cassoleta also goes by the names Sala-
ditro Valenciano, Queso de Puçol, and
Queso de Burriana. The special molds
into which the cheese is pressed give it
the appearance of a volcano with a
crater.

Servilleta or Tovalló

Fresh cheese made from
cow's and goat's milk
45–8% FDM

ORIGINS AND HISTORY

The cheese is produced in Costera de
Ranes, south of Valencia, and is sold
mainly at the Xátiva market. Servilleta
or Tovalló means "serviette" or "towel."
It was not that long ago that the
goatherds from Valencia used to graze
their herds throughout this country
region every morning, milking the
animals on the roadside whenever
necessary. The goatherds' wives used
some of the milk to produce a moist,
sweet fresh cheese using serviettes or
towels as molds.

PRODUCTION

The cheese is shaped in cloths that are
knotted together and gently squeezed.
This produces the typically rounded
shape that the cheese still has today.
The cheese industry in the Valencia
region has fortunately revived the old
traditions, especially the production
method, although today a combination
of cow's and goat's milk is used. The
further molding of the cheese is then
done by hand. The ripening period is at
least 15 days for a young cheese, while
a medium-aged cheese ripens for one to
two months.

CHARACTERISTICS

Shaped like a flattened sphere, imprints
of the knots in the cloth visible on the
upper side. Fresh Servilletta is white on
the outside and has practically no rind.
When ripe, the rind takes on a yellow-
orange color. Weight up to 6½ lb (3 kg).
A soft but firm cheese with a yellowy
color and a sweet-sour taste; fatty and
creamy on the palate. Only slightly salty.

SERVING SUGGESTIONS

In its home region the cheese is baked
in oil and eaten with fried peppers. It
goes well with a Muscatel from the
Alicante DO or a fruity rosé from
Navarra.

Queso de Murcia

Semi-hard cheese made from
goat's milk
45–50% FDM

ORIGINS AND HISTORY
The most important production area in
the Murcia region is located right in the
west near the town of Jumilla. Herds of
Murcian or Murcian-Granadian goats
graze on the fragrant herbs in the extensive highlands. Queso de Murcia is
produced in numerous small handcraft
cheese dairies. This cheese from Murcia
is a very recent creation, but it already
enjoys protected designation of origin
within Spain. Its introduction at the end
of the 1980s received regional government support, thus also successfully
preventing the decline of the local
Cabra Murciana breed of goats.

PRODUCTION
The bulk of the cheese is produced in
Jumilla's cooperative dairy according to
the usual semi-hard cheese production
method. There are several varieties of
Queso de Murcia, which differ in terms
of ripening period and refinement.
Murcia cheese ripens for at least three
weeks (*fresco*). As *curado* it has to
ripen for between one and two months.
Queso de Murcia al Pimentón is rubbed
with olive oil and ground paprika during
the ripening period. Queso de Murcia al
vino (PDO) is a ripe Murcia that has
been refined with tannin-rich red wine
from Jumilla.

CHARACTERISTICS
Cylindrical cheese weighing 2–4½ lb
(1–2 kg) with a zigzag pattern on the
edges. Murcia curado has a delicate,
white consistency and an acidic, creamy
flavor. It is similar to a young Manchego
in terms of shape and flavor. Murcia al
Pimentón has an orange rind, is soft and
delicate, and has a pleasant, slightly
acidic-creamy flavor. Due to its red wine
treatment, Queso de Murcia al vino is
much more delicate than the normal
Murcia. It has a slight red wine aroma,
and is mildly sweet and buttery in taste.
It has a deep, dark-brown color.

SERVING SUGGESTIONS
The fresh cheese is often used for tapas.
Murcia is also an important caper-grow-
ing region and these are very well suited
to this cheese. In terms of wine, the
region's Yecla DO is to be recommended.

Mahón-Menorca (PDO)

Hard cheese made from
cow's milk
38–45% FDM

ORIGINS AND HISTORY
Minorca
Cheese was made from goat's and
sheep's milk in Minorca way back in the
Moorish era for sale to the Berbers. The
conversion to cattle breeding took place
in the eighteenth century under English
rule.

PRODUCTION
After curdling the curds are placed in a
cloth (*fogasser*) that is knotted to form
a bag. The whey is squeezed out and the
cheese is dipped in brine. The cheese is
then removed from the cloth and left to
ripen, during which time it is turned
regularly. The rind is often rubbed with
butter or olive oil mixed with ground
paprika. Mahón ripens for two to six
months. The *afinadores* (affineurs)
often buy it as a fresh cheese from the
farmers in order to let it ripen according to their customers' requirements.

CHARACTERISTICS
Cuboid in shape with rounded corners,
height 2–3½ in (5–9 cm), side length of
8 in (20 cm), weight 2–9 lb (1–4 kg).
Smooth, fatty rind with a pale-yellow to
orange-red color. The cheese is ivory
colored and firm with small, uneven
holes. The flavor varies according to the
degree of ripeness, with a slightly

acidic, slightly salty, and distinctively
aromatic taste being characteristic. As
a *curado* it has a full-bodied, pleasantly
spicy and strong aroma with piquant
nuances. A semi-ripe Mahón is lighter,
and an older Mahón spicier in taste.

SERVING SUGGESTIONS
Depending on the degree of ripeness,
this cheese is suited to a light white wine
from the Rueda DO or young rosé wines
from Penedès or Navarra. An older
Mahón is suited to a full-bodied red wine
from the Binissalem DO in Majorca or a
rosé or red wine from the Tramuntana
mountains in Majorca—such as a
Castell Miquel.

SIMILAR CHEESE VARIETIES
A similar cheese is produced on the
neighboring island of Majorca under the
name Mallorquín. With the onset of the
tourist influx the local residents have
been producing this traditional cheese
from cow's milk instead of sheep's.

Majorero (PDO)

Semi-hard cheese made from
goat's milk
55% FDM

ORIGINS AND HISTORY

Majorero from Fuerteventura is perhaps the best goat's milk cheese in the Canary Islands. The name Majorero comes from *maxorata*, the Berber name for one of the Guanche tribes considered to be the original inhabitants of the Canary Islands. The residents of Fuerteventura refer to themselves as Majoreros. Majorero was the first of the islands' cheeses to receive protected designation of origin.

PRODUCTION

The Majorero goat is an undemanding and therefore very adaptable animal providing thick, aromatic milk. Sheep's milk is sometimes added to it for cheese making. The cheese is made according to an old, traditional handcraft method: The curd is not heated but is squeezed very thoroughly. There are several stages of ripeness: Fresh cheese (*tierno*—ripened for seven to ten days), semi-ripe (*semicurado*—ripened for three months), and ripe (*curado*—ripened for four months). Ripe Majoreros are sometimes treated with olive oil and ground paprika or with *gofio* (roasted wheat or maize meal).

CHARACTERISTICS

Flat cylinder with slanting, engraved sides and weighing 2½–9 lb (1.2–4 kg). The rind is naturally brown-yellow in color, but if it is treated as described above the color changes accordingly. The upper surface and underside have a characteristic grooved pattern caused by the shaping of the cheese using straps, which are traditionally woven out of palm leaves. Majojero is a fatty cheese which is compact, creamy, and ivory colored. It has a piquant and slightly acidic flavor, as well as appealing rust aromas with increasing ripeness.

SERVING SUGGESTIONS

A fruity white wine from Somontano or an older red wine from the Valdepeñas DO is to be recommended. A white wine from La Palma, with its bouquet reminiscent of nutmeg, goes exceptionally well with this cheese.

CANARY ISLANDS AND GOAT'S MILK CHEESE

Each of the seven volcanic Canary Islands is a world of its own. High mountains like those on Tenerife and the dry lava flows of Lanzarote, or desert-like stretches as on Fuerteventura, provide extreme conditions in which only animals such as goats feel at home. Traditional goat farming is therefore widespread throughout the Canaries, and the cuisine of the Canary Islands would be unthinkable without cheese—the Canary Islands have the highest cheese consumption per capita in Spain. Each island produces its own variety, but they do have a number of features in common. All of the cheeses are made from the raw milk of Canary Island goats. They are usually large, cylinder-shape cheeses made from compressed curds and weigh over 6½ lb (3 kg). The rind has the characteristic diamond-shape pattern that comes from wrapping the cheese in bands woven from palm leaves. On El Hierro the sweet and fatty fresh cheese is used to make the characteristic quesadilla dessert, a kind of frothy cheesecake. The cheese is smoked using pine twigs and bark and left to ripen, after which it has a pleasantly mild and slightly acidic taste.

Queso Palmero (PDO) or Queso de la Palma (PDO) from La Palma is the second of the islands' cheeses to be awarded a PDO—after Majorero from Fuerteventura. On La Palma this goat's milk cheese is eaten fresh or else smoked with almond shells and/or pine needles before being left to ripen. It then has a buttery consistency with a distinct but mild flavor. The cheese is made from the milk of the Cabra Palmera goat, a breed that is unique to the island. The goats are not only expert climbers but they are also extremely undemanding. They produce rich milk that is ideal for cheese making. Palmero is produced by individual handcraft dairies.

On La Gomera the goat's milk cheese is smoked using twigs and heather before being left to ripen fully for about two months. This piquant cheese is usually grated and used to make *almogrote*, a thick cheese sauce served with papas arrugadas, the region's small, wrinkly potatoes. This local potato variety, which is traditionally cooked in sea water, is served with almost everything in the Canaries.

The residents of Lanzarote refer to themselves as *conejeros*, which means "rabbit hunters." Hence the island's cheese is known as Queso Conejero. It comes in three versions: With an oily rind, with a paprika rind, or with a rind treated with roasted wheat or maize meal—a rind that gives the cheese an unmistakable flavor. As an unsmoked fresh cheese Conejero has a slightly acidic, mild flavor.

On Tenerife traditional production is dominated by raw goat's milk. Industrially manufactured products are often made from mixed milk. The cheese is usually enjoyed fresh but can also be eaten after it has ripened.

The village of Guía in the northeast of Gran Canaria is home to the flower cheese (Queso de Flor). It is produced in the island's highlands, and comprises a mixture of raw sheep's and cow's milk that is curdled using rennet from thistle leaves. This cheese is atypical for the Canary Islands, where mainly goat's milk cheeses are produced and eaten. It is only in the Guía area that cow's milk cheeses are produced. They have an unadulterated, full-bodied flavor with an acidic, buttery aroma. The cow's milk is mixed with sheep's milk from January to May. When produced on farms, Queso de Flor is made using a combination of vegetable and goat's rennet (Queso de Mediaflor).

PORTUGAL
Undiscovered delicacies

Despite the fact that millions of tourists visit Portugal each year, Portuguese cuisine, outstanding though it is, has never really taken off in other countries. This is a pity since Portugal can offer some notable culinary specialties, one of which is cheese—or *queijo* as the Portuguese call it. However, it must be said that the bulk of Portuguese cheese production focuses on standard cheese varieties that are spin-offs of foreign cheeses and produced by subsidiaries of major international dairy firms.

As far as the Portuguese themselves are concerned, cheese, by and large, means "Flamengo," a mild slicing cheese produced from a Dutch recipe, which accounts for 50% of overall cheese production. Next in line are other types of cow's milk cheese or cheeses that are made from a combination of ewe's and cow's milk and resemble Emmentaler or Camembert—not to mention fresh cheese and melting cheese. Cheese consumption is on the increase in Portugal, a development that has in turn benefited traditional specialty and locally made products. For decades, these have coexisted on the fringes of cheese production and been at risk of disappearing altogether because it was more profitable for the herdsmen and farmers to sell their milk to the large dairies. Nowadays, however, recipes—some of which date back to the fourteenth century—are being revived by young, enthusiastic dairy experts. Ewe's milk and goat's milk cheeses figure most prominently in this respect, while the production of cow's milk cheese is mainly centered about Lisbon and northwest Portugal.

Left: A tram journey through Lisbon is a popular tourist attraction.

Queijo de Azeitão (PDO)

Semi-hard slicing cheese
made from raw ewe's milk
45% FDM

ORIGINS AND HISTORY
Near Lisbon
Azeitão, a somewhat sharp cheese, is named after a small village in the foothills of the Arrabida mountains, south of Lisbon. A cheese maker from northern Portugal happened to settle and establish a small cheese dairy there early in the nineteenth century.

PRODUCTION
The unique combination of climate and vegetation in the environs of Setubal, Palmela, and Sesimbra has bestowed its unmistakable qualities on the ewe's milk and the Azeitão cheese produced here. Maturing time: About 30 to 90 days. Azeitão cheese is produced by coagulating ewe's milk with rennet extracted from thistle flowers. During the ripening process, the cheese wheels are washed and turned regularly, which gives them their distinctive appearance.

CHARACTERISTICS
Flat, cylindrical wheels, 3–4 in (7–9 cm) in diameter, about 2 in (4–5 cm) thick, and weighing 9–11 oz (250–300 g). The cheese has a thin, yellow rind that is often hard and cracked. Inside, the cheese is creamy when young, becoming runny with age. It has a rather sharp and slightly acidic taste, and a very delicate aroma of ewe's milk.

SERVING SUGGESTIONS
Sommelier's recommendation: Moscatel de Setubal, port, and other fortified dessert wines make good companions for this cheese.

Cabra Transmontano (PDO)

Hard cheese made from
raw goat's milk
45–60% FDM

ORIGINS AND HISTORY
Northern Portugal
The home of Cabra Serrano Transmontano is in northern Portugal, not far from the Spanish border, in an area where there are large herds of goats. This cheese is not very well known even within Portugal itself. It is produced in only very small quantities by the shepherds themselves and their families.

PRODUCTION
The cheese is produced by coagulating unpasteurized goat's milk by the addition of animal rennet. After maturing for at least two months, the water content in the fat-free dry matter is no more than 25–35%, which means that Cabra Serrano Transmontano is unequivocally one of Portugal's hardest cheeses. It is matured for at least two months.

CHARACTERISTICS
Round wheel, about 2 in (5–6 cm) thick, with a diameter of about 8 in (20 cm), weighing about 1 ½ to 2 lb (600–900 g). It has a hard rind and a firm, almost crumbly consistency. Its strong and very definite flavor of goat make it a must for dedicated cheese enthusiasts.

SERVING SUGGESTIONS
Sommelier's recommendation: In Portugal this cheese is usually cut into small pieces, eaten with bread, and accompanied by wine. Its hard texture also makes it ideal for grating. A local vinho verde wine is a good choice to serve with this cheese as it brings out the aromas of the cheese without drowning them.

Castelo Branco (PDO)

Soft/semi-hard cheese made from
raw ewe's milk or goat's milk
45% FDM

ORIGINS AND HISTORY

Beira Baixa / Central Portugal
Castelo Branco is produced in an area to
the south of the Serra da Estrela.

PRODUCTION

An infusion of cardoon enzymes is used to
curdle the milk. After being shaped into
circles, the cheese is usually left to mature
for at least 40 days. Depending on what
stage of ripeness it has reached, it may be
categorized either as a soft cheese or a
semi-hard cheese. Occasionally, cheese
makers subject the cheese to the somewhat unusual process of sprinkling it with
ashes after a few days of ripening and then
leaving it to mature for a further three
months, brushing it regularly.

CHARACTERISTICS

Small, round wheels, about 2 in (5–6 cm)
thick, 4–6 in (10–15 cm) in diameter,
weighing about 2 lb (1 kg). The rind is
straw yellow with a slightly reddish tinge.
It has the piquant, spicy flavor of ewe's
milk. If the cheese has been treated with
ash, it has an even more piquant taste and
a stronger aroma.

SPECIAL FEATURES

Goat's milk Castelo Branco is sold as fresh
cheese under a variety of names that differ
from region to region. It can be stored for

several months, which results in a harder
cheese with a strong flavor of goat.

SERVING SUGGESTIONS

Sommelier's recommendation: Red and
white wines from the Beira Interior region
make good companions for this type of
cheese. Tawny ports tend to work well
with the riper, more intensely flavored
cheeses.

Evora (PDO)

Semi-hard cheese made
from raw ewe's milk
45% FDM

ORIGINS AND HISTORY
Southwest Portugal (Alentejo)
Evora cheese takes its name from the
small, provincial town of the same name
situated in the hot, dry, and barren
province of Alentejo (southern Portugal).
The recipe dates back to ancient farming
traditions. Even as recently as the twentieth century, shepherds in Alentejo were
still being paid part of their wages in the
form of these small cheeses, which formed
a nutritious part of their daily provisions.

PRODUCTION
Evora is mainly made between the months
of November and March. Like most traditional Portuguese cheeses, it is produced
in small local cheese dairies using milk
from local animals. The milk is curdled
using plant rennet (thistle extract) and
the maturing time is 30–90 days.

CHARACTERISTICS
Tiny, round wheels ranging from 2–3 oz
(60–90 g) in weight. The natural rind is
light yellow to whitish-grey in color.
Depending on its degree of maturity, the
cheese is semi-hard to hard in consistency,
with a creamy center and occasional small
air bubbles. The taste is slightly acidic,
spicy to sharp, often somewhat salty.

SERVING SUGGESTIONS
Sommelier's recommendation: A specialty
to look out for in the markets of Alentejo
is mini-Evora wheels, preserved in olive oil
to keep them soft. The Portuguese are
fond of eating this cheese at the end of a
meal or as a snack. It can be grated to add
a piquant flavor to pasta, sauces, and many
other dishes. Evora goes well with white
wines with residual sugar or robust,
mature red wines low in tannins.

SIMILAR CHEESE VARIETIES
Merendeira, at 4–11 oz (120–300 g) in
weight, is another semi-hard cheese that
is made in exactly the same way but differs
in form, consistency, and size.

Nisa (PDO)

Semi-hard cheese
made from raw ewe's milk
45% FDM

ORIGINS AND HISTORY
Northern part of Alentejo
This origin protected cheese was originally made primarily by the farmers in northern Alentejo for their own consumption. It is named after the small town of Nisa, where the majority of cheese dairies producing this cheese happen to be situated. It may also be produced in Crato, Castelo de Vide, Marväo, Portalegre, Montforte, Arronches, and Alter de Chão.

PRODUCTION
Nisa is made from raw sheep's milk. Like Evora, its close relative, it is coagulated by an infusion of cardoon, a type of thistle extract. The resulting curds are then carefully cut and finally transferred into molds, but not pressed. The cheese is then matured for an average of 45 days.

CHARACTERISTICS
Round cheeses that vary in size up to 8 in (20 cm) in diameter, weighing on average about 2 lb (1 kg), although some weigh 7–11 oz (200–300 g). The rind is white, sometimes slightly reddish. The cheese is yellow, dense, and supple in texture, often with small holes. Young Nisa has a delicate flavor of sheep's milk, a taste that becomes stronger the longer the cheese is matured. Although Nisa has much in common with Evora during the production stage, its final form—which is generally considerably larger than that of Evora—allows it to develop its own unique aroma.

SERVING SUGGESTIONS
Sommelier's recommendation: The distinctive aroma of Nisa cheese is particularly pronounced when shaved into wafer-thin slices. A delicacy served with bread and a delicious white wine—such as one of the modern, fruity varieties currently enjoying great popularity in Portugal. A mature, stronger-flavored Nisa is ideally accompanied by a wine with residual sugar, for example a typical Moscatel.

Rabaçal (PDO)

Semi-hard cheese made
from sheep's or goat's milk
60% FDM

ORIGINS AND HISTORY
Central Portugal / coastal region
This protected origin cheese is produced
in central Portugal in a small coastal region
bordering on the Beira Baixa region. It is
made according to a 150-year-old recipe
that originated in local cheese dairies in
the region and has survived to this day.

PRODUCTION
An important element in the production
of Rabaçal is the combination of 80%
sheep's and 20% goat's milk. The cheese
is traditionally made by very small farm
dairies and family-run concerns. The milk
is coagulated with rennet from the goat's
stomach. The cheese is matured for a few
weeks.

CHARACTERISTICS
Flattish cylinder, measuring about 2 in
(4 cm) in thickness, 4–5 in (10–12 cm) in
diameter, weighing 11–18 oz (300–500 g).
The cheese has a yellowish rind and is pale
or almost white in color with a relatively
firm yet supple texture, punctuated by a
few small holes. It has a relatively sharp
flavor.

SERVING SUGGESTIONS
Sommelier's recommendation: Rabaçal,
which is at its best between March and
April, is generally served as a table cheese.

White wines and light, fruity reds make
good companions to serve with this
cheese.

CHEESES OF BEIRA BAIXA

The Beira Baixa region is home to
numerous regional cheese specialties
that are made from pure sheep's or
goat's milk, or sometimes a mixture of
both. In addition to Castelo Branco,
described on page 412, Amarelo da
Beira Baixa and Picante da Beira
Baixa also carry the PDO seal.

Serra da Estrela (PDO)

Semi-hard/hard cheese
made from sheep's milk
45% FDM

ORIGINS AND HISTORY

Central Portugal

This cheese has been produced by shepherds in the eastern mountain regions of central Portugal since the twelfth century. It is named after the 6,600 ft (2,000 m) or so mountain range of the same name in the province of Beira. Generally speaking, production is limited to a handful of cheeses produced each day by small local, family-run dairies.

PRODUCTION

Flowers and leaves from a wild species of thistle are traditionally used to curdle the milk, which is supplied exclusively by sheep of the Bordaleira breed. The curds are cut by hand and eventually transferred to ripen in caves, where the cheese matures, initially in very humid, then later very dry conditions. Before it is sold, the cheese—which develops a light mold—is washed and, in many cases, rubbed with olive oil. Ripening time is one to four months.

CHARACTERISTICS

Flat, round disks, 2–3 in (6–7.5 cm) thick and 6–7 in (16–18 cm) in diameter, weighing 2–4 lb (1–2 kg). The cheese has a smooth, thin rind, which is pale yellow to orange-brown in color. After a short time maturing, the pale-yellow cheese is so soft that it is easily spreadable. It becomes firmer the longer it is matured, but retains its suppleness nonetheless. The delicate, sweet taste of sheep's milk with its caramel overtones gives this cheese a unique flavor and aroma. Young cheeses of this type are very mild in flavor, while longer aging produces a more piquant and stronger taste.

SERVING SUGGESTIONS

Sommelier's recommendation: It should be served with bread and, depending on the degree of ripeness, combined with fruity or robustly mature red wines from the neighboring Dão region.

SIMILAR CHEESE VARIETIES

Similar cheeses to this include the somewhat stronger Serpa (PDO; see entry), Alcobaça—a mountain cheese made from sheep's milk—Nisa (PDO; see entry) and Feliciano, a semi-hard cheese with a natural rind (45% FDM).

Mestiço de Tolosa (PDO)

Semi-hard cheese from
sheep's and goat's milk
45–60% FDM

ORIGINS AND HISTORY
Eastern part of central Portugal
Production of this cheese is limited to the province of Portalegre, incorporating the districts of Tolosa, Castelo de Vide, Nisa, Marvão, Crato, Alter do Chão, Arronches, and Montforte. A specific and unique method of cheese production that has remained unchanged since time immemorial has been developed in these areas.

PRODUCTION
Sheep's and goat's milk in proportions of 20:80, 40:60, or 60:40 is filtered through a white cloth before being heated, either in the traditional way (in water over a wood fire while stirring) or in special containers. As soon as the temperature of the milk reaches 86 °F (30 °C), it is coagulated using animal or plant rennet, transferred to special molds, and pressed. The cheese is then salted. After being left to mature for 20 to 25 days, some cheese makers like to rub the cheese all over with a mixture of ground paprika and water, which gives the cheese its distinctive color and typical flavor.

CHARACTERISTICS
Round wheels, 1–2 in (3–4 cm) thick with a diameter of 3–4 in (7–10 cm), and weighing 5–14 oz (150–400 g). The yellow to orange-colored cheese has an homoge-

neous consistency and is fairly soft with small holes. It has a rather sharp, pronounced, and piquant flavor with a pleasant and distinctive aroma.

SERVING SUGGESTIONS
Local white and red wines from adjoining regions go well with this cheese.

Serpa (PDO)

Soft/semi-hard cheese
made from sheep's milk
45% FDM

ORIGINS AND HISTORY

Extreme southeastern corner of Portugal
This cheese, which is made entirely from
sheep's milk, is named after the small town
of Serpa in the far southeastern corner of
Portugal.

PRODUCTION

Serpa is made from unpasteurized milk
from the Merino breed of sheep. It is
mainly produced between January and
April. Extract from the flowers and leaves
of *Cynara cardunculus*, a type of thistle
available from most local markets, is used
to coagulate the milk. Serpa wheels are
often wrapped in white cotton cloths. The
maturing time varies depending on the
consistency desired.

CHARACTERISTICS

Round drums of cheese, measuring up to
12 in (30 cm) in diameter and weighing
7 oz–5 lb (200 g to 2.5 kg) or more. The
rind is light yellow. The cheese can be soft
and runny (*amanteigada*) or hard
(*curado*) in consistency, with some small,
irregular air holes. Depending on how long
it has matured, its taste varies from mild
and creamy to quite strong.

SERVING SUGGESTIONS

Sommelier's recommendation: Full-
bodied Alentejo wines. A more complex

Moscatel may be drunk with very ripe
cheese of this type.

POCKET-SIZE
MINI-CHEESES

What is striking about the range of
typical Portuguese cheeses is that
many of them are very small, often
weighing no more than 1–3 oz
(40–90 g). There is a good reason
for this: They were originally
produced mainly as sustenance for
shepherds and goatherds, and
their small size and keeping
qualities made them ideal for this
purpose.

Terrincho (PDO)

Semi-hard cheese made
from raw sheep's milk
45% FDM

ORIGINS AND HISTORY
Northern Portugal
Terrincho comes from northern Portugal,
from an area near to where Cabra Transmontano is made. Terrincho, like Cabra
Transmontano, is only produced in very
small quantities. It is named after the
Churra da Terra Quente ("Terrincha" for
short) breed of sheep. The traditional local
recipe has been handed down through
generations of farmers and is used by small
family-run dairies.

PRODUCTION
Animal rennet is used to coagulate the
unpasteurized sheep's milk. The cheese is
ripened in humid conditions for about 30
days.

CHARACTERISTICS
Small, flattened drums, 1–2 in (3–6 cm) in
thickness, varying in diameter up to 8 in
(20 cm) and weighing 2–3 lb (0.8–1.2 kg).
Its smooth rind encloses a white, homogeneous cheese with a soft, supple consistency. It has a distinctive, full flavor while
older cheeses have more bite.

SERVING SUGGESTIONS
Robust, local red and white wines.

PORT WINE

The Port Wine Institute was
specifically created to oversee
and guarantee the origin and
quality of every bottle of port. The
basic wines used in port must
originate exclusively from a strictly
defined cultivation area that
extends from the Spanish border
in the east across approximately
62 miles (100 km) of country to
the towns of Vila Real and
Lamego.

São Jorge (PDO)

Hard cheese made from
raw cow's milk
45% FDM

ORIGINS AND HISTORY

São Jorge Island/Azores

There were small herds of cattle in the
Azores as long ago as the fifteenth century.
Cow's milk remains to this day the basis for
Queijo da Ilha (island cheese), a Cheddar-
style cheese that is named after the island
of São Jorge, where it is made. The inhabitants of this last landfall en route to America not only had to be self-sufficient in
terms of supplying their own food, but also
had to provision passing seafarers. Even
today, this type of cheese remains
extremely popular with ocean-going
yachtsmen who stop off in the Azores.

PRODUCTION

High-quality, unpasteurized cow's milk is
used in the production of São Jorge
cheese. It is produced in an almost identical way to Cheddar, although methods
differ slightly from one cheese dairy to
another with regard to preferred temperatures and coagulating and souring times.
As a result, the finished cheeses may vary
considerably in quality. The length of
maturing time is a further significant
factor that influences the properties and
flavor of the finished cheese. São Jorge is
generally matured on average for three to
five months.

CHARACTERISTICS

Cylindrical wheels, 4–8 in (10–20 cm) in
height, 12–14 in (30–5 cm) in diameter,
usually weighing about 18–26 lb (8–12 kg).
The rind is dry, fairly smooth, and hard—
sometimes displaying cracks—and yellowish-brown in color. The cheese itself is
supple and hard to slightly crumbly in
texture, with irregular slits and air holes.
Its flavor is dubbed "seafarers' favorite"
and is quite strong or piquant, occasionally
rather sharp.

SPECIAL FEATURES

There is no way of pinpointing exactly
when the recipe for Cheddar cheese found
its way to the Azores, but it is thought to
have been some time in the early nineteenth century. Apart from similarities in
the way it is produced, São Jorge is a
completely unique variety of cheese that
resembles Gouda in appearance and
Cheddar in taste.

Pico (PDM)

Semi-hard cheese made from
raw cow's milk
45% FDM

ORIGINS AND HISTORY
São Pico island / Azores
This very small cheese from the island of
São Pico—which also boasts the highest
mountain in the Azores, Monte Pico
(7,713 ft/2,351 m)—is a typical Portuguese
cheese. It has been in production since the
eighteenth century in small farmhouse
dairies, and is consumed exclusively in the
Azores themselves, in Portugal, and in
Brazil.

PRODUCTION
This cheese is produced from high-quality milk supplied by cows that are reared
outdoors and grazed on lush meadows,
rich in natural herbs. The unpasteurized
cow's milk, which may occasionally be
combined with a little goat's milk, is
curdled by adding animal—usually
calf's—rennet. The cheese is then left to
mature for at least 30 days.

CHARACTERISTICS
Small, flat disks, 1–2 in (3–4 cm) thick
with a diameter of about 4 in (9–10 cm),
weighing 18–28 oz (500–800 g). The
smooth yellowish to brown rind conceals
a supple, soft, pale-yellow cheese, which
has a pleasantly mild, not too intense
flavor. Queijo do Pico is usually sold
unwrapped in the Azores.

SERVING SUGGESTIONS
Sommelier's recommendation: Pico works
very well with a wide range of different
types of wine, ranging from fresh vinho
verde to complex whites and fruitier reds.

GREECE
Sheep's and goat's milk

Olives, bread, wine, and cheese are some of the delights traditionally associated with Greece. In poorer times, Feta and other sheep's milk cheeses formed an important part of a Greek family's diet. Sheep's cheese and goat's cheese are widely used in Greek cuisine, imparting a distinct and hearty flavor to the food. Cheese also figures prominently as a popular element of "Mezedes." These small snacks are particularly appetizing accompanied by a glass of wine during an evening get-together with friends in the tavern.

Greek cheese is made mainly from sheep's and goat's milk. The rich flora of the grazing pastures provides the animals with a perfect diet, which guarantees the unique quality of their milk. Greece has a long history of cheese making, descriptions of which date back to classical times. Homer's *Odyssey*, for example, tells of Polyphemus the Cyclops milking sheep in his cave and turning their milk into cheese, placing it in small woven baskets.

Today, the amount of cow's milk cheese produced by the Greek dairy industry is growing steadily, but for the true Greek cheese enthusiast sheep's and goat's milk cheeses will always be the preferred choice. The most popular and best known cheeses are also those with the longest history. Feta cheese accounts for two-thirds of overall cheese production, and an average of 26 lb (12 kg) per capita is consumed in Greece each year.

Left: The Greek islands, including Chios—pictured here—enjoy a cuisine based on simple, traditional dishes.

Feta (PDO)

Soft cheese made from
sheep's and goat's milk
45% FDM

ORIGINS AND HISTORY

The origins of Feta cheese can be traced back to the days of ancient Greece. For shepherds, this simple cheese represented the only means of preserving the milk supplied by their roaming herds. Feta is mainly produced in the mountainous regions where the old traditions still prevail and the animals are left to roam and graze freely. Authorized production zones include Macedonia, Thrace, Thessaly, central Greece, Epiros, the Peleponnese, and Mytilini.

PRODUCTION

Regulations permit Feta cheese to contain up to 30% goat's milk. Feta stored in wooden barrels according to traditional methods is known as Barelisia, but most modern producers now use steel containers.

CHARACTERISTICS

Feta cheese comes in rectangular blocks weighing 4¼ lb (2 kg). The cheese is rindless and soft but remains firm enough to slice. It is white with a compact, crumbly consistency and creamy texture. It has a slightly tangy, piquant flavor and is fairly salty. The addition of goat's milk gives Feta a stronger, more piquant aroma. It is ready to eat after one month's maturing time but will develop a stronger flavor if left to mature for longer.

SPECIAL FEATURES

Since October 2007, only white cheese from the specified designated regions is entitled to bear the name "Feta." Similar brine cheeses made from cows' milk—which are made all over the world—are no longer permitted the "Feta" title but must now be marketed as "white cheese in brine," for example.

SERVING SUGGESTIONS

Feta is ideal for fillings and toppings, and perfect as a substantial salad component, or served on its own with olives and country-style bread. Feta cheese would go well with a subtly aromatic Malagouzia or Sauvignon Blanc white wine. A mature, smooth red wine, such as Nemea, also combines well with this cheese. Ouzo likewise makes an interesting companion.

Batzos (PDO)

Semi-hard/hard cheese made from
goat's and/or sheep's milk
45% FDM

ORIGINS AND HISTORY
*Thessaly, Central and Western
Macedonia*
Batzos, once widely available, is now
found only in a few parts of Macedonia.

PRODUCTION
Made from the curds of goat's or sheep's
milk, or a combination of the two,
Batzos is cut, stirred, and heated to
113 °F (45 °C). It is then scooped out
and left to drain in a large tub until the
following day, when it is cut into blocks
and salted. After five days, the blocks
are placed in metal containers filled
with a 10–12% saline solution and left
to mature for at least three months.

CHARACTERISTICS
White cheese with plenty of air holes
and a tangy flavor.

SERVING SUGGESTIONS
This cheese tastes delicious accompanied by local white wines from the
Drama region, which are produced from
modern Sauvignon Blanc grapes
blended with native Assyrtiko or Athiri
varieties.

FETA

Feta is practically a national dish
in Greece. Packed in brine, it can
keep for months even in a hot
climate. For a long time Feta
remained unknown outside the
Balkan countries, but the wave of
Greek emigration resulted in its
fame spreading to all parts of the
world.

Kefalotiri (PDO)

Semi-hard/hard cheese made from
raw sheep's and/or goat's milk
45% FDM

ORIGINS AND HISTORY

*Macedonia, Peleponnes, Thessaly,
Crete, Epirus, Ionian Islands,
Cyclades*

Kefalotiri, a cheese that is very popular among the Greeks themselves, is regarded as the father of Greek hard cheese. It gets its name from its shape, which resembles a hat or human head (*kefalo*). In contrast to Feta, Kefalotiri's history can be traced back only a mere few hundred years.

PRODUCTION

The curd is pressed, then salted and pressed again. The manner and duration of maturation varies but, generally speaking, it is left to ripen for two to three months in a cool, damp cellar.

CHARACTERISTICS

This cheese comes in drums weighing around 22 lb (10 kg) each. Depending on the ratio of sheep's and goat's milk used, the cheese is whitish or yellowish in color with a fairly firm consistency and lots of small air holes. It has a pronounced, very piquant, salty flavor.

SERVING SUGGESTIONS

Mature Kefalotiri cheese is used for grating. It is delicious served with a wine that has some residual sugar.

SIMILAR CHEESE VARIETIES

The best known Kefalotiri comes from the island of Crete. If it is made in the Pindos mountains, it is called Pindos. Skyros cheese, on the other hand, comes from the island of the same name, while Vouscous is produced on Limnos. Xynotiro is also regarded as part of the Kefalotiri family.

Kasseri (PDO)

Stretched curd cheese made from
sheep's and/or goat's milk

ORIGINS AND HISTORY
Macedonia, Xanthi, Lesbos, Thessaly
This cheese was first made in the nineteenth century. It is believed to have been introduced into Greece as Kaskaval cheese from Bulgaria. There are altogether 14 different ways to spell "Kasseri." After Feta, it is the most popular cheese in Greece.

PRODUCTION
Kasseri is made from fresh Kefalotiri. The latter is cut into strips and left to ripen for several hours, after which the strips of cheese are plunged into hot brine, heated to around 160 °F (70 °C), and the cheese mass is then kneaded and shaped. Kasseri takes about six months to mature.

CHARACTERISTICS
The cheese has no rind and is yellowish-white in color with a buttery consistency. It is a mild cheese with an aromatic, slightly piquant, buttery flavor.

SERVING SUGGESTIONS
Kasseri is often used in the traditional Greek dish known as Saganaki. It is baked in butter or olive oil and sprinkled with lemon juice. It goes well with a glass of Ouzo but also combines successfully with modern white wines such as Sauvignon Blanc and Chardonnay.

OUZO

Sooner or later, every visitor to Greece will encounter the delights of Ouzo, Greece's world-famous national drink. Not only does it serve as an excellent digestif to settle the stomach after a meal, but it also makes a perfect companion to Feta or Kopanisti. Ouzo is made according to a traditional recipe that involves grape must being distilled several times. Its distinctive flavor is due to the addition of star of anise, fennel, cardamon, seeds of the mastic tree, ginger, aniseed seeds, angelica roots, or cloves. Each producer has his own secret recipe that gives the ouzo either a predominantly dry or, sometimes, a sweet flavor. Connoisseurs never drink Ouzo cold and always dilute it with water. In this way, its fine aroma is allowed to develop its full potential. When water is added to Ouzo, it turns milky as the essential oils in the herbs and spices are released.

Graviera (PDO)

Hard cheese
made from cow's milk
40% FDM

ORIGINS AND HISTORY
Agrafon, Naxos, Crete
Graviera made its debut as a new kind of hard cheese at the beginning of the twentieth century, when it was created by the dairy institute of Ionnina. Today it is one of Greece's best known and most popular varieties of cheese. There are now three protected designations of origin: Graviera Naxou (Naxos), Graviera Kritis (Crete), and Graviera Agrafon (Agrapha).

PRODUCTION
Graviera is made in the traditional manner of Emmentaler-style cheeses. Graviera from Naxos is made from cow's milk, sometimes combined with small amounts of sheep's or goat's milk. Graviera from Crete and Agrafon, on the other hand, is made from sheep's milk, to which a small amount of goat's milk may be added. As with Emmentaler, ripening is triggered by propionic acid bacterial cultures and takes at least three months.

CHARACTERISTICS
Aromatic, fruity, mild taste with a slightly sweet undertone. The cheese is soft in consistency and produces a creamy sensation on the tongue.

Formaella (PDO)

Hard cheese
made from cow's milk
32% FDM

ORIGINS AND HISTORY
Arachova/Parnassus
This traditional hard cheese has been produced in the Mount Parnassus region and around the town of Arachova for more than 100 years.

PRODUCTION
This cheese is usually made from sheep's milk, occasionally with the addition of a small amount of goat's milk. After coagulation, the curds are heated, cut into large chunks, and placed in molds. The packed molds are then immersed in hot whey for an hour. The cheese mass is removed from the mold and placed in the hot whey for a further hour, after which it is lifted out, left to dry, and transferred to caves on Mount Parnassus to mature for several months.

CHARACTERISTICS
Formaella is sold in small cylinder-shape portions weighing 14 oz (400 g). Traditional Formaella has a strong, piquant flavor.

SPECIAL FEATURES
Virtually all of the Formaella produced is sold to local inhabitants and to tourists who visit Delphi in summer or the Parnassos skiing centre in winter.

When bought, the cheese will unfortunately only have matured for a few days, if at all.

SERVING SUGGESTIONS
Why not try a good Retsina with this cheese? Aromatic, full-bodied white wines are also delicious companions.

Mitzithra

Soft or hard cheese made from
sheep's or goat's milk
50% FDM

ORIGINS AND HISTORY

Like the Romans with their Ricotta, the
ancient Greeks were skilled at using up
every drop of their precious milk.
"Mitzithra" is also the Greek collective
name for cheese produced from whey.
Mitzithra was originally made from the
whey left over from making cheeses
such as Kefalotiri or Feta. The whey is
enriched with a little milk or cream.

PRODUCTION

Like all whey-based cheeses, it is made
from heated whey, usually from sheep's
or goat's milk, and consequently it is a
seasonal cheese, available only between
June and December. Different varieties
vary depending on factors such as the
type of milk used, whether milk or
cream is added to the whey, the temperature to which it is heated, and the acid
content of the whey.

CHARACTERISTICS

Mitzithra has a mild, fresh flavor and
can be consumed after just a few days
as a soft cheese. Left to age for several
months, it becomes a hard cheese.

SERVING SUGGESTIONS

Light, mild red wines go best with
Mitzithra, although a more mature hard
cheese deserves robust white wines or
even wines with a slight residual sweetness.

SIMILAR CHEESE VARIETIES

Manouri (PDO) is also made from the
whey of sheep's or goat's milk. Probably
the most unusual traditional whey-
based cheese, it has been produced in
central and western Macedonia and
Thessaly for over 100 years. It has a
creamy quality that melts on the
tongue, as well as a milky, fresh taste—
all of which quickly cemented its popularity in Greece and the adjoining
Balkan countries. The whey for high
quality Manouri must have a fat content
of at least 2.5%, which is achieved by
enhancing it with cream. The combined
whey and cream are heated with the
addition of coagulating agents and
placed in cloth sacks to drain. The
cheese then matures at a temperature
of 39–41 °F (4–5 °C).

CYPRUS

Cyprus in ancient times was a major commercial center for the Aegean, Syria, and Egypt. This "island of the sun" has been occupied by a succession of conquerors, including Romans, Byzantinians, Arabs, Turks, and not least the British. Today, three-quarters of the population of Cyprus are Greeks and one-third are Turks. These two national groups remain completely separate, not only geographically, but also in terms of religion and politics. The strictly guarded border runs right through the vibrant center of Nicosia. Despite all political differences, however, the national cheese of Cyprus is known as Halloumi in both the Turkish and the Greek sector alike.

Halloumi

*Soft cheese
made from sheep's milk
43% FDM*

ORIGINS AND HISTORY

For many centuries, shepherds and farmers on this eastern Mediterranean island relied on Halloumi as part of their staple diet, roasting it over an open fire up in the Cypriot mountains. Nowadays, virtually all the island's Halloumi is produced in large factories using the latest technology.

PRODUCTION

The cheese acquires its distinctive properties during the making, when the curds are dipped in hot water, kneaded, and flavored with fresh mint. Like Feta, Halloumi is sold in blocks and stored in brine. It takes only a few days to mature and can be kept for three months in the refrigerator.

CHARACTERISTICS

A white, rubbery cheese with an unmistakable flavor of mint. Halloumi is traditionally folded over before being packaged for sale. It has a mild, slightly salty taste.

SERVING SUGGESTIONS

If the cheese is too salty, it can be soaked in milk. Grilled Halloumi goes best with a light red wine or a full-bodied local white wine.

SIMILAR CHEESE VARIETIES

Many spin-offs from the original Cypriot Halloumi have sprung up in the meantime, particularly in the eastern Mediterranean and in the New World. It is popular in Lebanon and Romania as a Bedouin cheese, known as Halloum. It is also made in Australia (Halloumy) as well as in California (Haloumi).

TURKEY
Cheese for the Ottoman rulers

In the past the Turks often lived in nomadic tribes that, together with their roaming herds (primarily horses, sheep, and goats), only ever stayed in one place for a short period of time, depending on the weather conditions and the pasture available. The most important of their foodstuffs and trading goods were based on milk, leather, and meat. Products such as ayran (yogurt drink), cheese, and yogurt remain set features of Turkish cuisine today.

Turkey is a cheese country: No cheese means no breakfast, lunch, or supper—and no invitations as Mezeler, small appetizers, are always served by the traditionally hospitable Turks. Cheese is an established feature on a platter of Mezeler, next to olives or stuffed vine leaves. It is sometimes served as it is, and sometimes forms an ingredient of appetizers.

Cheese production is the work of the women in Turkey. In the village communities and within nomadic families cheese is usually produced for home requirements and for sale in local markets. This Turkish handcraft tradition is becoming more and more a thing of the past, however. The range of Turkish cheeses extends from traditionally produced specialties that are available only at the local, weekly markets through to varieties that are now produced on an industrial scale and sold in supermarkets throughout the country. In Turkey, too, the milk is usually collected, sometimes from farms with no more than four or five animals. Mountain village dairies or large cheese dairies then use it to produce cheeses that often bear the name of their town or region.

Left: Hospitality plays an important role in Turkey.

Beyaz Peyniri

Beyaz Peyniri is the Bei cheese, *Bei* being the Turkish name for a high ranking civil servant. Often simply referred to as Beyaz or just Peynir (= cheese), it is a soft brine cheese made from sheep's milk and also one of the best known Turkish cheese varieties internationally. It originates from the Black Sea coast and is today produced in a number of different regions in Turkey. Products from Thrace (western Turkey) and Marmara enjoy the best reputation. Like its Greek counterpart, Feta, Beyaz is a kind of national cheese. The curd is squeezed for several hours, cut into pieces, and then squeezed again. The pieces are then layered in metal containers, salted, and covered with brine in which Beyaz will keep for up to six months. It needs to be desalted before eating.

Mihalic

Mihalic is considered to be one of Turkey's best cheeses. Western palates are more familiar with this cheese than with many of the more down-to-earth Turkish cheeses. The classic Mihalic region comprises the area between the towns of Balikesir and Bursa, where it is produced from the milk of a local breed of sheep. It has a mild Cheddar flavor, uneven holes, and is white in color when young. With increasing ripeness it becomes firmer and more aromatic, the holes more even, and the cheese takes on a flax color. Mihalic may be kept for up to two years, at which point it is as suited to grating as a well-matured Italian Pecorino. Mihalic is ripened not in a tulum or teneke but on racks in places with high humidity. It develops a rind that becomes thicker and harder with age. Mihalic goes well with a rosé wine or, served in small pieces, with a fresh beer. If you want to try the subtle cheese flavor with a strong counterpart, combine it with a robust Merlot.

Kasar

One of the best known Turkish cheeses is Kasar, related to Kaskaval, which is native to the Balkans and eastern Europe. Legend has it that it was brought to Turkey by the Cossacks. It is more likely, however, that it came to Thrace with the Jews, who produced it traditionally. They were renowned for the outstanding cheeses that they produced in the vicinity of Istanbul until about 1930. Originally made from sheep's milk, it is now available in a number of varieties made from cow's milk. Kasar is similar to Gruyère or Cheddar, can be semi-hard to hard, and can ripen for a few months or up to almost two years. Younger Kasar cheeses (*Yeni Kasar*) are produced industrially, ripened in vacuum packaging, and have a square, loaf-like shape. Old (*Eski*) Kasar is placed in round molds and develops a rind, something that tends to be unusual for Turkish cheeses, and has a spicier flavor than the young cheese. Some Kasar varieties have holes the size of rice grains. Cheese mold may sometimes develop spontaneously on the very thick rind.

Lor

Lor is a fresh cheese that is somewhat similar to Italian Ricotta. It keeps for just a few days and tastes best when made from sheep's milk. As sheep's milk is very fatty, however, it is often replaced by cow's or goat's milk. Its somewhat insipid taste means that in Turkish cuisine it is mainly used for cooking or baking and seldom served at the table. Lor is a popular ingredient for stuffed, fried pastry rolls (*sigara böregi*).

Erzincan Peyniri/ Erzincan Tulumu

This tulum cheese made from sheep's milk is named after its home region surrounding the attractive town of Erzincan. It goes back to the era when farming families moved to the cooler mountain pastures at the beginning of the summer and spent the summer stocking up on supplies for the coming winter. Sheep's milk cheese from the mountainous region of Erzincan has many fans throughout Turkey and, as it is produced only locally, it is a rare delicacy. Erzincan can ripen in the tulum for up to two years. It is moist and relatively firm but becomes increasingly crumbly with age, and has a strong, piquant aroma. It is ready to be eaten after about five to seven months, when it has a spicy, full-bodied aroma and a creamy color.

LEATHER POUCH AND TIN DRUM

Turkish cheese production is closely tied to two terms that in fact refer to the containers in which the cheeses ripen. Today they are indicative of two groups of cheeses that are produced throughout the country, albeit with slight regional variations: tulum and teneke.

A *tulum* is an untreated leather pouch in which the cheese ripens, thus developing a very special aroma and characteristically firm consistency. Originally made from goat's or sheep's leather, today they often comprise plastic sheeting in which the curd is squeezed and ripened for up to two years, depending on the variety. The tulum has a capacity of about 26–30 lb (12–14 kg). The fatty spring milk from sheep at the start of the lactation phase is particularly preferred for tulum cheeses, which ripen for up to 20 months, and is often diluted with cow's milk. The large, square cheeses placed in tin drums are called *teneke* for the metal containers in which they are salted. These cheeses keep for longer.

Plaited cheese

Plaited cheese, a salty relative of Mozzarella, comes from southeastern and eastern Anatolia. It is made by hand using the same time-consuming process as that used for *pasta filata* cheese and then woven into a plait. The plaits are boiled briefly in salt water and left to ripen in brine for a day. The very spicy plaited cheese has a characteristically salty flavor.

Salamura

The Salamura cow's milk cheese from Anatolia is to be found most frequently in the eastern part of Turkey, where it often serves as a kind of buffer against the hot, spicy, Arab-influenced food. This mild fresh cheese, which is usually eaten within 12 hours of being made, is a popular breakfast cheese. Salamura

used in a variety of ways as a spread, a sandwich filling, or an appetizer.

means "preserved in brine," but this applies only when salt is added to the cheese to extend its shelf life. In this case it is kept in a teneke-like metal container and salted. It ripens before, usually, being exported to other parts of Turkey and sold as Beyaz Peynir. When unripened it tastes rather bland but it is considered to be very healthy due to its low salt content. Salamura may be

DIYARBAKIR

There are an estimated 200 villages around the town of Diyarbakir making cheese and milk products. The majority of them comprise small farms with only 25 to 30 milk-producing sheep. Diyarbakir is known for its thriving market specializing in cheese and milk products. The cold climate means that cheese production is more closely tied to the seasons than is the case in the warmer western regions. Many cheeses are produced between April and June only, owing to the later onset of the lactation phase. The most popular varieties in Diyarbakir are the local Salamura and the plaited cheese known here as Örme. Herbs (ot) are often used in cheese production in this region, such cheese being known as Otlu Peyniri. They are available in a variety of ages from just a few days through to several months old.

ENGLAND & WALES

Although the Romans may have been instrumental in establishing cheese as a popular food in the British Isles, its history dates back to even earlier times. After 1066, the diversity of English cheeses grew thanks to the influence of Cistercian monks. By 1500 cheese making in England had become a flourishing industry. By the beginning of the sixteenth century, almost every county was producing its own type of cheese. In those days, the best cheeses are reputed to have come from Cheddar, Cheshire, Shropshire, Banbury, Suffolk, and Essex. After the Second World War, regional specialties initially disappeared completely until farmers began resurrecting the old traditions. England's farmers—like those in Scotland, Wales, and Northern Ireland—are once again returning to recipes that have been handed down through generations. The countryside of England, Scotland, Wales, and Ireland is well nigh a dairy farmer's paradise, featuring a mild climate warmed by the Gulf Stream and generous rainfall. Succulent pastures provide perfect grazing for dairy cattle. Whereas in former times the majority of cheese was made with goat's and sheep's milk, most modern cheeses are made with cow's milk from traditional breeds of cattle. Since the 1980s an increasing number of cheese specialties, some of them handmade, are being crafted by small farm businesses or artisanal dairies and sold alongside the standard cheeses marketed by the major producers. Even so, the market continues to be dominated by hard and semi-hard Cheddar-style cheeses and varieties of popular foreign cheeses such as Gouda, Emmentaler, and Maasdamer.

Left: Local farmhouse cheese specialties are becoming increasingly popular.

BLUE-VEINED RARITIES

Buxton Blue (PDO) is a hard, cylindrical, cow's milk cheese that is produced in Derbyshire, Nottinghamshire, and Staffordshire. Its russet interior is blue veined as a result of special starter and blue-mold cultures being added to the milk. Annatto is used to produce the russet coloring. The curds are finely cut, rinsed in hot water, and drained. The cheese mass is then salted, ground, and placed in ripening molds in which the cheese is shaped and pressed. Buxton is matured in muslin cloth and regularly pierced with a long needle during its six-week maturation period to encourage the development of blue mold.

There are some indications that Dorset Blue (PGI) was being made in Dorset as early as 1800 BC. During the eighteenth and nineteenth centuries, skimmed milk or milk left over from butter making was used to make cheese. Skimmed milk is still used to this day. This semi-hard slicing cheese is gently pressed to produce a firm, compact texture with irregular blue and green veining. Beneath its dry, rough, brownish rind, the cheese has a piquant, peppery, mild to tangy flavor. The curds are cut and stirred during heating, after which the curd mass is left to stand in the whey overnight. Once the whey has drained off, the cheese is stacked in blocks until the desired degree of acidity is achieved. After four days of pressing and draining in the cheese mold, it is moved to the maturing room, where it is tended for a further three to five months. After four weeks, the cheese is pierced to stimulate the formation of mold.

The production of Exmoor Blue (PGI) is limited specifically to the counties of Somerset and Devon. It is a farmhouse cheese that has been in production since 1986, and is made using traditional methods. This blue-veined soft cheese is a rich yellow in color and has a buttery texture. It is made exclusively from the untreated milk of Jersey cows, which spend much of their time outdoors grazing on lush pastures and consequently produce high-quality aromatic milk. Plant rennet and blue-mold cultures are added to the milk. The cheese is pierced and the surfaces sprayed with a solution containing white-mold cultures. Exmoor Blue takes three to six weeks to mature.

Dovedale cheese (PDO) is another soft, blue-veined cheese, and comes from Derbyshire, Nottinghamshire, and Staffordshire. Milk from these areas is enriched with lactic acid bacteria, rennet, and blue-mold cultures. Once the whey has drained off and the curd has been immersed in brine, the cheese is pierced from top to bottom to encourage the growth of mold cultures. Dovedale is left to mature for three to four weeks.

Cheshire

Hard cheese made from
cow's milk
48% FDM

ORIGINS AND HISTORY
Cheshire, Shropshire, Staffordshire
Cheshire is reputedly one of the oldest English cheeses, and its recipe is thought to date back to the time of the Celts. Imitations of Cheshire are produced in many other countries under the name "Chester."

PRODUCTION
It is produced in much the same way as Cheddar. Although most cheese is now industrially manufactured, a considerable amount of farmhouse production still takes place. Farm-produced Cheshire is made according to ancient, traditional methods that involve wrapping it in muslin to mature. Maturing time is at least two to three months, but sometimes longer.

CHARACTERISTICS
This cheese is cylindrical with a diameter and height of around 12 in (30 cm), weighing approximately 50 lb (22 kg), although considerable variations do occur. The rind is sometimes covered with a wax coating and muslin cloths are often used to protect the natural rind. The interior of the cheese is white with a satiny sheen. It has a slightly crumbly consistency and is relatively moist. Annatto may be added to give the cheese a strong yellow or reddish color. It has a fresh, tangy flavor, and is slightly salty with a hint of oranges.

SERVING SUGGESTIONS
Sommelier's recommendation: Traditionally, Cheshire cheese is eaten with blackcurrant jam. A glass of beer or cider goes well with this cheese; otherwise an extra-fruity white wine with residual sugar makes a good partner. A mature, sweet wine can also be drunk with Blue Cheshire.

SIMILAR CHEESE VARIETIES
Firm, denser versions of Cheshire are produced to cater for the large-scale demand for pre-packaged cheeses, which are very popular in England. Popular variations of Cheshire include Blue Cheshire and Shropshire Blue made from untreated milk, both semi-hard, blue-veined cheeses.

Cheddar (PDO)

Hard cheese made from
cow's milk
48% FDM

ORIGINS AND HISTORY
*Somerset, Dorset, Devon, Cornwall
(southwest England)*
The first mention of a cheese from the
village of Cheddar in the western English
county of Somerset dates back to 1170.
Hundreds of farms and estates situated
in Cheddar and the surrounding areas
produced cheese to their own individual
recipes for centuries until it began to be
mass produced during the nineteenth
century.

PRODUCTION
Only cow's milk from the designated
area may be used in West Country
Farmhouse Cheddar. No coloring
agents, flavorings, or preserving agents
are permitted in this cheese. The
cutting of the curds into small pieces is
followed by what is called "scalding," in
other words, heating the curd mass.
After the whey has been drained off,
the curds are cut into blocks that are
stacked on top of one another and
turned (cheddaring) at brief intervals.
This results in the whey being
completely squeezed out by virtue of
the cheese's own weight. The raw
cheese blocks are then cut into smaller
pieces (known as "milling") before salt
is added. The individual portions are
placed in molds lined with muslin and

pressed for a further 24 hours. Plung-
ing the freshly molded cheese rounds
into hot water encourages the development of a rind. The cheese is rubbed
with pork fat, wrapped in a gauze cloth,
and left to ripen for at least nine months.
Cheddar reaches its peak of maturity in
one to two years.

CHARACTERISTICS
Traditionally sold in large cylinders
14–15 in (35–38 cm) in diameter, measuring 13–15 in (33–38 cm) in height and
weighing around 60 lb (27 kg). It has a
dry, firm rind that conceals a compact,
firm, creamy white cheese (a little
darker in the case of an older cheese)
with a few slit-shape holes. It has a rich,
full-bodied and slightly nutty flavor.

SERVING SUGGESTIONS
Sommelier's recommendation: A well-
matured Cheddar demands partners
such as beer (Guinness or "Bockbier"),
cider, or full-bodied or mature red wines
such as Bordeaux, Burgunder, Cabernet Sauvignon, or Shiraz/Syrah wines.

CHEDDAR—PRIDE OF THE BRITISH

Cheddar is one of the most popular types of cheeses of all time. Since neither its name nor its production method is protected—with the exception of West Country Farmhouse Cheddar—it is imitated all over the world. The large majority of Cheddar is now produced in modern industrial cheese dairies using methods based largely on traditional recipes. It is usually foil ripened. Industrially produced Cheddar is largely made from pasteurized cow's milk, which is coagulated by the addition rennet and starter cultures of lactic acid bacteria. The Cheddar that is sold in the shops is often colored with annatto, a natural coloring agent. This is partly due to an old tradition: In former times, only affluent Cheddar lovers were able to afford this relatively expensive full-cream cheese with its creamy-yellow color. Cheese makers therefore added saffron, and later annatto, to skimmed milk to give it the desired color. Coloring agents are still used to this day as consumers tend to prefer their Cheddar to be fairly strongly colored. The older the cheese, the sharper and stronger its taste. Cheddar combines extremely well with fruit and can be used in warm and cold dishes.

Derby and Sage Derby

Semi-hard cheese made from
cow's milk
48% FDM

ORIGINS AND HISTORY
Derbyshire
Derby is one of the first cheeses to be industrially produced. The county now boasts a handful of small cheese dairies that make cheese by hand and according to old traditions. The custom of adding sage to the cheese originated in the seventeenth century when people began to recognize the herb's medicinal properties. Sage Derby used to be served as a thanksgiving offering at harvest time and at Christmas.

PRODUCTION
Derby is a member of the Cheddar family and is produced in a similar manner to other cheeses of this type. Derby curds are softer and fluffier, however, which gives the finished cheese a fairly loose texture. In the case of Sage Derby, finely chopped sage is added to the curds. This is either mixed in evenly with the curd or else the cheese is built up of alternating layers of "green" and "white" curds (i.e. with or without sage). Sage Derby takes one to six months to mature.

CHARACTERISTICS
The cheese comes in a round loaf measuring up to 15 in (38 cm) in diameter, 6 in (14 cm) in thickness, and weighing 33 lb (15 kg). The natural rind (which can be covered in wax or foil) is pale yellow in color. Sage Derby sometimes has the imprint of sage leaves on its flat surfaces. Derby cheese has a smooth, elastic finish and an open texture, while Sage Derby also has attractive green marbling. The taste of Derby is buttery, mild, and aromatic while Sage Derby is a little more piquant.

SPECIAL FEATURES
Derby cheese is sold in England in a range of different flavors, including herbs, onions, garlic, raisins, and nuts.

SERVING SUGGESTIONS
Sommelier's recommendation: The British tend to drink beer with all variations of Derby cheese, but aromatic white wines, such as Muscatel, Gewürztraminer, or similar grape varieties also go well with this cheese. Red wines should be fruity but low in tannins. Wines with residual sugar go best with Sage Derby or Derby flavored with other kinds of herbs.

Lancashire cheese (PDO)

Semi-hard cheese made from
raw cow's milk
48% FDM

ORIGINS AND HISTORY
Lancashire
Lancashire milk is of exceptionally high
quality with a flavor that perfectly
reflects the character of the county's
hilly, green countryside close to the sea.

PRODUCTION
Farmhouse Lancashire is a Cheddar-
style cheese produced in the traditional
fashion. The curds—already slightly
soured—from two or often even three
consecutive days are placed in layers on
top of one another. This produces variations in flavor and a unique consistency. Traditional Lancashire ripens for
at least three to six months.

CHARACTERISTICS
Tall cylindrical cheeses, measuring up
to 14 in (36 cm) in height and diameter,
weighing up to 49 lb (22 kg). Smaller
cheeses are also available with a diameter of about 8 in (20 cm) and 6–7 in
(15–18 cm) in height, weighing up to
10–12 lb (4.5–5.5 kg). The rind is hard,
thin, light in color, usually oiled in order
to prevent cracking, and covered in a
waxed cloth. Young Lancashire, also
known as Creamy Lancashire, is white,
semi-hard, and fairly crumbly in texture.
It has a delicate flavor, mildly acidic and
slightly salty in taste. Only as it ages

does the cheese become harder and
firmer and develop the unique, full,
intense flavor of "tasty Lancashire."

SERVING SUGGESTIONS
Sommelier's recommendation: Young
Farmhouse Lancashire goes well with
dry, aromatic white wines while the
mature version benefits from being
paired with sweeter wines, or even a
good Tawny Port.

Red Leicester

Hard cheese made from
cow's milk
48% FDM

ORIGINS AND HISTORY
Leicestershire

This mild, sweet cheese with its distinctive orangey red coloring was produced in large quantities during the eighteenth century, and it remains hugely popular throughout Great Britain to this day. It takes its name from the place where it was originally produced: The famous cheese-producing county of Leicestershire. In order to distinguish true Leicester from the insipid version produced during the war years, it was renamed Red Leicester towards the end of the 1940s.

PRODUCTION

In terms of production technique, this cheese is another spin-off from the Cheddar family. Its characteristic color is achieved by adding annatto, which has gradually replaced carrot juice as a coloring agent. Maturing time is three to nine months.

CHARACTERISTICS

Cylindrical in shape, Red Leicester is traditionally 18 in (46 cm) in diameter with a height of 4 in (10 cm). Nowadays, smaller cheeses are also marketed—for example, with a diameter of 12–13 in (30–34 cm) and measuring 4 in (10 cm)

in thickness. Depending on the size of the cheese, its weight can vary between 28–40 lb (13–18 kg). Though usually rindless, Red Leicester is occasionally found with a thin, grayish-brown natural rind. It has a firm, open-textured consistency and is bright reddish-orange in color. Its mild flavor becomes sweeter with age.

SERVING SUGGESTIONS

Red Leicester makes an ideal dessert cheese, but it can also be grated and used as a topping. Sommelier's recommendation: Fine low tannin red wines, such as a German Spätburgunder or Dornfelder, or an Austrian Sankt Laurent, combine well with this cheese, while luscious, barrel-aged Chardonnays also make delightful companions. Beer is regarded as the traditional accompaniment to Red Leicester.

Single Gloucester (PDO)

Semi-hard cheese made from
raw cow's milk
48% FDM

ORIGINS AND HISTORY

Gloucestershire

The history of Single Gloucester cheese goes back a long way. If cheese historians are correct, it was one of the country's most popular varieties even as early as the eighth century and was much prized for its sweet and spicy taste. Although it grew steadily in importance from the sixteenth century onward, it is now only made by hand by a few local producers. Double Gloucester is much more widely available but it lacks protected origin status.

PRODUCTION

Single Gloucester is made from the evening's skimmed milk combined with whole milk from the following morning. It is made in the same way as Cheddar and matures for four to six months.

CHARACTERISTICS

In the shape of a flat millstone, 14 in (36 cm) in diameter, 3 in (7–8 cm) thick, weight 30 lb (14 kg). Smaller versions are available at just 13–15 lb (6–7 kg). It has a thin, natural rind covered with a light mold that is sometimes oiled or waxed and wrapped in gauze. This firm, straw-colored cheese has a moist, smooth texture and a clean, slightly sweet, mild, yet tangy flavor.

SERVING SUGGESTIONS

Sommelier's recommendation: Eaten with bread and cider, this was a favorite with farmers during haymaking. It also goes well with aromatic white wines.

SIMILAR CHEESE VARIETIES

Twice as big as the Single variety, Double Gloucester is called "double" because it is not skimmed like Single Gloucester, but made from full-cream milk. It is made mainly in southwest England, using pasteurized milk. Traditional farmhouse cheeses are ripened for three to six months in their natural rind, while foil-ripened varieties can be eaten earlier. Double Gloucester is a firm, dense, light-yellow cheese without holes. If the cheese is light orange in color, it indicates that annatto has been added. The taste is similar to Cheddar, cylindrical in shape with a diameter of 14 in (36 cm), and up to 6 in (15 cm) in height, weight 62 lb (28 kg).

Staffordshire Cheese (PDO)

Semi-hard cheese made from
cow's milk
50% FDM

ORIGINS AND HISTORY
Staffordshire
The origins of this cheese date back to
the time of the Cistercian monks, who
settled in Staffordshire during the thirteenth century. This traditional
specialty was produced up until the
Second World War, after which it largely
disappeared until its revival during the
1980s. The milk is supplied by cows
from local farms.

PRODUCTION
The secret of this type of cheese lies in
the creamy milk and cream with its
succulent aroma of grasses and herbs
reminiscent of the meadows of Staffordshire. The fresh, raw milk is left
overnight in a chilled room at a temperature of 32–41°F (0–5 °C). Cream is
added the following day and the milk/
cream combination is enriched with a
special mix of starter cultures and
rennet. The resulting curds are cut and
heated while stirring. The mass is then
salted and placed in molds. Wrapping
the cheese in cloth during maturation
gives Staffordshire its unique texture.
The cheese is turned daily for at least
two to four weeks, and it is not uncommon for the cheese to be left to mature
for up to twelve months.

CHARACTERISTICS
This smooth, slightly crumbly cheese
can be semi-hard or hard, depending on
its age. Creamy white in color and leaving a creamy feel in the mouth, it has a
fresh and pleasantly acidic flavor. The
cylindrical drum weighs about 18–22 lb
(8–10 kg) and is marketed wrapped in
a muslin cloth.

SERVING SUGGESTIONS
Sommelier's recommendation: Pleasant companions to this cheese are
aromatic, dry Muscatel wines, Gewürztraminer, or other similar types of wine.
Fruity, low tannin reds are also suitable
accompaniments.

Blue Stilton (PDO)

Semi-hard cheese made from
cow's milk
48% FDM

ORIGINS AND HISTORY

Leicestershire, Derbyshire, Notting-hamshire (central England)

Stilton is named after a village in Cambridgeshire and is regarded as the "King of English cheeses." Legend has it that the recipe was developed around 300 years ago by a certain Elizabeth Scarbrow, who began producing an improved version of a cheese known as "Lady Beaumont's Cheese," named after its inventor. Stilton was not actually made in the village of Stilton, however, but was sold to travellers at an inn there. Writers such as Daniel Defoe and Alexander Pope, who immortalized it in his work "Imitations of Horace," have also popularized this cheese.

PRODUCTION

A veil of secrecy hangs over the precise details of how Stilton is made. Pasteurized cow's milk is—with a few exceptions—enhanced with blue-mold starter cultures. The curd is not pressed but placed instead in forms furnished with drainage holes around the edge. The curd mass is turned regularly and left for one week while the remaining whey drains off. The cheese is then wrapped in a muslin cloth and later moved into the ripening room, minus the cloth, for a further three months.

CHARACTERISTICS

This tall, cylindrical cheese is 6–9 in (15–23 cm) wide, 12–15 in (30–9 cm) deep and weighs 14–18 lb (6.5–8 kg). Its yellowish rind is marked with white patches and becomes increasingly brown, coarse, and crusty with age. The ivory-colored cheese is creamy and slightly crumbly with fine blue veining. Young cheese has a mild flavor, while maturer versions are creamier and have a characteristic, strong aftertaste.

SPECIAL FEATURES

White Stilton (PDO) is an immature "Blue" Stilton that has not yet acquired its blue veining. It is mild and fresh tasting with no distinctive character.

SERVING SUGGESTIONS

Stilton tastes delicious served with celery or pears. There is an old tradition of scooping out a hole in a Stilton cheese and filling it with port or Madeira.

Swaledale (PDO)

Hard cheese made from
cow's or sheep's milk
45% FDM

ORIGINS AND HISTORY

This hard cheese has been produced in North Yorkshire for many centuries. The recipe has been passed down from generation to generation. Nowadays, only a handful of people know how to make this hard cheese specialty.

PRODUCTION

Swaledale cheese is made entirely by hand. After the curds are heated and stirred, they are left to rest for a while before being cut into blocks. After draining, the curds are cut once more and stacked on top of each other. Finally, the cheese is broken into small nuggets, which are placed in a muslin-lined mold and pressed gently for 18 hours. After immersion in a salt bath, the molded cheese is left to mature for three to four weeks.

CHARACTERISTICS

This creamy white cheese is dry in texture and covered with a greenish, blueish-gray natural rind, which is sometimes waxed. The flavor of Swaledale cheese is produced by the unique composition of the aromatic pasture—found only in this region—on which the cows and sheep feed.

SERVING SUGGESTIONS

Sommelier's recommendation: Full-bodied white wines with low acidity go well with this cheese. Red wines should be fruity and have mature tannins.

LONDON'S FINEST CHEESE STORE

A visit to Paxton & Whitfield at 93 Jermyn Street is an absolute "must" for all cheese enthusiasts. Established in 1797, this traditional, specialist cheese shop not only has a remarkable atmosphere but also sells a fantastic range of cheese specialties from all over the world, the main focus of which is an impressive selection of typical, craftsman-made English, Scottish, and Welsh cheeses.

Wensleydale

Semi-hard cheese made from
cow's or sheep's milk
48% FDM

ORIGINS AND HISTORY
Region around York
Wensleydale was first made in England
by monks who came to the York region
with the Norman conquerors. It was
originally a sheep's cheese with blue
veining (Blue Wensleydale). Today, it is
the white Wensleydale without the blue
mold that prevails, despite the fact that
it is only just over 100 years old. Once
on the brink of disappearing altogether,
this delicious cheese made a comeback
in the 1990s.

PRODUCTION
It is produced in a similar manner to
Cheddar although Wensleydale is
generally made by smaller dairies, occasionally from unpasteurized cow's milk
(or even sheep's milk in the case of some
farmhouse-produced cheeses). It is
matured in cool ripening cellars. When
making Blue Wensleydale, the cheeses
are pierced with steel needles to
encourage the growth of mold. White
Wensleydale takes three weeks to
mature while Blue Wensleydale usually
takes 8-10 weeks.

CHARACTERISTICS
Usually in the shape of a cylinder with
a diameter of 8 in (20 cm) and a height
of 12 in (30 cm). White Wensleydale is

usually the same, but is occasionally
found measuring 3–5 in (8–12 cm) deep
with a diameter of 3–4 in (8–10 cm) and
weighing about 10–12 (4.5–5.5) kg. The
cheese has a slightly crumbly, moist,
and supple texture. It is very pale in
color with small irregular holes. Blue
Wensleydale also features blue veining.
White Wensleydale has a mild, aromatic
flavor with an aftertaste that is tinged
with honey. The Blue version is full
flavored and rich, without any trace of
acidity or bitterness. Blue Wensleydale
is one of the hardest varieties of blue
cheese.

SERVING SUGGESTIONS
Sommelier's recommendation: The
English like to eat White Wensleydale
with a slice of apple pie. Cider makes a
suitable companion for this cheese
although beer and complex, mellow red
wines combine equally well with it.

Caerphilly

Semi-hard cheese made from cow's milk
48% FDM

ORIGINS AND HISTORY
South Wales
This cheese has its origins in the small town of Caerphilly, where it was first produced in 1832. This moist, gently pressed cheese quickly became a popular source of nourishment with Welsh miners as it helped them replace body fluid and salt lost during their labours underground. In the event of a surplus of cow's milk, the production of Cheddar—which took several months to mature—was supplemented with Caerphilly, which ripened within a few weeks and could be consumed much sooner.

PRODUCTION
Caerphilly is similar to the other crumbly cheeses such as Cheshire and Wensleydale. After the milk has coagulated, the curds are lightly pressed and placed in a salt bath for a while, a process that locks the moisture within the cheese. The characteristic round cheeses typically weigh about 8 lb (3.5 kg), although other sizes are now also available. Maturing time is one to three weeks.

CHARACTERISTICS
Flat wheels with a diameter of around 10–14 in (25-35 cm), 3 in (7-7.5 cm) thick and weight about 8 lb (3.5–3.7 kg). The rind, which is smooth, thin, and pale whitish in color, conceals a semi-hard, moist, white cheese without holes. A young Caerphilly is mild and fresh tasting with a hint of lemon. Its aroma intensifies as it ages and develops a thick covering of mold on the outside.

SPECIAL FEATURES
Since industrially produced Caerphilly made from pasteurized milk does not possess the traditional qualities of this cheese, it is better to buy farmhouse-produced Caerphilly, which is often still made from untreated milk.

SERVING SUGGESTIONS
Sommelier's recommendation: Dry white wines with fresh acidity—for example Riesling, Silvaner, Grüner Veltliner, or similar wines—make good partners for young Caerphilly. More robust wines, such as barrel-aged Chardonnay, Gewürztraminer, or Muscatel, should be drunk with older cheeses.

RAW MILK SPECIALTIES

The only traditional Welsh cheese still produced in Wales is Caerphilly. Cheese making does nevertheless have a long tradition in Wales and many early cheeses resembled the famous Caerphilly. Many local cheese dairies have sprung up in Wales since the 1980s, specializing in handmade organic and raw milk cheeses, including many made from sheep's milk. One of the main production centers is in Abergavenny. After many years of being out of the limelight, cheese is once again being produced in the town of Caerphilly itself. In the north of Wales, the Llyn peninsula likewise has an excellent reputation for its cheese making.

A typical example of Welsh cheese production is Tyn Grug, made from untreated cow's milk. The recipe and production technique are reminiscent of the way in which Cheddar is made. After five months of ripening, the resulting round, hard cheese with its grainy texture and nutty aroma weighs approximately 17–33 lb (7.5–15 kg). Llanboidy from Pembrokeshire is produced in a similar fashion. Its pungent aroma becomes stronger with age. A characteristic feature of this particular cheese, weighing approximately 10 lb (4.5 kg), is its crusty, yellowish rind with its light covering of mold. Teifi, a semi-hard cheese made from untreated milk, bears comparison with Gouda. After a lengthy period of maturing, it becomes very hard and develops a pronounced flavor of celery. Teifi is also available as a smoked cheese or with the added flavoring of nettles or caraway. Pant Ys Gawn is one of a handful of goat's milk cheeses and is also available with additional flavorings such as fresh herbs, chives, black pepper, or garlic. Another example is Celtic Promise, a cheese which was "invented" just a few years ago. This semi-hard cheese made from raw cow's milk is shaped like a dumpling and weighs only about 1 lb (500 g). It has a distinctive orange rind and a particularly piquant taste.

SCOTLAND
Strong sense of tradition

Our image of Scotland is one of magnificent landscapes—such as the Highlands with steep, rocky cliffs, rushing rivers, and wide expanses of moorland and heather; and the Lowlands region with its gently rising hills, separated by rivers meandering slowly through meadows filled with herds of sheep or cows.

It is a tribute to the Scots' strong sense of tradition that recipes, not to mention cultivation and production methods, have been passed down from generation to generation. This is equally true of the dairy industry and cheese making. With the exception of one or two fresh cheeses, there was virtually no cheese production to speak of until the eleventh century. This situation did not change until the monasteries and the Vikings began to develop an interest in cheese making, followed later by the establishment of the royal estates. Today, in addition to Dunlop cheese, Scotland produces a further 30 or so different cheeses of its own. Some of these—such as Caboc and Crowdie fresh farmhouse cheeses, Isle of Mull hard cheese, and the Scottish Cheddars—are still made according to traditional recipes. Some of the new cheeses developed by small local dairies include Bishop Kennedy, Bonchester, Cairnsmore, Dunsyre Blue, Lanark Blue, Gowrie, and St. Andrews.

Left: Eilean Donan Castle is the family seat of the McRae clan.

Bishop Kennedy

Soft cheese made from
raw cow's milk
45% FDM

ORIGINS AND HISTORY
Perthshire
Bishop Kennedy, which is also known as
"Scottish Munster," has only been in
production since the 1990s. It gets its
name from a fifteenth-century Scottish
bishop. Its creators, who were keen to
develop a cheese which was typically
Scottish, modelled it on Munster-style
red bacterial rind cheese.

PRODUCTION
Production is similar to the methods
used for other soft, red smear cheeses.
During the ripening stages, the rind is
washed with a special solution which
includes a generous amount of malt
whisky. Maturing time lasts three to four
weeks.

CHARACTERISTICS
Flat, round wheels weighing about 3 lb
(1.3 kg). The reddish, lightly smeared
rind conceals a pale-yellowish cheese
with a creamy consistency. It has a
strong flavor with a distinct aftertaste.

SERVING SUGGESTIONS
Sommelier's recommendation: Malt
beer makes an excellent accompaniment to Bishop Kennedy, but a glass of
cider or Scotch whisky also combines
exceptionally well with this cheese. A
glass of Gewürztraminer or similar
aromatic wine would also be a suitable
companion.

Caboc

Fresh cheese made from
cow's milk
70% FDM

ORIGINS AND HISTORY
Scotland
Caboc, a traditional and once fairly
common cheese variety, was thought to
have disappeared altogether until it was
rediscovered and revived during the
1960s.

PRODUCTION
The unusual feature of this semi-hard,
double-cream fresh cheese is that it is
rolled in a mixture of roasted oatmeal
as a finishing touch. Maturing time is
just a few days.

CHARACTERISTICS
The rindless cheese is shaped into logs
weighing approximately 2 lb (1 kg).
This white, semi-hard cheese has a
slightly acidic and nutty flavor.

SERVING SUGGESTIONS
Sommelier's recommendation: The
Scots eat this cheese with oatcakes or
oatmeal biscuits. Try a fine, dry white
wine or one with residual sugar. A
smooth rosé or a rich, strong white wine
with velvety mellowness, such as
Australian Chardonnay, would also
make an excellent companion.

Crowdie

Fresh cheese made from
cow's milk
70% FDM

ORIGINS AND HISTORY
Scotland
Crowdie (also known as "Gruth" in Gaelic) has been popular throughout Scotland for centuries. Nowadays it is only produced in small quantities by individual producers. The original recipe is thought to have been handed down from the Vikings.

PRODUCTION
As soon as the skimmed milk has curdled, the cheese is placed in a sieve lined with muslin to allow the whey to drain. Several hours later it is transferred to a basin without being pressed, and mixed with salt. Cream or double cream is often added to the mixture to increase the fat content. Some versions of this cheese are sprinkled with oats or peppercorns. Maturing time is just a few days.

CHARACTERISTICS
Crowdie is sold in 4 oz (125 g) tubs. It is white and creamy, sometimes slightly crumbly. It has a mild, fresh, and pleasantly acidic taste.

SERVING SUGGESTIONS
The Scots are fond of Crowdie as a breakfast cheese.

Dunlop

Hard cheese made from raw cow's milk
48% FDM

ORIGINS AND HISTORY
Scotland
This Cheddar-style cheese is thought to have been invented by Barbara Gilmour, an Irish immigrant who came to Ayrshire in the seventeenth century, bringing with her a recipe from her native Ireland. After reaching a peak of popularity in the eighteenth century, this cheese largely disappeared until around 20 years ago, when Ann Dorward began producing it again on her family-run farm. Dunlop is Scotland's best known cheese.

PRODUCTION
The milk for this cheese comes from Ayrshire cows. In some respects, the production of Dunlop cheese—which involves adding plant rennet to coagulate the milk—is similar to that of Cheddar. Dunlop takes six to eight weeks to mature.

CHARACTERISTICS
A cylindrical cheese, measuring 16 in (40 cm) in diameter and 9 in (23 cm) in height, it weighs around 60 lb (27 kg). It has a thin, relatively pale, natural rind which has a light covering of mold. Very mature cheeses are often covered in a gray-green mold. Dunlop is creamy white to pale yellow in color with a firm, yet supple, soft consistency and irregular holes. Dunlop is distinctly moister than Cheddar. It has a pleasantly mild taste that does not deteriorate with age.

SERVING SUGGESTIONS
Sommelier's recommendation: Dunlop is generally eaten while still very young, either on its own or accompanied by buttered oatmeal bread. Try a fruity, aromatic red wine or a glass of brown ale with this cheese.

OTHER SCOTTISH CHEESE VARIETIES

Cheddar and other Cheddar-style cheese varieties are just as popular in Scotland as they are in England, Wales, and Ireland. There are several variations of Cheddar that deserve a special mention in this respect. Orkney Extra Mature Cheddar, for example, originates, as its name suggests, in the Orkney Islands. It is matured for at least 12 months and has a particularly strong, spicy taste. Seriously Strong Cheddar, which is undoubtedly a specialty, takes even longer to mature and has a consistency reminiscent of Parmesan. Another Cheddar imitator is Isle of Mull cheese, an extremely spicy cheese that comes from the island of that name in western Scotland. Cairnsmore is a hard cheese made from raw untreated sheep's milk. It has a nutty flavor with slight caramel overtones. Bonchester (PDO) is a soft cheese made from untreated milk supplied by Jersey cows living within a radius of 60 miles (90 km) around Peel Fell in the Cheviot Hills. This cheese, which is not pressed and takes 6 to 12 days to mature, has a creamy, buttery yellow interior with a mild flavor and a fine aroma, recalling the grasses and herbs of local pastures. Similarly, Teviotdale Cheese (PGI), produced in the same area, is made from rich, untreated milk supplied by Jersey cows. In contrast to Bonchester, Teviotdale is a harder cheese. The curds are pressed several times before being placed in a mold, plunged in a salt bath, and dried for 4 days before finally being left to mature for 15 days. The rind is covered with white mold that encloses a golden-yellow interior with a mild, spicy, slightly salty flavor. Dunsyre Blue from Lanarkshire is one of Scotland's few blue cheeses and Lanark Blue from the same region is a particular rarity as it is made from ewe's milk. St. Andrews cheese comes from Perthshire and is similar to the French Epoisses cheese. It is made from untreated cow's milk with the addition of red smear cultures. The cheese itself is relatively soft, becoming almost runny later, thanks to the strongly acidic lactic coagulation process.

In Scotland, tradition is highly cherished—even with regards to cheese.

IRELAND
Late bloomer

The Irish landscape is a seemingly endless panorama of gentle hills and lush green meadows. The country's relatively unpolluted environment and the temperate climate that combines comparatively cool summers with very mild winters are good news for around a million cows. Almost 80% of agricultural land is used for grazing, and the Irish people are not the only ones who believe that their country boasts the best conditions in Europe for dairy farming. Probably the most successful and certainly the most famous dairy product to come from the Emerald Isle is Irish butter, made from cream from the milk of cows that graze outdoors virtually all year round. Irish butter is famous for its spreading qualities and popular all over the world for its natural golden-yellow color and its distinctive, creamy taste. Meanwhile, astonishing as it may seem, cheese making remained a virtually neglected industry for centuries on end. It was not until after the Second World War that the situation changed and the Irish began to take greater interest in producing cheeses, especially imitations of European specialties. Eventually, in the late 1970s and early 1980s, a small group of cheese makers began producing the typically Irish cheeses that we enjoy today. Many of these are based on almost forgotten recipes while others are new creations.

Left: The "emerald isle" is famous for its dairy products.

Cashel Blue

Semi-hard cheese made from
cow's milk
45% FDM

ORIGINS AND HISTORY
Tipperary region
Cashel Blue is named after the Rock of
Cashel, a rocky hill that is visible for
miles around. It is the only Irish blue
cheese of any significance.

PRODUCTION
This typical farmhouse cheese is
produced in the traditional manner of
blue-veined cheese and ripens in eight
weeks.

CHARACTERISTICS
It comes in cylinders 6 in (15 cm) across
and about 5 in (12–13 cm) high, weighing up to 3–4 lb (1.5–2 kg). Its crusty
rind is covered in mold and conceals a
pale-yellow cheese with cracks and
holes filled with green to bluish-green
mold. This strongly flavored cheese is
spicy and slightly salty with tangy overtones.

SERVING SUGGESTIONS
Sommelier's recommendation: Wines
with residual sweetness go well with
Cashel Blue. Riesling Auslese wines,
Vendanges Tardives from the Alsace,
Tokaji Aszu of at least 5 puttonyos, or
Sauternes make excellent companions.

SIMILAR CHEESE VARIETIES
Cashel Blue is closely related to
Chetwynd Blue.

Blarney

Semi-hard cheese made from
cow's milk
50% FDM

ORIGINS AND HISTORY
Ireland
Blarney is one of the few Emerald Isle
cheeses that can look back on a relatively long tradition. Because of its similarities with some Swiss cheeses, it is
often nicknamed Irish Gruyère.

PRODUCTION
Blarney takes 8 to 12 months to mature.

CHARACTERISTICS
This is a round, flattish cheese, measuring about 14 in (35 cm) across, 3–4 in
(8–10 cm) in height, and weighing 22 lb
(10 kg). It has a reddish natural rind
that conceals a pale-yellow, fairly dense
cheese with small, round holes. It has a
mild, slightly acidic to sweetish taste.

SERVING SUGGESTIONS
Sommelier's recommendation: Fresh
and fruity white wines, such as Riesling,
Grauburgunder, and Chardonnay, or
mellow, full-bodied Bordeaux-type red
wines, make the best partners for this
cheese.

Milleens

Semi-hard cheese made from
raw cow's milk
45% FDM

ORIGINS AND HISTORY
Cork
Milleens is a fairly modern cheese made
in the area around Cork. It has very
quickly established a reputation for
itself and is now regarded as one of
Ireland's top cheese varieties. Veronica
and Norman Steel first began producing small quantities of this cheese in
1978 at their farm in County Cork.

Maturer cheese goes much better with
wines with a delicate residual sweetness.

PRODUCTION
The production method for Milleens is
similar to that of many other Trappist
monastery cheeses. It takes a minimum
of three to four weeks, but ideally ten
weeks, to mature.

CHARACTERISTICS
This cheese is flat and round in shape and
weighs about 3 lb (1.5 kg). Its light red,
washed rind conceals a pale-yellow,
compact, supple cheese with a sweet-
sour, mild, and aromatic flavor. At its peak
of maturity, it becomes very soft and its
flavor intensifies, becoming strong and
spicy.

SERVING SUGGESTIONS
Sommelier's recommendation: A young
Milleens is best partnered in terms of
aroma by fine white wines that are not
too dry, or by rounded, fruity red wines.

OTHER VARIETIES OF IRISH CHEESE

The rapid upturn in fortune experienced by Irish dairies and cheese producers during the second half of the twentieth century was due almost entirely to the production and export of popular varieties such as Cheddar, Gouda, Emmentaler-type cheeses, Maasdamer, and Trappist cheese. Any visitor to Ireland who has the opportunity to taste local cheeses on site will encounter many interesting farmhouse-produced specialties. Ardrahan, a washed-rind cheese produced in West Cork, is similar to Gruyère. The same is true of Gabriel, a hard cheese from the same region, which has Swiss-style holes. Blue Rathgore is a blue-veined goat's milk cheese made in Northern Ireland. It is similar to Corleggy, a hard cheese, containing only plant rennet and produced specifically with vegetarians in mind. Croghan is another semi-hard goat's milk cheese (made from non-pasteurized milk and with a nutty flavor). Coolea from West Cork is a cow's milk cheese resembling Gouda with a consistency that is a little harder than Durrus, Orla, or Gubbeen, a red smear cheese with a full-flavored, nutty aroma. Lavistown, on the other hand, is very similar to Cheddar, as is Ryefield, a small, slow-maturing cheese.

DENMARK
Adopted specialties

The Scandinavian countries have much in common in terms of climate, landscape, history, language, and culture. Nevertheless, each nationality has retained a high degree of individuality. This is also true of the culinary specialties that are typical of each country. Denmark produces very few original cheeses of its own and Danish cheese making focuses mainly on foreign-inspired imitations and variations, many of which by now carry Danish name tags. The tradition of making cheeses modeled on German and Dutch recipes began many centuries ago. Since then, English, French, and Swiss cheeses have also been copied by Danish cheese producers and, more recently, even Greek and Italian cheeses have been added to the list. It is not surprising, therefore, that there is hardly any variety of cheese that is not produced in Denmark.

Left: Denmark's symbol—the Little Mermaid statue in Copenhagen.

Danablu (PGI)

Blue-veined cheese made from
cow's milk
50–60% FDM

ORIGINS AND HISTORY
Danablu is now recognized as the world's most famous blue-veined cow's milk cheese. It was first produced in 1920 when Danish cheese producers were experimenting with different mold cultures. Danablu was created by Marius Boel.

PRODUCTION
The curds are made from full-cream, pasteurized cow's milk and injected with *Penicillium Roqueforti*, a blue-mold culture that produces the blue-green veining. Danablu ripens relatively quickly (two to three months). It is also salted for export.

CHARACTERISTICS
It is sold in tall, round cylinders measuring 6–7 in (16–18 cm) in diameter, or sometimes in rectangular blocks, weighing on average about 6½ lb (3 kg). Its yellowish, natural rind conceals a white cheese with a network of blue veins. Young Danablu has a very creamy consistency that becomes harder and even crumbly as it matures. It has a strong aroma and a taste that is spicy and occasionally almost metallic.

SERVING SUGGESTIONS
Danablu goes well with fruit, in sauces, or crumbled onto salads. If the cheese is too strong or salty, it can be crumbled and mixed with butter or cream. In this form it can be spread on bread. Sommelier's recommendation: Danablu pairs perfectly with fine, sweet wines, full-bodied, mature reds, or a sweet sherry.

Esrom (PGI)

Semi-hard cheese made from
cow's milk
45–60% FDM

ORIGINS AND HISTORY

In the 1930s, the State Institute for
Dairy Research in Hillerø revived a long
forgotten recipe for Esrom cheese. It
was named Port Salut because of its
similarities with that cheese, but was
renamed Esrom in 1952 after the
cheese made by the monks of the Esrom
monastery on the island of Seeland.
Although Esrom is mainly mass
produced in factories, a small amount
is still handmade by small (organic)
cheese dairies.

PRODUCTION

Esrom takes about three weeks to
mature and is washed regularly with red
smear solution.

CHARACTERISTICS

Loaf-shape cheese, about 2 in (4–5 cm)
in thickness, 8 in (21–2 cm) long, 4–5 in
(10–12 cm) wide, and weighing about
3 lb (1.2–1.5 kg). The cheese has a thin,
natural rind that is sometimes covered
with yellow wax. It is white or ivory
colored with a supple, elastic texture
and numerous, small, irregular-shape
holes. Young Esrom is very mild and
slightly sweet. As it matures, it develops
a strong, piquant aroma.

SPECIAL FEATURES

Esrom is often called Danish
"Butterkäse" (Butter Cheese).

SERVING SUGGESTIONS

Esrom can be eaten with or without its
rind. However, eating it with the rind
allows the cheese's characteristic
aromas and flavors to be fully appreciated. Sommelier's recommendation:
Fruity white wines combine well with
this cheese, as do light red wines. Excellent alternatives are a glass of chilled
lager or cider.

Havarti

Semi-hard cheese made from
cow's milk
45% FDM

ORIGINS AND HISTORY

Havarti, currently one of Denmark's most popular export cheeses, was invented by Hanne Nielsen, a farmer's wife. In the mid-1900s she went traveling through Europe, collecting numerous recipes, new techniques, and information on the art of cheese making along the way. Upon returning to her farm, she began creating cheeses, the most successful of which was Havarti cheese, named after her farm—it was even sold to the royal court. To this day, Havarti remains one of the leading cheeses produced by the major dairies although a farm-produced version is also available in some places.

PRODUCTION

It is made in much the same way as most semi-hard cheeses. Havarti should mature for about three months to achieve its optimum degree of ripeness.

CHARACTERISTICS

Havarti is sold in rectangular, loaf-shape blocks, measuring 2–5 in (5.5–12 cm) high, 12 in (30 cm) long, 5 in (12 cm) across, and weighing 10 lb (4.5 kg). It has a pale, washed, lightly smeared rind, often coated with wax or covered in foil. Inside, the cheese is white to pale yellow in color. It is supple in texture with small, irregular holes. The taste is slightly sour and becomes increasingly spicy, sharp, and strong as the cheese matures.

SPECIAL FEATURES

A more piquant version of Havarti, flavored with dill or caraway, is also available. Havarti enriched with cream has a softer consistency and a milder flavor.

SERVING SUGGESTIONS

Sommelier's recommendation: Fruity white wines, such as Weißburgunder or Grauburgunder, make ideal companions to serve with young Havarti, while a more mature cheese is better served by a rosé or full-bodied white. Dill- or caraway-flavored Havarti tastes delicious accompanied by a glass of Aquavit.

Danbo

Semi-hard cheese made from cow's milk
45% FDM

ORIGINS AND HISTORY

Danbo is an imitation of a type of cheese known as "Steppenkäse," which was and still is very popular in southeastern Europe, Austria, and Russia, as well as in Scandinavia and Germany. Danbo is one of the Danes' favorite cheeses as well as a popular export. In the USA, Danbo is known as "King Christian II cheese," a reference to the fact that this sixteenth-century Danish ruler's efforts to improve the quality of cheese during his reign included importing Dutch cheese makers into the country.

PRODUCTION

Danbo is part of the Samsø family of cheeses (see entry). Both mass-produced and farm-produced versions are available. Maturing time is at least six weeks but can be as long as two years.

CHARACTERISTICS

Danbo is sold as a square block 10 x 10 in (25 x 25 cm), about 2 in (4–6 cm) thick, and weighing 13–15 lb (6–7 kg). It has a dry, yellowish rind, usually coated in a layer of light yellow or red wax. The cheese is semi-hard and whitish-yellow in color with medium-size holes. It varies in aroma and taste, depending on whether it has been ripened with or without cheese flora.

SPECIAL FEATURES

Extra-mature Danbo is known as Gammelost. It is considered a specialty and is characterized by its strong flavor.

SERVING SUGGESTIONS

Sommelier's recommendation: Suitable accompaniments for young Danbo are light, fruity wines, such as Rieslings or Kerners, rosé wines, or—more traditionally—a glass of lager. Mature Danbo is best partnered with aromatic wines such as Gewürztraminer or wines with subtle residual sweetness.

Samsø

Semi-hard cheese made from
cow's milk
45% FDM

ORIGINS AND HISTORY
Samsø was named after the Danish island of the same name, where it was originally developed by Swiss cheese makers as an imitation of Emmentaler. Since the nineteenth century, this ancestor of several Danish cheeses has acquired a unique character of its own, and despite its alpine associations it remains a cheese that is typically Scandinavian.

PRODUCTION
It is produced in a similar way to Emmentaler and takes three months, often longer, to ripen.

CHARACTERISTICS
Large disks (or sometimes blocks) weighing 30–5 lb (14–16 kg) and measuring 16–18 in (40–5 cm) in diameter and about 4 in (9–10 cm) in height. This pale, rindless cheese is supple and elastic in texture with a few small air holes, the size of cherry pits. Young Samsø has a sweet aroma with a hint of nuttiness while older cheese acquires a sweet-sour or even sharpish flavor with distinct hazelnut overtones. After six months of maturing, Samsø will have developed its full, rich flavor.

SERVING SUGGESTIONS
Sommelier's recommendation: Samsø pairs well with wines that have nutty overtones, such as Chardonnay, Grauer Burgunder, dry Silvaner Spätlese wines, or even cask-aged white wines. Robust rosé wines or a traditional glass of lager also make excellent companions.

SIMILAR CHEESE VARIETIES
Fynbo (a semi-hard cheese made on the island of Fynbo), Tybo (a loaf-shape or rectangular, semi-hard cheese with a mild, faintly acidic taste made in the northern part of Jutland), Molbo (a round cheese made in Jutland with a slightly acidic flavor), Danbo (see entry), and numerous other varieties of Danish cheese.

Maribo

Semi-hard cheese made from
cow's milk
45% FDM

ORIGINS AND HISTORY

Maribo, named after the monastery
town of the same name, is made on the
island of Lolland and is very similar to
the Finnish cheese known as Turunmaa. It is available throughout Denmark
but is little known outside the country.

PRODUCTION

It is produced in much the same way as
other semi-hard cheeses (Gouda,
Edam). Maribo is usually foil ripened
and takes about four months to mature.

CHARACTERISTICS

Square or round in shape 15 x 15 in
(38 x 38 cm) 4 in (10 cm) in thickness,
16 in (40 cm) across and weighing about
30 lb (14 kg). Maribo is usually rindless
and coated with wax. Its relatively firm,
yellowish-white interior is dotted with
numerous little irregular holes. Maribo
has a slightly sour flavor that is a little
reminiscent of Gouda. There are
stronger versions of Maribo on the
market, such as a red smear version and
caraway-flavored Maribo.

SERVING SUGGESTIONS

Sommelier's recommendation: Young
Maribo combines well with fine, fruity
white wines. More mature, stronger
cheese is better suited to aromatic and
full-bodied wines. Caraway-flavored
Maribo tastes delicious if accompanied
by a chilled Aquavit.

CAVE-RIPENED CHEESE

One of the most recent success stories in
Denmark's cheese-making industry is the
development 25 years ago of "cave
cheese." The unusual feature of this cheese
is that it is ripened in limestone caves in an
old Danish chalk mine, which provides an
ideal environment in terms of temperature
and constant humidity. These conditions,
as well as the high level of carbonic acid,
give this cheese its inimitable, characteristic flavor. The cheeses, which take several
months to ripen, are still turned by hand in
keeping with traditional methods.

SWEDEN

Swiss sponsors

Sweden's agriculture—and hence the production of dairy products and cheese—is concentrated in the central and southern parts of the country, where there is ample grazing pasture for cows and goats. Although various central European cheese recipes had been introduced to this part of the country by monks and missionaries during the ninth century, cheese making on any sort of scale remained largely the preserve of the monasteries. Until the beginning of the nineteenth century, most of the cheese consumed in Sweden consisted of foreign imports. It was not until the mid-1800s that farms and estates, drawing on the expertise of Swiss cheese makers, began making a determined effort to build up Sweden's cheese-making industry. Early attempts to produce Emmentaler led to the creation of cheeses such as Herrgårdost, Svecia, and Västerbottenost. Thanks to the advent of collective dairies toward the end of the nineteenth century and increasing foreign influence, Sweden is now producing a wide variety of different cheeses.

Left: Sweden's rocky coast is lined with innumerable islands and skerries (rocks).

Svecia (PGI)

Semi-hard cheese made from
cow's milk
45% FDM

ORIGINS AND HISTORY
The name Svecia comes from the Latin
for Sweden. This traditional Swedish
cheese is reputed to be a copy of a
Dutch cheese.

PRODUCTION
The milk is coagulated with rennet and
the resultant curds are pressed—but
not heated—before being placed into
molds. The cheese generally takes eight
to ten weeks, but sometimes up to one
year, to mature.

CHARACTERISTICS
Although occasionally found in block
form, Svecia generally comes in round
drums, measuring 4–6 in (11–15 cm) in
thickness, 12–14 in (30–5 cm) across,
and usually with a weight of 26–36 lb
(12–16 kg). It has no rind and is foil
wrapped or else coated with red or
yellow wax. The cheese is light yellow
in color and has a moist, supple texture
with numerous small slits and holes. Its
mild, slightly acidic taste becomes more
strong and piquant the longer it
matures. A one-year old Svecia, with its
fresh and very pronounced aroma, is
considered a real delicacy.

SERVING SUGGESTIONS
Sommelier's recommendation: Young
Svecia tastes delicious with lighter,
fruity types of white and red wine.
Mature Svecia, on the other hand,
works best with full-bodied, dry white
wines or moderately robust, mature,
red Bordeaux, Tuscan, or Rioja wines.

Hushållsost (TSG)

Semi-hard cheese made from
cow's milk
60% FDM

ORIGINS AND HISTORY

The history of Hushållsost, whose name literally means "household cheese," stretches back more than 700 years. This cheese variety from southern Sweden used to be considered something of a rarity since it was made, unlike traditional cheeses from that part of the country, from skimmed milk or whey. This former farm cheese has now become one of the Sweden's most popular, mass-produced, standard cheeses.

PRODUCTION

Rennet and lactic acid bacteria are used to coagulate the milk. The curds are pressed and the resulting cheeses are placed in humid ripening cellars, where they are left to mature for one to two months.

CHARACTERISTICS

Small, round, cheeses shaped like drums, 4–6 in (10–15 cm) deep, about 5 in (13–14 cm) across, weighing 4–7 lb (2–3 kg). The cheese usually has a natural rind unless it is foil ripened, in which case it is sold without a rind. This pale, straw-colored cheese has a smooth, open texture with numerous slits and air holes. It has a pleasant, milky flavor with a subtle hint of lemon.

SERVING SUGGESTIONS

Sommelier's recommendation: Ideally, Hushållsost should be accompanied by a fresh, dry or medium-dry Riesling, but a classic Chasselas would also go well with it.

WHEY-BASED CHEESE

Sweden also produces a substantial number of whey-based cheeses that are called Mesost or sometimes Getost and Getmesost. This traditional cheese has a creamy, caramel flavor with a slightly bitter aftertaste. With a fat content of just 10–20 %, the cheese is extremely low in calories.

Herrgård

Semi-hard cheese made from
cow's milk
45% FDM

ORIGINS AND HISTORY

Herrgård is one of Sweden's most popular cheeses. Literally translated, its name means "knight's house" and, until the late eighteenth and early nineteenth century, its production was indeed confined to the great estates. The great aim in those days was to develop a cheese that would be on a par with Swiss cheeses. To this day, Herrgårdsost has much in common with Emmentaler and Gruyère cheese.

PRODUCTION

This cheese is made in much the same way as other semi-hard cheeses. It takes four to ten months for the cheese to mature properly.

CHARACTERISTICS

Herrgård cheese comes in the form of a wagon wheel and measures 4–6 in (10–14 cm) in height, 14 in (35 cm) in diameter, and weighs about 22–30 lb (10–14 kg). It has a natural rind and is often protected by a covering of yellow wax. Underneath, the cheese is light yellow in color, supple in texture, and contains a moderate number of holes. The taste is mild with a hint of nuttiness.

SERVING SUGGESTIONS

Sommelier's recommendation: Its excellent melting qualities make Herrgård an ideal cheese for cooking purposes. Suitable companions are dry, fruity white wines and low-tannin red wines.

Västerbotten

Hard cheese made from
cow's milk
45–50% FDM

ORIGINS AND HISTORY
Originally known as Burträsk, this
cheese was first made about 1860 in the
small town of Burträsk and later copied
throughout the entire region. This "king
of Swedish cheeses" was eventually
renamed Västerbotten after its place of
origin.

PRODUCTION
It is produced in a similar way to Svecia,
but takes much longer to mature and is
often stored for up to a year, which
makes it a much harder cheese.

CHARACTERISTICS
A round cheese with slightly convex
sides, 6–7 in (14–18 cm) in height, 16 in
(40 cm) in diameter, and weighing
40–44 lb (18–20 kg). Its smooth, waxed
rind conceals a relatively firm, somewhat crumbly cheese with some small
holes. It has a very aromatic, spicy taste.

SERVING SUGGESTIONS
Sommelier's recommendation: Its high
ratio of dry matter makes Västerbotten
an ideal grating cheese to cook with.
Moderately robust red wines, such as
Dornfelder, Spätburgunder, or Caber-
net-type wines, make good partners for
this type of cheese, as do mature
Bordeaux, Tuscan, or Rioja wines.

THE WORLD'S MOST NORTHERLY CHEESE

Lappernas Renost is an interesting, if very
rare, cheese made from extremely high-fat
reindeer milk. It is based on a recipe that
has been passed down through centuries
of tradition. If ever the opportunity arises to
sample this cheese, seize the chance for
this is indeed a true rarity. Lappernas is
made in very small quantities because the
yield of milk from a reindeer is less than
7 gallons (about 25 l) of milk per year. In
Lapland this cheese is usually accompanied by coffee, in which small pieces are
dunked prior to eating.

NORWAY
Pure nature

Norwegians are fond of describing their homeland as "that somewhat individual country in northern Europe." In the past, Norwegians derived a living from agriculture, even though only a small portion of the land was agriculturally viable—which is why people soon turned their attention to the sea. Seafarers were the first to bring home cheese recipes from foreign parts and, later on, it was for the most part Irish monks and missionaries who helped expand Norway's cheese culture. To this day, the country's milk still comes from goats in the mountainous interior and from cattle grazing on the higher-quality pastures near the coast. The Norwegians learned a great deal about dairy farming from the Swiss. The first cooperative cheese factory was established in 1856, and in 1928 a farmers' association was set up to handle the export trade. This is still operating under the name of Norske Meierier (Norwegian Dairy Association). The range of products now covers traditional cheeses and domestic standard cheeses, as well as 50 varieties that have been newly developed over the past ten years.

Left: Borgund stave church is one of the oldest wooden buildings in Europe.

Jarlsberg

Semi-hard cheese made from
cow's milk
45% FDM

ORIGINS AND HISTORY
Jarslberg cheese, which takes its name from "Jarl," a Viking prince or earl, comes from the land of the fjords. It is based on old traditional recipes for a variant of Emmentaler cheese. After almost disappearing altogether, it was rediscovered in the twentieth century by a group of emergent cooperatives, backed by Ås University, which successfully revived Jarlsberg cheese. The success was so resounding that it has become not only one of Norway's most popular cheeses but also a major export favorite.

PRODUCTION
Summer milk supplied by cows grazing on succulent upland pastures is used to make Jarlsberg cheese, which matures for at least 100 days, and often much longer, in Norway's fjord region.

CHARACTERISTICS
Jarlsberg is produced in large, round wheels with a diameter of about 12 in (30 cm) and weighing 22 lb (10 kg). The cheese has a smooth natural rind coated in yellow wax and a firm, golden-yellow interior with fairly large, irregular holes. It has a mellow, nutty, creamy flavor and is a little sweeter than Emmentaler.

SERVING SUGGESTIONS
Jarlsberg is an excellent melting cheese and is therefore ideal for toppings or for use in raclette or fondue dishes. Fruity white wines, rosé wines, and light red wines make the best companions, although lager is a good alternative.

Norvegia

Semi-hard cheese made from cow's milk
45% FDM

ORIGINS AND HISTORY

Norvegia, like Jarlsberg, is a cheese with a very old tradition. The recipe for Norvegia, a cheese that was originally a copy of Dutch Gouda, was revived toward the end of the nineteenth century by small farm dairies.

PRODUCTION

In contrast to most hard and semi-hard cheeses, the cheeses are not washed with saline solution during the ripening process. The cheese is left to mature for at least seven months before being released for sale.

CHARACTERISTICS

This cheese with its dry, yellow rind comes in round wheels, 2–5 in measuring (6–12 cm) in thickness, 10–15 in (25–37 cm) across, and weight 9–26 lb (4–12 kg). It is also available in block form coated in hard, black wax, weighing 11–15 lb (5–7 kg). The cheese itself is white to pale yellow with evenly distributed holes and its firm texture makes it easy to slice. Cheese that has matured for a certain time develops a pronounced, piquant, creamy taste. Because it is not washed with saline solution, Norvegia is considerably less salty than many other cheeses.

SERVING SUGGESTIONS

Sommelier's recommendation: Norvegia is often used in cooking because of its excellent melting properties. It is delicious accompanied by fruity white wines such as Sauvignon Blanc, but also combines well with light, spicy red wines like Dornfelder, Blaufränkisch, and Lagrein.

Nøkkelost

Semi-hard cheese made from
cow's milk
45% FDM

ORIGINS AND HISTORY
The Dutch recipe for Nøkkelost was
brought to Norway by seafarers, as
evidenced to this day from the trade
mark of crossed keys, which is also
found on Leiden cheese. Its name is
derived from the Norse word "nökkel,"
meaning keys. Nøkkelost has been
produced in Norway since the seventeenth century, but it is now mainly
factory produced.

PRODUCTION
As far as production techniques are
concerned, it is a typical semi-hard, cow's
milk cheese. One unusual feature of this
cheese is the addition of cumin seed. It
takes about three months to mature.

CHARACTERISTICS
The cheese comes in the shape of a round
cylinder, 3–6 in (8–15 cm) in thickness,
12–16 in (30–40 cm) across, and weighing 26–33 lb (12–15 kg). It is also available in blocks weighing 11–15 lb (5–7 kg).
This light yellowish, supple, semi-hard
cheese contains numerous little air holes
and cumin seeds, which give this mild-
tasting cheese a unique flavor.

SERVING SUGGESTIONS
Sommelier's recommendation: Nøkkelost is particularly delicious melted over
potatoes cooked in their skins. The
aromatic elements pair well with
medium-dry Rieslings, Grüner Veltliner
with peppery overtones, or mild, cask-
aged wines such as red Languedoc. The
classic companion, however, is lager.

NORWEGIANS LOVE
THEIR GOAT'S CHEESE

Norwegians are particularly fond of goat's
milk cheeses. One such product is
Hardanger, which the Norwegians also
call Rosendal. The curds for Hardanger
cheese are hand pressed before it is left to
mature for at least two months and coated
with a black wax rind. Its name, Snofrisk,
reflects its appearance: It is a snow-white,
fresh goat's cheese. It is made from 80%
goat's milk and 20% cream from cow's
milk. Its taste is fresh and mild.

Gammelost (Gamalost)

Sour-milk, blue-veined cheese
made from cow's or goat's milk
3–5% FDM

ORIGINS AND HISTORY

The cow's milk cheese Gammelost comes from Hardangerfjord, while a goat's milk version is made in Sognefjord. Its name—literally translated—means "old cheese," but why it should be so called remains a mystery. It has been suggested that this is a reference to its long keeping qualities, which, in centuries past, meant it could be stored well into the winter. On the other hand, it could be an allusion to the greenish-brown mold that quickly appears on the rind of a maturing Gammelost.

PRODUCTION

Gammelost is made from sour skimmed-milk curds. The crucial factor is the addition of fungal cultures that cover the cheese with a light coating of delicate, downy mold. This is pressed or inoculated into the interior of the cheese itself so that the mold cultures spread throughout the whole cheese. In the past, the mold developed unaided in the residue of the previous day's production, which was left in wooden barrels containing fungal spores.

CHARACTERISTICS

Round, cylindrical cheeses measuring 4–8 in (10–20 cm) in height, 5–8 in (12–20 cm) in diameter, and weighing 2–7 lb (1–3 kg). The cheese has a hard, cracked, greenish-brown, natural crust that conceals a brownish-yellow to brown, semi-hard cheese without holes. The consistency of a young cheese is relatively soft, whereas a mature Gammelost can be extremely hard. Depending on how long it has matured, Gammelost has a strong taste with a spicy, sharp, and aromatic flavor. Smell and taste are also determined by the type of milk used. The cheese is sometimes wrapped in straw or in cloths previously soaked in gin with juniper berries. This makes it ripen even better from the inside out and protects it against undesirable bacteria.

SERVING SUGGESTIONS

To this day, farmers sometimes heat a piece of cheese in whey and drink the mixture as a remedy for coughs and colds. One particular specialty involves scooping out a hole in a whole cheese and filling it with gin, Aquavit, or with beer before consumption. Sommelier's recommendation: Schnapps or lager is the classic companion for this cheese. Alternatively, mature port, wines with residual sugar, or robust white wines are also suitable.

FINLAND
Rarities

Cheese has been made in Finland since the sixteenth century, when the main cheeses produced consisted predominantly of fresh farm cheese destined for home consumption and mature types of cheese produced by the country estates of Åland and the southern Finnish islands. Reindeer-milk cheese was also produced. Only very few of these early cheeses have survived. Although Turunmaa still retains a degree of commercial importance, other traditional varieties are now only craft produced on farms and are very difficult to get hold of. The Finnish dairy industry grew significantly in terms of output in the mid-nineteenth century, when the Swiss cheese master Rudolf Klossner began producing Emmentaler cheese at the Sippolas estate. Gradually, cheese recipes from neighboring countries, as well as from England and The Netherlands, were also introduced into Finland.

Left: Uspensky Cathedral is the largest Orthodox church in Western Europe.

Turunmaa

Semi-hard cheese made from
cow's milk
50% FDM

ORIGINS AND HISTORY

Turunmaa, also known as Korsholm or
Ålands Special, is an ancient type of
Finnish cheese that has been made on
the big country estates since the
sixteenth century. Its recipe is said to be
modelled on Dutch or Danish cheeses.
All three of its names refer to the areas
where it was originally produced.

PRODUCTION

This cheese is produced in much the
same way as Gouda and takes about two
to three months to mature.

CHARACTERISTICS

The cheese is cylindrical in shape, 8 in
(20 cm) in height, 9 in (22 cm) in diameter, and weighing about 13 lb (6 kg).
Turunmaa is rindless and pale yellow in
color with a smooth, semi-hard consistency, and numerous unevenly spaced
holes. Young cheese is mild and slightly
acidic in taste, but develops a fuller,
slightly sharp aroma as it ages.

SERVING SUGGESTIONS

Sommelier's recommendation: Turunmaa is best served with a moderately
robust, dry white, or red wine. Extra-
mature cheese deserves a full-bodied,
mature red wine with low tannins or a
wine with residual sweetness.

Lappi

Semi-hard cheese made from
cow's milk
45% FDM

ORIGINS AND HISTORY

This typically Finnish cheese, which is
very similar to Edam, is produced in the
heart of Finland in a thinly populated
region of unspoilt nature, famous for its
lakes and forests. It gets its name from
the small village of Lapinlehti.

PRODUCTION

Lappi is mainly mass produced. The
cheese matures in about five weeks.

CHARACTERISTICS

Generally sold in 12 x 6 x 4–5 in blocks
(30 x 15 x 9–12 cm) with a weight of
10–11 lb (4.5–5 kg), or in lighter, rindless rounds (foil ripened or waxed). It
is a pale-yellow, semi-hard cheese with
a few pea-size holes. It is a mild tasting
but nevertheless aromatic cheese.

SERVING SUGGESTIONS

Dry, mature white wines with a delicate
bouquet or dry, fruity, velvety red wines
make the best partners for this type of
cheese, as does a glass of lager.

FINNISH EMMENTALER (SWISS FINLAND)

Emmentaler production began in Finland in
the mid-nineteenth century when the recipe
and method were introduced by the Swiss
cheese expert Rudolf Klossner. Finland has
for many years been one of the world's
major producers of Emmentaler. Thanks to
the excellent quality of Finnish Emmentaler,
it has become one of the country's main
export products. The USA is one of its best
customers in this respect. Pasteurized milk
is curdled in giant vats that produce up to
ten or more wheels, each weighing about
175 lb (80 kg), which are then matured for
3 to 12 months. During this time they are
automatically turned and washed on a
regular basis and finally divided into
portions and packaged.

Juustoleipä

Fresh cheese made from
cow's milk
Less than 10% FDM

ORIGINS AND HISTORY
Juustoleipä is produced in several
regions in central Finland. It is both
farm produced in small quantities and
mass produced. There is also a very rare
version made from reindeer milk. Juustoleipä, roughly translated, means
"cheese bread" in Finnish, which is a
reference to the way in which it is made.

PRODUCTION
The fresh curds from skimmed milk are
drained of whey before being placed in
a flat mold and gently heated over a fire
or in the oven. It is then left to mature
for several days.

CHARACTERISTICS
Juustoleipä, which is available in various shapes and sizes (usually in 9 oz/
250 g portions), has a lightly toasted,
brown surface, beneath which is an
almost white, creamy, smooth, soft
cheese. It is mild or slightly sweet in
taste.

SERVING SUGGESTIONS
The Finns eat Juustoleipä for breakfast
or as a dessert with jam or wild berries.
It goes down well with coffee, fruit juice,
or milk.

Ilves and Munajuusto

Fresh cheese made from
cow's/reindeer milk
45% FDM

ORIGINS AND HISTORY
Munajuusto is a traditional regional
cheese that is produced by a few small
farmhouse dairies. The mass-produced
version of this cheese is known as Ilves.
The traditional variety is made from rich
reindeer milk.

PRODUCTION
Eggs are added to the milk at the beginning of the process. The mixture is
heated to induce curdling. Once the
whey has drained off, the curds are
gently pressed into molds. The cheese
can be toasted in front of an open fire
before being left to mature for a short
period.

CHARACTERISTICS
Ilves is usually sold as a round cheese
weighing 2–3 lb (1–1.3 kg). It is a relatively firm, whitish fresh cheese with a
high-water content. Its pale-colored
surface is marked with irregular brown
patches caused by the toasting. It has a
mild, slightly sweetish flavor.

SERVING SUGGESTIONS
Sommelier's recommendation: A cask-
aged white wine or, alternatively, a top-
fermented beer combine particularly
well with this cheese.

ICELAND
From the age of the Vikings

The mountainous, occasionally barren, Icelandic landscape is characterized by huge glaciers, high volcanic peaks, and vast lava fields. Even so, a good 20% of the country is used as grazing land for more than 500,000 sheep, about 70,000 Icelandic horses, and over 35,000 cows, which produce top-quality milk of the highest standard. The earliest Icelandic cheeses, which are believed to date back to the days of the Vikings, were made from sheep's milk. Skyr, a fresh, whey-based cheese frequently mentioned in Icelandic folklore, is one such cheese, which has survived to this day.

Left: Hallgrímskirkja is one of Reykjavik's main landmarks.

Skyr

Whey-based cheese made
from cow's milk
10% FDM

ORIGINS AND HISTORY

The first mention of a fresh cheese made from sheep's milk occurs in old Icelandic legends dating from the days of the Vikings. Skyr was originally produced on every farm for the family's own consumption. Nowadays, the cheese is made increasingly from the pasteurized skimmed milk, whey, or buttermilk of cows. Although a small amount of Skyr is still farm produced, most of it is now mass produced.

PRODUCTION

Skyr was originally made as a fresh cheese without the addition of rennet. To induce curdling, a little Skyr from the previous day was simply added to the heated milk. Once the whey had drained off, the fresh cheese was ready to eat the following day. Mass-produced Skyr relies on the addition of calf's rennet in order to promote coagulation, however. In addition, special bacterial cultures are added to the milk to improve the cheese's quality and shelf life.

CHARACTERISTICS

Skyr, a soft, white cheese, is somewhere between yogurt and Quark in taste. It is marketed in tubs and pots of varying sizes.

SERVING SUGGESTIONS

Skyr is popular as a breakfast cheese or as part of the evening meal. It can also be eaten as a dessert or simply as a snack—in its natural state, sprinkled with sugar, mixed with fruit, or stiffly beaten with milk.

SIMILAR CHEESE VARIETIES

Avaxtstyr is a version of Skyr mixed with fruit. Rjomaskyr is another version of Skyr, enriched with cream.

OTHER TYPES OF ICELANDIC CHEESES

In addition to Skyr, Iceland produces many other types of cheese, almost all of which are based on imported recipes yet still retain their individuality. One of these is Mysingur and another is the brown, relatively creamy Mysoustur, made from heated, skimmed cow's milk. Various whey-based, Norwegian-style cheeses are also available. Modern cheese factories also produce imitations of Edam (Barudostur), Tilsiter (Tilsitter), Emmentaler (Odalostur), Havarti (Buri), Brie (Dla-Brie), Blue Cheese (Gradaost), Camembert, and Port Salut. Their exceptional flavor and extremely enticing aroma are due to the high-quality milk used in their production.

POLAND
Sheep's cheese from the mountains

Only a handful of traditional cheeses have survived Poland's eventful history. Most of the cheese making takes place in southern Poland's mountain region, which adjoins the border with the Czech Republic and Slovakia. Nowadays, most cheeses in Poland are imitations of Western European cheeses, such as Butterkäse (butter cheese), soft, white mold cheeses, and Gouda. Nevertheless, Poland does produce a few traditional cheeses, among them Oscypek and Bryndza Podhalanska, which have now been registered as EU-protected regional products. Podhalanski cheese, a semi-hard cheese made from cow's or sheep's milk, with small holes and a hard rind, is another cheese to have survived and is also available as a smoked version. Tylzscki cheese is one of the few remaining traditional cheeses still being produced in Poland. It resembles Tilsiter, from which it gets its name, and is the only cheese not to come from the mountainous region in the southern part of the country.

Left: Warsaw's controversial landmark: The Cultural Palace built by Stalin.

Bryndza Podhalańska PDO

Soft cheese made from
sheep's milk
38% FDM

ORIGINS AND HISTORY

The first mention of Bryndza cheese from the Podhale region was recorded in 1527. The production of cheese made from ewe's milk has, for many centuries, been a direct by-product of sheep farming in the Podhale region. After driving their flocks up to the high pastures every year, the shepherds would spend several months in the mountains, during which time they practically lived on sheep's milk and its related products. The basic method for producing Bryndza Podhalańska has been passed down from generation to generation—so much so that it has become a skill for which the region's cheese makers are renowned. It may only be made in Nowy Targ (Neumarkt) and Tatra (Powiat Tatrzański) regions and in six villages in the Zywiec district. This region in the foothills of the Tatra range is known as Podhale, and from it Bryndza Podhalańska gets its name.

PRODUCTION

Bryndza Podhalańska is made only between May and September. The milk has to come from ewes of the Polska Owca Górsla (Polish mountain sheep) breed. If cow's milk is used at all (maximum 40% permitted), it must come from Polska Krowa Czerwona (Polish Red) cows. After the milk has been coagulated by the addition of rennet, the whey is drained off, and the curds are fermented (preripened), then cut into small chunks. The crumbly cheesy curds are pounded into a firm mass, mixed with salt, and placed in a container. What makes Bryndza ewe's milk cheese so special is the high quality of its ingredients and its traditional production techniques, which are exclusive to the Podhale region.

CHARACTERISTICS

White or cream-colored cheese, sometimes a delicate shade of willow green. It has a piquant, somewhat salty, and occasionally slightly sour taste.

Oscypek PDO

Stretched-curd cheese
made from sheep's milk
45% FDM

ORIGINS AND HISTORY
The High Tatra national park in the region around Zakpane is home to one of Europe's oldest shepherd communities. Sheep farming in this area has a history dating back as far as the thirteenth century, whilst the production of Oscypek cheese can be traced back to the fourteenth century. Shepherds, or *batza*, from Wallachia introduced sheep breeding and milk processing techniques into the region from the Carpathian mountains.

PRODUCTION
This hard, smoked cheese, which comes in a unique spindle shape, is made up in the mountain dairies from fresh ewe's milk. The milk is heated in a copper vat and curdled by the addition of rennet. The resulting curd is cut, transferred to wooden containers, and rinsed with hot water. The mass is thoroughly kneaded by hand, immersed once more in hot water, and then kneaded again. Once the cheese has developed an elastic consistency, it is pressed into characteristic spindle molds that have decorative designs carved on the inside. These leave a distinctive imprint pattern on the cheese. Oscypek cheese is dried and matured on wooden shelves in the smoke room for two to three months.

CHARACTERISTICS
Its flavor is reminiscent of chestnuts. Each cheese weighs between 1½ lb and 2 lb (600–800 g) and is about 8 in (20 cm) long. Oscypek is popular as a grilled dish in Poland. The smoking process gives the surface of the cheese a golden shimmer and a distinctive smoky aroma.

SPECIAL FEATURES
After a long dispute regarding the cheese's protected origin registration, Poland and Slovakia have now reached agreement that both designations—Oscypek (Poland) and Slovenskýštiepok (Slovakia)—are legitimate.

CZECH REPUBLIC
A bishop's breakfast

The Czech Republic with its famous spas and health resorts, its many castles, palaces, cultural monuments, and historic towns—including its capital city of Prague—is well worth exploring as a tourist destination. Unlike Slovakia, the Czech Republic had close connections with Austria and Germany, associations that are also reflected in its cheese culture. The country's most traditional cheese is Olomoucké tvarůžky, a small sour-milk cheese of the red smear variety. Abertam, too, is a typical farm cheese, made in Karlovy Vary (formerly known as Karlsbad) in Bohemia. This distinctively ball-shape, strong-flavored hard cheese is made from sheep's milk and takes about two months to mature. Czech dairies also produce standard European cheeses.

Left: The Gothic Teyn Church stands in the heart of Prague's Old Town.

Olomoucké tvarůžky

Sour-milk cheese made from
cow's milk
10% FDM

ORIGINS AND HISTORY

There is evidence to indicate that Olomoucké tvarůžky has been produced in the Haná region of northern Moravia with its economic center of Olomouc since the end of the fifteenth century. Archbishop Johannes von Morara is reputed to have been breakfasting on this cheese as long as 900 years ago. Commercial production of the cheese began in Olomouc around 1770, but today there is only one producer left—in Loštice, the home, coincidentally, of a cheese museum. Olomoucké tvarůžky is the only cheese of Czech origin and it is now one of the country's most famous indigenous varieties. Its roots do indeed go back to Austrian Moravia, so it is not surprising that Austria, a country that has been producing this cheese under the name of Olmützer Quargel for over 100 years, also lays claim to having "invented" it. Olmützer Quargel has also been produced in Germany since the end of the Second World War.

PRODUCTION

Olomoucké tvarůžky is made from sour-milk curds. The curds, which have a characteristic crumbly structure with large, tough grains, are distinctly acidic with a high level of biological activity.

The curds are ground and table salt is added before the curd mix is preripened in sealed containers. The cheese mass is subsequently mixed with lactic acid cultures and molded to the required shape. During the first stage of the ripening process, the cheeses are placed on grids and matured in conditions of controlled temperature and humidity. Subsequent rinsing during the second stage produces a golden yellow smear on the surface of the cheese.

CHARACTERISTICS

The activity of the special microflora which form on the surface during ripening gives the cheese its typical, unique, sharp, piquant, and complex taste, flavor, and smell. The riper the cheese, the stronger these qualities. It has a golden-yellow smear rind that conceals a semi-soft to soft cheese with a lighter center. It usually takes the form of 4 oz (125 g) rolls, divided into several slices, each weighing about 1 oz (20–30 g).

KASHKAVAL—A CHEESE THAT UNITES NATIONS

Kashkaval is a type of semi-hard cheese that is both familiar and very popular in many Eastern European countries and the eastern Mediterranean region. This semi-hard cheese is one of the traditional cheese varieties found in Bulgaria, Turkey, Hungary, and Romania and is made either from sheep's milk or cow's milk. Both natural and smoked versions are available. Depending on which type it is, its smooth, dry rind conceals a pale, delicate yellow cheese or a brownish interior, typical of smoked cheese. It is piquant, spicy, and often a little salty in flavor. Kahkaval belongs to the *pasta filata* group of cheeses, in which the curds are kneaded in hot water. This semi-hard cheese is ideal on bread, as part of a cheese board, as a snack, as a topping on oven dishes, or added to salads.

SLOVAKIA
Individuality and character

The tradition of cheese making is an important aspect of life in this small country with its picturesque landscape. Slovakia has always maintained close links with Hungary and Eastern Europe, and this explains why ewe's milk cheese of the Bryndza (Brimsen) variety and stretched-curd cheese of the Bulgarian Kashkaval variety are part of its culinary heritage. Nevertheless, the cheese specialties produced in the country's mountain regions have an individuality and character all of their own, as demonstrated by the applications for Bryndza and Parenica to be assigned protected origin status.

OTHER TYPES OF SLOVAK CHEESES

Korbacik is a salted, stretched-curd cheese made from cow's or sheep's milk. Sometimes likened to a whip, it consists of lots of thin strands and is sometimes artistically braided. It was originally farm produced for home consumption. It comes in smoked and unsmoked versions. For hundreds of years shepherds in the Carpathian mountains have been making Oschtjepka cheese (45% FDM) from the milk of their ewes. Meanwhile, it is now made from cow's milk or a combination of the two. The shepherds traditionally made the cheese themselves by pressing and shaping sour-milk curds into large rounds, weighing about 2 lb (1 kg) each. These were then left to mature in brine for several days before being hung up to dry in cloths from the ceilings of their mountain huts. This cheese is smoked over an open wood fire. The thin, brownish, natural rind of this semi-hard cheese bears the imprint of the cloth and has a sweet and aromatic taste.

Left: St. Martin's Cathedral in Bratislava is a national cultural monument.

Slovenská bryndza

Fresh cheese made from
sheep's milk
25–50% FDM

ORIGINS AND HISTORY

This cheese is made in Slovakia's mountain region, where milk is produced by sheep of the Valaška, Zošľachtená valaška, Cigája and Východofrízska ovca breeds that graze in the area. Barrel-aged cheese made from sheep's milk and Slovenská bryndza were nutritional mainstays for the people who lived in Slovakia's mountain regions. Whenever a milk surplus occurred, shepherds up in the high pastures would produce a simple quark, which was shaped into clumps and left to mature in sealed wooden barrels. In 1787 the first factory to produce the cheese on an industrial scale was established in Detva and, even prior to the First World War, exports of Slovenská bryndza were being made to Hungary and Austria in particular.

PRODUCTION

The basic ingredient of Bryndza is curds from ewe's milk cheese, although cow's milk is also permitted. The individual chunks of cheese, each weighing about 7–15 lb (3–7 kg), are placed on a mat, where they sour for two to three days in warm conditions and then ripen for a further four to six days. The cheeses are then transferred from the alpine huts to the production plants down in the valley. Here, they are washed, cut into smaller portions, and milled before being stirred into a soft mass and seasoned with salt.

CHARACTERISTICS

The distinctive features of this cheese are its delicate aroma and taste, which includes pleasantly acidic, somewhat piquant, salty overtones. Its unique flavor is produced by naturally occurring microorganisms present in the sheep's milk produced in this region. The cheese is sold in little containers, prepackaged blocks, or a sausage-shape plastic wrap. It has a delicate and slightly crumbly consistency and is easy to spread.

SPECIAL FEATURES

An application has been made for this cheese to be registered for an EU protected geographic indication.

SERVING SUGGESTIONS

Bryndza is used to prepare traditional dishes such as Bryndzové pagáiky (cheese dumplings) or Pirohy pinené bryndzou (pierogi stuffed with cheese).

SIMILAR CHEESE VARIETIES

Brinza (Romania), Brynza (Hungary), Brundza Podhalańska (Poland).

Parenica

A *pasta filata* cheese made from
cow's or sheep's milk
50% FDM

ORIGINS AND HISTORY

Parenica was first produced by sheep farmers in the early eighteenth century for their families' own consumption. By the nineteenth century, it was being sold not only in the area now known as Slovakia, but also in Vienna and other cities. Page 180 of the chapter on cheese in Part III of the *Codex Alimentarius Austriacus* (published in Vienna in 1917) states that Parenica is a steamed, stretched cheese that is cooked in hot water and pulled into strings and strands before being twisted and smoked. The cheese unquestionably originated in upper Hungary—in other words, Slovakia.

PRODUCTION

After coagulation has taken place, the lumps of sheep's cheese, each weighing between about 7 and 11 lb (3–5 kg), are cut into smaller pieces of around 1 lb (0.5 kg) each. These are placed in a wooden tub filled with hot water and kneaded until a fine cheesy mass forms. The resultant cheesy mass is lifted out and the remaining liquid is pressed out by hand before the cheese is repeatedly kneaded and pulled out into strings. This elastic mass of cheese is pulled into strands and shaped on wooden boards, using the edge of the hand. The strands are plunged briefly into a brine solution, then wound from opposite ends and connected in an "S" shape and bound with string. Once the cheese has dried, it is lightly smoked.

CHARACTERISTICS

Sold in individual packages of 1¼–2 lb (450–500 g), Slovenská parenica is marketed as an "S"-shape cheese, about 2–3 in (5–8 cm) in height and 2–3 in (6–8 cm) across. The traditional practice is to wind two rolls together with cheese thread. The cheese has a distinctive smell of sheep's milk and smoke. It is mild and pleasantly salty to taste and its elastic, white to butter-yellow body has a fibrous structure that produces a stringy cheese when pulled apart. The rind is darkened by smoking to yellow or brown.

SPECIAL FEATURES

An application has been submitted for protected origin status.

HUNGARY

Delicious products from sheep's milk

Hungary's history has been extremely eventful. A succession of invaders and conquerors and, most importantly, centuries of Turkish rule led to the introduction of Bryndza, a Feta-type sheep's cheese, preserved in brine. Hungary actually has very few native or traditional cheese specialties of its own and cheese making as such, modelled on German and Swiss cheeses, only became underway just before the Second World War, when Hungary began to produce its own versions of standard European cheeses. The Hungarian dairy institute did however develop new varieties of cheese, including a Tilsiter imitation known as Óvarí.

Óvarí has meanwhile become one of Hungary's best known Tilsiter-style cheeses. This red smear ripened cheese is typically spicy and salty in taste. Anikó is a soft, cow's milk cheese. Kashkaval, the traditional *pasta filata* cheese of the Balkans, is also produced in Hungary. Parenyica Sajt is a coiled, lightly smoked sheep's milk cheese, occasionally produced from cow's milk. Hundreds of years ago, shepherds in the Tatra mountains used to make a simple sheep's cheese known as Gomolya. This traditional shepherd's cheese is delicate and light in consistency and tastes of sweet sheep's milk. Liptoi is made by small cheese dairies from chunks of Gomolya curds. It makes an excellent topping on a slice of bread. This snack is popular not just in Hungary but in the Czech Republic, Slovakia, and Austria as well.

Left: The Fisherman's Bastion in Budapest is one of Hungary's main tourist attractions.

RUSSIA

A form of curd cheese, made by curdling milk naturally, was known in Russia as far back as the Middle Ages. The first cheese dairy was set up in Moscow in 1795, but production was minimal. It was nearly another century before an intensive cheese industry developed about 1870. The large dairies in the central Russian regions of Tver, Yaroslavl, Vologda, Novgorod, and Kostroma became established within a short space of time and hard cheeses from these regions—such as Kostromski, Uglitschsky, and Poschechonsky—continue to enjoy a good reputation throughout the country today. There were about 100 cheese varieties being produced in Russia in 1913, with production being based on cheese techniques from The Netherlands and Switzerland, as is indicated today by cheese designations such as Gollandsky and Gouda (Dutch) and Shveytsarsky (Swiss). The best Shveytsarsky, as the Russian equivalent of Emmental is called, is still produced in the northern Caucasus. The Caucasian cheese makers claim that the mountain pastures there provide conditions for the cows similar to those of the Swiss alpine pastures. During the Soviet era processed cheese in all its forms was popular, largely due to its cheapness. There were also the élite varieties, however, such as Sovietsky, which is still produced in the Altaj region, albeit to a lesser extent. Almost all the world's cheese varieties are to be found at Russian cheese markets today. In addition to the local Rossijsky, Kostromsky, and the processed cheese Druschba, Gouda, Maasdam, Edam, and Tilsit are very popular. The greatest demand is for semi-hard and processed cheeses.

Left: St. Basil's Cathedral in Red Square in Moscow.

Sovietsky

Semi-hard cheese made
from cow's milk
50% FDM

ORIGINS AND HISTORY

The Sovietsky brand has been in existence since the 1930s, but its production is based on an older Shveytsarsky Syr recipe—a Swiss cheese that has been produced in the Altaj region since the second half of the nineteenth century. Sovietsky is an "élite cheese," and even during the Soviet era it was one of the best known and most widely produced varieties. Today production is limited to a few small dairies in Altaj.

PRODUCTION

Sovietsky is produced by the dairies in the mountainous region of Altaj. Production takes place almost solely in summer and fall because it is only during this period that the milk gives the cheeses the required flavor. The curds are cut and reheated before being shaped into large sticks, salted, and then ripened for a month in wooden molds. The cheese is then packed in a wax covering and stored for a further four to six months.

CHARACTERISTICS

Spicy, sweet, and nutty taste. The straw-colored cheese is homogeneous and elastic with small, round holes. So-called "tears" sometimes form in the holes, indicating that the cheese has ripened thoroughly. The sweetness becomes more distinct the longer the cheese ripens, and the cheese becomes somewhat sharper.

SERVING SUGGESTIONS

In Russia this cheese is eaten cut into thin slices for breakfast, lunch, and supper. It is served with tea, coffee, or cocoa, or with a semi-sweet or dry white wine. Its sweet flavor makes it ideal for making desserts.

Kostromski

Semi-hard cheese made from
cow's milk
40–50% FDM

ORIGINS AND HISTORY
The production of Kostromski began in
the Volga region of Kostroma at the end
of the nineteenth century and the
cheese is named after this region. Today
the cheese is produced by several
dairies in central and southern Russia.

PRODUCTION
Salt, pure culture acid starter, and
rennet are added to the milk. The curds
are reheated at a low temperature.
Ripening takes at least six weeks.

CHARACTERISTICS
Round cheese weighing about 11–26 lb
(5–12 kg). It is subtly acidic both in
flavor and aroma. The flavor becomes
more distinct and slightly piquant if the
cheese is ripened for more than two
months. Elastic and homogeneous,
cream to pale-yellow-colored cheese
with small oval or square holes. Thin,
soft, and elastic rind.

SERVING SUGGESTIONS
This cheese is eaten as it is or else with
bread, and is also ideal for use in the
kitchen.

USA
Moving forward by looking back

It was in about 1700 that European immigrants brought their cows and their art of cheese making to the United States. What began on small farms for home use went on to develop into a major industry, particularly with the wave of immigration in the nineteenth century. Today the USA is the world's largest cheese producer and the diversity of cheese varieties has never been as extensive. It was the industrial production of Cheddar, Gouda, Brie and Camembert, Mozzarella, Provolone, and other varieties that made this development possible. "Processed cheese," created by John Kraft at the start of the twentieth century, also made a significant contribution to establishing this leading market position. There are only a few cheese varieties that can claim to be of truly American origin, however.

Over the last ten years, America's cheese producers have developed a new self-confidence. The American Cheese Society promotes the establishment of a cheese culture, providing advice and support for producers, and integrating the interests of the different parties. The reversion to old European traditions of cheese production has meant tremendous progress in terms of product quality and cheese culture, with the states of Wisconsin, California, and Vermont leading the way. Slowly but surely American consumers are realizing that cheese can be enjoyed as it is and not only for cooking, melting, and in salads.

Left: A gift from France—the Statue of Liberty in New York harbor.

CHEESE WITH STYLE—THE MOST IMPORTANT CHEESE CATEGORIES IN THE USA

FRESH CHEESE
Fresh cheese can be produced from any type of milk but the milk must always be pasteurized. This category includes Italian-style Mascarpone and Ricotta, Chevre, Feta, cream cheese, curd cheese, and cottage cheese.

SOFT RIPENED CHEESE
In the United States soft ripened cheeses are usually made from pasteurized milk. This category includes French Brie and Camembert-style cheeses as well as triple cream category cheeses, the Triple Crèmes.

SEMI-SOFT CHEESE
The term "semi-soft" refers to cheese varieties with a soft, creamy interior, and hardly any or no rind. These cheeses generally have a high water content. Their flavor ranges from very mild through to piquant and spicy. Depending on the ripening duration, these cheeses can be made from raw or pasteurized milk. This category includes most of the blue cheeses, Colby, and Monterey Jack, as well as Italian-style Fontina cheese or the Danish Havarti. Washed rind cheeses also fall under this category.

FIRM/HARD CHEESE
The flavor range extends from very mild through to spicy and piquant. The cheese is elastic in the case of firm cheeses and with hard cheeses is hard enough for grating. These cheeses can be made from both raw and pasteurized milk. This category includes Gouda-style cheeses, Cheddars, Dry Jack, Swiss-style (Emmental) Gruyère-style cheeses, as well as many Tomme and Parmesan kinds.

BLUE CHEESE
The classic representatives are French (Roquefort), Italian (Gorgonzola), and Danish-style cheeses.

PASTA FILATA CHEESE
Pasta filata cheeses are primarily of Italian origin and are mostly based on the example of Mozzarella, Provolone, and Scamorza.

NATURAL RIND CHEESE
This category comprises those cheeses whose rind forms by itself due to the natural microflora. Typical examples are Tomme, based on the French Tomme de Savoie, and cheeses based on the French Mimolette. This category also includes English Stilton and Lancashire-style cheeses.

WASHED RIND CHEESE
The rind is treated with brine, beer, wine, brandy, or red mold bacteria. These are cheeses based on the French Epoisses and Livarot, or the Italian Taleggio. It also includes a number of Tomme, Triple-Crème, and soft cheese varieties.

PROCESSED CHEESE
The term "processed" describes cheese products derived from a wide variety of cheese varieties that are enhanced with stabilizers, emulsifiers, and flavor enhancers in order to achieve the characteristic consistency and long shelf life. This category includes American cheese, processed cheese spreads, and cheese-flavored spreads.

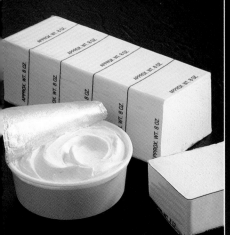

American Cheese

The Americans' favorite cheese is bright yellow, rather sticky, and soft—namely processed cheese. This high flying cheese which went on to conquer the world was invented in New York at the start of the last century by Mr. James L. Kraft, who sold cheese from door to door. The cheese's smell became stronger with age and the cut edge dried out quickly, problems for which Kraft needed to find a solution, and he experimented until he found one. The cheese (originally Cheddar or Colby) was cut up, heated, colored with annatto, and shaped into a block. This product became an instant success. Kraft then came up with another novel idea when the Americans developed their penchant for sandwiches in the 1940s. He cut the block of cheese into slices and repacked the slices as a block. The individually packed slices, known as Cheese Singles, were on the market in 1965 and they, too, became a sales hit. Mr. Kraft's family of processed cheeses was soon extended to include Velveeta, a pasteurized, spreadable processed cheese in a block shape, and Cheez Wiz,

a spreadable processed cheese in a jar. American cheese is a feature of cheeseburgers and sandwiches.

Cottage Cheese

The grainy cream cheese known as cottage cheese is made without adding rennet, the heated milk being left to curdle on its own. Different styles are made from milk with different fat content. The very soft curd is cut into cubes 0.5 cm in size which are heated in the whey until the required consistency has been achieved. The whey is then drained off. The now lumpy mixture is rinsed with cold water and any remaining whey removed. The grainy substance is salted, enhanced with milk or cream, and optionally flavored with spices or herbs. Cottage cheese has a creamy, grainy consistency—there are large and small curd kinds. It has a slightly sour, delicate, creamy, and very neutral flavor and is sold in tubs, beakers, or in plastic bags. Cottage cheese goes well with a rosé

THE AMBITIONS OF A NEW GENERATION

With the "new" generation of cheese specialties the focus is on the individuality, quality, and authenticity of the products. Specialty cheeses are produced in small quantities, the main focus of attention being natural flavor and natural texture. The cheese can be produced from any type of milk and often contains natural flavors and ingredients such as herbs, spices, fruit, and nuts. Artisan cheeses—cheeses made using handcraft methods—are also produced in small quantities and largely by hand. Here there is a special focus on the cheese makers' skills and the traditional production methods. According to the American Cheese Society's definition, a farmhouse cheese has to be made from the milk of animals living on the farm that come from the farmer's own herd. The buying in of milk for production purposes is not permitted. The farmers usually use raw milk in order to retain the full flavor and aroma of the cheese.

wine or in small quantities with fresh beer. If you would like to offset the subtle cheese flavor with a strong counterpart, combine cottage cheese with a robust Merlot.

Cream Cheese

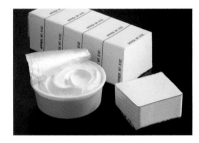

Cream cheese became popular in around 1880, an era that saw a revolutionary technical development in dairies. The technique used is based on a process used from the 1850s in Normandy. A separator meant that the whey could be separated from the cheese solids straight away, even when heated. The fresh curd could therefore be packaged immediately while still hot (thus sterilizing it, so to speak), doubling the shelf life of the fresh cheese. Cream cheese has a soft, creamy texture with a full-bodied, nutty, slightly sweet milk aroma. So-called Neufchâtel is slightly firmer in terms of consistency and has a lower fat content. Unlike cottage cheese, cream cheese requires the addition of a starter culture for it to curdle.

WISCONSIN
Cheese as a part of history

The state of Wisconsin is the largest cheese producer in the USA. Cheese is part of Wisconsin's history, forms part of its identity, and is the pride of the state as a whole.

Wisconsin's rise as a cheese-producing state began when wheat farming started to stagnate in the mid-nineteenth century. The soil was depleted and pests were continually reducing yields. Immigrants, a large proportion of those in Wisconsin from Germany and Switzerland, brought their cheese-making recipes and methods with them and got down to work. The climate and landscape were ideal for livestock farming and in 1910 Wisconsin overtook the state of New York in terms of cheese production, there being as many as 2,807 cheese dairies in Wisconsin by 1922. The residents of Wisconsin have long since given up their irritation with the nickname "cheese head" and now carry the name with pride.

America's first dairying qualification was established at the University of Wisconsin while the Wisconsin Cheese Makers' Association has been in existence for over 100 years and is the only authority providing certification as Master Cheese Maker. The midwest state has set itself the goal of becoming the leader in the production of quality cheese. The producers' focus is on upscale specialties, handcraft production, organic products, and cheeses with very long ripening periods. High quality specialties already currently make up 15% of Wisconsin's total cheese production, even though committed producers only started paying serious attention to this segment five years ago.

Left: The state of Wisconsin is the largest cheese producer in the USA.

Brick Cheese

flavor and aroma develop to the full. This cheese goes well with sweet onion, with mustard, and even with Liverwurst, in sandwiches.

Wine tip: Harmonizes very well with American beer. In terms of wine, a rounded, mature Chardonnay with distinct barrique character makes a good match. Aromatic wines such as Viognier or Gewürztraminer are also well suited.

Brick cheese is a Wisconsin original that was first produced by John Jossi from Switzerland in about 1877. He used the Limburg (Germany/Belgium) recipe for his Brick cheese but altered the moisture content by squeezing the curd between bricks. It is now made in a brick-shape form, also known as a square. The reduced water content made the cheese milder and the name of the cheese derives from this production technique. The shape of the cheese is also similar to that of a brick.

Brick is made from cow's milk, and is semi-hard with small, uneven holes and an open texture. A young brick has a mild, sweet, and buttery flavor; if it is left to ripen for longer it becomes spicy and piquant. Its smell is less intense than that of the original. The rind is treated with red mold as with Limburg. Reddish-brown, somewhat dry rind/crust; cheese ranging from pale yellow to white. Softer than Cheddar but firmer than Limburg, with numerous, uneven holes; it crumbles easily and is slightly sticky when sliced. A significantly mild and slightly sweet taste when young. The ripening period is several months, during which time the

Cheddar

Cheddar is America's favorite cheese by far. Wisconsin is the USA's largest Cheddar producer with almost half of overall production. Industrially produced Cheddar is available in a variety of ripeness stages and colors. West of the Mississippi the preference is for this cheese with a subtle orange-red color (with the natural colorant annatto). East of the Mississippi it is the creamy white version that is popular.

The wax coatings have different colors in order for the different stages of ripeness to be recognized from the outside: a pale wax rind means a young, mild cheese that has ripened for less than four months. The piquant version ripens for four to ten months and has a red wax coating. A fully ripened, sharp Cheddar needs to ripen for longer than ten months and the ripeness duration is indicated by a black wax coating.

Wine tip: The younger version is well suited to Californian wines such as Sauvignon Blanc, Chardonnay, or Viognier. The riper type needs a great deal of smoothness and the Chardonnay should therefore have been matured in the barrel. In terms of red wines, mellow Pinot Noir from California or Oregon, as well as mature Merlot, is a suitable accompaniment.

Colby

Colby was the first truly American new cheese. Created in 1874 by cheese maker Joseph Steinwand, this semi-hard cheese was intended to be a milder, less dry, and firmer version of Cheddar. The creation bears the name of the town in which it was produced for the first time. Full-cream milk is used to make this traditional, creamy cheese with a block or cylinder shape. Colby is made using the same method as that for Cheddar, with one important difference: the curd is washed separately in cold water, which prevents "caking."

This treatment makes the texture of Colby significantly more elastic than is the case with Cheddar. Colby ripens for about four weeks. It yields to pressure and has a mild, sweet taste. It keeps for a short time only and is often used as a snack, as well as for salads, sandwiches, or for cooking. Colby Jack is made from two cheese varieties that ripen as one cheese, namely Monterey Jack and Colby. The two types are easily recognized by their characteristic orange-creamy white marbling. Colby Longhorn refers to the 16½ lb (7.5 kg) Colby shaped like a long, narrow cylinder.

Wine tip: The somewhat fruity, aromatic white wines from Finger Lakes such as Gewürztraminer, Riesling, or Sauvignon Blanc harmonize just as well with this cheese as the white wines from Washington state. The wine should not have too much of a wooded influence, however. Also recommended is a white Zinfandel with its fresh fruit. Red wines are more difficult, Pinot Noir being the best option.

Cold Pack

Cold Pack cheese was invented by a bar owner from Wisconsin who wanted to be able to offer his customers a spreadable cheese as a snack. This cheese is also known as Club or Crock cheese. It is usually based on a combination of mature Cheddar cheese and nutty Swiss cheese, but other mixtures are also common. The cheeses used are finely ground, mixed together, and often flavored with other ingredients as well (vegetables, fruit, sausage, spices,

herbs). Unlike processed cheese, this mixture is neither heated nor treated and therefore needs to be kept in the refrigerator. Cold Pack cheese always tastes like the original cheese from which it was made. It's the flavors that distinguish this cheese—try jalapeno, smoky bacon, horseradish, garlic and herb, port wine—and many more. They are ideal for snacks, and good with pasta or rice dishes.

Maytag Blue was one of the first American cheese varieties produced on the farm. Made from the milk of Holstein cows and ripened for five months, the outstanding quality of this cheese soon made it very well known. Maytag Blue is a favorite of gourmet chefs throughout the USA, being suitable both for serving at the table and for use in salad dressings. Maytag Blue is still produced by hand in small quantities on the Maytag family farm in Iowa. The cylindrical cheese is moist and crumbly with a spicy flavor and a lemony finish.

Wine tip: A late harvest is the ideal accompaniment, preferably with the fresh, citrus nuances of the Riesling or Sauvignon-Blanc grape varieties.

Maytag Blue

RAW-MILK CHEESE— BUT RIPENED

The Maytag family began producing blue cheese in Iowa in 1941. The production method derives from a scientist at Iowa State University.

Federal Department of Agriculture regulations require that every cheese that ripens for less than 60 days be made from pasteurized milk. Cheeses with a ripening period of longer than 60 days can be made from either raw or pasteurized milk.

Above: Wonderful location — the capital Madison with the state Capitol.

Right: The Native Americans of Wisconsin have a great deal to offer.

Below: A typical mid-West house.

CALIFORNIA
Spanish heritage

California owes its cheese expertise to the Spanish missionaries who came from Mexico, bringing their cows and the art of cheese making with them. These cheeses were the predecessors of Monterey Jack, a "real" American cheese and one that symbolizes cheese production in California like no other.

Cheese has been made in California for over 200 years, about as long as the history of wine making in the state. Industrial production began about 1850, at the start of the Gold Rush, but only much later, about 1970, did cheese production really begin to boom.

There are about 50 cheese makers today, producing around 130 different cheese varieties, mainly from cow's and also from sheep's milk. The Californian cheese industry reflects the extremes of the Sunshine state. At one end of the scale there are the small producers making the finest, award-winning cheeses by hand, and at the other end there are the highly modern dairies producing several million lb/kg of cheese daily.

The Spanish priest Junipero Serra founded the agricultural industry in California in 1769, bringing not only fruit and vegetables but also dairy cows and the art of cheese making with him. More than 25 types of Hispanic cheese—the most common being Queso Fresco, Panela, and Cotija—are produced in California. In addition to the omnipresent Cheddars and Bries, California's cheese masters are increasingly producing smaller, finer cheese specialties. California occupies second place among the United States cheese producers right behind Wisconsin.

Left: California owes its cheese-making skills to the Spanish missionaries.

Dry Jack

Dry Jack coming back into favor. Today Dry Jack is one of the best cheeses in the USA. Its production center is in Sonoma, where the cheese is produced by two companies using traditional methods.

The ripened version of Monterey Jack came about by chance. In the First World War cheese wholesaler D.F. DeBernardi in San Francisco made the mistake of leaving a delivery of Monterey Jack lying about for too long. The cheese had hardened, while its pale yellow color and crumbly consistency resembled Italian Parmesan. DeBernardi placed the cheese, weighing about 9 lb (4 kg), in a brine-soaked cloth and later rubbed the rind with a mixture of oil, pepper, and cocoa. The semi-black coating on the rind was a natural preservative and also looked like the earlier blackened rind of the Italian cheese. The "mistake" came at just the right time, supplies of hard cheeses such as Parmesan or Pecorino from Italy having been interrupted as a result of the war. The "dry" Jack with its fruity-sweet and nutty flavor was quickly accepted as an alternative by the Italians in San Francisco. Dry Jack declined in importance once supplies of the Italian original resumed at the end of the war but renewed pride in local, traditional products has seen

Californian Teleme

Teleme is a Californian original developed by Greek immigrants in 1920 based on the Touloumotyri cheese made from goat's milk. The Greek immigrants living near San Francisco used cow's milk for want of goat's milk and created an entirely new version with their young, very soft, gently fragrant aromatic cheese. The natural rind features mold and yeast and is sprinkled with rice flour. The ripening period is at least ten days and can take up to two months.

Wine tip: A fresh white Californian wine, such as an unoaked Chardonnay or Sauvignon Blanc, or else a Viognier, harmonizes well with this cheese. If not too sweet a white Zinfandel can also be a good partner. Riper cheeses can also harmonize with red wines that have little tannin and a sweet smoothness.

Monterey Jack

Legend has it that Spanish missionaries, who came to California in the eighteenth century, had already produced an early form of Jack, which they called "Queso del Pais" or country cheese. The farming families continued with this type of cheese making after the missionaries left. The cheese could be produced economically even from small quantities of milk and with little equipment. In around 1882 David Jacks, a Scottish immigrant and dairy owner in Monterey, began selling his cheese in San Francisco and on other markets in the west of the USA. He named the cheese after his surname and the town where it originated: Monterey Jack. Since its commercial launch more than 100 years ago, Monterey Jack has developed into one of the best known cheese varieties in the USA. More than one third of the some 50 Californian cheese makers in total produce Jack in all its variations. This hard cheese can be made from either full-cream milk or from skimmed milk. A young Jack ripens for one week up to one month. The soft, mild version is the best known but there are also spiced and flavored variations (with pepper, dill, pesto, onion, garlic Jalapeño chili, for example) available. The flavor and consistency vary with the duration of the ripening. Monterey Jack generally has a mild, buttery flavor, a creamy consistency with medium-size holes, and a very high water content. It is characterized by outstanding melting qualities and is therefore very popular in the kitchen. Monterey Jack is also known as California Jack or Sonoma Jack.

Wine tip: a Chardonnay, preferably from Monterey, as well as a Pinot Noir or Petite Sirah with a mature character, harmonizes especially well.

VERMONT
Country idyll

Vermont is idyllic: Vast, green meadows, lush pastures with cows, farms, and then the panorama of the Green mountains. Vermont's model dairy industry supplies the whole of New England with milk and milk products.

There is a long tradition of cheese making in New England, the first settlers in Plymouth in the state of Vermont having made their own cheese as far back as 1620. They brought not only their dairy cows but also their expertise and equipment with them to their new homeland and supplied their own milk, butter, and cheese. They made Cheddar based on the English example: Huge wheels of cheese measuring 20 in (50 cm) in diameter. The farm producers disappeared over the course of time and even in Vermont the bulk of the Cheddar degenerated into a mass-produced product in plastic wrapping. The rich, flavorsome Cheddar of the early years became a rarity, but its tradition was maintained by family enterprises such as Crowley and the Grafton Village Cheese Company, as well as by larger concerns such as the Cabot Creamery and Shelbourne Farms. Good Cheddar from Vermont, sometimes ripened for years, has the best of reputations today. A recent revival of interest in traditional, handcraft production led to a renaissance of farm cheeses in other enterprises as well. The University of Vermont even has its own research and training institute for handcraft cheese production. The production of goat's cheese (chèvre) and sheep's milk cheese has now also become particularly popular.

Left: Idyllic country life with green meadows and lush pastures.

Vermont Cheddar

opulent, wood-matured Chardonnay, or red wines from the Merlot, Cabernet Sauvignon, or Zinfandel grape varieties.

Crowley

Hard cheese made from raw cow's milk, 50% FDM. Vermont almost has a monopoly over New England's Cheddar production. You will search in vain for bright orange Cheddars colored with annatto in Vermont. It is part of Vermont's cheese tradition not to use artificial colorants for Cheddar or any of the other cheeses. The milk comes from Jersey cows and is processed as raw milk. The flavor varies from mild to very strong and piquant, sometimes even sharp. Depending on the age of the cheese, its texture ranges from smooth to dry and through to almost crumbly. The Cheddars generally ripen for between 6 and 36 months. Vermont Cheddar experienced a renewed boost in popularity due to the smoked versions and those refined with spices or herbs. Young Cheddar is ideal for adding to soups and sauces and can be used in the kitchen in a number of ways. It can weigh up to 110 lb (50 kg).

Wine tip: The young, fresh cheese goes well with fresh white wines such as unwooded Chardonnay and Sauvignon Blanc. A riper Cheddar needs an

Crowley was first produced in Healdville in the state of Vermont in 1824. Crowley is the only remaining original among Vermont's cheeses. The recipe has been altered and improved time and again since 1882. Today it is still produced in the Winfield Crowley cheese dairy, where it is made by hand without the use of any kind of machinery. Only about 200 lb (90 kg) are produced each day. The washing of the curd with spring water makes this cheese especially aromatic, while the use of raw milk makes it soft and creamy. Crowley is nowhere near as dry or acidic as Colby or Cheddar. It develops its characteristically strong and robust flavor after ripening for a period of six months.

Plymouth Cheese

This cheese made from raw milk is an old-fashioned relative of Cheddar and characteristic of the colonial era farm cheeses, its history going back to 1890. The grainy cheese with its rustic, natural rind has a moist, creamy texture and develops complex, full-bodied aromas. Made in the small village of Plymouth only, it is produced in small quantities as a round cheese weighing 2–45 lb (1–20 kg). The curd is coagulated with vegetable rennet and washed before being kneaded. The mixture is then salted by hand and pressed into molds, ripening thereafter for a minimum of two months but usually for much longer (up to 12 months). These well-ripened cheeses are only produced in limited quantities, however.

Cougar Gold

Cougar Gold, a semi-hard cheese made from cow's milk, was developed at Washington State University in Pullman in 1948. The US government wanted to have a cheese in closed containers that could be dispatched to troops all over the world without any problem. Plastic was not available at this time and the wax coating often crumbled, resulting in the cheese going off. Today Cougar Gold is produced and sold in the university's own dairy, set up in 1992. Half of the production is sold directly from the university dairy shop and by local wholesalers, while the other half is exported worldwide. The name derives from Cougar (puma), the university mascot and the name of the former project manager, N.S. Golding. The starting product for Cougar Gold is a cheese made using the Cheddar process. Ripening in closed containers, this cheese initially emitted gases that caused the containers to burst. Golding discovered that fermentation of the cheese could be prevented by adding specific lactobacilli strains. The ripening process lasts for a minimum of a year. The cheese can be kept almost indefinitely if stored unopened in a cool place. Cougar Gold is packed in 32 oz (900 g) tins. Although Cougar Gold is made from Cheddar cheese, it does not taste like Cheddar. It has distinct nutty nuances reminiscent of Gouda and Emmental, has a rich flavor, and becomes distinctly piquant with age.

The white cheese is smooth with a piquant flavor.

Wine tip: Wines from Washington are to be recommended here. Riesling or Sauvignon Blanc, as well as unoaked Chardonnay, go with the young versions, while the mature cheese harmonizes well.

further raised the quality of Tillamook. This cheese is made solely from raw milk. Today the Tillamook County Creamery Association, where Tillamook production makes up three quarters of the overall output, comprises 196 dairies. The association processes one third of the total milk output of the state of Oregon.

Wine tip: Chardonnays matured in the barrel or the renowned Pinot Noirs from Oregon are unbeatable as companions for this specialty.

Tillamook

Tillamook County in the northwest of Oregon has a long tradition of cheese making. The numerous Holstein, Jersey, and Guernsey cows graze the fertile land and provide the milk for this medium-ripe, exclusive Cheddar cheese, said to be one of the best in the USA. The settlers discovered soon after their arrival that the milk from their cows was of a very high quality in their new homeland. The Canadian Peter McIntosh arrived in the area toward the end of the nineteenth century and introduced the Cheddar process that

Creole Cream

The fresh cheese specialty Creole Cream cheese is a set feature of New Orleans' culinary tradition. Its origins go back almost 200 years to when the first French settlers arrived in the southern states. Today Creole Cream cheese enjoys special Slow Food protection as a flavor legacy worthy of being conserved.

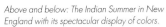

Above and below: The Indian Summer in New England with its spectacular display of colors.

Right: Sailing in lobster paradise is also on offer in New England.

CANADA
Inspired by France and England

Cheese making in Canada began when the first French settlers arrived in the country. In New France the French initially started their cheese making with soft cheeses based on the recipes and traditions of their homeland. In 1783 the next wave of immigrants brought the English, who largely limited themselves to Cheddar production. The production of milk and milk products improved the incomes of the farmers living under difficult conditions. In order to stimulate demand and to promote the cheese-producing area of Ontario worldwide, the authorities decided to have the largest cheese in the world made for the world fair in Chicago. A significant amount of effort resulted in the production of a giant Cheddar weighing 11 tonnes. The Canadian Cheddar held the record as the largest cheese in the world until 1964, when Wisconsin beat the record for the New York World Fair with a 17-tonne cheese.

The wave of immigration following the Second World War saw increased demand for Feta, Mozzarella and Edam, Provolone, Münster, and Raclette. The cheese makers quickly learnt to produce these varieties as well. As in the USA, Canada is witnessing increasing interest in specialties and cheeses based on traditional handcraft methods. The provinces of Ontario and Québec are home to more than 80% of Canadian dairy farms.

Left: Canada has long been the embodiment of wilderness and wide open spaces.

Cheddar

Cheddar remains the Canadians' favorite cheese and it is available in all varieties from mild to strongly flavored. Cheddar makes up over one third of Canada's overall cheese production. One of the first and best known cheese brands in Canada is "Black Diamond Cheddar" with its black rind. It is produced in Ontario by a long established company of the same name using raw milk. The best Cheddars ripen for 18 months to 2 years. Industrially produced Canadian Cheddar is generally rindless, has a smooth, shiny surface, is pale yellow to orange in color, and has a smooth, slightly elastic texture. It has a characteristic, buttery aroma and a strong, nutty flavor that becomes more intense with age. Age groups: mild (ripened for 3 months), medium (ripened for 4–9 months), sharp (ripened for 9 months and up to 5–7 years). Well-ripened Cheddar has a strong, acidic flavor.

Wine tip: A Canadian beer goes well with this cheese, but wine is perhaps more interesting—a Chardonnay from the Niagara peninsula, for example,

which accentuates the nutty flavor of the cheese. Combination with aromatic varieties such as Gewürztraminer is also appealing. Riesling harmonizes very well with the younger, fresher Cheddar types.

Dragon's Breath

A surface-ripened blue cheese with a black, wax rind. Its consistency ranges from soft and creamy through to hard. The cheese spends a while in a highly concentrated brine and has a strong, sharp flavor. In order to be able to enjoy the flavor to the full it is best to remove the wax rind, underneath which is the blue mold, and then leave the cheese to ripen further for a few days so that the mold can spread.

Wine tip: The wine needs to be a fairly robust one. Mature white wines are to be recommended, with residual sweetness being a definite plus, while an ice wine is simply delicious served as an accompaniment.

Curds

Curds are different pieces of cheese about the size of a grape. They are rindless, smooth, and shiny, and white or orange in color with a soft and very elastic consistency. These fresh, creamy cheese snacks with a milky flavor are generally made from Cheddar, Swiss Cheese, or young Gouda.

Marble

Marble is a semi-hard cheese comprising two varieties: The most common combination is that of Brick cheese or a white Cheddar with an orange-colored Colby or Cheddar. Rindless, smooth and

shiny, with white and orange marbling and a closed, compact, texture. A buttery aroma and a nutty flavor that varies depending on the types of cheese used.

Wine tip: The white wines from the Niagara peninsula or from British Columbia are recommended here, preferably a Chardonnay with a touch of wood. Fruity Pinot Noirs also harmonize well.

Niagara Gold

The milk for this rich, luxuriant soft cheese is provided by a single herd of Guernsey cows in the mild wine-producing region of Niagara. Soft, melting, cream-colored cheese with a golden brown rind. Nutty, earthy aromas. The young cheese has a mild, sweet flavor, becoming stronger and sharper when ripened.

Wine tip: The Niagara peninsula has a great many wines on offer as accompaniments. The young cheese is best suited to a dry white wine such as a Chardonnay, Sauvignon Blanc, or Riesling. The ripened cheese is better suited to a mature, opulent, barrel-nuanced

Chardonnay or a classic Pinot Noir from the region. Ice wine made from the Vidal grape variety can make an interesting combination with this cheese.

Oka

The monks in the Oka monastery near Montreal have been producing their aromatic semi-hard cheese ever since the arrival of the Trappist monk Alphonse Juin in 1893. Brother Alphonse had learnt his handicraft as a cheese master in France and brought the recipe for this cheese, based on the famous Port du Salut, with him to his new homeland. Oka is one of the very few original Canadian cheeses and is very popular both in Canada and in the USA. It is made by squeezing but not heating the curd. The cheese ripens from the outside inward and the natural, straw- to orange-colored rind is oiled during the ripening. The ripening takes place in the monastery cellar. The cheese has a creamy, smooth, homogeneous texture that yields to pressure. Oka has a clean, aromatic smell and a complex aroma with slightly fermented nuances. It has a nutty, fruity, and fresh

flavor, these flavor nuances becoming more distinct with increased ripeness. Oka is best used for serving at the table but it is also valued as a kitchen ingredient due to its good melting properties.

Wine tip: Riesling and Sauvignon Blanc are recommended as accompaniments for a young Oka, while the ripened version goes well with robust Chardonnays or expressive Pinot Noirs.

La Sauvagine

In the fall Quebec is home to more than 13 million ducks, geese, and teals, a time known to the Canadians as Sauvagine. The handcraft soft cheese of the same name has a rustic flavor derived from the fact that the white mold is additionally treated with red mold. Moist, orange-colored rind, ivory-colored, melting cheese. Its flavor includes a touch of mushroom.

Wine tip: Aromatic wines such as Gewürztraminer or Vidal are the ideal accompaniments, while mild red wines with low-key tannins are also to be recommended.

CHEESE PRODUCTION IN QUEBEC

Practically all of the well-known European varieties are produced in Québec on a large scale. It is primarily cow's milk cheese that is produced in Quebec, but the proportion of goat's and sheep's milk cheese is on the rise. Over 90% of the dairy cows are Holstein cows, the rest being made up of Ayrshire, Jersey, Brown Swiss, and Canadienne breeds. A return to nature and traditional values has been in evidence since the 1980s, however, and specialties, farmhouse, and artisan cheeses from cow's, sheep's and goat's milk are enjoying a renaissance. Small cheese dairies have sprung up all over the French-speaking province, with about 100 enterprises producing all types of goat's milk cheese with all kinds of flavors. Sheep's milk cheese represents a relatively new but promising niche market for Quebec's cheese makers, with about 12 farms currently making cheese from sheep's milk. Québec's cheese makers exhibit a great deal of imagination, refining their cheeses with brown ale or mead, or smoking the cheese over maple wood. The cheese creations have imaginative names such as Pied-de-Vent (foot of the wind) from Iles de la Madeleine, Coureur des Bois (wood messenger) from Saint-Antoine-de-Tilly, Diable aux Vaches (cow devil) from Mont-Laurier, or Fumirolle (smoke) from Cote de Beaupré.

MEXICO
A Spanish past

The Spanish conquerors brought milk-producing animals and therefore cheese to Mexico, the Mexicans' diet having comprised mainly fruit, vegetables, fish, and poultry up until that point. Independent cheese production has developed in many parts of Mexico, with *queso ranchero*, the generic term for a range of cheese varieties, still being produced today according to farm tradition. Cheese production has become an important economic sector in northern Mexico. Large-scale production of what have since become the local cheese varieties, but especially the imitation of the well-known European cheese types, began in about 1980. As a result, the Trappist cheeses, Camembert, Manchego, Edam, and hard cheese based on the example of Gruyère are all available in Mexico. Retailers also sell the regional specialties from the main cheese areas of Oaxaca, Chiapas, and Quertaro.

In addition to the all-pervasive Oaxacas String cheese (Queso Oaxaca) there are also a number of fresh cheeses that are sold in small pots. The best cheeses are the farm cheeses to be found at the local markets packed in small baskets or wooden containers, tied together as spheres of all sizes, wrapped in straw or cut into flat, white slabs. These cheeses are definitely worth trying should the opportunity present itself. Industrially produced Mexican cheeses such as the imitations of the European originals are to be found prepackaged in the supermarkets.

Left: Chichén Itzá on the Mexican Yucatán peninsula.

Queso blanco

Fresh cheese made from cow's milk. Different shapes and sizes, often block shape. This creamy, white cheese is made from skimmed cow's milk or whey and is slightly similar to Mozzarella and cottage cheese. It is traditionally curdled with lemon juice, giving it a fresh, unmistakable flavor. The industrially produced cheese is usually made from full-cream milk curdled with rennet. Queso blanco is popular as a filling for enchiladas. It is characterized by a mild, creamy taste with fresh citrus nuances.

Queso Panela

Fresh cheese made from cow's milk. This cheese is also known as Queso de Canasta because it bears the imprint of the woven basket in which it is placed to drain and which gives it its shape. The soft, snow-white, young cheese easily absorbs other aromas. It is often coated with a garlic-chili paste or served in roasted avocado leaves as an aperitif. Requeson is related to Ricotta and is sold in the markets packed in fresh maize straw.

Queso fresco

Fresh cheese made from cow's and/or goat's milk. The Queso fresco recipe is based on Spanish Burgos (see entry). The soft, slightly delicate cheese is eaten within a few days of being made. It has a very mild, fresh, and pleasantly acidic flavor. It is usually made from a mixture of cow's and goat's milk. The Mexicans like to use it to make enchiladas and taquitos. Queso Anejo is a ripened version of Queso fresco. It is soft when in the early stages of ripeness, becoming very firm and hard if the curd is salted. This aromatic cheese is often used for grating in the kitchen. When rubbed with chili powder Anejo has a red rind and is known as Enchilado.

popularly used for Mexican fondues (queso fundido), which are normally served as an evening meal using a multitude of ingredients.

Oaxaca and Asadero

A cooked and kneaded cheese made from cow's milk. Oaxaca string cheese, also known as Quesillo, has been made on farms in Oaxaca in southern Mexico since the early days. It is a slightly melting fresh cheese and is very popular as an ingredient for quesilladas (tacos filled with cheese and heated so that the cheese in the middle melts). Oaxaca has similar properties and a similar production method to that of Italian Mozzarella. It is available in a variety of shapes, namely as spheres, strands rolled into spheres, or as woven strips. Queso Asadero is a version of Oaxaca and is similar to Italian Provolone. With its good melting properties, Asadero is

Hard cheese

Queso Chihuahua is made from cow's milk and comes from the town of the same name in the north of Mexico. The Mennonites were the first to produce this cheese, which is why it is also known as Queso Menonita. Unlike the majority of Mexican cheeses, it is not white but pale yellow in color and varies in flavor from mild to slightly sharp. It is used for queso frito (crumbed, fried cheese) in particular. Queso Cotija is a very sharp, piquant goat's milk cheese that becomes hard and crumbly with age, which is why it is also referred to as "Mexican Parmesan." Cotija is popularly sprinkled over beans and salads.

Asia

Tibet

The women milk the Dris (female yaks) in the morning and turn the fatty milk into yogurt, butter, and cheese. In the Himalayan region buttermilk is used to make a crumbly cheese that can be kept for years when dried and which, cut into cubes, serves as supplies for travelers. The cheese, which is made from fresh, full cream milk, is curdled and the curd is squeezed between stones before being dried by the wind and the sun.

Mongolia

Cow's or yak's milk is used to make Mongolian Bjaslag. The milk is boiled and a small amount of kefir is added instead of rennet. Once curdled, the junket is placed in a large cloth and the whey is allowed to drain off. The junket in the cloth is squeezed between stones or weighted planks, giving the cheese a rounded or almost square shape measuring about 10 in (25 cm) in diameter

Many Mongolian nomads are traditional livestock breeders and dairy farmers.

and 2 in (5 cm) in height. It is cut into strips and dried to make it keep longer.

The curdled junket popularly eaten as a snack in Mongolia is known as Eezgii. It has a slightly sweet flavor and the firm cheese pieces create a grainy, mealy sensation on the tongue. Bjaslag is made by adding a little kefir to the milk. Once the whey has drained off, the curd is boiled until all the liquid has evaporated. The dry curd is then

Sweet Eezgii is popularly enjoyed as a snack between meals.

roasted gently over the fire until it disintegrates into golden-yellow pieces with a grainy consistency. The pieces of cheese are hard enough to be stored in a cloth sack for long periods of time.

The firm, flat cubes of dried curd are known as Aruul in Mongolia. They are made by leaving the milk to turn sour before removing the curd with a cloth and allowing the whey to drain off. The curd is then placed between two wooden planks which are weighted down with stones. Having been squeezed in this manner, the cheese forms a broad "cake" which is then cut into pieces about 4 in (10 cm) in length, and these are left to dry on a board in the sun. The dried Aruul pieces can be kept almost indefinitely and are so hard

Aruul is cut into pieces about 4 in (10 cm) long and left in the sun to dry.

that they have to be sucked. They vary in flavor depending on the region and on the milk used, but usually range between slightly sweet and sour. Together with Borts (dried meat cut into strips or ground), Aruul is an indispensable component of the shepherd's supplies.

India

The best known Indian cheese is Paneer, a straightforward fresh cheese made from cow's milk for which the curd is squeezed to a greater or lesser extent, depending on the degree of firmness required. As cows are sacred to the Hindus, lemon juice or vinegar is used to coagulate the milk instead of rennet. The curd is placed in a cloth and the whey squeezed out. Paneer is usually eaten fresh within a few days of being made.

The Philippines

Kesong Puti, a grainy, cream cheese, is very popular in the Philippines. Also known as Filipino cottage cheese, it is made from the milk of the carabao, a domesticated breed of water buffalo.

The milk is curdled with rennet and the curd is salted. Kesong Puti is soft with a salty and slightly acidic taste. It is especially popular served for breakfast.

Japan

Naturally ripened cheeses have been produced in Japan for only about the last 30 years, but consumption has continued to increase since then. Today there about 80 Japanese farmers producing their own cheese, initially copying the European varieties, but creations exhibiting characteristically Japanese aroma and flavor components have gradually been developed. The soft Japanese Sakura cheese ripens on the leaves of the Japanese mountain cherry, thus acquiring its unique aroma. The upper surface of the cheese is decorated with cherry blossom. Another soft cheese, named Sakagura, is refined with sake in order to give it a particularly strong aroma.

China

Simple, very flat cheeses are produced in the Yunnan province in southwestern

Naturally ripened cheeses have been produced in Japan for only about the last 30 years.

China. So-called Rubing cheese is a fresh cheese made from goat's milk that is fried in flat slices in a skillet. This crispy cheese is served either with sugar or with black pepper and salt.

Rushan is another cheese from Yunnan and is a flat cheese with a leathery consistency, usually made from cow's milk. The slices are also fried, and then wrapped around a wooden stick prior to eating. Rushan is to be found as a snack at street kiosks and is usually filled with chocolate, honey, or puréed fruit.

The sour milk from the day before or else rice vinegar is used for curdling. This flat Yunnan cheese is made by shaping the curd into small balls and heating them in the whey. The elastic cheese balls are then pulled apart and placed on a bamboo mat. The flat cheese is covered with a second mat and the cheese is then rolled. The cheese can be eaten fresh but it will keep for several weeks if it is left to dry for a day. These traditionally produced cheeses have a very low lactose content.

Armenia

Motal, a special cheese made from goat's milk and wild herbs, is produced in the provinces of Aragazotn and Ararat, provinces which are dominated by imposing 13,000 ft (4,000 m) high mountains. The shepherds keep the cheese in terracotta containers sealed with beeswax or lavasi (a traditional bread), which are then placed upside down in ash in cool, dry cellars. The cheese keeps for many months when preserved in this way.

Africa

Nigeria

Choukou is a traditional cheese from the Sahel region which is produced by women only.

Namibia

In Namibia milk products are produced only in those regions with high rainfall and consequently the majority of cheeses are imported. However, local cheeses are made on a small scale from the milk of Karakul sheep and from the milk of goat breeds ideally suited to the barren landscape.

Cape Verde Islands

On the Cape Verde Islands the shepherds in the almost uninhabited mountain region of Planalto di Bolona on the island of Santo Antão produce cheese made from goat's milk by hand. The goats are semi-wild and the shepherds produce the rennet themselves.

Mauritania

The small Tiviski dairy in the capital Nouakchott has been producing the Caravane cheese made from camel's milk since 1994. It is similar to a Camembert in terms of appearance and to a goat's milk cheese in terms of flavor. The cheese was intended for the European market, but as yet there are no regulations governing the import of camel's milk products.

South Africa

Mild cheeses are the traditional preference in South Africa. The industrially produced cheeses are mostly processed cheeses. South Africa produces some 82,000 tons/tonnes of cheese, more than half of which is made up of Cheddar and Gouda. The remaining varieties comprise cheese types based on European examples, with Mozzarella and white cheese in brine (Feta), Feta cheese, and cream cheese being the most popular. The new specialties are largely based on Italian varieties but French-style cheeses are also becoming increasingly popular.

Australia

Until the end of the 1950s only butter and Cheddar cheese were made from milk produced in Australia. The wave of immigration after the Second World War saw the start of the production of other varieties, such as blue cheese, cream and cottage cheese, Camembert, Edam, Feta, Gouda, Halloumi, Mozzarella, Parmesan, Pecorino, Provolone, Ricotta, and Swiss-style hard cheese. The Australian Specialist Cheese Makers' Association was founded by a group of young cheese makers in 1994 and these Australian cheese specialists have established an international reputation for their products within a short space of time, the proportion of their products growing by 10% annually. In addition to using cow's milk, they also make their cheeses from sheep's, goat's, and buffalo milk.

Despite the high quality of the milk supplied by the animals grazing the clean, intact meadows, the production of raw-milk cheeses is unfortunately prohibited in Australia, meaning the loss of much of the true character and aroma of the carefully produced cheese specialties.

New Zealand

New Zealand's dairy industry produces all cheese varieties from ripened Cheddar to aromatic soft cheeses, from Gruyère to Mozzarella. Local cheese specialties that were not copies of European examples were produced in New Zealand earlier than in other New World countries. One of the pioneers was Ross McCallum, who founded his own company, Kapiti Cheese, in 1985. His cheese varieties bore Maori names and all had their own New Zealand character. There are surprisingly few sheep's milk cheeses in New Zealand. In 1990 the first Feta-style sheep's milk cheese to come onto the market was Hipi Iti, meaning "small sheep" in the indigenous language. It was a huge success.

Middle and Far East

The living conditions for milk-producing animals in these dry regions with only sparse vegetation are difficult, hence cheese production mainly uses

Simple cheeses made from sour milk have been produced for thousands of years.

Testouri is widespread in all of the countries of the Middle East. It is shaped like an orange and is made from sheep's or goat's milk. It is lightly salted and is preferably eaten as fresh cheese.

Syria and Lebanon

milk from goat and sheep breeds that have adapted to their surroundings. Simple cheeses based on sour milk have been produced in these regions for thousands of years. They are eaten either as fresh cheeses or dried to enable them to be kept for longer. The cheeses are usually rather heavily salted. Cheese factories are to be found everywhere in the Middle and Far East countries, but it is still the farmers, nomads, and Bedouins who produce cheese using the very traditional methods.

Halloumi is a typical Bedouin cheese made from sheep's milk. A delicate, slightly yellowy cheese, it keeps for a very long time and has a rather salty flavor. It is found throughout the Middle and Far East, as is Labneh (*laban* = Arabic for yogurt) or Lebenen. A soft, creamy cheese, Labneh is made simply by extracting water from the curdled, yogurt-like milk, to which salt is added before draining it in a cloth. It is often rolled in herbs or spices. The spherical cheese is popularly eaten for breakfast. It is known as Lebneh in Lebanon and Israel, as Lebney in Syria, and as Labaneh in Jordan. The general Arabic term for this type of cheese is Gibne.

Baladi, a white cheese with a crumbly texture, is very popular in Lebanon. It is available both salted and unsalted and is made from cow's milk. Akkawi or Ackawi is made solely from cow's milk. It has a mild, salty taste and is soft to semi-hard in consistency. Akkawi originally comes from Palestine. Today Ackawi refers to a semi-hard cheese found throughout the Middle East region. It is a smooth, white cheese with a mild, salty flavor. It is used for serving at the table and goes well with fruit. Ackawi is the most widely sold cheese among Americans of Arab descent.

Darfiyeh is a traditional goat's milk cheese with an unusual flavor and

In the Middle and Far East cheese is usually eaten fresh or dried.

comes from the mountainous region in northern Lebanon. It is made by the shepherds and farmers, using the milk from the goats that roam widely in this region. The cheese ripens in a cleaned, salted goatskin pouch (*darrif*).

Alternating layers of cheese and fresh curd are placed in the goatskin pouch and salted, and the pouch is then closed so that it is airtight. Its long shelf life means that Darfiyeh is available all year round, despite its seasonal production. Attempts are now being made to produce this traditional cheese at a dairy at the North-René Moawad Foundation agricultural center in order to be able to promote it amongst the population outside the region and thus to support the farmers through sales in the mountain areas.

Like many cheeses in the Middle and Far East, Jibne Baida, a very salty hard cheese, is boiled first before eating. Shanklish (Shinklish, Shankleesh, Sorke, or Surke) is a characteristic cheese made from cow's or sheep's milk in Syria and Lebanon. The tennis-ball-size cheeses are rolled in spices or herbs (usually thyme) and ripen in this aromatic coating. It is soft and mild as a fresh cheese, becoming harder and sharper with increasing ripeness. In Syria, in particular, this cheese is popularly rolled in chili powder as well.

South America

The high altitude climate of the Andes is not ideal for dairy farming and simple fresh cheeses have tended to predominate. They are suited to the living conditions and are easy to produce. In Peru, for example, an animal skin pouch containing fresh curd made from goat's milk is simply hung next to the fire and the whey is allowed to drain off. Argentina boasts vast herds of livestock, but the animals are bred primarily for their meat. Italian immigrants had a major influence on cheese production in Argentina and it is therefore no wonder that the majority of cheese creations have Italian-sounding names. For example, the Argentinean Quartirolo is similar to the Italian Mozzarella, while Reggianito or Saltido is a somewhat salty Parmesan-style cheese. In Venezuela the cheese platter has a distinctly Spanish influence (although Cuajada, the Spanish sheep's milk curd cheese, is made from cow's milk there). In Brazil there is of course a perceptible Portuguese influence.

GLOSSARY

Affinage, Affineur: Refinement.
Handling and care of the cheese while
it is maturing. The term comes from
affiner (French = to refine). Affineurs
buy the fresh cheese and age it in their
own maturation cellar.

Alpkäse: Refers to those cheeses that,
unlike Bergkäse, are produced solely in
the high altitude mountain pastures
during the summer while the animals
are out to pasture.

Annatto: Vegetable colorant obtained
from achiote seeds. Gives Cheddar, for
example, its yellow-orange colour.

AOC: (French) abbreviation for
Appellation d'Origine Contrôlée,
protective designation of origin. In
France and Switzerland it refers to
cheeses produced in a defined region
according to traditional, handcrafted
methods. AOP refers to cheeses that
have European protective designation
of origin.

Artisanal: (French) handcrafted
production.

Ash: Powdered charcoal often used in
France to dust goat's milk cheese
(cendré).

Bacteria linens: Bacterial strain used
together with brine or other liquids to
produce the red rind on the surface of
washed-rind cheeses.

Bergkäse: Cheese that is produced all
year round in the Alps or alpine valleys. The milk is usually delivered to
larger dairies in the valleys, where it is
made into cheese.

Casein: The protein contained in milk.

Centrifugation: Spinning the milk at a
very high speed in order to separate
the fat globules as cream. What
remains is skimmed milk.

Chèvre: (French) goat's milk cheese.

Cooked curds: The curd mass is
heated in order to solidify the curd
grains further for hard cheeses with an
extremely long shelf life, and to extract
the liquid. The higher the temperature,
the harder the cheese will be later.

Cultures: Mixture of selected micro-organisms with specific functions in the production of cheese.

Curd: Liquid and solid components of curdled milk that have separated once the milk has curdled.

Fat content: Classification of cheese according to its fat content. Low fat is less than 10% FDM, full fat at least 60% FDM. The fat content changes in proportion to the water content because the cheese loses moisture, and therefore weight, during the maturing process and is therefore not a fixed measurement. The dry weight undergoes practically no change at all during maturation, however.

FDM: Abbreviation for "fat in dry matter."

Handling: Brushing, washing, and turning the cheeses until they have reached the required degree of maturity.

Junket: Milk that has been curdled (set) by souring and/or the addition of rennet.

Lactase: Enzyme that breaks down lactose.

Lactation time, stage: Breastfeeding period when the mother provides milk to her young.

Lactic acid: Lactic acid separates the milk protein, coagulates the milk, and protects the cheese from decomposing bacteria at the same time.

Lactobacilli: Naturally present in fresh milk and in the ambient air. Lactobacilli play a key role in the formation of aroma and holes in maturing cheese, and have a positive influence on both shelf life and quality. Lactobacilli convert lactose into lactic acid.

Lactose: Sugar found in milk.

Lactose intolerance: Lack of the lactase enzyme in the intestine, without which human beings are unable to break down lactose. Derives from the fact that if no milk or milk products are consumed after weaning, this enzyme is no longer produced by the body.

Microorganisms: Enable the conversion of lactose into lactic acid.

Milk breed: Animals bred to produce high milk yields.

Milk pre-ripening: Prolongs the milk's freshness. Lactic acid bacteria cultures are added for pre-ripening.

Milk-producing animals: Mammals providing milk for human nutrition.

Mold, mold cultures: Selected cultures for forming internal and external mold. The most well known are *Penicillium camemberti* (they ensure the white bloomy rind on soft cheeses) and *Penicillium roqueforti* (responsible for the blue mold veins in Roquefort).

Natamycin: Rind of hard and semi-hard cheese often contains traces of natamycin, a preservative applied to the surface to protect against mold.

PDO: Protected Designation of Origin.

PGI: Protected Geographical Indication.

Propionic acid bacteria: Bacterial strain responsible for distinct holes in cheese owing to its ability to produce carbon dioxide gas.

Quark: Curd cheese.

Rennet (animal), rennet ferment, the enzyme rennin: Enzyme traditionally derived from the calf's stomach. Rennet ferment is present in the stomachs of other young animals as well. The rennin enzyme causes the coagulation of casein and the separation of the cheese substance from the milk, as well as converting milk into a junket-like substance within a short period of time.

Rennet (microbial): Rennet substitute derived from mold.

Rennet (vegetable): Plant extracts such as the juice of the fig tree or thistle petals, for example, have been used since antiquity as a milk coagulant.

Rennet stomach: Stomach in ruminants in which the enzyme rennin is excreted during digestion.

Salt additives: Used together with heat treatment, salt additives make a processed cheese physically, chemically, and bacteriologically stable.

Salt bath: Cheese is placed in 15% to 20% saline solution after draining, shaping, and compressing, if required.

Salting: Salt extracts further liquid from the curd, enhancing the flavor of the cheese and ensuring that the rind is firm. Salting may be done dry by hand or in a salt bath.

Serum: see Whey.

Skimmed milk: Fat-free milk.

TSG: Traditional Speciality Guaranteed.

WFF: "Water fat free," international criterion for distinguishing the basic cheese types on the basis of the residual water content (hard cheese, fresh cheese, etc.).

Whey: Liquid portion of the milk that separates from the solid components (curds) following coagulation.

Whey protein: May be separated only by heating to a minimum of 158 °F (70 °C).

LITERATURE

Androuet, Pierre
Guide du fromage, Editions Stock, Paris 1971

Anifantakis, Emmanuel
Greek Cheeses – A Tradition of Centuries, National
Dairy Comittee of Greece, Athens 1991

Chenel, Laura and Siegfried Linda
American Country Cheese, Addison-Wesley
Publishing 1989

Courtine, Robert
Larousse des fromages, Larousse, Paris 1973

Eekhof-Stork, Nancy
Der große Käseatlas – Geschichte, Sorten,
Herstellung, Rezepte, Hallwag Bern and
Stuttgart 1979

ENIL (ed.)
Les fromages de la connaissance à la passion,
Amicale des Anciens Elèves (ENIL), Mamirolle 1996

Eprim Edition, Crémier Fromager:
www.fromag.com

Fiori, Giacomo
Die Käse Italiens, Eos Editrice 1999

Gluatteri, Fabiano
Käse—Genuss and Vielfalt aus Europa, Kaiser,
Klagenfurt 2006

Greek Cheese
Hellenic Export Promotion Organisation

Harbutt, Juliet
A complete illustrated Guide to the Cheeses of the
World, Lorenz Books New York, 1999

Harbutt, Juliet
Guide to the Finest Cheese of Britain, The Specialist
Cheesemaker Association

Il Portale del Formaggio
www.formaggio.it

Italian Institute for Foreign Trade
Formaggi, Käsespezialitäten aus Italien, ICE
Düsseldorf 1991

Kielwein, Gerhard, and Hans Kurt Luh,
Internationale Käsekunde, Stuttgart 1979

Mair-Waldburg, Heinrich
Handbuch der Käse, Käse der Welt von A-Z, Eine
Enzyklopädie, Volkswirtschaftlicher Verlag Kempten
1974

Masui, Kazuko and Yamada, Tomoko
French Cheese, Dorling Kindersley,
Munich 2006

Ministero Agricoltura e Foreste
DOC Käse aus Italien, Franco Angeli,
Milan 1992

Nantet, Bernard, Rance, Patrick and others
Alles Käse! Die besten Sorten der Welt,
DuMont, Cologne 1998

Official Journal of the European Union,
1998–2008
http://eur-lex.europa.eu

Olivier, Philippe
Fromages des pays du nord, Jean-Pierre Tailliendier,
Paris 1998

Sperat-Czar, Arnaud
Cheeses of the World, Hachette,
London 2004

Runet, Pierre (ed.)
Histoire et géographie des fromages, Université de
Caen, 1987

Sanz, Mariano and Enric Canut,
Käse aus Spanien, Vereinigung zur Förderung der
Käse aus Spanien, APQE Madrid and ICEX
Düsseldorf

Scholz, Wolfgang
Käse aus Schaf- und Ziegenmilch, Ulmer, Stuttgart
1995

Wisconsin Cheesecyclopedia
Wisconsin Milk Marketing Board 2006

ACKNOWLEDGMENTS

Bernard Anthony, fromager et affineur, Vieux-Ferrette/France

Hermine Hackl, Agrarmarketing Austria (AMA), Vienna/Austria

Eva Gschösser, Agrarmarketing Tirol, Innsbruck/Austria

Matthias Meichsner, aicep Portugal Global, Berlin

Arla Foods, Viby/Denmark

Vanessa Henry, Bord Bia—Irish Food Board, Dublin/Ireland

Commercial Section of the Embassy of the Republic of Cyprus, Berlin

Federal Ministry of Food, Agriculture, and Consumer Protection, Milk/Cheese Department, Dr. Umstedt, Angelika Metzen, and Antje Preussker, CMA, Bonn

Renate van Dijk, CONO Kaasmakers, Westbeemster / The Netherlands

Marianne Kalriis, Danish Dairy Board, Arhus/Denmark

Marie Ange Cortellino, Photo Library—Information Division Food and Agriculture Organization of the United Nations (FAO), Rome/Italy

Armando Lopes, Fonseca, Hagen

Dorothée Cocco, Fromi GmbH, Kehl

Selda Kirli, Garmo AG, Stuttgart

Genussregion Österreich

Pericles Alexandrakis, Greek Embassy, Commercial Section, Berlin

Elisabeth Häfner, Saarbrücken

Hellenic Foreign Trade Board (HEPO), Athens/Greece

Gertrud Schmitz and Sarah Nühlen, ICE, Düsseldorf

Inge Adolphs (Düsseldorf), Juan Carlos Sanz (Madrid/Spain), Spanish Consulate General (ICEX)

Izabella Kaminska, IJHARS—Agricultural and Food Quality Inspection, Warsaw/Poland

Josef Stemmer, Landesvereinigung der Bayerischen Milchwirtschaft, Munich

Graça Leite, Editorial Verbo, Lisbon/Portugal

Philippe Paranteau and Natacha Thévenin, Maison de la France, Frankfurt

Max Rubner—Institut (formerly Federal Milk Research Institute), Kiel, Dr. Klaus Pabst (Public Relations) and especially Gisela Kordes (Library)

Stephan Seul, Milch-Marketing, Bad Breisig

Milchindustrie-Verband (MIV), Berlin

Chuluun-Erdene Sosorbaram and Georg Mischler www.mongolfood.info (Mongolia)

Käse-Import Müller-Moers, Moers

Natur Genuss Österreich

Norrost GmbH, Hanau

Aad Vernooij, NZO Niederländisches Büro für Milcherzeugnisse, Zoetermeer

Oberwalliser Landwirtschaftskammer, Visp (Switzerland)

Philippe Olivier, Affineur, Boulogne-sur-Mer/France

Nadine Maaßen, OTG Oberstdorf Tourismus GmbH

Margarete and Alois Payer, Offerdingen http://www.payer.de

Helmut Pöschel, Würchwitz

Christopher Ratschka, Warsaw/Poland

Anna Kurizina, www.Russland-Aktuell.ru, Moscow/Russia

Ovidiu Sopa, www.sibiul.ro and Oana Fofiu, Sibiul/Romania

Sopexa, Düsseldorf

Helena Lindmark, Claes Henriksson, Swedish Dairy Association, Uppsala/Sweden

Switzerland Cheese Marketing, Baldham

Hannah Buck, The Specialist Cheesemakers Association, London/England

Tholstrup Cheese, Ratingen

Frederik Vandermersch, VLAM, Brussels/Belgium

Dietmar Wiedemann, Weidner—Käse GmbH, Friedberg/Bavaria

Franz Wimmers, Herzogenrath (Pikantje van Antje)

Mary Litviak, Wisconsin Milk Marketing Board, Excelsior/USA

Dr. Kerstin Keunecke, ZMP Zentrale Markt- und Preisberichtstelle, Bonn

Karin Zuck, European Cheese Center, Hanover

Nigel White, British Cheese Board, Surbiton, Surrey/England

Rakel Korsvuld, TINE B.A., Oslo/Norway

Gerard Durling & Jennifer McGinnis, igourmet.com

PHOTO CREDITS

The publisher wishes to thank the archives, organizations, and photographers concerned for the reproduction approval granted and for the help and support they have given in producing this book. The publisher has made every effort to identify all of the owners of illustration rights. Persons and institutions who may not have been contacted and who claim rights to images used are requested to contact the publisher in retrospect.

INDEX

MAJOR CHEESE VARIETIES LISTED BY CATEGORY*

*In some cases, individual cheeses belong to several groups (example: as well as being a semi-soft cheese and a blue-veined cheese, Roquefort is also a sheep's milk cheese). To avoid repetition, the cheeses are listed according to the categories by which they are best known.

Soft cheese with white mold

MAJOR CHEESE VARIETIES ACCORDING TO COUNTRY AND REGION OF ORIGIN

ALPHABETICAL INDEX